Feelings
and
Emotions

PERSONALITY AND PSYCHOPATHOLOGY

A Series of Monographs, Texts, and Treatises

Feelings
and
Emotions

The Loyola Symposium

Edited by
Magda B. Arnold

ACADEMIC PRESS  New York and London

1970

ACADEMIC PRESS, INC.
111 Fifth Avenue, New York, New York 10003

United Kingdom Edition published by
ACADEMIC PRESS, INC. (LONDON) LTD.
Berkeley Square House, London W1X 6BA

LIBRARY OF CONGRESS CATALOG CARD NUMBER: 70-97482

PRINTED IN THE UNITED STATES OF AMERICA

List of Contributors.

Silvano Arieti, *Psychiatrist, New York, New York*

Magda B. Arnold, *Professor of Psychology, Loyola University, Chicago, Illinois*

James R. Averill, *Department of Psychology, University of California, Berkeley, California*

Joseph V. Brady, *Deputy Director, Division of Neuropsychiatry, Walter Reed Army Medical Center, Washington, D.C., and Professor of Behavioral Biology, Johns Hopkins University School of Medicine, Baltimore, Maryland*

K. L. Casey, *Department of Physiology, University of Michigan, Ann Arbor, Michigan*

Joel R. Davitz, *Professor of Psychology, Teachers College, Columbia University, New York*

Otto Ewert, *Professor of Psychology, Ruhr University, Bochum-Querenburg, West Germany*

Nico H. Frijda, *Professor of Psychology, University of Amsterdam, Holland*

James Hillman, *Director of Studies, Psychiatrist, Zurich, Switzerland*

D. Stanley Jones, *Director, Full Circle Foundation for Education and Research, Hayle, Cornwall, England*

Richard S. Lazarus, *Professor of Psychology, University of California, Berkeley, California*

Robert W. Leeper, *Professor of Psychology, University of Oregon, Eugene, Oregon*

Ronald Melzack, *Professor of Psychology, McGill University, Montreal, Canada*

Vincent Nowlis, *Professor of Psychology, University of Rochester, New York*

Edward M. Opton, Jr., *Department of Psychology, University of California, Berkeley, California*

Richard S. Peters, *Professor of Philosophy, University of London, Institute of Education, London, England*

Robert Plutchik, *Director, Evaluation Research Program, Bronx State Hospital, and Department of Psychiatry, Albert Einstein College of Medicine, Bronx, New York*

Karl H. Pribram, *Professor of Neuropsychology, Stanford University School of Medicine, Stanford, California*

Stanley Schachter, *Professor of Social Psychology, Columbia University, New York*

Pavel V. Simonov, *Senior Research Scientist, Institute of Higher Nervous Activity and Neurophysiology, USSR Academy of Sciences, Moscow, USSR*

S. Strasser, *Professor of Philosophy, University of Nijmegen, Holland*

Silvan Tomkins, *Professor of Psychology, Livingston College, Rutgers University, New Brunswick, New Jersey*

Albert Wellek, *Professor of Psychology, Director of Psychological Institute, Joh. Gutenberg University, Mainz, West Germany*

Preface

The *Loyola Symposium on Feelings and Emotions*, at which the papers collected in this volume were presented, was the third in a distinguished sequence. The first and second symposia were organized by Dr. Martin L. Reymert; the one in 1927 (Wittenberg Symposium), the other in 1948 (Mooseheart Symposium). Dr. Reymert said in his preface to the first symposium volume:

"Our Symposium, it seems to me, has two valid *raisons d'être*. First of all, we shall be taking stock internationally of our present status; secondly, from the platform thus afforded, we should arrive at a clearer and more fruitful perspective which in turn may show problems as well as ways and means which should occupy our attention in the immediate future. In this connection I am glad to announce to you that our present meeting is not meant only as a passing show in the history of psychology, but that, with the hearty endorsement of the administrative authorities of this institution and, as we hope, with the continuous interests of all psychologists, it is our hope to repeat such an International Symposium on Feelings and Emotions . . . .

"Considered from all angles, we cherish the hope that the Wittenberg Symposium on Feelings and Emotions of 1927 will prove to be of real value to the history of our science" (1928, pp. xxii-xxiii).

That first symposium certainly left its mark on the then young science of psychology. The collection of papers published in 1928 became a standard work in the field and was consulted by succeeding generations of psychologists. But a second symposium did not materialize until 1948, when the Loyal Order of Moose underwrote the conference. Dr. Reymert said in a talk he gave at the second symposium:

"At the first Symposium held 20 years ago at Wittenberg College, I said that it might be advisable to have a symposium every decade not only to inventory progress but to turn attention toward and to furnish incentive in this very important field. I felt then, as I feel now, that this field constitutes the very 'heart core' of man's problems in relation to himself and other men at every level of interaction from the strictly personal up to the international . . . .

"Feelings and emotions, since they represent an exceedingly complex field, are not readily subject to precise experimental control. Therefore, after the academic psychologists (with a strictly introspective emphasis) had catalogued the emotions and described their subjective feeling tone, and after the behaviorists had similarly catalogued the behavioral expression of the emotions, research in feelings and emotions went into eclipse for quite a while. Twenty years ago some of the papers even addressed themselves to the issue of whether emotions had any scientific implications beyond description and classification.

"However, since that time we have been observing what might be referred to as the mobilization of all the natural and social sciences toward new knowledge of human development and understanding of the total individual as a unit . . . In the first Symposium, even though we had some physiological contributions, the emphasis was largely psychological, and *academic* psychology at that. In the present Symposium, we have not only academic psychology represented but physiology, anthropology, sociology, biochemistry, clinical psychology, psychiatry, and psychoanalysis . . ." (1950).

In the twenty years following that talk, emotion was once more eclipsed.

Before 1927, emotion was viewed with suspicion because its value for scientific psychology appeared doubtful. However, in the second symposium, a goodly number of workers from other disciplines showed that the topic of emotion was of vital interest to them; also, despite the meteoric rise of behaviorism, there was still a considerable number of psychologists who — though not necessarily specializing in the field of emotion — had a great deal to say about it. But after that time, a wall of silence began to close off emotion from the general theoretical and experimental endeavor of psychologists, particularly in this country. Behavior theory, as it now began to be called, had finally succeeded in banishing all thought of what might be going on in the "black box" by convincing psychologists that any concern with "mentalistic" events was thoroughly unscientific.

It took a new generation of behavior theorists to realize that the black box would have to be opened sometime, somehow, if the science of psychology was not to become strangled in formalisms. In the early sixties, a few collections of articles (Candland, 1962; Knapp, 1963) and research reports (West and Greenblatt, 1960) appeared which concentrated mainly on bodily changes in emotion — the one aspect that could not easily be disregarded. Gradually, behavior theory began to readmit into the front parlor of academic respectability at least some "covert" psychological activities that had been banished to the back rooms of clinical psychology far too long. In short order, even theoretical treatises on emotion began to appear again. Together with the promising neurophysiological research that had been carried on for several decades and produced findings with considerable bearing on feelings and emotions, there now seemed enough promising material and, particularly,

enough eminent scientists interested in this field, to think of organizing a Third
International Symposium in October 1968.

The field of psychology had proliferated to such an extent that rather careful
selection of the contributors seemed to be required. To invite professionals from
other disciplines (physiology, anthropology, sociology, biochemistry) as in the
second symposium, would have increased the scope of the conference to such an
extent that even a week would not have allowed sufficient time for all the
papers. Even within psychology, specialization had become so great that it was
decided to invite only scientists who had made important contributions to this
field.

Since there had been some recent symposia dealing mainly with experimental,
particulary neurophysiological, research connected with emotion, it was further
decided to concentrate on theoretical approaches because they would give a
more accurate picture of the stand of knowledge at the present time. To allow
discussion among the contributors themselves and to encourage general audience
participation, the number of papers was drastically reduced, as compared to the
second symposium. In line with this attempt to provide some self-criticism was
the invitation to two philosophers, Professor R. S. Peters and Professor S.
Strasser, to participate in the symposium. Both had done important work in this
field, critically evaluating scientific contributions and suggesting new theoretical
approaches. Unfortunately, several invited participants from France were unable
either to come to the conference or to prepare a paper because the urgent
reorganization of French universities in the summer and fall of 1968 required all
their time and energy.

It is perhaps a sign of the times that it was neither a university nor a private
foundation that was willing to support such a symposium in 1968, but the
Section on Personality of the National Institutes of Mental Health in
Washington, D. C. The thanks of myself and all contributors are due to this
agency, and particularly to Dr. David Pearl, Head of the Section, who from the
beginning showed warm interest in this project and was as pleased when support
was granted as were the rest of us. I would also like to express my warmest
appreciation to Dr. R. E. Walker, chairman of the Department of Psychology,
Loyola University, who made our guests feel so at home; to Mundelein College,
especially the President, Sister Ann Ida, who so graciously welcomed the
meetings to their auditorium; to all administrators and colleagues at Loyola
University, particularly the Academic Vice President, Rev. R. W. Mulligan, S.J.,
who helped to make this conference a success. Finally, I owe a debt of gratitude
to Rev. J. H. Mead, S.J., my executive assistant, who first suggested the
symposium and later, through his unflagging labor and attention to all the
necessary details, was responsible for its smooth functioning. Thanks are also
due to all the students who, under his competent leadership, took over many
necessary duties and acted as efficient guides, hosts, and hostesses.

I hope that this volume of symposium papers, like its predecessors, will give the reader some idea of the present stand of knowledge in the field of emotion. The discussions proved to be too sporadic and disconnected to be included here. Hence, I have simply attempted to indicate in the introduction to each section what were the main points covered and how they fitted into the plan of the whole symposium. If the symposium and the symposium papers again prove their value, I hope that in another twenty years there will be a Fourth International Symposium to look forward to.

REFERENCES

Candland, D. K. (Ed.) (1962). *Emotion: Bodily changes, an enduring problem in psychology: Selected readings.* Van Nostrand, New York.

Knapp, P. H. (Ed.) (1963). *Expression of the emotions in man.* International Univ. Press, New York.

Reymert, M. L. (Ed.) (1928). *Feelings and emotions. The Wittenberg symposium.* Clark Univ. Press, Worcester, Massachusetts.

Reymert, M. L. (Ed.) (1950). *Feelings and emotions. The Mooseheart symposium.* McGraw-Hill, New York.

West, L. J. and Greenblatt, M. (1960). Explorations in the physiology of emotions. *Am. Psychiat. Assoc., Psychiat. Res. Rep.* No. 12.

Contents

PART III
COGNITIVE THEORIES OF FEELING AND EMOTION 123

Chapter 8

Chapter 9

Chapter 10

Chapter 11 166 - 167

Chapter 12

Chapter 13

Chapter 14

Chapter 15

Chapter 20

Feelings
and
Emotions

Part I

Theories Based
on Biological Considerations

INTRODUCTION

In the study of emotion, it was one of the first observations that there are a limited number of well-defined emotional patterns. It was not surprising that psychologists soon assumed that there must be a few basic patterns that are the foundations of the numerous subtle emotions found in human adults. In Plutchik's paper, these basic patterns represent responses to the few standard situations every animal is bound to encounter. He suggests that these "prototype emotions" run through all levels of animal life and can be recognized as emotions from the most primitive vertebrate to man. D. Stanley-Jones, on the other hand, traces the development of love and hate from more primitive physiological states, namely, feelings of heat and cold.

To be sure, these are *theories*, that is, attempted explanations of the origin of some emotions. But unlike other theories, they are based not on evidence, scientific or otherwise, but on another theory, the theory of evolution. For this reason, it should perhaps be stressed that these are not the only possible explanations. It is true that there are certain situations every living organism will encounter (enemy, food, mate, frustration), but the situation does not necessarily determine the response. It will depend on the animal's interpretation of the situation whether he will attack or turn tail; and the emotional expression will be appropriate to the kind of interpretation — which easily accounts for the increasing number and subtlety of human emotions. Similarly, it need not be assumed that higher emotions will develop "out of" more primitive responses. They may develop according to the perceptual capabilities of a given species or individual; and the peripheral changes shown in emotions may be initiated over some of the pathways used in other responses without developing out of them.

1

Emotions, Evolution, and Adaptive Processes

Robert Plutchik*

During the past century there evolved three major traditions concerned with the nature of emotion. The first stemmed from Darwin's theory of evolution which implied that there has been an evolution not only of physical structures, but of "mental" and expressive characteristics as well. Darwin gathered a great deal of evidence, mostly observational and anecdotal, to illustrate the basic continuity of emotional expression in lower animals and in men. The baring of the fangs of a dog, or wolf, he noted, is related to the sneer of the human adult, and flushing of the face in anger has been reported in widely diverse races of man as well as in certain species of monkeys. Defecation and urination during fear has been observed in rats, cats, dogs, monkeys, and humans. "Even insects express anger, terror, jealousy and love," Darwin wrote.

He used four kinds of evidence for his conclusions about the innate basis of emotional expressions: (a) emotions appear in very young children in the same form as in adults; (b) they are shown in identical ways by those born blind; (c) they appear in widely distinct races and groups of men; and (d) they appear in related forms in many kinds of lower animals. These views and their elaboration have had a tremendous impact on the development of modern ethology by zoologists, but have had relatively less influence on the development of American Behaviorism.

The second major tradition in the psychology of emotion began with William James' analysis of the sequence problem. James suggested that "we do not run because we are afraid, but rather that we are afraid because we run." In essence, his view was that an emotion is a conscious feeling arising from sensations in the

*Albert Einstein College of Medicine, New York.

viscera and skeletal muscles, which comes after a state of bodily arousal and not before it. The major concern was with the sequence of events relating perception, feeling, and bodily states.

James' viewpoint eventually triggered the critique by Cannon who claimed to find the origin of emotional feeling in the thalamus rather than in the viscera. The controversy led to two important results. First, it stimulated a great deal of research concerned with autonomic changes under conditions of stress and emotion, a concern which continues to exist at the present time. Secondly, it led to increasing numbers of studies dealing with the effects of brain lesions and stimulation of subcortical brain areas. The current strong interest in hypothalamic and limbic structures reflects this.

The third major tradition in the psychology of emotion is based upon Freud's view that emotions might be considered "archaic discharge syndromes" that are part of the biological inheritance of man, and which can be identified in infants as well as adults. In addition, emotions or affects (the two terms are usually used interchangeably), may be unconscious and not directly accessible to awareness. Freud thus de-emphasized the feeling aspect of emotion. Psychoanalytic theory has much to say about the development of emotions and their vicissitudes, but psychoanalysts have been more preoccupied with a theory of anxiety than with a theory of affect-in-general.

The closest approach to a general psychoanalytic theory of affect is the work of Rado (1956) who talks about "adaptational psychodynamics." Like Freud, he places less emphasis on emotions as feelings and stresses the need for "contextual inference." Such inference enables a distinction to be made between various emotional patterns such as escape, combat, submission, defiance, brooding, expiation, etc. He thus ends up talking a language very much like that of the ethologists.

The three traditions that I have described might be summarized in the following way: the Darwinian approach has been largely concerned with the expressive and behavioral aspects of emotion; the James-Cannon approach has been mostly concerned with reportable feelings, visceral physiology, and brain structure; and the Freudian approach has been primarily interested in inferences about the complex mixture of emotional states found in man. Each of these approaches has something important to contribute, and yet there have been few attempts made to integrate them. A general theory of emotion should have relevance to all of these areas of concern.

WHAT SHOULD A THEORY OF EMOTION DO?

There are lots of burdens we can place upon a theory of emotion. First and foremost, it should stimulate our thinking and guide our research. It should suggest fruitful lines of investigation. The James theory, for example, stimulated considerable research on autonomic activity; psychoanalysis stimulated research dealing with infants, with child development, and with personality.

Secondly, a theory should act as an integrator of facts already known. It should attempt to place them within a single framework and to account for them in terms of a small number of basic concepts. This implies, for example, that certain ethological observations and certain psychoanalytic ones can be shown to be either related or based on the same principles.

A third function of theory is to show relations between apparently diverse areas. Any approach that successfully brings together two realms of phenomena increases the generality of our concepts. If, for example, behavioral observations or fantasy productions can be related to hormones, diet, brain chemistry or limbic system functioning, we increase the generality of our concepts. We do the same if we can show relations between emotions and personality, child development, or evolution. Finally, a theory should predict some new relationships.

These four functions of theory — i.e., to stimulate research, integrate known facts, incorporate diverse areas, and predict new relations — are not the only important characteristics of theories. Basically, any theory of emotion should attempt to answer (even if tentatively) a whole series of questions which psychologists have been asking for a long time, such questions as the following: "What is an emotion?" "What functions do emotions have?" "What is the relation between feelings and bodily states?" "Are emotions learned or innate?" "Are there differences between emotions?" "What is the effect of maturation and learning on emotion?" and so on.

WHAT A THEORY OF EMOTION IS NOT

If what I have said so far seems reasonable then I can now suggest what a theory of emotion is not. In general, any attempt to answer only one of the above questions is not a theory of emotion. At best it would be either a correct or incorrect fact, but not a theory. Similarly, a viewpoint which is limited to only one of the three major traditions described above, would not be a general theory of emotion. More specifically, however important William James' viewpoint was historically, it really is not a theory of emotion; it is simply a statement about a presumed sequence of events relating perception, bodily states and feelings.

There are several current approaches to emotion which are also not general theories in the sense that I have suggested. For example, a point of view which has been called "activation theory" proposes that the traditional categories of emotion be eliminated and that all behavior be described solely in terms of whether it is intense or not and whether it shows approach or avoidance (Duffy, 1962).

This view has been criticized on several grounds: that correlations between arousal indices are typically low and sometimes paradoxical (Lacey *et al.*, 1963);

that no attempt has been made to distinguish, in terms of this conception, between different emotions such as love, hate, anger, fear or depression; and that it has not proposed answers to the kinds of questions already listed. At best, activation theory is a statement of an important variable to be considered within the Jamesian tradition.

Another current approach to emotion is the concern with "emotionality" in general rather than with emotions in particular. Within this framework attempts are made to relate, for example, a variety of stress variables in infancy to "emotionality" in adult life, or relations are established between certain conditioning variables or operant schedules and "emotionality."

If we look more closely at such studies we find that the dependent variables or measures of emotionality have little to do with what ethologists or psychoanalysts or laymen call emotion. They are usually measures of learning such as rate of bar pressing or number of trials to learn an avoidance task. The term "emotionality" as used by different investigators actually implies very different kinds of overt behaviors. Such usage of the term probably reflects an urge for standardization as well as the tendency "to exclude direct observations of animals" as part of the methods of research (Lorenz, 1967). However, the tendency to label widely different behavioral reactions by a single term such as "emotionality" can only lead to confusion or can propagate those that already exist.

Still another approach to a theory of emotion is the view that a satisfactory analysis of emotion is provided by a knowledge of brain structures and of the pathways by which the excitations travel. Thus we have a theory based upon the identification of hypothalamic nuclei involved in eating, sex, and aggression (Gellhorn and Loofbourrow, 1963), or theories which try to identify the limbic system structures that are related in some way to emotional expression (MacLean and Ploog, 1962; Delgado 1966).

There are several reasons why such an approach can never provide a complete theory of emotion. For one thing, this view tends to be species-dependent. The brain structure of man is not identical to that of squirrel monkeys, or rats or fish. Yet behavior patterns expressive of emotion are identifiable in all these animals as well as birds and insects. There are only 250 neurons in an ant's brain and 900 in the brain of a bee, yet both are capable of exceedingly complex social organizations, aggressive behavior, reproductive behavior, exploration and even communication. Obviously, a description of brain pathways involved in emotion for the bee cannot apply to the rat or to man. Secondly, an approach which focuses on brain structure tends to ignore the stimulus variables and the expressive patterns which are distinctive for different emotions. The ethologists have already made clear that there are many subtle releasing mechanisms and trigger stimuli which produce emotional behavior. Emotional patterns are dependent on both stimulus situations and brain mechanisms.

It is reasonable to expect that we will eventually have more-or-less complete knowledge of brain structures involved in emotional expression. We will then have more facts at our disposal. But these facts are not, in themselves, a theory of emotion. Theories are not equivalent to facts, but are ways of organizing them systematically and producing useful implications and guides for research.

There is one other approach which I should like briefly to describe. This is the view that as long as a person is aroused, the labeling of emotional states by human adults depends only on the nature of the situation (Schachter and Singer, 1962). This view is in the Jamesian tradition of concern with reportable feeling states in relation to autonomic changes; it completely ignores both the ethological and psychoanalytic traditions.

The major evidence on which this theory is based has been criticized on methodological grounds (Plutchik and Ax, 1967; Stein, 1967). In addition, the reputed lack of clearcut differentiation of emotional stress can be easily explained in terms of the proven fact that most emotional states are mixed. In the recent ethological text on animal behavior, Hinde (1966) writes, "For much of the time a tendency to show one type of behavior is in conflict with tendencies to show others . . . . The evidence is considerable that the diversity of behavior shown in threat and courtship can be understood in terms of ambivalence between a relatively small number of behavioral tendencies." Lorenz (1967) puts the case more strongly. He says, "It is important to realize that behavior determined by only two drive components is almost as rare as that caused by the impulse of a single instinct, acting alone." Inconsistent results are largely due to the fact that investigators often ignore the complex, mixed emotional states and focus on only one or another emotion-component.

Despite the difficulty of doing research, due to the conflict of emotions, there have been many reports which apparently show some differentiation of emotional states (Almy, 1951; Arnold, 1945, 1960; Ax, 1953; Darwin, 1965; Davis *et al.*, 1955; Engel *et al.*, 1956; Funkenstein *et al.*, 1957; Gellhorn, 1960; Gellhorn and Loofbourrow, 1963; Grace *et al.*, 1951; Landis and Hunt, 1939; Mahl, 1949; Schachter, 1957; Schneider and Zangari, 1951; Wolf and Wolff, 1942; Wolff, 1953). These reports have likewise been ignored by those who assume that all states of arousal are physiologically identical. Finally, the situational approach is basically a description of only one of the many factors which influence the verbal labeling of feeling states by human adults. It hardly qualifies as a general theory of emotion.

Let me summarize the points I have made. A general theory of emotion should attempt to relate the three great traditions dealing with emotions, that is, the expressive tradition, the physiological tradition, and the dynamic tradition. Any viewpoint which does not do this ignores some important areas of concern. In addition, we have to consider whether some of our basic questions about emotion are capable of being answered within the proposed framework.

EVOLUTION AND EMOTION

Darwin's theory of evolution has been described as the most general and important idea in biology (Bonner, 1962; Simpson *et al.*, 1957). His concept of natural selection implies that almost every feature of each existing species has survival value, and this is as true of an animal's behavior, including his emotional behavior, as it is of his bodily structures. In other words, "Behavior, like all of the other features of an animal, is a product of evolution" (Barnett, 1967). From an evolutionary point of view, we should, therefore, study the specific ways in which emotions function adaptively, as well as the forms they take in different species.

For example, Lorenz (1967) discusses the function of intraspecies aggression and suggests that some of the functions are: (a) production of a balanced distribution of animals of a given species over an available environment; (b) selection of the strongest animals by rival fights for protection of the young and of the herd; and (c) establishment of a ranking order to limit fighting between members of a group. Many different mechanisms may produce the same function.

In some ways the question of function is more significant than the question of mechanism. For example, the eye of a honey bee and that of a man differ considerably in mechanism, yet they function in very similar ways. It is likewise reasonable to discuss the functions of aggression, threat, protection, courtship and mating in different species including man, without assuming that the causal mechanisms are in any way identical. Yilmaz (1966), a theoretical physicist, puts the general issue in the following way, "Most of the current work in neurology ... is directed toward the study of mechanism .... This is of course a most useful activity; otherwise, how could we repair an organ when it is damaged or out of order? However, not all of us are doctors. Some of us may want to know why the organ is there in the first place. Others might wonder if it could have been evolved differently and perhaps in a better way. Such questions lead us to consider a class of possible mechanisms which will perform a given task or function."

There are a number of implications of these views. All organisms, in order to survive, encounter certain common problems. These problems are created by the nature of the environment, which in certain ways is similar for all animals. In order to survive, any organism must take in nourishment and eliminate waste products. It must distinguish between prey and predator, between a potential mate and a potential enemy. It must explore its environment and orient its sense organs appropriately as it takes in information about the beneficial and harmful aspects of its immediate world. And in organisms which are relatively helpless at birth and for a while thereafter, there must be ways of indicating the need for care and nurturance. The mechanisms by which these functions are carried out will vary widely throughout the animal kingdom, and various rituals may become associated with them, but the basic prototypic functions will remain invariant.

This functional approach to emotion implies that the recognition by an animal of the beneficial or harmful aspects of its environment means that it must *evaluate* its environment in some way (Arnold, 1960). This evaluation process represents the cognitive aspect of emotions, and it influences the type of response pattern actually observed. For example, if a lower animal or a human being perceives a stimulus as potentially harmful, there are several reactions possible. One is to retreat from it, another is to fight it, a third is to vomit it out, and a fourth is to cry for help. Each of these reactions represents a distinct type of negative evaluation, and the appropriate responses for each evaluation represent distinct classes of prototype emotions.

So-called "cognitive" approaches to emotion are mainly concerned with the nature of the evaluation process, but it should be recognized that an evaluation or a perception is not an emotion. Evaluations are only a part of the total process which involves an organism interacting with its environment in biologically adaptive ways.

THE CONCEPT OF PROTOTYPE EMOTIONS

"There is only a limited number of modes of dealing with danger available to the individual that have proved of general applicability exploitable in phylogeny. With respect to stimuli arising from within the organism, survival is favored by expulsion or by isolation. With respect to stimuli referring to a source of (potential) danger arising from the outer environment, survival is favored by flight, fight, submission, reversal, and vocalization, in the order of apparent phylogenetic development" (Turner, 1957).

This concept of a small number of modes of dealing with danger or with problems posed by the environment has been elaborated by Scott (1958). He suggests that there are only a few classes of adaptive behavior found in many species and phylogenetic levels. He talks about ingestive behavior, agonistic behavior, eliminative behavior, investigative behavior, etc.

Several years ago, in the book I wrote called *The Emotions: Facts, Theories and a New Model* (1962), I tried to develop this concept of basic adaptive patterns in a more systematic way. I noted that the functional analysis of emotions must relate in some reasonable way to the subjective or introspective aspects. At the same time it was necessary to recognize that most emotions were actually mixed states made up of more primary emotions, in the same sense that all colors can be considered to result from a mixture of just a few primary colors.

As a guide to the organization of relations among emotion concepts, I used the fact that emotions vary in at least three systematic ways. Emotions vary in *intensity*, as reflected by the distinctions we make between fear and panic or irritation and rage. They vary also in degree of *similarity* to one another. We note, for example, that shame and guilt are more similar than joy and disgust. Such similarity relations are implicit in all emotions. Finally, emotions have the character of *polarity*. We recognize that joy is the opposite of sadness, and hate is the opposite of love. We can also conceive of polarity itself as being a matter of degree.

These three implicit relations between emotions: intensity, similarity, and polarity, can be represented simultaneously by means of a three-dimensional model which looks like an inverted cone.

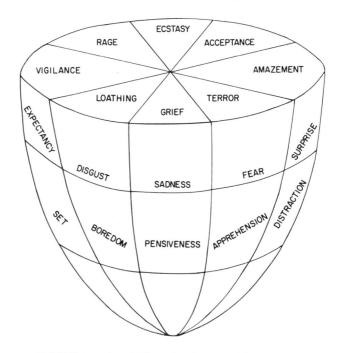

FIGURE 1. A multidimensional model of the emotions.

Figure 1 presents a schematic view of this three dimensional model of the emotions. Each "slice" of the inverted cone represents a different primary emotion, with the vertical dimension implying an intensity variable. Emotions placed near one another are more similar than those which are farther apart or are opposite.

Figure 2 shows a cross-section of the inverted cone. The "*C*" at the center is used to represent the idea of conflict which results when opposite emotions are mixed. However, as would also be the case with colors, degrees of mixture are possible. The mixture of opposite emotions produces greater conflict than the mixture of adjacent emotions, thus implying a potential scaling of the concept of conflict.

FIGURE 2.   A cross-section of the emotion-solid.

It is important to note that the words used are only approximate terms borrowed from the introspective language. It is perfectly possible to use the same model without these words since a more general, nonsubjective language is available. This is the language of functions.

TABLE I
THE THREE LANGUAGES USED TO DESCRIBE EMOTIONAL STATES

Subjective Language	Behavioral Language	Functional Language
Fear, Terror	Withdrawing, Escaping	Protection
Anger, Rage	Attacking	Destruction
Joy, Ecstasy	Mating, Possessing	Reproduction
Sadness, Grief	Losing Contact	Deprivation
Acceptance, Greed	Eating	Incorporation
Disgust, Loathing	Vomiting, Defecating	Rejection
Expectancy, Watchfulness	Sensing	Exploration
Surprise, Astonishment	Stopping	Orientation

Table I provides a list of the basic adaptive or prototype functions. These functions have the same general properties as human feeling states; namely, intensity, similarity, and polarity. If we focus on the polarity aspect, we note the following pairs: protection (withdrawal) is opposite destruction (attack);

incorporation (eating) is opposite rejection (eliminating); reproduction (possessing or mating) is opposite deprivation (loss); and exploration (sensing) is opposite orientation (stopping).

The table emphasizes another fundamental point — emotions can be described in terms of several different languages. From a broad, phylogenetic, evolutionary point of view, the functional (adaptive) language is the most general and applies to humans as well as lower animals. The behavioral language is also quite general and can be used to describe both humans and lower animals. The subjective language is applicable only to humans who have had certain language experiences.

Unfortunately, this makes the subjective language most variable and subject to numerous kinds of biases. For example, in some subcultures, people may be taught that it is unmanly to express fear, and such people may not report fear even when the behavioral evidence would suggest that it exists. As another illustration of this point, the psychoanalysts frequently cite evidence that subjective reports of feeling states do not match those inferred on the basis of free associations, dreams, slips of the tongue, expressive movements and the like. There are many reports by psychoanalysts and others of a complete incongruity between a person's verbalized feelings and his expressive behavior or medical condition. Thus, important as subjective experiences of emotions are for humans, they are the least reliable from a scientific point of view. This does not imply that they are not of great use when obtained under appropriate conditions.

The layman tends to think of emotions in terms of subjective feeling states, but it is evident that feelings are neither reliable enough nor general enough to serve as a *general* basis for a theory of emotion. In order to provide a general definition of emotion we need to use the functional or adaptational language, and within that framework the following definition is proposed: an emotion is a patterned bodily reaction of either protection, destruction, reproduction, deprivation, incorporation, rejection, exploration or orientation, or some combination of these, which is brought about by a stimulus.

This definition emphasizes the basic prototype patterns of adaptation that are used by all organisms, including man, in their struggle for survival. It implies a cognitive process in connection with the evaluation of stimuli. It makes the study of emotion a central aspect of evolutionary biology, with implications for the ethologists as well as for the Jamesians and the psychoanalysts. In addition, it emphasizes the idea that emotions, as actually observed in humans and in lower animals, are typically mixtures of the primary or prototype ones and thus often difficult to recognize or understand without special methods. It also implies the possible development of a science of emotion-mixture just as there is a science of color-mixture. Last, but not least, it represents a guide for research by pointing to areas and relationships that have not yet been adequately explored.

FIGURE 3

All these points have been elaborated in my book and in subsequent publications (Plutchik, 1962, 1965, 1966a).

SOME IMPLICATIONS OF THE THEORY

In the time I have remaining I will briefly describe some recent researches. During the two years I was at the National Institute of Mental Health, I studied the effects of brain stimulation in rhesus monkeys. Various subcortical areas were systematically explored. Electrodes were permanently implanted in areas from which interesting effects were obtained, such as food intake, erection of the penis, urination, defecation, aggression, withdrawal, lipsmacking, grunting, tremor, etc. (Plutchik *et al.*, 1966).

Seconds before the photograph shown in Fig. 3 was taken, the monkey, who previously would not spontaneously eat, began to fill his mouth and pouches with dry pellets because of brain stimulation of a particular part of the brain. After the brain stimulation was discontinued, the monkey immediately ejected all the food pellets.

Figure 4 shows what happened when a region near the central midline gray area was stimulated. The monkey suddenly turned his head and bit viciously at the plastic headholder. As soon as stimulation was discontinued, the monkey stopped biting and turned his head away.

In general, we found that stimulation of many brain sites produced more than one kind of behavior (erections plus lipsmacking, or food intake plus grunting) suggesting that some very different emotional states are represented in nearly the same brain location. In addition, we found that stimulation of several different locations could produce the same kind of reaction, such as eating or erection of the penis. Finally, we had evidence that stimulation of various discrete brain areas could produce patterns of behavior identified by the functional labels already mentioned, that is, incorporation, rejection, protection, destruction, etc. It is worth noting that similar findings have been reported by Delgado (1966), MacLean and Ploog (1962), Wasman and Flynn (1962), and Robinson and Mishkin (1961).

More recently, at the Jackson Laboratories, I decided to critically examine the nature of "emotionality" in dogs. Many previous studies have considered "emotionality" a single dimension that can be measured by some simple index such as defecation frequency or amount of exploratory activity. An increasing number of studies, however, are showing that emotionality is an extremely complex state which is reflected by dozens of different indices, many of which correlate either negatively or not at all with each other. Several factor-analytic studies using multiple measures have reported anywhere from four to ten independent factors (Billingslea, 1942; Brace, 1962; Furchtgott and Cureton, 1964; Willingham, 1956).

FIGURE 4

In our study, we focused on patterns of approach and withdrawal ("timidity") in dogs. In order to do this we randomly selected from the animal colony eight animals from each of four breeds: beagle, basenji, sheltie and wire-haired fox terrier, making a total of 32 dogs studied. Each animal was individually exposed to 17 different test stimuli in a specially constructed chamber. The stimuli included: food, a live puppy, a red ball, a rubber snake, a mechanical dog, a model of the head of a clown, a mirror, and others. For each stimulus we measured such things as contact time with the object, amount of activity, tendencies to approach or avoid the object, and number of defecations and urinations.

FIGURE 5

Figure 5 shows a basenji who literally turned his back on the stimuli and put his head between his paws. This pattern of reaction occurred only among basenjis. Although the beagles also obtained high timidity scores, they simply backed into a corner and watched the stimuli as they were introduced one by one. Most of the shelties and wire-haired terriers approached the objects and licked or sniffed them.

We found highly significant differences among breeds of dogs in their tendencies to approach, avoid, or ignore the objects, as well as in their mean contact time and mean activity level. Significant sex differences were also found. Factor-analysis suggested that three or four independent factors were needed to reasonably account for the data (Plutchik and Stelzner, 1966).

There are several implications of these findings: (a) breed differences in timidity and approachfulness ("curiosity") were clearly evident; these differences were related to the types of functions (e.g., pack hunting, solitary hunting, or sheepherding) for which the breeds were originally developed; (b) no emotion can be unequivocally measured by a single behavioral index alone; this emphasizes the point that particular emotions be studied rather than a global something called "emotionality"; (c) there were some individual differences that were larger than breed differences; for example, although the dogs with the highest scores on contact or approach were terriers and shelties, there was one beagle among the high scorers. This is the kind of variability on which natural selection operates.

A third study that I want to describe briefly was concerned with the relations between emotions and personality traits. In my book, I had suggested that personality traits could be conceptualized as resulting from the mixture of emotions.

Several investigators had already proposed a circular organization of personality traits (Freedman *et al.*, 1951; Lodge, 1953; Lorr and McNair, 1963). Since I had also proposed a circular organization for emotions, an attempt was made to relate these two sets of concepts (Schaefer and Plutchik, 1966). This was done by asking a group of experienced clinicians to indicate the extent to which each of a series of diagnostic constructs implies or is associated with each of a sample of traits and emotions. For example, for a diagnostic concept such as paranoia, ratings were obtained from the judges on the extent to which it implies the existence of such traits as *kind, assertive, or suspicious*, or emotions such as *joyful, angry,* or *sad.* From these ratings intercorrelations were computed and factor-analyzed.

Among other things, the results showed that the relationships between traits as well as emotions could be organized in terms of a circular configuration using a circumplex (Guttman, 1954). This is shown in Fig. 6. We find here in the empirical data good agreement with the theoretical model. For example, *agreeable* and *accepting* (incorporation) are opposite *disgusted* and *resentful* (rejection); *joyful* and *sociable* (reproduction) are opposite *sad* and *timid* (deprivation); and *angry* and *quarrelsome* (destruction) are nearly opposite *cautious* and *fearful* (protection). The concept of polarity is thus shown to be part of clinicians' conceptions of traits and emotions.

Theoretically, every trait or emotion concept could be shown to fall somewhere along the circle; we thus have the basis for a parsimonious description of the relations between the hundreds of trait and emotion terms which are part of our vocabulary. This has implications for psychiatric practice as well as for personality test construction.

Partly as a result of this work, I then helped develop a test which was designed to evaluate the relative strengths of each of the eight primary emotions in a person (Kellerman, 1964; Kellerman and Plutchik, 1968). After extensive pretesting, a set of 12 terms such as sociable, quarrelsome, and obedient was selected to represent all quadrants of the personality-trait universe as defined by the circumplex already obtained. The two major emotion components in each trait were determined on the basis of clinical judgment and then the traits were paired in all possible combinations. The final index consisted of 66 paired items in a forced-choice format.

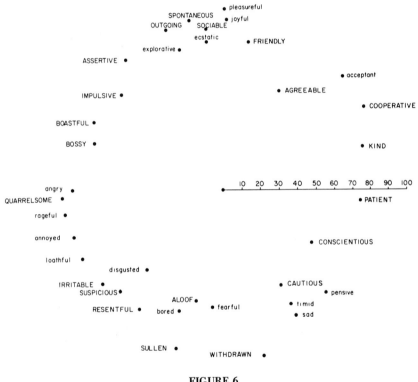

FIGURE 6

Since each trait is assumed to be made up of at least two emotions, each time a subject chooses one trait out of a pair to describe himself, he implicitly tells us something about his emotional dispositions. Although subjects respond to trait items, their responses are scored for the underlying component emotions.

In the first study using the Emotions Profile Index or EPI, three groups of subjects were chosen: a normal, a moderately maladjusted, and a severely maladjusted one, all equated on I.Q., age, sex, and socio-economic level. Analysis of the data showed that a conflict measure based upon the test responses increased as a function of degree of maladjustment of the patients. In addition,

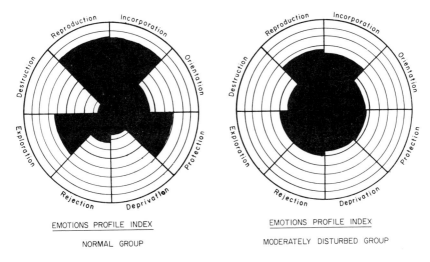

EMOTIONS PROFILE INDEX

NORMAL GROUP

EMOTIONS PROFILE INDEX

MODERATELY DISTURBED GROUP

FIGURE 7

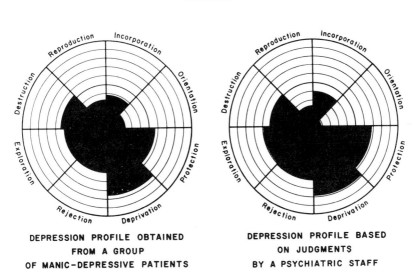

DEPRESSION PROFILE OBTAINED
FROM A GROUP
OF MANIC-DEPRESSIVE PATIENTS

DEPRESSION PROFILE BASED
ON JUDGMENTS
BY A PSYCHIATRIC STAFF

FIGURE 8

the results of a factor-analysis were interpreted as showing a greater restriction of expression of emotions in the more maladjusted patients. Figure 7 illustrates the differences in emotion profiles between the normal and one of the maladjusted groups. In the latter group, there is an obvious reduction in the pleasure dimensions of *reproduction* and *incorporation,* and an increase in the *destruction* dimension. The overall patterns look quite different.

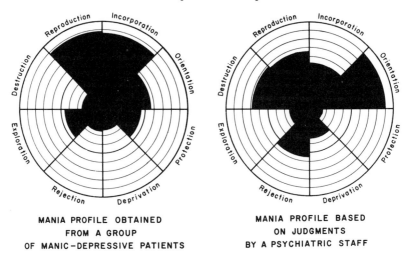

MANIA PROFILE OBTAINED
FROM A GROUP
OF MANIC–DEPRESSIVE PATIENTS

MANIA PROFILE BASED
ON JUDGMENTS
BY A PSYCHIATRIC STAFF

FIGURE 9

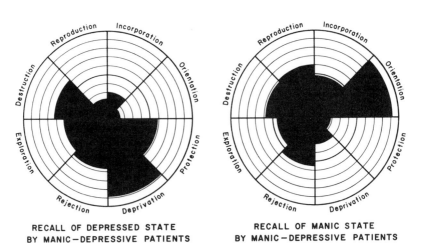

RECALL OF DEPRESSED STATE
BY MANIC–DEPRESSIVE PATIENTS
WHEN WELL

RECALL OF MANIC STATE
BY MANIC–DEPRESSIVE PATIENTS
WHEN WELL

FIGURE 10

This test, the EPI, has been used quite widely by now with a variety of groups including children. An interesting recent application concerns its use with manic-depressive patients (Platman *et al.*, 1968). In this study, a comparison was made between EPI emotion profiles obtained from a group of manic-depressive patients and profiles based upon staff ratings. Patient profiles agreed with staff judgments remarkably well for depression but poorly for mania (Figs. 8 and 9). When the patients were well and functioning normally in an interval phase, they again provided emotion profiles based on the EPI in terms of how they recalled their manic or depressed experiences. These *remembered* profiles showed very high agreement with the judgments of the staff (Fig. 10).

EMOTIONS PROFILE INDEX

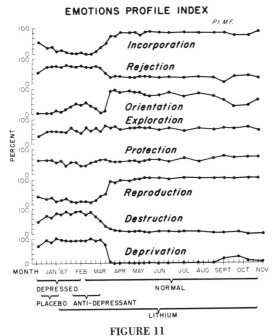

FIGURE 11

We concluded that manic states seem to be associated with strong denial or confusion, while depressed states are reported accurately. In addition, we noted that it is possible to consider mania and depression not only in terms of the affects of sadness and loss, but also in terms of other affects, for example, aggression and disgust. The data could be interpreted to mean that the manic patient is denying his feelings of destruction and rejection while the depressed patient is willing to admit these feelings. This would presumably be related to the fact that the manic perceives the source of his anger and rejection in the external world, while the depressed person usually sees the source of his anger in himself. In any case, only through the use of multidimensional affect measurement can such hypotheses be tested.

The complex relations between emotions for one patient are illustrated in Fig. 11. During a period of almost one year this patient took the EPI almost weekly as a measure of his current emotions. During the initial three-month period that he was in the hospital and severely depressed, his *deprivation* score was extremely high, but so were his *destruction* and *rejection* scores. At the same time his *reproduction, incorporation,* and *orientation* scores were extremely low. As the patient recovered, reciprocal changes took place in all these emotions, although with somewhat different time-courses. These patterns emphasize the very complex nature of the emotion-mixtures that exist in individuals.

The conceptions underlying the EPI have been used in other contexts. For example, Kellerman (1966) developed a way of evaluating the eight prototype dimensions in dolphins and produced emotion profiles for several animals. Recently a technique has been developed for evaluating the eight emotional prototypes from the content of early memories (Wynne and Schaffzin, 1965; Peterson, 1965); this technique can be adapted to any kind of written material including dreams and interviews.

To conclude: the theory of emotion that I have proposed is based on evolutionary considerations. It focuses on the reality and ubiquity of conflict of emotions in man and animals and proposes a conceptual framework for the analysis and synthesis of behavior and experience. It has relevance to all the major traditions in the psychology of emotion (Plutchik, 1965, 1966a, b) and has proven to be an integrator of facts as well as a stimulator of research.

REFERENCES

Almy, T.P. (1951). Experimental studies on the irritable colon. *Am. J. Med.,* 10, 60-67.
Arnold, Magda B. (1945). Physiological differentiation of emotional states. *Psychol. Rev.,* 52, 35-48.
Arnold, Magda B. (1960). *Emotion and personality.* Columbia Univ. Press, New York.
Ax, A.F. (1953). The physiological differentiation of fear and anger in humans. *Psychosomat. Med.,* 15, 433-442.
Barnett, S.A. (1967). *Instinct and intelligence.* Prentice-Hall, Englewood Cliffs, New Jersey.
Billingslea, F.Y. (1942). Intercorrelational analysis of certain behavior salients in the rat. *J. Comp. Psychol.,* 34, 203-211.
Bonner, J.T. (1962). *The ideas of biology.* Harper, New York.
Brace, C.L. (1962). Physique, physiology and behavior: An attempt to analyze a part of their roles in the canine biogram. Doctoral dissertation, Harvard University, Cambridge, Massachusetts.
Darwin, C. (1965). *The expression of the emotions in man and animals.* Univ. of Chicago Press, Chicago, Illinois.
Davis, R.C., Buchwald, A.M., and Frankman, R.W. (1955). Autonomic and muscular responses, and their relation to simple stimuli. *Psychol. Monographs,* 69, No. 405.

Delgado, J.M.R. (1966). Emotions. In: *Introduction to psychology: A self-selection text book.* Brown, Dubuque, Iowa.

Duffy, E. (1962). *Activation and behavior.* Wiley, New York.

Engel, G.L., Reichsman, F. and Segal, H.L. (1956). A study of an infant with gastric fistula. Behavior and the rate of total hydrochloric acid secretion. *Psychosomat. Med.,* 18, 374-398.

Freedman, M., Leary, T., Ossorio, A. and Coffey, H. (1951). The interpersonal dimension of personality. *J. Personality,* 20, 143-161.

Funkenstein, D.H., King, S.H. and Drolette, M.E. (1957). *Mastery of stress.* Harvard Univ. Press, Cambridge, Massachusetts.

Furchtgott, E. and Cureton, E.E. (1964). Factor analysis of emotionality and conditioning in mice. *Psychol. Reports,* 15, 787-794.

Gellhorn, E. (1960). Recent contributions to the physiology of the emotions. *Psychiat. Res. Rep.,* 12, Jan.

Gellhorn, E. and Loofbourrow, G.N. (1963). *Emotions and emotional disorders.* Hoeber, New York.

Grace, W.J., Wolf, S. and Wolff, H.G. (1951). *The human colon.* Hoeber, New York.

Guttman, L. (1954). A new approach to factor analysis. In P.F. Lazarsfeld (Ed.), *Mathematical thinking in the social sciences.* Free Press, Glencoe, Illinois.

Hinde, R.A. (1966). *Animal behavior.* McGraw-Hill, New York.

Kellerman, H. (1964). The development of a forced-choice personality index and its relation to degree of maladjustment. Ph.D. dissertation. Yeshiva University.

Kellerman, H. (1966). The emotional behavior of dolphins, Tursiops Truncatus: Implications for psychoanalysis. *Intern. Mental Health Res. Newsletter,* 8, 1-7.

Kellerman, H., and Plutchik, R. (1968). Emotion-trait interrelations and the measurement of personality. *Psychol. Reports,* 23, 1107-1114.

Lacey, J.I., Kagan, J., Lacey B.C., and Moss, H.A. (1963). The visceral level: situational determinants and behavioral correlates of autonomic response patterns. In: P.H. Knapp (Ed.), *Expression of the emotions in man.* International Univ. Press, New York.

Landis, C. and Hunt, W.A. (1939). *The startle pattern.* Farrar and Rinehart, New York.

Lodge, G.T. (1953). A method for the dynamic representation of personality data. *J. Projective Techniques,* 17, 477-481.

Lorenz, K. (1967). *On aggression.* Bantam, New York.

Lorr, M., and McNair, D.M. (1963). An interpersonal behavior circle. *J. Abnormal and Social Psychol.,* 67, 68-75.

MacLean, P.D. and Ploog, D.W. (1962). Cerebral representation of penile erection. *J. Neurophysiol.,* 25, 29-55.

Mahl, G.F. (1949). Effect of chronic fear on the gastric secretion of HCL in dogs. *Psychosomat. Med.,* 11, 30-44.

Peterson, E.H. (1965). A comparison of affects in early memories, recent memories and thematic material. MA Thesis, Queens College.

Platman, S.R., Plutchik, R., Fieve, R.R. and Lawlor, W. (1969). Emotion profiles associated with mania and depression. *Arch. Gen. Psychiat.,* 20, 210-214.

Plutchik, R. (1962). *The emotions: facts, theories and a new model.* Random House, New York.

Plutchik, R. (1965). What is an emotion? *J. Psychol.,* 61, 295-303.

Plutchik, R. (1966a). Emotions as adaptive reactions: Implications for therapy. *Psychoanalyt. Rev.,* 53, 105-110.

Plutchik, R. (1966b). Psychophysiology of individual differences with special reference to emotions. *Ann. N. Y. Acad. Sci.,* 134, 776-781.

Plutchik, R. and Ax, A.F. (1967). A critique of "Determinants of Emotional State" by Schachter and Singer (1962). *Psychophysiol.*, 4, 79-82.

Plutchik, R. and Stelzner, D. (1966). Individual and breed differences in timidity and approach in dogs. *Proc. Am. Psycholog. Assoc.*, 149-150.

Plutchik, R., McFarland, W.L., and Robinson, B.W. (1966). Relationships between current intensity, self-stimulation rates, escape latencies and evoked behavior in rhesus monkeys. *J. Comp. Physiol. Psychol.* 61, 181-188.

Rado, S. (1956). *Psychoanalysis of behavior.* Grune and Stratton, New York.

Robinson, B.W. and Mishkin, M. (1961). Alimentary responses evoked from forebrain structures in macaca mulatta. *Science,* 136, 260-262.

Schachter, J. (1957). Pain, fear and anger in hypertensives and normotensives: A psycho-physiological study. *Psychosomat. Med.,* 19, 17-24.

Schacter, S. and Singer, J.E. (1962). Cognitive, social and physiological determinants of emotional state. *Psychol. Rev.,* 69, 379-399.

Schaefer, E.S. and Plutchik, R. (1966). Interrelationships of emotions, traits, and diagnostic constructs. *Psychol. Reports,* 18, 399-419.

Schlosberg, H. (1954). Three dimensions of emotions. *Psychol. Rev.,* 61, 81-88.

Schneider, R.A. and Zangari, V.M. (1951). Variations in clotting time, relative viscosity, and other physiochemical properties of the blood accompanying physical and emotional stress in the normotensive and hypertensive subject. *Psychosomat. Med.,* 13, 289-303.

Scott, J.P. (1958). *Animal behavior.* Univ. of Chicago Press, Chicago, Illinois.

Simpson, G.G., Pittendrigh, C. and Tiffany, L. (1957). *Life, introduction to biology.* Harcourt, Brace, New York.

Stein, M. (1967). Antonomic nervous system and behavior. In: D.C. Glass (Ed.), *Neurophysiology and emotion.* Rockefeller Univ. Press, New York.

Turner, W.J. (1957). Some phylogenetic roots of human behavior. *Trans. N. Y. Acad. Sci.,* 20, 192-198.

Wasman, M., and Flynn, J.P. (1962). Directed attack elicited from hypothalamus. *Arch. Neurol.,* 6, 220-227.

Willingham, W.W. (1956).The organization of emotional behavior in mice. *J. Comp. Physiol. Psychol.,* 49, 345-348.

Wolf, S. and Wolff, H.G. (1942). Evidence on the genesis of peptic ulcer in men. *J. Am. Med. Assoc.,* 120, 670-675.

Wolff, H. (1953). *Stress and disease.* Thomas, Springfield, Illinois.

Wynne, R.D., and Schaffzin, B. (1956). A technique for the analysis of affect in early memories. *Psychol. Reports.,* 17, 933-934.

Yilmaz, H. (1966). A program of research directed toward the efficient and accurate machine recognition of human speech. NASA-ERL Report C-68336, Cambridge, Massachusetts, December.

Chapter 2

The Biological Origin of Love and Hate

D. Stanley-Jones*

RAGE AND THE SYMPATHETIC NERVOUS SYSTEM

The two primary emotions are love and hate. These are founded on the physiological reactions of lust and rage. Lust and rage are seen in decerebrate cats and dogs, animals bereft of their cerebral cortex, in whom there is no question of feeling, or affect, or any conscious awareness that an emotion is being experienced. Only the bodily expression is there, not the mental experience. Lust and rage, therefore, are much simpler to deal with than love and hate, less complicated by problems of consciousness at a higher level.

The rage-reaction of a decerebrate cat is familiar. The animal snarls and spits, lashes with its claws and its tail, stands with its back arched and its legs extended as part of the pattern of decerebrate rigidity. The special feature of this rage-reaction are over-activity of the antigravity extensor muscles, acceleration of the heart, constriction of the blood vessels, and a rise of blood pressure. The cardio-vascular components are mediated by the sympathetic, and coordinated by the posterior hypothalamus. Rage is therefore a sympathetic emotion.

Rage-reactions of this impersonal pattern occur in man. Like similar reactions in a decerebrate cat, they are blind, impersonal, undirected. The brevity of the response, with no duration beyond the immediate stimulus, indicates that there is no involvement of the cerebral cortex through which the neural circuits could reverberate, and no actual experience of hate as a projected or directed personal emotion. It is doubtful whether there is any conscious experience of affect.

Rage occurs as a fully integrated and conscious reaction in an angry man. He stands with his knees braced, his trunk erect, his hands clenched in a fist, his jaws clenched and possibly grinding his teeth. The general pattern is that of

*Full Circle Foundation for Education and Research, Hayle, Cornwall, U.K.

overactivity of all the antigravity extensor muscles. The clenching of the fist, anatomically, is flexion; but in the tree-climbing primates from whom man is descended, the flexors of the forearm are part of the antigravity system, and take part both in decerebrate rigidity and the expression of rage. In the sloth, which hangs upside-down on the trees, it is the flexor muscles which go rigid. In the pigeon, decerebrate rigidity affects the pectoral muscles that raise the bird against gravity while in flight.

All these muscular movements in the rage-reaction of the human are self-limiting — the bracing of knees, the arching of the back, clenching of fists and jaws — and therefore completely harmless. They allow the diversion of a great quantity of neural dynamic, or nervous tension, away from a potentially dangerous projection of hate onto the outside world. They enable a man to turn his aggressions inwardly upon himself, using a pattern of muscular response which does no harm to anyone.

Perhaps I could suggest, at this point, a few definitions which I have found helpful.

Rage is the physiological response of a decerebrate animal, or a man in the solitude of his own company. Its bodily components are muscular and cardio-vascular — an acceleration of the heart and constriction of the blood-vessels. The affective component (when the cortex is intact) is an intransitive hate.

When rage is directed outward to an external object, it becomes hate. When hate leads to muscular action directed outwardly instead of inwardly, it is aggression. When it leads only to words (a wonderful safety-valve, though potentially dangerous) it could be called anger. When a man loses his temper, his emotions are out of control, he is starting a kybernetic runaway under the influence of positive feedback which may lead him to destruction.

All these responses involve the sympathetic nervous system; all are associated with constriction of the blood-vessels and acceleration of the heart which is itself a magnified blood-vessel.

LUST AND THE PARASYMPATHETIC NERVOUS SYSTEM

Lust in decerebrate animals is not nearly so familiar. It needs a special two-stage preparation, in which a cat is first decerebrated and then reduced to a spinal animal (Dusser de Barenne and Koskoff, 1932, 1934). The limbs, especially the hindlimbs, are held in a spring-like flexor rigidity, and this is accompanied (in male cats) by genital erection. As the cat is manipulated, the flexor rigidity and genital erection come and go exactly in step with each other.

Spinal man can exhibit a massive flexor movement of his trunk and limbs, together with genital erection and emission of seed. There seems to be no sexual or affective component, no consciously felt desire or feeling; it is merely a physiological response having as its principal components flexion of the trunk and limbs, and vasodilatation of the genital vessels.

Lust in a fully conscious man is mediated by the parasympathetic, through the nervi erigentes or nerves of genital erection. These nerves cause dilatation of the blood-vessels. The parasympathetic in general, and the vagus in particular, cause a slowing of the heart, a lowering of the blood pressure, and dilation of the arterioles. The action is thus the direct opposite of the sympathetic; but it is not only in opposition, it is a cooperative opposition. In the antagonism between parasympathetic and sympathetic, the essential point is that it is a balanced antagonism.

EMOTION AND THE HYPOTHALAMUS

These two halves of the autonomic nervous system have their headquarters in the hypothalamus: the sympathetic in the posterior, the parasympathetic in the anterior hypothalamus. The hypothalamus has long been regarded as a see-saw (Eppinger and Hess, 1910). This is not only a figure of speech, it is in fact a very accurate description. The general function of the hypothalamus is to preserve the constancy of the internal environment, that is to preserve homeostasis, whether it be glucostasis through the balanced antagonism of insulin and adrenalin; or thermostasis through the balanced antagonism of vasodilatation and vasoconstriction; or emotional homeostasis through the balanced antagonism of lust and rage, of love and hate. Its every reaction is patterned on that of a see-saw, either-or; and it achieves this in a downward direction by coordinating the opposing actions of the parasympathetic and the sympathetic.

Looked at from this viewpoint, the real muscles of emotional expression are not the recently acquired facial muscles that are related to the platysma, but the far older vascular muscles that encircle the arterioles. These muscles control the blood pressure, and thus determine the amount of work done by the heart, that is its oxygen consumption and thermal output.

Among these many homeostatic duties of the autonomic and the hypothalamus, the primary function seems to be temperature control. The posterior hypothalamus and the sympathetic mobilize the defenses against over-cooling by constriction of the blood-vessels and increasing the thermal output of the heart. The anterior hypothalamus and the parasympathetic defend against over-heating, by slowing the heart and by vasodilatation which sends the blood to the surface.

When an animal is cold, the heart-rate increases and the blood-vessels constrict. These sympathetic reactions occur also in the expression of rage. When an animal is hot, its parasympathetic helps it to cool by vasodilatation. This is also the essential mechanism of lust.

The suggestion is therefore made that the human emotions of love and hate, of lust and rage, have their biological origins in the mammalian defenses against heat and cold (Stanley-Jones, 1966b).

There are several lines of evidence in support of this thermostatic theory of the origin of emotion. First, the autonomic centers in the hypothalamus for sympathetic and parasympathetic are virtually identical with those for temperature control. This alone would account for the either-or pattern, the balanced antagonism which is such a feature of the hypothalamic see-saw; because an animal is either too hot or too cold — it cannot be both at once.

Secondly, in cold-blooded animals the polarity of the autonomic is reversed because the direction of heat-flow is reversed. The sympathetic and adrenalin protect against over-heating, the parasympathetic and acetylcholine defend against over-cooling. Autonomic control of the pupil and of the heart-rate are also reversed.

Finally, in certain cold-blooded animals (frogs and lizards), thermal defense is effected by change of color, and thermostasis is the principal determinant of behavior. Whether a lizard comes out into the open, or whether it rests in the shade, is decided almost entirely by the question of temperature. And among the reptiles (lizards and chameleons) the same color-changes which help them to regulate their temperature are much in evidence during their displays of emotion.

There is thus an unbroken chain of evidence linking the thermostatic defenses and emotional responses of cold-blooded vertebrates, as seen in their color-changes, with the thermostatic and emotional responses of man; for throughout the range of terrestrial animals, both those reactions are mediated by the two halves of the autonomic having their controlling headquarters at one or other end of the hypothalamus.

The thermostatic theory of emotion explains also the immediacy of our emotions, that is their essential relation to the immediate present. An emotion cannot be frozen or preserved like a bottle of fruit, it is nothing if not for here and now. Whenever lust or rage are taken out of context with the living present they constitute a risk to mental health. Rage and fear are the sympathetic emotions for fight or flight. In their crude forms they have no other function. So also with our thermal responses: it is useless to shiver today because tomorrow will be cold, or to sweat now in memory of the heat of yesterday. Thermal responses, like the primary emotional responses, are of use only in the immediate present.

ROLE OF THE PARASYMPATHETIC NERVOUS SYSTEM

So much for the basic physiology of emotional expression. The flux of neural impulses can be traced from their origin in the stretch-receptors of the carotid sinus, up as far as the hypothalamus, then downwards to the muscles of the heart and the blood vessels. We must now trace them upwards, from the hypothalamus to the cortex, where alone these physiological responses can become conscious mental events, where emotions are first experienced as affects or feelings.

The first thing to note is that only the parasympathetic has direct access to the cortex. Little is known of the sympathetic afferents, they have not been fully traced or understood; but a great deal is known of the parasympathetic afferents: where they come from, how they get to the cortex, what they do when they get there, and how they influence our feelings.

When the cut end of the vagus is stimulated, there is general motor inhibition, ranging from suppression of the knee-jerk (Cragg and Evans, 1960) to almost total paralysis (Schweitzer and Wright, 1937). So these parasympathetic afferents, ascending to the cortex, must ultimately relay to the motor Areas 4 and 6.

The prime source of neural dynamic for the parasympathetic is probably the carotid sinus, at the bifurcation of the carotid artery. Stretch-receptors here are sensitive to changes in the pressure of the blood. If the carotid sinus is artificially distended (in a dog) by perfusion with fluid under pressure, the dog will nearly fall asleep as the pressure is raised, and will awake as the pressure falls (Koch, 1932). That this is a parasympathetic effect is known by the constriction of the pupil.

The inhibitory role of the parasympathetic is well in evidence in diving animals. A duck has to hold its breath while under water, and this can be imitated by pouring cold water onto its beak. Respiration stops, and the afferent channel here is the glossopharyngeal nerve. When a seal dives, its heart-rate slows from 60 to 15 a minute. The dominance of the parasympathetic in the life of the seal may be related to the complete absence of sympathetic emotions, especially fear of man and response to pain.

So also in the contrast between the rabbit and the hare. The rabbit has a rapid heart-beat with poor parasympathetic control, and seems to live in perpetual fear. The hare has a slow pulse, is vagotonic and stays motionless almost until it is actually trodden upon. The absence or presence of sympathetic fear may be related to the activity or nonactivity of the parasympathetic.

ORBITAL CORTEX AND FEELINGS

From the stretch-receptors in the carotid sinus and the aortic arch, the parasympathetic neural input ascends to the 9th and 10th nerve nuclei in the medulla, thence to the anterior hypothalamus and ultimately to Area 13 in the orbital cortex. Area 13 is known to be the cortical projection area for the vagus and parasympathetic (Bailey and Bremer, 1938); the orbital region is also the reception area for the chorda tympani, probably carrying taste-impulses which are intimately connected with the parasympathetic reflexes of salivation and digestion (Patton and Amassian, 1950).

When Area 13 is excised in monkeys, there ensues a profound change in behavior (Ruch and Shenkin, 1943). The monkeys become unnaturally restless, and exhibit hypermotility of a remarkable pattern: the restlessness works up to a noonday peak, then subsides in the evening and permits normal sleep at night (Livingston *et al.*, 1947). This restlessness — may we call it hypomania? — is thus closely geared to the rhythm of day and night.

From this it may be concluded that the normal function of Area 13 is to restrain the appearance of restlessness or mania. The area of cortex which is kept under this perpetual restraint is probably Areas 9 and 10, the actual frontal poles of the brain, for these seem to be the areas responsible for the most highly integrated movements released by destruction of Area 13.

What happens when Area 13 is overactive? Knowing that Area 13 is the projection area of the vagus, knowing also that overstimulation of the vagus leads to generalized motor inhibition, or depression, we may conclude that overactivity of Area 13 leads to depression, and that underactivity leads to mania.

Mania and depression are intimately related to feeling. Mania is accompanied by feelings of elation and euphoria, as well as by motor restlessness. Depression is essentially a feeling of sadness and often of guilt, with generalized motor and mental retardation.

THE SENSE OF GUILT

The problem of guilt deserves a moment of exploration. Guilt, especially sexual guilt, is expressed as a blushing of the face; that is, by vasodilatation. It may therefore be regarded as a parasympathetic emotion. There seems to be a mutual exclusiveness between guilt and lust, an either-or pattern or secondary see-saw at the parasympathetic end of the hypothalamus.

If lust is active, as expressed by genital erection, there is no sense of guilt; and if guilt is active, there cannot be an erection. It seems as if the parasympathetic is rather short of supplies of neural dynamic, that it cannot send out vasodilator impulses to both ends of the body at once. It is another case of either-or; either to the pelvis and the sacral nervi erigentes, or to the face as the blush of sexual guilt.

Guilt is an unhealthy emotion, and is possibly due to blockage of parasympathetic lust by sympathetic fear. At a higher level, guilt may be sublimated as a sense of responsibility, it forms the basis of our ethical sense of moral values. It is just this ethical sense which is so notably lacking in mania and after leucotomy, and this ties up with the belief that leucotomy acts by interrupting the parasympathetic inflow into the orbital cortex via Area 13. At the other extreme, guilt is a prominent feature of psychotic depression, and may be regarded as due to overactivity of the parasympathetic, directed upwards as guilt instead of downwards as lust.

THE STRUCTURE OF CYCLOTHYMIA

Mania and depression are the two halves of the cyclothymic rhythm. They are related to each other as mirror images, or plus and minus. Mania is caused (I believe) by underactivity, and depression by overactivity of the ascending influence of the parasympathetic, which enters the cortex at Area 13.

This theory of the origin of cyclothymia affords a rational explanation for prefrontal leucotomy, especially as a treatment for psychotic depression. Leucotomy acts presumably by interrupting either the inflow or the output of Area 13, thus cutting off from the cortex the stream of parasympathetic afferents whose overactivity has caused the depression.

Cutting off the parasympathetic afferents in this way may have unfortunate results. It may leave a patient with the postleucotomy syndrome which is in effect a surgically produced mania. Patients after leucotomy sometimes exhibit Rylander's triad of extraversion, elevation of mood, and overactivity. They have a much reduced sense of social responsibility, and little or no sense of guilt.

If the phases of cyclothymia are related to waxing and waning of parasympathetic input into the cortex, and if the origin of neural dynamic for the parasympathetic is in the carotid sinus, it might be possible to interrupt the endless cycles of this disease by a "debuffering" operation on the carotid sinus. This would cut off at its source the main input into the parasympathetic, instead of cutting its output into the cortex as in leucotomy.

A surgical treatment of cyclothymia on those lines has been suggested (Stanley-Jones, 1966a), but so far the operation has not been carried out. Experiments on mice have been conducted at Loyola University, by Doctors Scudder and Richardson, in an endeavor to test this hypothesis. It was found that bilateral section of the glossopharyngeal nerves was followed by changes in behavior.

FEELINGS AND WILLED BEHAVIOR

Finally, I would like to say something on the influence of feelings on behavior. It has long been known that the principal determinant of human behavior is emotion, that when the emotions and the intellect are in competition for control of the will, it is usually the emotions that win. Is there any neural or anatomical explanation for this?

The first thing to note is that there is no center in the cortex for willed movements. For all those psychological faculties such as conation, striving, desire, I want, I will, there has been discovered no anatomical correlate whatsoever. The cortex has by now been explored in sufficient detail for it to be stated that there *is* no cortical center for the will. On the other hand, it is inconceivable that the neural focus for our highest faculty should be elsewhere than in the cortex. The only conclusion is that it must be in the cortex, but that we are looking for the wrong thing, we are asking the wrong question.

Voluntary movement has been described as a change from posture to posture. The first step in any willed movement is the inhibition of tonic posture, to allow phasic or voluntary movement a brief spell of action. The first step in voluntary movement in inhibition.

This has been tested and proved in the human. A man was asked to make a voluntary movement, keeping his arm flexed and to extend it on the stimulus of light touch. Recording electrodes were placed on biceps and triceps. It was found that voluntary contraction of the triceps was preceded always by involuntary relaxation or inhibition of the opposing biceps, and that this unconscious suppppression of the biceps preceded voluntary contraction of the triceps by about 50 milliseconds (Hufschmidt, 1954) — again the importance of suppression or inhibition as the first action of the will.

This identification of the voluntary aspect of movement with muscular inhibition not only gives a physiological basis for the faculty of conation, but also brings into line the important but neglected "Law of reversed effort" enunciated by Baudouin (1920) and Coué. Little attention has been given to Coué's discovery, which tallies closely with everyday experience, because hitherto there has been no explanation whether in terms of psychology or neurology.

As enunciated by Baudouin (1920, p.116), "the law of reversed effort is revealed in all its simplicity to everyone who is learning to ride a bicycle. When we are at length able to wobble painfully along, should we see a big stone lying in the middle of the road, we know that all our attempts to avoid it serve only to direct our steering wheel towards the obstacle, upon which it impinges with deadly precision.... The stone has attracted our attention, suggestion is at work, and our efforts to counteract it serve merely to reinforce it."

The operation of this law is familiar to anyone faced with the problem of getting out of bed on a cold morning. There is a conflict between conation ("I want to get up") and affect ("I like the warmth of my bed"); the issue is heavily weighted in favor of the desired comfort. If however the mind is cleared for a moment by active suppression of the desire, getting out of bed will be found to be almost effortless.

The greater the effort of the will in its struggle against a contrary desire, the less the result. The effect of voluntary effort, in these circumstances, may indeed be diametrically reversed. Voluntary movement in the face of a contrary desire is impeded by enhancement of that desire, and facilitated by inhibition of that desire. Structurally this is similar to the hindrance to willed movement by muscular rigidity (as in Parkinson's disease) and to the release of voluntary movement by inhibition of postural tone. In both cases, voluntary movement is associated with a process of inhibition or suppression.

The origin or focus of voluntary movement could therefore lie concealed in the motor suppressor system. This starts from certain suppressor strips in the cortex, Areas 2S, 4S, 8S, 19S (McCulloch, 1949) not well located in the human but definitely known to exist (Bucy, 1954, Penfield and Jasper, 1954). The suppressor downfall from these small areas converges onto the cingular gyrus Area 24 at the bottom of the midline cleft. Area 24 is the principal outlet for motor suppression. From here the suppressor downfall suffers a triple bifurcation, and ends up finally in the ventromedial nucleus of the hypothalamus. Here it is directed either to the anterior hypothalamus, or to the posterior hypothalamus, but not to both ends at once.

It is the ventromedial nucleus which determines the set of the hypothalamic see-saw, the either-or mechanism that balances parasympathetic against sympathetic; and its mode of action is by direction of suppressor dynamic to one end or the other of the see-saw.

This mechanism, which has been discovered by extirpation experiments, tallies closely with Benzinger's (1964) views on the thermostatic function of the hypothalamus; he postulates an interaction between the two ends, that is between the defenses against overheating and overcooling, an interaction that is based on mutual inhibition.

The ventromedial nucleus, therefore, determines the general set of our behavior: whether we react positively, creatively, sublimating the libido through the parasympathetic and the anterior hypothalamus; or negatively, destructively, giving vent to our sympathetic emotions of rage or fear.

Destruction of the ventromedial nucleus in animals releases either the posterior or the anterior hypothalamus from its tonic inhibitory influence. If the posterior hypothalamus is released from suppression, the animal exhibits very pronounced rage-reactions (Schreiner and Kling, 1953). If, on the other hand, the anterior hypothalamus is released, the animal develops an enormous appetite and puts on weight (Anand *et al.*, 1955). The appetite for food is closely related to the appetite for sex, and these voracious animals display greatly exaggerated libidinal behavior at both the oral and the genital level.

WHY EMOTION OVERRULES REASON

Our problem is to discover how human behavior can be influenced by emotion. The pathway for voluntary movement is down the pyramidal tract direct from motor cortex to spinal cord; this is a throughway with no relays and little risk of interference from the hypothalamus and its emotions. There are, however, at least two other systems involved. Firstly, there is the motor suppressor system from Area 24 which has to inhibit postural tonus to allow voluntary movement to take place. The same suppressor downfall goes also to the ventromedial nucleus, which determines the general set of the hypothalamus, whether we react positively and creatively, or negatively and destructively.

But the problem is more than the question *how?* We want to know *why* emotion takes priority even over reason and the intellect. I think this is the answer. Once a voluntary impulse has left the motor areas and travelled down the pyramidal tract, it arrives at the spinal cord and continues on its journey to the muscles — this I regard as the outlet for willed movements guided by intellect. This mechanism is undisturbed by leucotomy. But the suppressor downfall reaches the hypothalamus, where it has a chance to return to the cortex, by the re-entrant circuit ascending to Area 13. There it can continue its influence over the general level of motor activity, in terms of mania and depression, hypermotility or retardation; thus it has an immense anatomical advantage over the pyramidal or voluntary impulses which, once they have left the cortex, have no chance to return.

So this is the final picture of the influence of feelings on behavior, interpreted in terms of neural dynamic. Neural impulses arise in the stretch-receptors of the carotid sinus, and enter the hypothalamus. Here they can go either to anterior or to the posterior end. At the posterior, sympathetic end there is another bifurcation, the fight-or-flight reaction, either rage or fear. At the anterior, parasympathetic end, the neural impulses can go either up or down. If they go down, they leave either by the sacral nervi erigentes as lust, or by the cranial parasympathetic as guilt, and also in relation to the appetite for food.

If they go up (that is upwards from the anterior hypothalamus to Area 13) the pattern changes. It is not a bifurcation, either-or, but a modulation of a sustained tonus, too much or too little — too much yields depression, sadness and sloth, too little releases hypermotility and feelings of elation.

The ventromedial nucleus determines the set of the hypothalamus. What determines the set of the ventromedial nucleus? This nucleus is specifically sensitive to blood-sugar — if the blood-sugar is too high, the level is reduced by parasympathetic insulin; if it is too low, supplies are replenished by sympathetic adrenalin. This is the neural and biochemical link with hunger in relation to our emotions, and explains why hunger, like sex, is one of the major determinants of human behavior.

THE BIOCHEMISTRY OF EMOTION

Biochemical determinants of emotion have been recognized for years. Testosterone, the male hormone, accentuates parasympathetic lust. Adrenalin is intimately connected with sympathetic rage and fear.

Adrenalin exists naturally in two forms. Adrenalin A from the medulla of the adrenal gland is secreted direct into the blood stream; its principal targets are the liver and voluntary muscle, where it is used to mobilize glycogen into glucose.

Adrenalin B (nor-adrenalin) is liberated at the adrenergic nerve endings of the sympathetic, especially the vasoconstrictor nerves that raise the blood pressure. Its action on glycogen is only one-twentieth as effective as that of adrenalin A (Schümann, 1949).

Adrenalin A predominates in timid animals, rabbits, guinea-pigs, frightened dogs, and herbivores in general. Adrenalin B is found more in agressive animals and carnivores (Ruesch, 1953). The clue to the hitherto unexplained difference between fear, the motive of flight, and rage, which supplies the dynamic for a fight, may well lie in the biochemical difference between adrenalin A and adrenalin B.

Fear and rage have differentiated out of the primitive sympathetic response to cold probably in relation to habits of feeding. Adrenalin A in herbivores is the basis of fear, whose cognitive trigger is "you are going to eat *me.*" Adrenalin B in carnivores stirs up the feelings of rage, supplying the dynamic for aggression with the aim of "I am going to eat *you.*"

The contrasting emotions of fear and rage, in their nutritional context, are reflected in the vascular behavior of the human stomach (Wolf and Wolff, 1947). Fear causes blanching by gastric vasoconstriction, thereby diverting the blood to the life-saving muscles of flight. Rage causes a blushing of the stomach by local vasodilatation, in anticipation of the meal that, in carnivores, follows a success-ful fight. Man on the biochemical level is still a carnivore.

Intravenous injection of adrenalin in humans yields results consistent with this biochemical basis of emotion. Student volunteers when injected with adrenalin A showed signs of anxiety (a variant of fear); adrenalin B caused feelings of "anger directed outward away from the self" (Funkenstein *et al.,* 1953).

Patients who are depressed and fearful show an excessive secretion of adrenalin A even in the absence of external stress. Paranoids, whose outlook on life is dominated by hostility, have an excess of adrenalin B.

The two principal types of anxiety are associated with thyroid disease and anxiety neurosis. Thyroid anxiety (for which there has never been even the beginning of an explanation, biochemical or otherwise) is due probably to repressed fear (Stanley-Jones, 1957) with excess of adrenalin A. Neurotic anxiety is related to repressed rage and to excess of adrenalin B.

The relation of glandular (A) to neural (B) adrenalin follows the pattern of the evolutionary hierarchy, in which the biochemical or glandular level is more primitive than the neural. Fear and flight from an aggressor is a life-saving response whose failure means death. Rage in the pursuit of a meal is merely for the satisfaction of hunger. Fear must therefore be regarded as a more primitive, more fundamental emotion than rage.

This conclusion is supported by a statistical analysis of the physiological responses to fear and anger in humans (Ax, 1953). The correlations between a group of physiological variables, measured in situations provoking either fear or rage, were significantly higher for rage than for fear. This suggests that rage is a more highly integrated, and fear a more primitive response, which tallies with the relative status of neural and glandular secretion.

REFERENCES

Anand, B.K., Dua, S. and Shoenberg, K. (1955). Hypothalamic control of food intake. *J. Physiol.* 127, 143-152.

Ax, A.F. (1953). Fear and anger in humans. *Psychosomat. Med.,* 15, 433-442.

Bailey, P. and Bremer, F. (1938). A sensory cortical representation of the vagus nerve. *J. Neurophysiol.,* 1, 405-412.

Baudouin, C. (1920). *Suggestion and autosuggestion.* Allen and Unwin, London.

Benzinger, T.H. (1964). The thermal homeostasis of man. *Symp. Soc. Exp. Biol.,* 18, 49-80.

Bucy, P.C. (1954). Discussion. *J. Neurosurgery,* 11, 26-28.

Cragg, B.G. and Evans, D.H.L. (1960). Reflexes mediated by vagal afferents. *Exp. Neurol.,* 2, 1-12.

Dusser de Barenne, J.G. and Koskoff, Y.D. (1932). Flexor rigidity and priapism in spinal cat. *Am. J. Physiol.,* 102, 75-86.

Dusser de Barenne, J.G. and Koskoff, Y.D. (1934). Further observations on flexor rigidity in hindlegs of spinal cat. *Am. J. Physiol.,* 107, 441-446.

Eppinger, H. and Hess, L. (1910). *Die Vagotonie.* Hirschwald, Berlin.

Funkenstein, D.H., King, S.H. and Drolette, M. (1953). The experimental evocation of stress. In *Symposium on stress,* March 16-18. U. S. Government Printing Office.

Hufschmidt, H. (1954). Antagonist inhibition as the earliest sign of a sensory-motor reaction. *Nature,* 174, 607.

Koch, E. (1932). Irradiation der pressorezeptorischen Kreislaufreflexe auf das animale Nervensystem. *Zeitschrift für Kreislaufforschung,* 24, 251-258.

Livingston, R.B., Fulton, J.F., Delgado, J.M.R., Sachs, E., Brendler, S.J., and Davis, G.D. (1947). Functions of the orbital surface. *Res. Publ. Assoc. Nervous Mental Disease,* 27, 405-420.

McCulloch, W.S. (1949). Cortico-cortical connections. In P. C. Bucy (Ed.), *The precentral motor cortex* (2nd ed.). Univ. of Illinois Press, Urbana, Illinois.

Patton, H.D. and Amassian, V.E. (1950). Cortical projection zone of the chorda tympani. *J. Neurophysiol.,* 15, 245-250.

Penfield, W. and Jasper, H. (1954). *Epilepsy and the functional anatomy of the human brain.* Little, Brown, Boston.

Ruch, T.C. and Shenkin, H.A. (1943). The relation of area 13 to hyperactivity in monkeys. *J. Neurophysiol.,* 6, 349-360.

Ruesch, J. (1953). *Symposium on Stress,* March 16-18, U. S. Government Printing Office.

Rylander, G. (1939). *Personality changes after operations of the frontal lobes.* Munksgaard, Copenhagen.

Schreiner, L. and Kling, A. (1953). Behavioral changes following rhinencephalic injury in the cat. *J. Neurophysiol.,* 16, 643-659.

Schümann, H.-J. (1949). Vergleichende Untersuchungen über die Wirkung von Adrenalin, Arterenol und Epinin auf Blutdruck, Milzvolumen, Darm und Blutzucker. *Archiv für Experimentelle Pathologie und Pharmakologie,* 206, 164.

Schweitzer, A. and Wright, S. (1937). Stimulation of the central end of the vagus. *J. Physiol.*, 88, 459-475.

Stanley-Jones, D. (1957). *Structural Psychology.* J. Wright, Bristol.

Stanley-Jones, D. (1960). *Kybernetics of natural systems.* Pergamon, Oxford.

Stanley-Jones, D. (1966a). Kybernetics of cyclothymia. *Progress of Brain Research,* 17, 151-168.

Stanley-Jones, D. (1966b). The thermostatic theory of emotion: A study in kybernetics. *Progress of Biocybernetics,* 3, 1-20.

Wolf, S. and Wolff, H.G. (1947). *Human gastric function* (2nd ed.). Oxford Univ. Press, London.

Part II

Physiological Correlates
of Feeling and Emotion

INTRODUCTION

In the five papers of this section, the focus is on the neural and physiological correlates of feelings and emotions.

In the first three papers, the discussion rests on the assumption that the activation of specific structures produces certain physiological changes that represent the emotion. Thus Pribram concludes from his findings on lesioning or stimulating the amygdala and hippocampus that these structures monitor and modulate organismic excitation and inhibition; and that this monitoring function is experienced as feeling. Melzack discusses the affective aspect of pain and suggests that it is mediated by reticular and limbic brain structures. Brady, finally, discusses the autonomic-endocrine patterns he obtained in various stress experiments, implying that they are correlated with emotional behavior.

The last two papers start out with the investigation of psychological correlates of the neurophysiological process. Thus Tomkins suggests that affect is the awareness of stimulation increments, a certain stimulus level, and stimulation decrements. In contrast, Schachter denies this "identity hypothesis" and concludes from his experiments with obese and normal subjects that among the former there is no necessary connection between the reported feeling of hunger, the stomach contractions during food deprivation, and eating behavior. He concludes that "the labels one attaches to a bodily state, how one describes his feelings, are a joint function of cognitive factors and of a state of physiological arousal."

Chapter 3

Feelings as Monitors

Karl H. Pribram*

"Emotion always focuses on the object, while feeling reveals my momentary state of mind" (Magda B. Arnold, 1969, Vol. 1, p. 21).

FEELINGS AND EMOTIONS

For the past decades I too have been struggling to clarify my thinking with regard to the neuropsychological problems encompassed by the term emotion. This struggle has not been an exercise in abstraction; rather, a series of experimental researches have been undertaken and their results systematized. These studies have focussed on the frontal and limbic formations of the forebrain. The bibliography which records these efforts is appended to this manuscript.

I am here today not to review once more the fruits of these efforts, but to voice my continuing dissatisfaction with them. One of the difficulties of re-*search* as opposed to re-search is the proper definition of the problem so that experimental analysis can be engaged. As yet the physiologically oriented community in psychology has failed to come to terms with this issue.

Let me give an example. Many of the students concerned with brain function in emotion are engaged with hypothalamic and limbic mechanisms. Implicit in their approach is the relationship between these structures and the autonomic nervous system. This implicit relationship has been voiced in the term "visceral brain," a term coined to make explicit the "gut" aspects of emotion. Papez (Bull, 1951) was initially responsible for calling attention to the limbic formations as a neural mechanism of emotion. He based his case to a considerable extent on the influences which the limbic systems can exert on hypothalamic structures; "the main central organ which evokes the visceral responses associated with emotional expression . . . ."

*Stanford University, California

However, taken out of context, this quotation does Papez a disservice. The statement is included in a series of others which are given equal weight. Here is a more complete and faithful reproduction:

" . . . In fact, the autonomic nervous system is involved at these lower levels in support of predisposition, attitude and motor adjustments appropriate to the needs of the organism. More elaborate controls are found in the bulbar reticular formation, especially for the regulation of respiration, vegetative and related functions.

"In the tectal and tegmental regions of the midbrain there are special mechanisms such as the tectospinal tracts and tectopontocerebellar paths for the control of the eyes and head, for shaping the attitudes of sex and defense, and for the exercise of inhibitor controls over locomotion, oral and autonomic activities. The tegmentum of the midbrain is notable for such structures as the red nucleus, rubrospinal tract, rubroreticuloolivary path and the nucleus profundus mesencephali with its numerous connections to the reticular formation, to the subthalamic nuclei and other parts. Of special significance for attitude and inhibition is the substantia nigra with its afferent connections from the cerebral cortex and pretectal nucleus, and its efferent connections to the basal ganglia.

"The ventral thalamus is situated between the tegmentum of the midbrain and the basal ganglia. Two of its major parts are concerned respectively with attitude and visceral activity. (a) In the subthalamus (under the dorsal thalamus) there are primitive subcortical connections from the optic and vestibular systems to the zona incerta. The fasciculus geniculatus interalis comes from the pars ventralis of the lateral geniculate body, a visual relay; and the fasciculus tegmentoincertalis comes from the vestibular region. Both probably exert an important subcortical influence on posture and attitude through the connections of the zona incerta with the basal ganglia. (b) The hypothalamus is an ancient region for the regulation of hypophyseal and autonomic activities. Its action is evoked by the medial bundle of the forebrain and visceral afferent impulses as well as impulses from the basal ganglia. Its efferent fibers pass down to the tegmentum of the midbrain, and in the central gray matter. The hypothalamus is regarded as the main central organ which evokes the visceral responses associated with emotional expression and the accompanying attitude."

The passage is taken from a chapter written by Papez for Nina Bull's *The Attitude Theory of Emotion* (1951, pp. 89-92) where he points to the "many parallel features" between his mechanism and attitude theory. Yet, despite this very specific published account, Papez has been repeatedly claimed as a proponent of the visceral theory of emotion, nor, suprisingly, did he deny this affiliation at any time. This is typical of the confustion displayed in this field of inquiry. Though investigators do not acknowledge it, it would seem to make a difference whether one thinks that the visceral-autonomic accompaniments of emotional expression are just that or whether gut responses and the messages signalled from them to the brain are *the* characteristics which define emotion.

My own views began with a visceral orientation but experimental results quickly disabused me of such a limited view. Gradually a more comprehensive position was developed – a position not too different from that of Nina Bull and the other great woman theorist on emotion, Magda Arnold, who states simply that "an emotion indicates my attitude . . . ." I am not at all surprised that in this field of inquiry two women should see clearly what has continued to befuddle males.

In my language, emotions are Plans (Miller *et al.*, 1960), neural programs which are engaged when the organism is disequilibrated. Equilibrium is ordinarily maintained through a more or less harmonious "motivated" execution of Plans; they are modified and grow by the consequences produced by their execution. When such execution is hampered, for whatever reason, a "hangup" results: mechanisms of internal adaptation and control such as the regulation of input channels (including those concerned with signals from viscera and those making up the "body image") are brought into play. These mechanisms of emotion are of two sorts. One tends to open, the other to close, the organism to further input. In either case, however, the orderly progression of the growth of the Plan being executed is brought to a halt. If the "hangup" goes on for any length of time because it continues to be infeasible to execute the Plan in its present form, then earlier, more rudimentary organizations become engaged in an attempt to "get the organism moving again." The hampered Plan is then gradually and selectively pruned back to a version which in the experience of the organism has proved feasible of execution. When execution continues to be blocked, considerable "regression" may occur.

In this sense emotion need not be expressed in behavior. When it is, emotional expression is more primitive and encompasses more basic responses than an organism's reasoned actions, i.e., those steered in detail by their consequences. But this is *not* to say that all emotion is "built in" to the organism, that emotion is what is genetically determined in behavior. Quite the contrary: the Plans engaged in emotion, just as motivational Plans, are shaped by the experience of the organism. In fact the "Plans in Action" and "Plans in the Passions" are the same: it is the *consequences of attempted or contemplated execution* which differ. In the language of attitude theory, my attitude toward a person or object remains for a time basically the same whether I can do something about it or not. As noted by attitude theorists, attitude has two aspects: attitude which is preparatory to action and attitude which involves self-regulation with respect to someone or thing.

Having attained some clarity in my thinking on these points, I found that others immediately arose to plague me. Some of these concerned a set of problems usually included under the rubric "emotion," which have to do with wide-ranging predispositions to behave in one or another fashion. The clinic especially is concerned with physiological determinants of such predispositions or moods — as for example, depression. And depression hardly fits what I conceive of as a Plan (though the more ambiguous term, attitude, would not necessarily encounter this difficulty).

Closely related to this set of problems is another which arises when one tries to detail what is meant by equilibration and disequilibration. Just how is the execution of Plans coordinated into an harmonious activity? And just how and what becomes disequilibrated when the execution of Plans is hampered? Elsewhere (Pribram, 1967a) I have detailed the evidence which suggests that disequilibrium, arousal, is a function of the amount of uncertainty (in the information-theorists's sense). This leaves unanswered the question of the mechanism of appraisal of the amount of uncertainty.

The answers to these questions became possible once it occurred to me that here the concern was primarily with organismic states — in my language with *Images* rather than with *Plans*. And so my focus of inquiry shifted from emotions to feelings. This shift allowed a fresh approach to be made, one which clarified for me a number of hitherto obscure facets. This paper serves as an introduction to this approach.

FEELINGS AND SENSATIONS

From the energy configurations which excite some of our receptors we are able to reconstruct an objective world. Sight and hearing especially give us images which we interpret as being distant from the receptors excited. Touch, taste and smell do not ordinarily allow this attribution of distance; localization is to the receptor surface. Yet even here the judgment is made that one touches, tastes or smells something other than one's own receptor reactions.

But there is another world, a subjective world of feelings. We feel hungry or sleepy or sexy. We feel happy or sad, contemplative or assertive. What distinguishes the objective from this subjective world?

The answer to this question becomes especially tacky when one considers neurological mechanisms. The naive realist can easily state that, indeed, sensations refer to things "out there" but that feelings refer to "internal states." But clinical experience with phantoms produced by limb amputation make it unlikely that our experience of receptor stimulation occurs where we are apt to localize it. Images of objects are formed *in the brain* — why then do we locate objects where we do?

Békésy (1967) has performed some critical experiments to answer this question. Using touch, which ordinarily is not interpreted as distant, he has created conditions under which such an interpretation is made. When one limb is stimulated, the source of excitation is localized to that extremity. When, however, symmetrical places on both limbs are stimulated, the subjects of his experiments begin to experience the sensation in a location *between* the limbs. The effect is similar to that produced when two loud-speakers replace a single source: the stereo effect localizes the sound source between the speakers.

These are, of course, only some of the conditions which determine objectivity; constancy in the face of movement on the part of the organism, intermodality validation, and recurrence, are others. The point here is, however, that the objective world must be constructed from this evidence because when it is lacking, the verdict is apt to be that the experience is subjective — i.e., felt.

APPETITES AND AFFECTS

Next, let me turn to the specific issues raised earlier. Do the results of recent neurobehavioral experiments clarify earlier obscurities? I believe they do. For instance, the relationship between emotion and motivation takes on new meaning when feelings become a legitimate focus of interest.

The early experiments on the neural control of motivation and emotion produced a major paradox: when lesions were made in the region of the ventromedial nucleus of the hypothalamus, rats would eat considerably more than did their controls and they became obese. But this was not all. Although rats so lesioned would eat a great deal when food was readily available, they were found to work less for food when some obstacle interfered. In addition, it was found that the more palatable the food, the more the lesioned subject would eat. Similar effects are obtained when drinking is studied. This gave rise to the notion that the *lesioned* animals were more "finicky," i.e., had less appetite than the controls. Further, recent experimental results obtained by Krasne (1962) and by Grossman (1966) show that electrical *stimulation* of the ventromedial nucleus *stops* both food and water intake in the deprived rats. Moreover, the animals learned an instrumental response to terminate such stimulation, suggesting that aversive, affective effects may have been produced. Grossman therefore suggests that the neurobehavioral results occur due to alterations in *affect* rather than *appetite* when the ventromedial nucleus is manipulated, that the lesioned animals show an *exaggerated sensitivity to all sorts of stimulation.*

Just the opposite sort of results are obtained when another area in the hypothalamic region is manipulated. Cessation of eating and drinking occurs when a far-lateral region of the hypothalamus is damaged. Here also more widespread effects are obtained, however. The results of a recent study by Bunnell and Thompson (in press) show that such lesions severely impair escape behavior — that the lesioned subjects are insensitive to shock.

Grossman notes that one discrepancy remains, however. How can stimulation of a *stop* mechanism *increase* affect? This remaining discrepancy is resolved if both "go" and "stop" mechanism are conceived to generate feelings — "go" mechanisms, the feelings of appetite and interest related to motivation, and "stop" mechanisms, the affects related to emotion.

APPRAISAL, AROUSAL, AND SALIENCE

The results of recent neurobehavioral research, when approached from the standpoint of an inquiry into feelings, have given equally clear answers to the second of my questions: the nature of the appraisal mechanism.

Some years ago we showed that the effects of temporal lobectomy on changes in temperament resulted from the removal of the limbic system structures contained within the temporal lobe: the amygdala and hippocampus (Pribram and Bagshaw, 1953; Pribram, 1954). Further analysis showed that these limbic formations were involved in a variety of behaviors labeled as "the Four F's" — an extension of Cannon's "Fight and Flight" label for sympathetic neural function (Pribram, 1960). Our Four F's included, in addition to Cannon's, feeding and sexual behavior. The close anatomical linkage between the limbic and hypothalamic structures made this result a reasonable one. The problem arose when I became dissatisfied with just a descriptive correlation between brain anatomy and behavior and tried to understand the mechanism of operation of this relationship. What I wanted to know was whether the amygdala regulated only functions ordinarily ascribed to the hypothalamic mechanism or were *other psychological process affected?*

The experiments performed therefore went far afield from the proverbial Four F's. In collaboration with Schwartzbaum (1960), with Bagshaw (1965), and with Hearst (1964a, 1964b), transfer of training experiments were undertaken. In one procedure, transposition behavior was studied; in the other, the reaction to stimulus equivalences. Stimulus generalization was analyzed as a control measure. The tasks were chosen because they seemed to us reasonably remote from hypothalamic influence.

Amygdalectomy affected performance in both transposition experiments but not in those testing stimulus generalization. My conclusion was therefore that the amygdala at least, influences processes other than those ordinarily ascribed to the hypothalamus.

A clue to what these processes might be came from an observation made while testing the monkeys on the transposition task. The amygdalectomized subjects neither transposed nor did they choose the absolute cue. Instead they treated the test trials as a completely novel situation, performing initially at chance (see Douglas, 1966).

Pursuing this observation Bagshaw and her collaborators working in my laboratory showed that amygdalectomy indeed altered monkeys' reactions to novelty (Bagshaw *et al.*, 1965; Kimble *et al.*, 1965; Bagshaw and Benzies, 1968;

Bagshaw and Coppock, 1968: Bagshaw and Pribram, 1968). Behavioral and some components of EEG habituation to novelty were markedly prolonged. On the other hand, the viscero-autonomic "arousal" indicators (GSR, changes in heart and respiratory rates) or orienting to novelty were wiped out by the lesions (without impairing the response mechanisms per se). These results led me to suggest that orienting to novelty proceeds through two hypothetical stages. The first, characterized by behavioral orienting reactions, "samples," scans the novelty. The second, characterized by viscero-autonomic "arousal" reactions, leads to "registration" of the novelty in experience and memory and so to its habituation (Pribram, 1969).

I have elsewhere (Pribram, 1967b) spelled out in detail a plausible neural mechanism to account for these results. The mechanism involves inhibitory interactions in the afferent channels of the nervous system; Bagshaw and Spinelli have shown that these afferent interactions can be influenced by electrical stimulations of the amygdala.

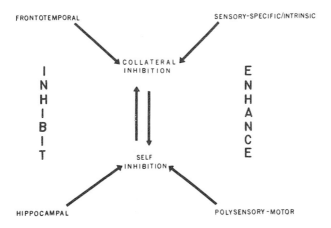

FIGURE 1.   A model of corticofugal control over input processing. Collateral inhibition is considered the basic process for the orienting reactions; self-inhibition is the basic process for habituation. Two corticofugal systems enhance and two inhibit this basic mechanism of afferent neural inhibition.

A good deal about the process of "registration" has been learned by Bagshaw and her group. In a classical conditioning situation, normal monkeys show a gradual incrementing of concurrent, and a lengthening of the period during which anticipatory, galvanic skin responses occur as trials are given. In amygdalectomized subjects no such incrementing or anticipating is observed. Thus "registration" apparently involves a selective enhancement of the intensity and the temporal extension of a process set into operation by the repetition of events. It is as if some sort of "internal rehearsal" were taking place in the normal organism without which registration does not occur (Bagshaw and Coppock, 1968).

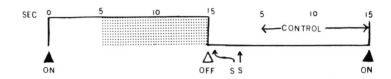

TRIALS	GRP	5-10 SEC ON	10-15 SEC ON	5-10 SEC OFF	10-15 SEC OFF
FIRST 40	NORM	3.7	7.0**	3.9	7.0
	AMX	3.2	3.3	3.9	6.3
SECOND 40	NORM	5.7**	8.8*	6.2	4.5
	AMX	2.7	4.8	3.5	4.3
All 80	NORM	9.3	14.5*	10.3	7.0
	AMX	5.8	8.2	7.3	6.3

$* = p < .08$

$** = p < .05$

MEAN NO. GSRS IN PERIODS PRECEDING SHOCK

(ANTICIPATORY RESPONSES)

FIGURE 2.   **Mean number of GSR occurring in 10-sec period of light on just preceding light offset (CS) in the first 40 and in the second 40 trials for each group.**

Note that I have been talking about experiencing. These data help explain an observation I made many years ago (Miller *et al.*, 1960, Chapter 14). A patient on whom a bilateral amygdalectomy had been performed a year earlier had gained much weight. She seemed to present a golden opportunity to find out directly what she *experienced* to make her eat so much. Her answer was always that she did *not* feel inordinately hungry, that in fact she could not describe her experience. Chances are that each experience was to her a novelty and therefore not identifiable as hunger.

The converse observation that déjà-vu phenomena, the "as if" experiences of familiarity, result when epileptiform excitations involve the amygdala is in this light also more understandable.

In problem-solving situations the "registration" function becomes manifest in the efficacy with which cues, reinforcers, and deterrents guide behavior. Douglas and I (1966) have detailed elsewhere the basis for invoking such a reinforce-register process. In short, amygdalectomized organisms appear to be

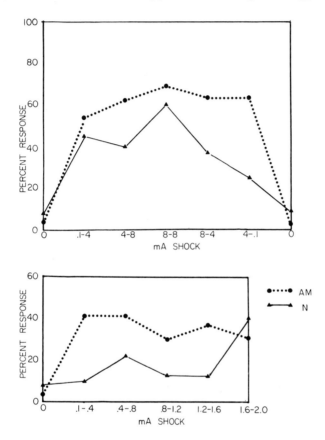

FIGURE 3. Above: Curves of percentage GSR generated by three runs of stimuli of ascending and descending intensity (in mamp) by the amygdalectomized (AM) and control (N) groups. Below: A finer breakdown of stimulus values from .1 to 1.0 mamp, pooled ascending and descending values.

insensitive to what is relevant, salient, correct — to what is the right response to make in a problem. Sensitivity can be achieved only when simpler go and stop mechanisms are modulated. There is ample evidence that in fact the amygdala performs such modulations.

In experiments designed to test psychophysical thresholds, Bagshaw and J.

Pribram (1968) have shown that the amygdalectomized monkey reacts in an all-or-none fashion to foot shock — threshold is if anything lower, but the reaction of the subject is the same for the lowest as for the highest intensities given, Roger Russell *et al.* (1968) has shown by similar psychological techniques that a quantitative relationship can be drawn between the amount of carbachol injected into the amygdala and the amount of water drunk by an already drinking animal, although such injections will neither initiate nor stop drinking.

If this is indeed the psychological process in which the amygdala is involved, what of the hippocampus? There is today much evidence that response-inhibition is primarily affected and that the neural process involved in the production of response-inhibition is akin to what Pavlov called internal inhibition (Gerbrandt, 1965; Kimble, 1969). But as Douglas (1967) has pointed out,

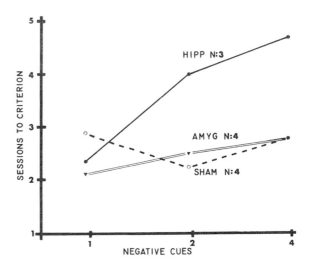

FIGURE 4.   Graph of the results of changing the number of negative cues in a set of discrimination problems. Note the effect on the hippocampectomized monkeys.

the response-inhibition hypothesis does not account for all of the data. There are situations — e.g., passive avoidance (Kimble and Kimble, 1965), discriminations in which both cues are reinforced (Webster and Voneida, 1964), distraction effects (Douglas and Pribram, in press) — in which hippocampectomized monkeys are shown to make as few or fewer responses than their controls. To account for these instances Douglas and I (1966) have ventured the thesis that hippocampectomized organisms cannot gauge what has become nonsalient, irrelevant. Ordinarily repetition of nonsalient occurrences leads to their being ignored. Behavioral habituation takes place and in a problem-solving situation responses are no longer made to the nonsalient, i.e., the wrong, the nonrein-forced cues. Hippocampectomized monkeys continue to make such wrong responses (Douglas *et al.*, 1969) and, in a learning situation in which the number of nonsalient cues was manipulated, their rate of acquisition was proportional to the number of nonsalient cues while that of normal subjects was independent of this manipulation.

I have come to the conclusion therefore that the amygdala and hippocampus provide for a sequence of processes to occur which allow us to appraise the amount of uncertainty. The mechanism which accomplishes this organizes hierarchically the salient within the context of the nonsalient, the reinforced within the context of the nonreinforced, the right within the context of the wrong. The neural mechanism by which these processes are achieved is most likely a modulation of afferent, hypothalamic, and probably, mesencephalic inhibitory interations — though evidence for the nature of hypothalamic and mesencephalic inhibitory organization has still to be investigated.

FEELINGS AS MONITORS

A final word about the specification of feelings and the third of my specific questions: the neural organization of predispositions or moods. There is a difference in the organization of the neuronal aggregates involved in feelings and those involved in sensory perception. Feelings arise from the operation of multiply interconnected core brain structures characterized by short fine-fibered, many-branched neurons. The pattern of organization of neural potentials can be expected to depart considerably from that which occurs in flat sheets of horizontally connected cells cutting across parallel lines of nerve transmission. Little is known as yet of the resultants of excitatory and inhibitory interactions which take place in such networks. From the anatomical picture one might conjecture that these interactions blend into a device which governs the reciprocity between excitation and inhibition (operating somewhat like a gyroscope to keep the system tuned), but this conjecture needs testing at the unit recording level. Because of the multisynaptic nature of the neuronal aggregates involved, they are in themselves especially sensitive to chemical substances circulating in the surrounding blood stream and thus are ideally constituted to serve as receptor sites. This special combination of control and sensitivity could be expected to make of these brain structures superb instruments for continuously monitoring their own state, a requirement basic to any conception of mood.

In conclusion, let me review the sets of problems which remained unanswered when my focus of inquiry was emotion. Does the shift in focus to feelings, and the evidence which makes it useful to consider feelings as monitors, give greater understanding of these problems?

Wide-ranging predispositions to behave, moods, were difficult to conceive as a set of Plans or programs. There is just nothing sufficiently precise about a depression, for example, to make of it a firm guide to behavior. It would be nonsense to indicate that one *plans* to be depressed. On the other hand, it is fair to say one *is* depressed or *feels* depressed. Treating Feelings as Monitors whose neuroanatomical, neurophysiological and neurobehavioral makeup has been developed here, makes eminent sense to me. Once this much is acknowledged, other feelings are admitted as legitimate entities for study. Feelings of hunger, thirst and sexiness; feelings of salience, of right and wrong, can and should be studied — and have already yielded a good deal to neurobehavioral analysis.

Thus Feelings as Monitors are well equipped to handle the problem of equilibration and disequilibration resulting from the successes and failures of motivated action. One does not plan to be involved or upset; one becomes, is and *feels* involved or upset and generally aroused when Plans succeed or fail to coordinate or when a Plan is adaptively implemented or falls short of execution. In each instance the salience of the outcome of the action, the reinforcement, is appraised and the process of appraisal monitored — i.e., felt. Feelings as Monitors, so conceived, readily encompass the problems raised by interest and commitment. One does not plan these psychological investments — one *feels* them; one either is or isn't interested or committed.

Feelings as Monitors are therefore Images rather than Plans. As such they form the matrix within which Plans are formed; the "go" Plans making up the motivations of the organism and the "no-go" Plans of which emotions are constituted. Concentrating on the experimental analysis of Feelings as Monitors, of "momentary states-of-mind" (Arnold, 1960), has thus proved rewarding, not only in its own right but in clarifying problems which a focus on emotions per se failed to resolve.

REFERENCES

Arnold, M.B. (1960). *Emotion and personality*. Columbia Univ. Press, New York.
Bagshaw, M.H. and Benzies, S. (1968). Multiple measures of the orienting reaction and their dissociation after amygdalectomy in monkeys. *Exp. Neurol.*, 20, 175-187.
Bagshaw, M.H. and Coppock, N.W. (1968). Galvanic skin response conditioning deficit in amygdalectomized monkeys. *Exp. Neurol.*, 20, 188-196.
Bagshaw, M.H. and Pribram, K.H. (1965). Effect of amygdalectomy on transfer of training in monkeys. *J. Comp. Physiol. Psychol.*, 59, 118-121.
Bagshaw, M.H. and Pribram, J.D. (1968). Effect of amygdalectomy on stimulus threshold of the monkey. *Exp. Neurol.*, 20, 197-202.
Bagshaw, M.H., Kimble, D.P. and Pribram, K.H. (1965). The GSR of monkeys during orienting and habituation and after ablation of the amygdala, hippocampus and inferotemporal cortex. *Neuropsychologia*, 3, 111-119.
Békésy, G. von (1967). *Sensory inhibition*. Princeton Univ. Press, Princeton, New Jersey.
Bull, N. (1951). *The attitude theory of emotion*. Nervous and Mental Disease Monographs, New York.
Bunnell, B.N. and Thompson, R. (in press). *Physiol. and Behavior.*

Douglas, R.J. (1966). Transposition, novelty, and limbic lesions. *J. Comp. Physiol. Psychol.*, 62, 354-357.

Douglas, R.J. (1967). The hippocampus and behavior. *Psychol. Bull.*, 67, 416-442.

Douglas, R.J. and Pribram, K.H. (1966). Learning and limbic lesions. *Neuropsychologia*, 4, 197-220.

Douglas R.J. and Pribram, K.H. (in press). Distraction and habituation in monkeys with limbic lesions. *J. Comp. Physiol. Psychol.*

Douglas, R.J., Barrett, T.W., Pribram, K.H., and Cerny, M.C. (1969). Limbic lesions and error reduction. *J. Comp. Physiol. Psychol.*, 68, 437-441.

Gerbrandt, L.K. (1965). Neural systems of response release and control. *Psychol. Bull.*, 64, 113-123.

Grossman, S.P. (1966). The VMH: A center for affective reactions, satiety, or both? *Physiol. and Behavior*, 1, 1-10.

Hearst, E. and Pribram, K.H. (1964a). Facilitation of avoidance behavior by unavoidable shocks in normal and amygdalectomized monkeys. *Psychol. Reports*, 14, 39-42.

Hearst, E. and Pribram, K.H. (1964b). Appetitive and aversive generalization gradients in normal and amygdalectomized monkeys. *Psychol. Reports*, 58, 296-298.

Kimble, D.P. (1969). Possible inhibitory function of the hippocampus. *Neuropsychologia*, 7, 235-244.

Kimble, D.P. and Kimble, R.J. (1965). Hippocampectomy and response perseveration in the rat. *J. Comp. Physiol. Psychol.*, 60, 474-476.

Kimble, D.P., Bagshaw, M.H. and Pribram, K.H. (1965). The GSR of monkeys during orienting and habituation after selective partial ablations of the cingulate and frontal cortex. *Neuropsychologia*, 3, 121-128.

Krasne, F.B. (1962). General disruption resulting from electrical stimulation of ventro-medial hypothalamus. *Science*, 138, 822-823.

Miller, G.A., Galanter, E.H. and Pribram, K.H. (1960). *Plans and the structure of behavior.* Holt, New York.

Pribram, K.H. (1954). Concerning three rhinencephalic systems. *Electroencephalog. Clin. Neurophysiol.*, 6, 708-709.

Pribram, K.H. (1960). A review of theory in physiological psychology. *Ann. Rev. Psychol.*, 1-40. Annual Reviews, Palo Alto.

Pribram, K.H. (1967a). The new neurology and the biology of emotion: a structural approach. *Am. Psychologist*, 22, 830-838.

Pribram, K.H. (1967b). The limbic systems, efferent control of neural inhibition and behavior. In W.R. Adey and T. Tokizane (Eds.), Progress in brain research (Vol. 27). *Structure and function of the limbic system*, 318-336. Elsevier, Amsterdam.

Pribram, K.H. (1969). Four R's of Remembering. In K. Pribram (Ed.), *On the biology of learning.* Harcourt, Brace, New York.

Pribram, K.H. and Bagshaw, M.H. (1953). Further analysis of the temporal lobe syndrome utilizing fronto-temporal ablations. *J. Comp. Neurol.*, 99, 347-375.

Russell, R.W., Singer, G., Flanagan, F., Stone, M. and Russell, J.W. (1969). Quantitative relations in amygdaloid modulation of drinking. *Physiol. and Behavior*, 3, 871-875.

Schwartzbaum, J.S. and Pribram, K.H. (1960). The effects of amygdalectomy in monkeys on transposition along a brightness continuum. *J. Comp. Phsyiol. Psychol.*, 53, 396-399.

Webster, D.B. and Voneida, T.J. (1964). Learning deficits following hippocampal lesions in split-brain cats. *Exp. Neurol.*, 10, 170-182.

Chapter 4

The Affective Dimension of Pain*

R. Melzack† and K. L. Casey‡

The problem of pain, since the beginning of the century, has been dominated by the concept that pain is a sensory experience. Yet pain has a unique, distinctly unpleasant, affective quality that differentiates it from sensory experiences such as sight, hearing, or touch. It becomes overwhelming, demands immediate attention, and disrupts ongoing behavior and thought. It motivates or drives the organism into activity aimed at stopping the pain as quickly as possible. To consider only the sensory features of pain, and ignore its motivational-affective properties, is to look at only part of the problem (Cantril and Livingston, 1963; Chapman *et al.*, 1965). Even the concept of pain as a perception, with full recognition of past experience, attention, and other cognitive influences (Livingston, 1953; Barber, 1959; Melzack, 1961), still neglects the crucial motivational dimension.

The motivational-affective dimension of pain is brought clearly into focus by clinical studies on frontal lobotomy, congenital insensitivity to pain, and pain asymbolia. Patients with frontal lobe lesions (Freeman and Watts, 1948) rarely complain about severe clinical pain or ask for medication. Since lobotomy does not disrupt sensory pathways (indeed, sensory thresholds may be lowered, King *et al.*, 1950), its predominant effect appears to be on the motivational-affective

*Portions of this paper have appeared in Melzack and Casey (1968) and Melzack (1967). Supported by contract SD-193 from the Advanced Research Projects Agency of the U.S. Department of Defense (to R.M.) and grant NB-06588 from the U.S. National Institutes of Health (to K.L.C.).

†McGill University, Montreal, Canada.

‡University of Michigan, Ann Arbor.

dimension of the whole pain experience. The aversive quality of the pain and the drive to seek pain relief both appear to be diminished. People reported to be congenitally insensitive to pain also appear to have no sensory loss, and are able to feel pricking, warmth, cold, and pressure. They give accurate reports of increasing intensity of stimulation, but the input, even at intense, noxious levels, seems never to well up into frank pain. The evidence (Ford and Wilkins, 1938; McMurray, 1950; Sternbach, 1963) suggests that it is not the sensory properties of the input but rather the motivational-affective properties that are absent. Similarly, patients exhibiting "pain asymbolia" (Schilder and Stengel, 1931; Rubins and Friedman, 1948) are able to appreciate the spatial and temporal properties of noxious stimuli — for example, they recognize pin pricks as sharp — but fail to withdraw or complain about them. The sensory input never evokes the strong aversive drive and negative affect characteristic of pain experience and response.

The neglect of the motivational features of pain underscores a serious schism in pain research. Characteristically, textbooks in psychology and physiology deal with "pain sensation" in one section and "aversive drives and punishment" in another, with no indication that both are facets of the same phenomenon. This separation reflects the widespread acceptance of von Frey's (1895) specificity theory of pain, with its implicit psychological assumption (see Melzack and Wall, 1962) that "pain impulses" are transmitted from specific pain receptors in the skin directly to a pain center in the brain. Although there is convincing evidence (Zotterman, 1959; Iggo, 1960; Burgess and Perl, 1967) that *physiological* specialization exists within the somesthetic system, the clinical, physiological, and psychological evidence reviewed by Melzack and Wall (1962, 1965) argues strongly against the assumption that activity in one type of receptor, fiber or brain center is uniquely responsible for the complex *psychological* experience of pain.

The assumption that pain is a primary sensation has, moreover, relegated motivational and cognitive processes to the role of "reactions to pain" (see Fig. 1), and has made them only "secondary considerations" in the whole pain process (Hardy *et al.*, 1952; Sweet, 1959). But the notion that motivational and cognitive processes must *follow* the primary pain sensation fails to account for even relatively simple data. For example, Beecher's observation that most American soldiers wounded at the Anzio Beachhead "entirely denied pain from their extensive wounds or had so little that they did not want any medication to relieve it" (Beecher, 1959, p.165) is interpreted (Beecher, 1959; Sweet, 1959) to mean that their joy at having escaped alive from the battlefield blocked only their reaction to pain, but not pain sensation itself. If this is the case, then pain sensation is not painful, even after extensive bodily damage. Rather than face the paradox of nonpainful pain (see Nafe, 1934), it seems more reasonable to say simply that these men felt no pain after their extensive injuries — that the input was blocked or modulated by cognitive activities before it could evoke the motivational-affective processes that are an integral part of the total pain experience.

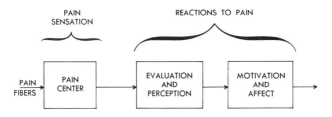

FIGURE 1. Conceptual model of pain sensation and reactions to pain.

Recognition of such interactions among widespread brain areas renders the "pain center" concept meaningless. The concept implies a "man-in-the-brain" who hears the alarm bell ring, evaluates the meaning of the input, decides on a response strategy, and pushes the appropriate response button. To avoid this sort of animistic thinking, we must postulate relationships among sensory, motivational, and cognitive systems to account for the facts of behavior.

THE MOTIVATIONAL DIMENSION OF PAIN

The theory that pain is a sensory modality is relatively recent. A much older theory, dating back to Aristotle, considers it to be an emotion – the opposite of pleasure – rather than a sensation. Indeed, this idea of pain is part of an intriguing and usually neglected bit of history (Dallenbach, 1939). At the turn of the century, a bitter battle was fought on the question of pain specificity. Von Frey argued that there are specific pain receptors, while Goldscheider contended that pain is produced by excessive skin stimulation and central summation. But there was a third man in the battle – H. R. Marshall (1894), an early philosopher and psychologist – who said, essentially, "a plague on both your houses; pain is an emotional quality, or *quale*, that cuts across all sensory events." He admitted the existence of a pricking-cutting sense, but thought that pain was distinctly different. All sensory inputs, as well as thoughts, could have a painful dimension to them, and he talked of the pain of bereavement, and the pain of listening to badly played music. His extreme approach was, of course, open to criticism. Sherrington (1900), for example, noted that the pain of a scalded hand is different from the "pain" evoked in a musicologist by even the most horrible discord. Marshall was soon pushed off the field. But if a less extreme view is taken of his concept, it suggests a new approach to pain. For pain does not have just a sensory dimension; it also has a strong negative affective dimension, and it drives us into activity. We must do something about it — avoid it, attack the source, and so on — and, of course, these response patterns are in the realm of emotion and motivation.

We (Melzack and Casey, 1968) have recently presented a conceptual model to account for the emotional and motivational dimension of pain, based in part in the gate control theory of pain (Fig. 2) proposed by Melzack and Wall (1965). The gate control theory suggests that there exists, in the spinal cord, a gate mechanism that modulates the amount of input transmitted from the peripheral fibers to dorsal horn transmission (or T) cells (Fig. 2) which project to the anterolateral pathway. The number of impulses transmitted per unit time by the T cells is determined by the ratio of large- and small-fiber inputs, and by brain activities which influence the gate control system through central-control efferent fibers. The output of the T cells is monitored centrally over a prolonged period of time; when it reaches or exceeds a critical intensity level, it triggers the Action System — those neural areas responsible for the complex, sequential patterns of behavior and experience characteristic of pain.

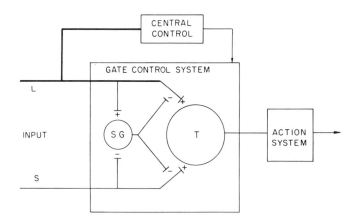

FIGURE 2.   Schematic diagram of the gate control theory of pain mechanisms: L, the
             large-diameter fibers; S, the small-diameter fibers. The fibers project to the
             substantia-gelatinosa (SG) and first central transmission (T) cells. The
             inhibitory effect exerted by SG on the afferent fiber terminals is increased
             by activity in L fibers and decreased by activity in S fibers. The central
             control trigger is represented by a line running from the large-fiber system to
             the central control mechanisms; these mechanisms, in turn, project back to
             the gate control system. The T cells project to the entry cells of the action
             system. +, excitation; -,inhibition. (From Melzack and Wall, 1965.)

We (Melzack and Casey, 1968) have noted that the output of the dorsal-horn T cells is transmitted toward the brain by fibers in the anterolateral spinal cord and is projected into two major brain systems: via neospinothalamic fibers into the ventrobasal and posterolateral thalamus and the somatosensory cortex, and via medially coursing fibers, that comprise a paramedial ascending system, into the reticular formation, the medial intralaminar thalamus and the limbic system (Mehler, 1957; Mehler *et al.*, 1960). Recent behavorial and physiological studies have led us (Melzack and Casey, 1968) to propose (Figure 3) that (a) the selection and modulation of the sensory input through the neospinothalamic projection system provides, in part at least, the neurological basis of the sensory-discriminative dimension of pain (Semmes and Mishkin, 1965; see Melzack and Casey, 1968), (b) activation of reticular and limbic structures by the paramedial ascending system underlies the powerful motivational drive and unpleasant affect that trigger the organism into action, and (c) neocortical or higher central nervous system processes, such as evaluation of the input in terms of past experience, exert control over activity in both the discriminative and motivational systems. It is assumed that these three categories of activity interact with one another to provide perceptual information regarding the location, magnitude, and spatio-temporal properties of the noxious stimulus, motivational tendency toward escape or attack, and cognitive information based on analysis of multimodal information, past experience, and probability of outcome of different response strategies. All three forms of activity, then, could

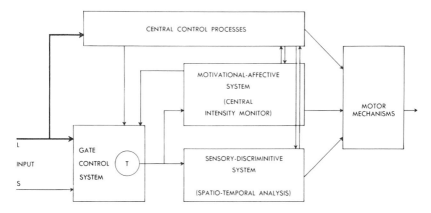

FIGURE 3.   Conceptual model of the sensory, motivational, and central control determinants of pain. The output of the T cells of the gate control system projects to the sensory-discriminative system (via neospinothalamic fibers) and the motivational-affective system (via the paramedial ascending system). The central control trigger (comprising the dorsal-column and dorsolateral projection systems) is represented by a line running from the large fiber system to central control processes; these, in turn, project back to the gate control system, and to the sensory-discriminative and motivational-affective systems. All three systems interact with one another, and project to the motor system.

influence motor mechanisms responsible for the complex patterns of overt responses that characterize pain.

There is convincing evidence that the brainstem reticular formation and the limbic system, which receive projections from the paramedial ascending system, are responsible for the aversive drive and affect characteristic of pain. At the mesencephalic level, stimulation of the central gray and some adjacent areas produces strong aversive drive and behavior typical of responses to naturally occurring painful stimuli (Hunsperger, 1956; Delgado, 1955; Spiegel *et al.*, 1954; Olds and Olds, 1963). Lesions of these areas, in contrast, produce marked decreases in responsiveness to noxious stimuli (Melzack *et. al.*, 1958; Skultety, 1958). At the thalamic level, "fear-like" responses, associated with escape behavior, have been elicited by stimulation of the medial-intralaminar nuclei of the thalamus (Roberts, 1962). In the human, lesions in the medial thalamus have provided relief from intractable pain (Hecaen *et al.*, 1949; Mark *et al.*, 1963).

Limbic forebrain areas have also been implicated in pain-related processes. Electrical stimulation of the hippocampus, fornix, or amygdala may evoke escape or other attempts to stop stimulation (Delgado *et al.*, 1956; Delgado, 1955). After ablation of the amygdala and overlying cortex, cats show marked changes in affective behavior, including decreased responsiveness to noxious stimuli (Schreiner and Kling, 1953). Surgical section of the cingulum bundle, which connects the posterior frontal cortex to the hippocampus, also produces a loss of "negative affect" associated with intractable pain (Foltz and White, 1962). This evidence indicates that limbic structures, although they play a role in many other functions (Pribram and Kruger, 1954), provide a neural basis for the aversive drive and affect that comprise the motivational dimension of pain.

Intimately related to the brain areas involved in aversive drive and sometimes overlapping with them are regions that are involved in approach responses and other behavior aimed at maintaining and prolonging stimulation. Such regions included the lateral hypothalamus, medial forebrain bundle, and septum (Olds and Milner, 1954; Olds and Olds, 1963). Stimulation of many of these areas, as well as some of the limbic forebrain structures, yields behavior in which the animal presses one bar to receive stimulation and another to stop it. These effects, which may be due to overlap of "approach" and "aversive" structures, are sometimes a function simply of intensity of stimulation, so that low level stimulation elicits approach and intense stimulation evokes avoidance (Grastyan *et al.*, 1965). In addition, complex excitatory and inhibitory interactions among these areas (Olds and Olds, 1962; Tsubokawa and Sutin, 1963; Stuart *et al.*, 1964) may explain why aversive drive to noxious stimuli can be blocked by stimulation of positive reward areas in the lateral hypothalamus (Cox and Valenstein, 1965).

We propose that these systems function as a *central intensity monitor*: that their activities are determined, in part at least, by the intensity of the T-cell output (the total number of active neurons and their rate of firing) after it has undergone modulation by the gate control system in the dorsal horns. Cells in the medial brainstem are capable of summation of input from spatially separate body sites and of temporally dispersed inputs (Amassian and deVito, 1954; Bell *et al.*, 1964), so that discrete spatial and temporal information is transformed into intensity information. In the medial medullary reticular formation of the decerebrate cat, neurons with large cutaneous receptive fields are activated principally by small-diameter myelinated cutaneous afferents. Some of these cells respond only to high intensity mechanical stimulation of the skin; others respond to mild skin deformation but give prolonged, higher frequency responses to heavy mechanical stimuli (Casey, 1969).

We suggest that the output of these cells, up to a critical intensity level, activates those brain areas subserving positive affect and approach tendency. Beyond that level, the output activates areas underlying negative affect and aversive drive. We propose, therefore, that the drive mechanisms associated with pain are activated when the somatosensory input into the motivational-affective system exceeds the critical level. This notion fits well with Grastyan's (1965) observations that animals seek low-intensity electrical stimulation of some limbic system structures, but avoid or actively try to stop high-intensity stimulation of the same areas. Signals from these limbic structures to motor mechanisms, together with the information derived from sensory and cognitive processes, could selectively activate or "prime" neural networks subserving adaptive response patterns.

There is convincing evidence (Barber, 1959; Melzack, 1961) that cognitive or "higher central nervous system processes" such as attention, anxiety, anticipation, and past experience exert a powerful influence on pain processes. These controlling influences may affect both sensory and affective experience or they may modify primarily the affective-motivational dimension. Thus, excitement in games or war appears to block both dimensions of pain (Livingston, 1953; Beecher, 1959), while suggestion (Hardy *et al.*, 1952; Melzack *et al.*, 1963) and placebos (Beecher, 1959) may modulate the motivational-affective dimension and leave the sensory-discriminative dimension relatively undisturbed. These complex processes, which must be subserved in part by neocortical functions, can act selectively on sensory or motivational mechanisms. It is now well established (see Melzack and Casey, 1968) that many forebrain structures can influence the activity of ascending pathways in the spinal cord, reticular formation, and limbic system. There is evidence, moreover, that the input is localized, identified in terms of physical properties, evaluated in terms of present and past experience, and modified before it activates the sensory or motivational systems. Men wounded in battle may feel little pain from the wound but may complain bitterly about an inept vein puncture (Beecher, 1959). Dogs that repeatedly receive food immediately after the skin is shocked, burned, or cut soon respond to these stimuli as signals for food and salivate, without showing any signs of pain, yet howl as normal dogs would when the stimuli are applied to other sites on the body (Pavlov, 1927, 1928).

The system performing these complex functions of identification, evaluation, and selective input modulation must conduct rapidly to the cortex so that somatosensory information can undergo further analysis, interact with other sensory inputs, and activate memory stores and preset response strategies. Moreover, it must be able to act selectively on the motivational and sensory systems in order to influence their response to the information being transmitted over more slowly conducting pathways. Melzack and Wall (1965) have proposed that the dorsal-column and dorsolateral (Morin *et al.*, 1963) projection pathways act as a *central control trigger* to form the input or "feed-forward" limb of this loop. The fast-conducting pathways have grown apace with the cerebral cortex (Bishop, 1959), carry precise information about the nature and location of the stimulus, adapt quickly to give precedence to phasic stimulus changes rather than prolonged tonic activity, and conduct rapidly (Morse and Towe, 1964) to the cortex, so that their impulses may begin activation of central control processes.

AFFECT AND EMOTION

This analysis of pain appears to apply to other phenomena characterized by strong affect, such as tickle, and, indeed, seem to describe the salient features of emotion. Most young children, for example, love to be tickled — by members of their family, but rarely by strangers. Our children (aged 3 to 9) often ask us to tickle them, which we do gladly, and they laugh uproariously, squirm around in delight, and ask for more when we stop. If we tickle too hard, or change our expression and pretend to scowl, they try to get away from us. If we persist, they become frantic in their attempts to escape, and their laughter may turn to tears. The moment our tickling movements become gentle again, or our scowl changes back to a smile, all is well, and the game continues as before. Some of our children are more ticklish than the others. Sometimes it is not even necessary for us to touch them; all we have to do is extend a hand and say that we are going to tickle them, and that is enough to get them laughing.

These events, we believe, contain in a nutshell a description of three salient features of emotion. (a) There is an emotion-provoking *sensory input* — in this case, repetitive, light touches applied to particular body areas in the context of play or games. (b) A *high level of arousal* or excitement pervades the whole behavior pattern — but it is not simply arousal, because it is clear that there is a strong affective coloring to the experience (Young, 1959) that is determined partly by the intensity of the tickling movements. At low intensity, the input is pleasurable but at a higher intensity it may become "too much," and behavior shifts from tickle-seeking to escape, indicating a switch in both affect and drive states. (c) *Central mediating processes* — such as the children's interpretation (based on experience and imagination) or our scowl or of the intentions of a stranger — play an astonishly powerful role in determining whether the tickle (with input intensity held constant) is very pleasant or very unpleasant.

These three features of emotion, with all the awesome complexity of their neural substrates (Pribram, 1967), stand in marked contrast with the simplicity of many earlier concepts. Emotion used to be neatly compartmentalized as a separate and distinct psychological entity, certainly deserving at least one major brain center. Conceptually, Gall and Spurzheim's (cited by Boring, 1950) phrenological maps characterize these notions by attributing a cortical center (which has a corresponding skull bump) to each emotion (or "affective faculty"). Although phrenological maps disappeared long ago, they left their mark on psychological concepts, and investigators have repeatedly sought one or more centers for the emotions. However, modern psychology and physiology make it virtually impossible to separate "emotion" from motivation, learning, memory, imagination, thought, and perception. Emotion is influenced by all these activities and contributes to them. Widespread portions of the nervous system are clearly involved in emotion, yet each portion has its specialized functions.

The history of the problem of emotion is a fascinating progression of ideas. The peripheralist theory of James and Lange, which places heavy emphasis on visceral activities and the autonomic nervous system, was replaced by the more centralist notions of Cannon and Bard and of Papez and MacLean, in which brain structures — the thalamus and the limbic system — play an increasingly prominent role. More recently, Hebb (1966) has emphasized the role of memory and experience in emotion, in which the cerebral cortex is involved, and has therefore provided a yet more centralist approach. The remembered outcome of previous actions, and past experience with similar configurations of events, are critical in determining our reactions in emotional situations. Emotion, then, once considered to be a holdover from our animal ancestry and unbecoming the mature human adult (excepting, perhaps, filial love and patriotism) is now seen to have a major cortical contribution.

Cognitive processes such as thoughts and past experience, however, may not only influence emotion; they may evoke it. The thought of war, of betrayal by a friend, of one's children, may all evoke strong emotion — anxiety, hate or love. Moreover, as Hebb (1966) has pointed out, cognitive processes hold the key to distinguishing such emotions as fear and anger. Both may involve the same intensity of arousal, yet both are subjectively and behaviorally different, and that difference lies, at least in part, in the cognitive processes that accompany each. The tendency to flee or to attack may be determined by past experience in similar situations, by the provoking agent being your boss or your wife, and so on.

This emphasis on mediating processes does not, of course, deny the importance of sensory events. There is, for example, a class of novel, strange, unusual objects that produces irrational or spontaneous fears (Hebb, 1946). These objects are characteristically incongruous with past experience: an umbrella pulled slowly across a lawn by a thin "invisible" thread often produces fright in dogs (Melzack, 1952); a death mask of a chimpanzee elicits fear in chimps (Hebb, 1946); the sight of a mutilated animal or person evokes horror in the human (Hebb, 1966). In general, however, even novel stimulation and orienting responses cannot be equated with emotion. Some novel inputs elicit exploration and curiosity (Hebb, 1955). Other forms impinge on us daily without any emotional impact; a "mutilated" chair rarely evokes fear. There is a gap between the sensory input and emotion that necessitates an understanding of the cognitive factors that obviously often mediate between input and emotional response.

An important clue to the role of the sensory input in evoking the affective dimension of emotion lies in the convincing evidence that many sensory inputs are desirable up to some intensity level (that is, are accompanied by positive affect), but that beyond this critical intensity, they become less desirable or even aversive. Pfaffmann (1960) has shown that animals make more approaches to a salt solution as the concentration increases, but beyond the critical concentration level they approach less often and finally avoid it. Records from peripheral nerve show increased firing rates proportional to the solution concentration. Similarly, rats work to get moderate levels of light stimulation — the brighter the light the harder they work (Stewart, 1960) — but actively avoid intense light (Kaplan, 1952). Intensity, then, plays an important role in affect and drive (Pfaffmann, 1960; Young, 1959). When the input, after it has undergone modulation by central mediating processes, exceeds some critical intensity level, motivational tendency shifts from approach to avoidance and, in terms of human experience, affect switches from positive to negative, from pleasantness to unpleasantness.

Perhaps the most characteristic feature of emotion is the high level of activation or arousal. Lindsley (1951), Hebb (1955), and others have stressed the critical role of arousal (and the reticular activating system), although arousal by itself must not be equated with emotion. Arousal is a vague term, even though we generally know what we mean by it psychologically. Physiologically, of course, it is identified with EEG activation, autonomic nervous system activity, and so forth. Psychologically, arousal seems to be more than this. There is also an affective component to arousal. High levels of arousal in the human are almost always accompanied by positive or negative affect. Excitement and interest, up to a certain level, are all moderately high arousal states with positive affect coloring. Nervousness and anxiety are high arousal states with negative affective coloring.

SUMMARY

We have proposed a conceptual model to account for the motivational-affective dimension of pain. The model also appears to encompass the salient features of emotion: (a) the inputs from the sensory systems, which provide discriminative spatio-temporal information; (b) arousal or activation, which is clearly a dimension of emotion, but which cannot be the whole answer to the problem of emotion; and (c) cognitive processes such as memory, against which the input is matched, and which provide the direction and course of emotional experience and response.

Within the framework of the model, the word "pain" is a label, a category, signifying a multitude of different, unique experiences. Pain varies along both sensory-discriminative and motivational-affective dimensions. The magnitude of intensity along these dimensions, moreover, is influenced by cognitive activities, such as evaluation of the seriousness of the injury. If injury or any other noxious input fails to evoke aversive drive, the experience cannot be labelled as pain. Conversely, anxiety or anguish without somatic input is not pain. Pain must be defined in terms of its sensory, motivational, and central control determinants. It is a function of the interactions of all three determinants, and cannot be ascribed to any one of them. It would be just as wrong to say that the limbic system is the "pain center" as to ascribe that function to the posterior thalamus. Clearly, each of the central nervous system areas involved in the total pain experience has specialized functions. In a model such as this, "function" does not reside in any one area. Rather, each specialized portion of the brain contributes to experience and response as a whole.

REFERENCES

Amassian, V.E. and DeVito, R.V. (1954). Unit activity in reticular formation and nearby structures. *J. Neurophysiol.*, 17, 575-603.

Barber, T.X. (1959). Toward a theory of pain: relief of chronic pain by prefrontal leucotomy, opiates, placebos, and hypnosis. *Psychol. Bull.*, 56, 430-460.

Beecher, H.K. (1959). *Measurement of subjective responses.* Oxford Univ. Press, New York.

Bell, C., Sierra, G., Buendia, N., and Segundo, J.P. (1964). Sensory properties of neurons in the mesencephalic reticular formation. *J. Neurophysiol.*, 27, 961-987.

Bishop, G.H. (1959). The relation between nerve fiber size and sensory modality: phylogentic implications of the afferent innervation of cortex. *J. Nervous and Mental Diseases*, 128, 89-114.

Boring, E.G. (1950). *A history of experimental psychology* (2nd ed.), Appleton, New York.

Burgess, P.R. and Perl, E.R. (1967). Myelinated afferent fibers responding specifically to noxious stimulation of the skin. *J. Physiol.*, 190, 541-562.

Cantril, H. and Livingston, W.K. (1963). The concept of transaction in psychology and neurology. *J. Individual Psychol.*, 19, 3-16.

Casey, K.L. (1969). Somatic stimuli, spinal pathways, and size of cutaneous fibers influencing unit activity in the medial medullary reticular formation. *Exp. Neurol.*, (in press).

Chapman, L.F., Dingman, H.F., and Ginzberg, S.P. (1965). Failure of systemic analgesic agents to alter the absolute sensory threshold for the simple detection of pain. *Brain*, 88, 1011-1022.

Cox, V.C. and Valenstein, E.S. (1965). Attenuation of aversive properties of peripheral shock by hypothalamic stimulation. *Science*, 149, 323-325.

Dallenbach, K.M. (1939). Pain: history and present status. *Am. J. Psychol.*, 52, 331-347.

Delgado, J.M.R. (1955). Cerebral structures involved in the transmission and elaboration of noxious stimulation. *J. Neurophysiol.*, 18, 261-275.

Delgado, J.M.R., Rosvold, H.E., and Looney, E. (1956). Evoking conditioned fear by electrical stimulation of subcortical structures in the monkey brain. *J. Comp. Physiol. Psychol.*, 49, 373-380.

Foltz, E.L. and White, L.E. (1962). Pain "relief" by frontal cingulotomy. *J. Neurosurgery*, 19, 89-100.

Ford, F.R. and Wilkins, L. (1938). Congenital universal insensitiveness to pain. *Bull. Johns Hopkins Hosp.*, 62, 448-446.

Freeman, W. and Watts, J.W. (1948). Pain mechanisms and the frontal lobes: a study of prefrontal lobotomy for intractable pain. *Ann. Internal. Med.*, 28, 747-754.

Frey, M. von (1895). Beiträge zur Sinnesphysiologie der Haut. *Ber. d. kgl. sächs. Ges. d. Wiss., math.-phys. K.*, 47, 181-184.

Grastyan, E. Czopf, J., Angyan, L., and Szabo, I. (1965). The significance of subcortical motivational mechanisms in the organization of conditional connection. *Acta Physiol. Acad. Sci. Hung.*, 26, 9-46.

Hardy, J.D., Wolff, H.G., and Goodell, H. (1952). *Pain sensations and reactions.* Williams and Wilkins, Baltimore.

Hebb, D.O. (1946). On the nature of fear, *Psychol. Rev.*, 53, No. 5, 259-276.

Hebb, D.O. (1955). Drives and the C.N.S. (conceptual nervous system), *Psychol. Rev.*, 62, 243-254.

Hebb, D.O. (1966). *A textbook of psychology* (2nd ed.). W.B. Saunders, Philadelphia.

Hécaen, H., Talairach, J., David, M., and Dell, M.B. (1949). Coagulations limitees du thalamus dans les algies du syndrôme thalamique. Résultats thérapeutiques et physiologiques. *Rev. Neurol.*, 81, 917-981.

Hunsperger, R.W. (1956). Affektreaktionen auf elektrische Reizung im Hirnstamm der Katze. *Helv. Physiol. Pharmacol. Acta*, 14, 70-9.

Iggo, A. (1960). Cutaneous mechanoreceptors with afferent C fibers. *J. Physiol.*, 152, 337-353.

Kaplan, M. (1952). The effects of noxious stimulus intensity and duration during intermittent reinforcement of escape behavior. *J. Comp. Physiol. Psychol.*, 45, 538-549.

King H.E., Clausen, J., and Scarff, J.E. (1950). Cutaneous thresholds for pain before and after unilateral prefrontal lobotomy. *J. Nervous and Mental Diseases*, 112, 93-96.

Lindsley, D.B. (1951). Emotion, Pp. 473-516. in S.S. Stevens (Ed.), *Handbook of experimental psychology*. Wiley, New York.

Livingston, W.K. (1953). What is pain? *Sci. Am.*, 88, 59-66.

Mark, V.H., Ervin, F.R., and Yakovlev, P.I. (1963). Stereotactic thalamotomy. *Arch. Neurol.*, 8, 528-538.

Marshall, H.R. (1894). *Pain, pleasure, and aesthetics*. Macmillan, London.

McMurray, G.A. (1950). Experimental study of a case of insensitivity to pain. *Arch. Neurol. Psychiat.*, 64, 650-667.

Mehler, W.R. (1957). The mammalian "pain tract" in phylogeny. *Anat. Rec.*, 127, 332.

Mehler, W.R., Feferman, M.E., and Nauta, W.J.H. (1960). Ascending axon degeneration following antero-lateral cordotomy. An experimental study in the monkey. *Brain*, 83, 718-750.

Melzack, R. (1952). Irrational fears in the dog. *Can. J. Psychol.*, 6, 141-147.

Melzack, R. (1961). The perception of pain. *Sci. Am.*, 204, (2), 41-49.

Melzack, R. (1967). Brain mechanisms and emotion. In D.C. Glass (Ed.), *Neurophysiology and emotion*. Rockefeller Univ. Press and Russell Sage Foundation, New York.

Melzack, R. and Casey, K.L. (1968). Sensory, motivational, and central control determinants of pain: a new conceptual model. In D.L. Kenshalo (Ed.), *The skin senses*. Thomas, Springfield, Illinois.

Melzack, R., and Wall, P.D. (1962). On the nature of cutaneous sensory mechanisms. *Brain*, 85, 331-356.

Melzack, R., and Wall, P.D. (1965). Pain mechanisms: a new theory. *Science*, 150, 971-979.

Melzack, R., Stotler, W.A., and Livingston, W.K. (1958). Effects of discrete brainstem lesions in cats on perception of noxious stimulation. *J. Neurophysiol.*, 21, 353-367.

Melzack, R., Weisz, A.Z., and Sprague, L.T. (1963). Stratagems for controlling pain: contributions of auditory stimulation and suggestion. *Exp. Neurol.*, 8, 239-247.

Morin, F., Kitai, S.T., Portnoy, H., and Demirjian, C. (1963). Afferent projections to the lateral cervical nucleus: a microelectrode study. *Am. J. Physiol.*, 204, 667-672.

Morse, R.W., and Towe, A.L. (1964). The dual nature of the lemnisco-cortical afferent system in the cat. *J. Physiol.*, 171, 231-246.

Nafe, J.P. (1934). The pressure, pain and temperature sense. In C. Murchison (Ed.), *Handbook of general experimental psychology*. Clark Univ. Press, Worcester, Massachusetts.

Olds, J., and Milner, P. (1954). Positive reinforcement produced by electrical stimulation of septal area and other regions of rat brain. *J. Comp. Physiol. Psychol.*, 47, 419-427.

Olds, M.E., and Olds, J. (1962). Approach-escape interactions in the rat brain. *Am. J. Physiol.*, 203, 803-810.

Olds, M.E., and Olds, J. (1963). Approach-avoidance analysis of rat diencephalon. *J. Comp. Neurol.*, 120, 259-295.

Pavlov, I.P. (1927). *Conditioned reflexes*. Milford, Oxford.

Pavlov, I.P. (1928). *Lectures on conditioned reflexes*. International Publishers, New York.

Pfaffmann, C. (1960). The pleasures of sensation. *Psychol. Rev.*, 67, (4) 253-268.

Pribram, K.H. (1967). Emotion: steps toward a neuropsychological theory. In D.C. Glass (Ed.), *Neurophysiology and emotion*. Rockefeller Univ. Press and Russell Sage Foundation, New York.

Pribram, K.H., and Kruger, L. (1954). Functions of the "olfactory brain." *Ann. N.Y. Acad. Sci.*, 58, 109-138.

Roberts, W.W. (1962). Fear-like behavior elicited from dorsomedial thalamus of cat. *J. Comp. Physiol. Psychol.*, 55, 191-197.

Rubins, J.L., and Friedman, E.D. (1948). Asymbolia for pain. *Arch. Neurol. Psychiat.*, 60, 554-573.

Schilder, P., and Stengel, E. (1931). Asymbolia for pain. *Arch. Neurol. Psychiat., Chicago*, 25, 598-600.

Schreiner, L., and Kling, A. (1953). Behavioral changes following rhinencephalic injury in cat. *J. Neurophysiol.*, 16, 643-659

Semmes, J., and Mishkin, M. (1965). Somatosensory loss in monkeys after ipsilateral cortical ablation. *J. Neurophysiol.*, 28, 473-486.

Sherrington, C.S. (1900). Cutaneous sensations. In E.A. Schafer (Ed.), *Textbook of physiology*. Pentland, Edinburgh.

Skultety, F.M. (1958). The behavioral effects of destructive lesions of the periaqueductal gray matter in adult cat. *J. Comp. Neurol.*, 110, 337-365.

Spiegel, E.A., Kletzkin, M., and Szekeley, E.G. (1954). Pain reactions upon stimulation of the tectum mesencephali. *J. Neuropath. Exp. Neurol.*, 13, 212-220.

Sternbach, R.A. (1963). Congenital insensitivity to pain. *Psychol. Bull.*, 60, 252-264.

Stewart, J. (1960). Reinforcing effects of light as a function of intensity and reinforcement schedule. *J. Comp. Physiol. Psychol.*, 53, 187-193.

Stuart, D.G., Porter, R.W., and Adey, W.R. (1964). Hypothalamic unit activity. II Central and peripheral influences. *Electroencephalog. Neurophysiol.*, 16, 248-258.

Sweet, W.H. (1959). Pain. In J. Field, H.W. Magoun, and V.E. Hall (Eds.), *Handbook of physiology*, 1, 459-506.

Tsubokawa, T., and Sutin, J. (1963). Mesencephalic influence upon the hypothalamic ventromedial nucleus. *Electroencephalog. Clin. Neurophysiol*, 15, 804-810.

Young, P.T. (1959). The role of affective processes in learning and motivation, *Psychol. Rev.*, 66, 104-125.

Zotterman, Y. (1959). Thermal sensations. In J. Field, H.W. Magoun, and V.E. Hall (Eds.), *Handbook of physiology*, 1, 431-458.

Chapter 5

Emotion: Some Conceptual Problems and Psychophysiological Experiments

Joseph V. Brady*

INTRODUCTION

The two distinguished predecessors of this historic conference, spanning almost half a century of investigative and theoretical endeavor, bear ample testimony to the abiding concern of biological and social scientists of all persuasions with the topic to which this symposium is addressed. Despite long-standing and dedicated attention, however, conceptual and experimental analysis of emotion has proceeded slowly and somewhat haltingly amidst a host of psychological and physiological complexities. Introspective emphasis has traditionally occupied a far more prominent place in psychological descriptions of emotion than the objective experimental analysis of behavior. And refinements in methodology emerging since the previous symposium in 1948 have only recently permitted biochemical and behavioral measurements appropriate to laboratory analysis of the complex psychophysiological relationships which characterize emotional processes.

SOME CONCEPTUAL CONSIDERATIONS

Conceptually, however, persistent semantic, linguistic, and taxonomic difficulties continue to compromise efforts to bridge the wide gap between scientific operations and systematic interpretations in the area of emotion. One continuing course of confusion in particular, to which no less a scholar than

*Johns Hopkins University School of Medicine, Maryland.

J.R. Kantor (1966) has recently addressed himself at length, would seem to require at least brief comment in relationship to the psychophysiological analysis which is to provide the central focus of this presentation. Indeed, the very title of this symposium and its predecessors alludes to an important distinction which has been all-too-often neglected in the endless polemic exchange occasioned primarily by failure to differentiate between two classes of psychological events, "feelings" or "affects" on the one hand, and "emotional behavior" on the other.

Although both feelings and emotional behavior involve psychological interactions between organism and environment, a useful and important distinction between the two can be made on the basis of the localizability of their principal effects or consequences. *Emotional behavior* seems most usefully considered as part of a broad class of *effective* interactions, the primary consequences of which appear to change the organism's relationship to its *external* environment. *Feelings* or *affective* behavior, on the other hand, can be distinguished as a generic class of interactions, the principal effects of which are localizable *within* the reacting organism rather than in the exteroceptive environment. Many different subclasses of feelings may be identified within this broad affective category, but emotional behavior seems uniquely definable in terms of a change or perturbation, characteristically abrupt and episodic, in the ongoing interaction between organism and environment.

In keeping with their internal orientation, the feelings can be intimately associated with autonomic-visceral, proprioceptive, and endocrine activity. A host of recent conditioning studies (Razran, 1961; Schuster and Brady, 1964; Slucki *et al.*, 1965; Katkin and Murray, 1968), have documented the ease with which such interoceptive events can acquire discriminative control over behavior and the flexibility which characterizes the loose integration of feeling responses with exteroceptive environmental stimuli. Under such conditions, the proliferation and variability of feelings appears limited only by the intricacies of an organism's conditioning history and the complexity of environmental stimulus situations. Of course, the labeling of such predominantly private feeling events presents many problems for the development of an appropriately objective verbal repertoire, and the wide-spread difficulty associated with affective communication provides ample testimony to the operational inadequacy of available vocabularies.

The persistent confusion between feelings and emotional behavior can in part be attributed to the prominence of interoceptive participation in at least some *effective* response patterns. But such psychophysiological activity need not constitute a defining property of emotional behavior characterized by the external localization of its primary effects and identified by abrupt changes in ongoing interactions with the exteroceptive environment. Figure 1 summarizes diagramatically some of the distinctions and interrelationships implied in this brief discussion and borrows generously from Kantor's conceptualization of the problem in modified form.

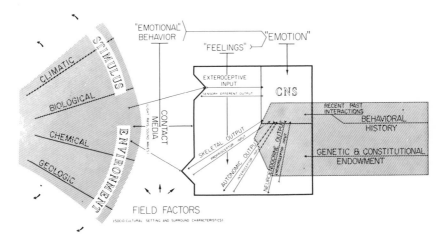

FIGURE 1. Diagramatic representation of conceptual schema emphasizing the distinction between feelings and emotional behavior.

Viewed in this way, such emotional changes in ongoing behavior become susceptible to a functional analysis of their conditions of occurrence in relationship to explicitly-defined experimental operations. Experimental analysis of the special character of these perturbations in the ongoing interaction between organism and environment has provided a starting point for the series of studies emphasizing relationships between distinguishable behavioral and physiological processes in emotion which are to be discussed in the present report.

SOME PSYCHOPHYSIOLOGICAL EXPERIMENTS

The basic laboratory setting in which these studies have been conducted is illustrated in Fig. 2 and has been previously described in considerable detail (Brady, 1965; Mason, 1958).

Briefly, the primate restraining chair situation provides for automatic and programmable delivery of food and water, administration of mildly punishing electric shock to the feet, a hand-operated electromechanical lever switch, and presentation of a variety of visual and auditory stimuli to the experimental animal. Blood samples and pressure measurements are obtained through chronically indwelling catheters. Urine samples are collected in a receptacle attached below the seat of the chair. Programming and control of all behavioral procedures is accomplished remotely and automatically with an electro-mechanical system of relays, timers, counters and recorders.

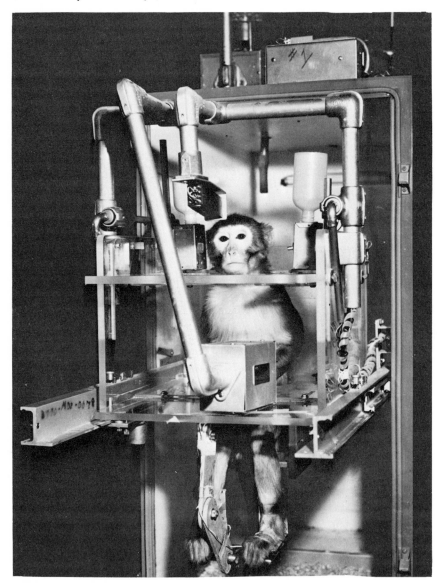

FIGURE 2.   Rhesus monkey in primate restraining chair.

Preliminary studies readily established that neither restraint in the chair following an initial 48-hour adaptation period nor performance of lever pressing for food reward alone on several different schedules of reinforcement produced any significant endocrine or autonomic changes in monkeys maintained for prolonged intervals under such conditions. When, however, emotional conditioning procedures were superimposed upon such performance baselines,

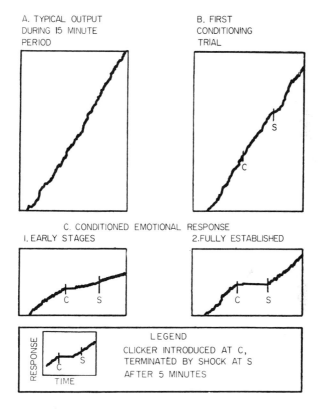

FIGURE 3.   The conditioned emotional behavior as it appears typically in the cumulative response curve.

significant changes were observed. The basic procedure which provided the focus for these initial studies is a modification of the Estes-Skinner conditioned suppression technique (Estes and Skinner, 1941; Hunt and Brady, 1951) and represents a convenient laboratory model for emotional behavior within the definitional framework discussed above. Conditioning trials consisting of five-minute continuous presentations of an auditory warning stimulus terminated contiguously with a brief shock to the feet are superimposed upon a lever-pressing performance for an intermittent food reward. Within a few trials, virtually complete suppression of the lever-pressing behavior occurs in response to presentation of the clicker, as illustrated in Fig. 3, accompanied by piloerection, locomotor agitation, and frequently urination and/or defecation.

The development of this conditioned "anxiety" response was first studied in relationship to changes in plasma 17-OH-CS levels occurring during a series of acquisition trials consisting of 30-minute lever-pressing sessions with auditory stimulus and shock pairing occurring once during each session approximately 15

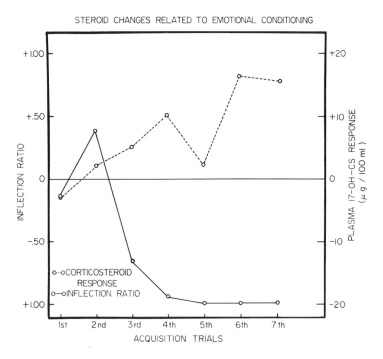

STEROID CHANGES RELATED TO EMOTIONAL CONDITIONING

FIGURE 4.   Changes in plasma 17-OH-CS levels related to emotional conditioning.

minutes after the start (Mason *et al.*, 1966). Seven such conditioning trials were accompanied by the withdrawal of blood samples immediately before and immediately after each 30-minute session and 17-OH-CS levels associated with successive stages in the acquisition of the conditioned emotional behavior were determined. Figure 4 shows the corresponding changes in lever pressing and 17-OH-CS throughout the series of seven conditioning sessions. The progressive suppression of lever pressing in response to presentation of the auditory stimulus during each successive trial is represented by the lower solid line on Fig. 4 in terms of an "inflection ratio" which provides a quantitative measure of the conditioned emotional behavior.* The upper broken line on Fig. 4 reflects the progressive increase in 17-OH-CS elevations occurring during each of the seven successive "anxiety" conditioning sessions.

This relationship between emotional behavior and the activity of the pituitary-adrenal cortical system has been further confirmed (Mason *et al.*, 1957) in a series of experiments with monkeys in which the conditioned suppression of lever pressing had been previously established. Five such animals were studied during one-hour lever-pressing sessions for food reward involving alternating 5-minute periods of auditory-stimulus-presentation and no-auditory-stimulus, as illustrated in Fig. 5. Blood samples taken before and after several such experiments with each animal, during which *no* shock followed any of the auditory stimulus presentations, revealed substantial corticosteroid elevations related to the *conditioned* emotional behavior alone. Figure 6 shows that the rate of rise of this behaviorally-induced steroid elevation is strikingly similar to that observed following administration of large ACTH doses in these animals, although such pituitary-adrenal stimulation appears to cease shortly after termination of the emotional interaction, hormonal levels returning to normal within an hour. Significantly, when the conditioned "anxiety" response is markedly attenuated by repeated doses of reserpine administered 20 to 22 hours before experimental sessions, the elevation of 17-OH-CS in response to the auditory stimulus is also eliminated (Mason and Brady, 1956).

When measurements of plasma epinephrine and norepinephrine levels were added to the corticosteroid determinations in experiments with this conditioned emotional behavior model, the potential contributions of a "hormone pattern" approach to such psychophysiological analyses became evident. Preliminary observations in the course of a rather rudimentary conditioning experiment involving a loud truck horn and electrical foot shock with monkeys suggested the differential participation of adrenal medullary systems in conditioned and

---

*The "inflection ratio" is derived from the formula $(B-A)/A$ in which "A" represents the number of lever responses emitted during the 5 minutes immediately preceding introduction of the auditory stimulus and "B" represents the number of lever responses emitted during the 5-minute presentation of the auditory stimulus. The algebraic sign of the ratio indicates whether output increased (plus) or decreased (minus) during the auditory stimulus, relative to the output during the immediately preceding 5-minute interval. The numerical value of the ratio indicates the amount of increase or decrease in output as a fraction (percentage in decimal form) of the output prior to introduction of the auditory stimulus. Complete cessation of lever pressing during the auditory stimulus yields a ratio of -1.00, and a 100 per cent increase a value of plus 1.00. A record showing essentially unchanged output obtains a ratio in the neighborhood of 0.00. The ratio thus indicates whether introduction of the conditioned stimulus produced an inflection in the output curve, how much of an inflection it produced, and in which direction.

unconditioned aspects of such emotional behavior patterns. Figure 7 shows, for
example, that exposure to the horn or the shock alone *prior* to the conditioned
pairing of the two produced only mild elevations in catecholamine levels.
Following a series of conditioning trials, however, during which horn-sounding
for 3 minutes was terminated contiguously with shock, presentation of the horn

CUMULATIVE RECORD OF LEVER PRESSING WITH SUPERIMPOSED CONDITIONED
EMOTIONAL RESPONSE IN THE MONKEY

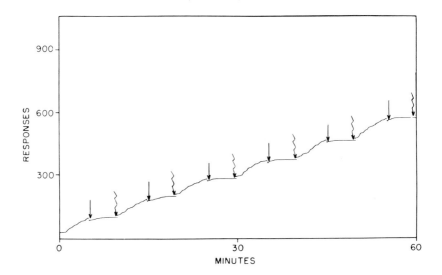

FIGURE 5.   Cumulative record of lever pressing with superimposed conditioned "anxiety" response. The straight arrows indicate the onset, and the jagged arrows
the termination of each five-minute clicker period. Between clicker periods
the lever-pressing response rate is maintained. During clicker presentations
lever pressing is suppressed.

alone markedly increased norepinephrine levels without eliciting any epinephrine
response. This hormone pattern approach has been extended in a series of
experiments in which concurrent plasma epinephrine, norepinephrine, and
17-OH-CS levels were determined during monkey performance on the alternating
5-minute "on," 5-minute "off" conditioned "anxiety" response procedure
illustrated in Fig. 5. The results summarized in Fig. 8 obtained during 30-minute
control and experimental sessions involving recurrent emotional behavior
segments confirm the differential hormone response pattern characterized by
marked elevations in both 17-OH-CS and norepinephrine but little or no change
in epinephrine levels (Mason *et al.*, 1961b).

Observations of autonomic changes related to this same conditioned emotional stress model have recently been obtained with a series of monkeys catheterized for cardiovascular measurements (Brady, 1967; Brady *et al.*, 1969). Heart rate and both systolic and diastolic blood pressure were recorded continuously during experimental sessions involving both lever pressing alone and exposure to the conditioned "anxiety" procedure. Figure 9 shows the

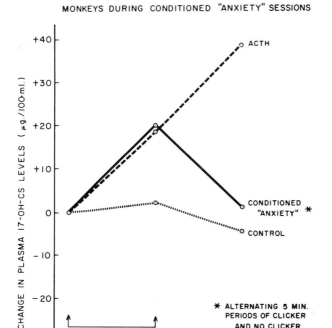

PLASMA 17-HYDROXYCORTICOSTEROID RESPONSE IN
MONKEYS DURING CONDITIONED "ANXIETY" SESSIONS

FIGURE 6.   Plasma 17-OH-CS response during conditioned "anxiety" sessions as compared to control sessons and I.V. ACTH (16 mg/kg) injection.

lever-pressing performance, heart rate, and blood pressure values obtained during approximately nine minutes of a one-hour control session prior to emotional behavior conditioning. The stable lever-pressing performance was accompanied by equally stable heart rate and blood pressure values throughout the session. By contrast, Fig. 10 shows the results obtained during an early experimental session following a series of only five conditioning trials involving 3-minute presentations of a clicking noise terminated contiguously with foot shock superimposed upon the lever-pressing performance. The complete suppression of lever-pressing during clicker presentation is accompanied by a dramatic drop in heart rate and by a somewhat less vigorous blood pressure decrease.

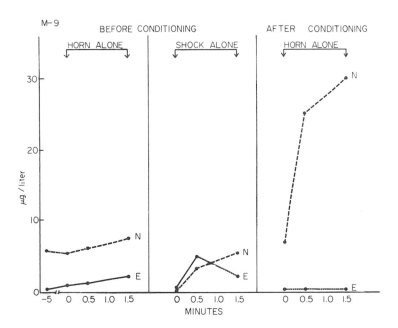

FIGURE 7.   Plasma norepinephrine and epinephrine responses before and after emotional conditioning.

Significantly, however, continued pairings of clicker and shock superimposed upon the lever-pressing performance produced abrupt reversals in the direction of these autonomic changes with cardiac acceleration and blood pressure elevation appearing and persisting in response to the clicker during the later stages of emotional conditioning. Figures 11 and 12 show the sequence of changes in the form of the autonomic responses for two of a series of five such animals in the course of fifty such emotional conditioning trials. Blood pressure, heart rate, and lever-pressing rate for successive conditioning trials are shown as changes during the 3-minute clicker period as compared to baseline values (the "O" point on each graph) representing averages for each measure of the 3-minute interval immediately preceding the clicker. The blood pressure and heart rate values are shown as absolute changes in millimeters of Mercury and beats per minute, respectively. The lever-pressing values are shown as percent changes in response rate during the clicker as compared to the preclicker baseline. Figure 11 shows complete cessation of lever pressing during the clicker developing by the third

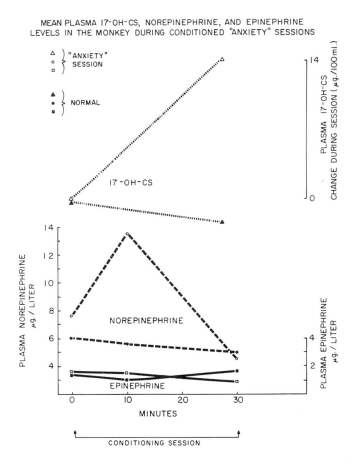

FIGURE 8. Mean plasma 17-OH-CS, norepinephrine and epinephrine levels during conditioned "anxiety" sessions.

conditioning trial for Monkey A and the maintenance of this behavioral suppression response throughout the entire course of 50 clicker-shock pairings. The autonomic changes can be seen to follow a more varied but nonetheless systematic course during this acquisition phase with Monkey A. A marked deceleration in heart rate first appeared during presentation of the clicker on the third conditioning trial corresponding to the initial development of complete

behavioral suppression. During the next four trials, a similar decelerative change
in heart rate accompanied the behavioral response with little or no change

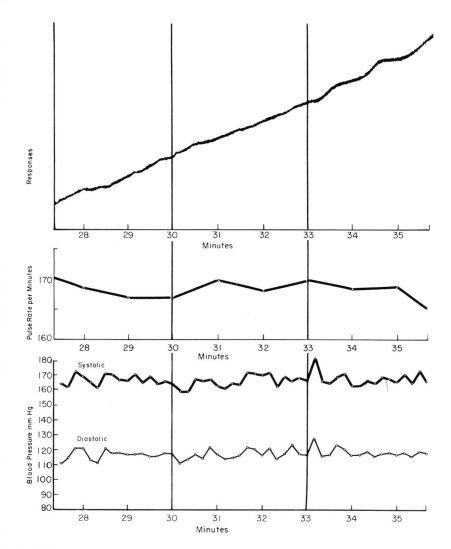

FIGURE 9.   Lever-pressing performance, heart rate, and blood pressure values during
control session prior to emotional conditioning.

apparent in either diastolic or systolic blood pressure. During the eighth
conditioning trials, however, an abrupt change in the direction of the cardiac
response to the clicker was reflected in both heart rate and blood pressure

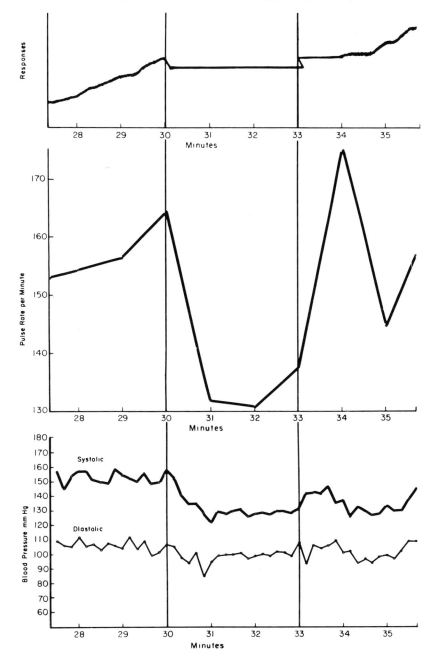

FIGURE 10.   Changes in lever pressing, heart rate, and blood pressure during conditioned
"anxiety" sessions after emotional conditioning.

measures. Increases in heart rate approximating 40 beats per minute developed
in response to the clicker by the tenth conditioning trial and persisted
throughout the remainder of the fifty acquisition trials. Both systolic and

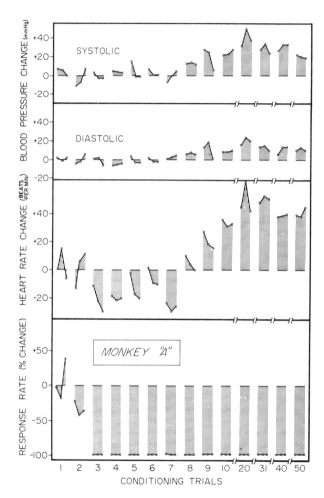

FIGURE 11.   Minute-by-minute changes in blood pressure, heart rate, and lever-pressing
response rate for Monkey A on successive 3-minute clicker-shock trials
during acquisition of the conditioned emotional response. The zero points
represent control values calculated from the 3-minute interval immediately
preceding the clicker.

diastolic blood pressure showed correspondingly consistent and dramatic
elevations in response to the clicker developing between the eighth and tenth

conditioning trial and persisting through trial fifty. Figure 12 shows a similar behavioral and autonomic response pattern for Monkey B during acquisition of

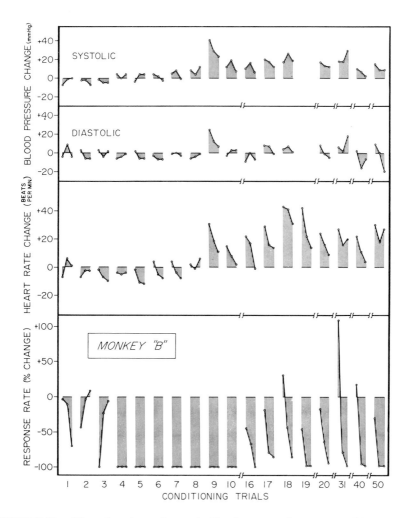

FIGURE 12. Minute-by-minute changes in blood pressure, heart rate, and lever-pressing rate for Monkey B on successive 3-minute clicker-shock trials during acquisition of the conditioned emotional response. The zero points represent control values calculated from the 3-minute interval immediately preceding the clicker.

the conditioned emotional response. Development of complete behavioral suppression by trial four is accompanied by the decelerative change in heart rate which appears repeatedly in response to the clicker through trial seven. Again, only minimal changes in blood pressure could be discerned during these early pairings of clicker and shock. And on trial nine, the cardiac accelerative response emerged precipitously in response to the clicker, persisting in the form of substantial elevations in both blood pressure and heart rate on succeeding acquisition trials.

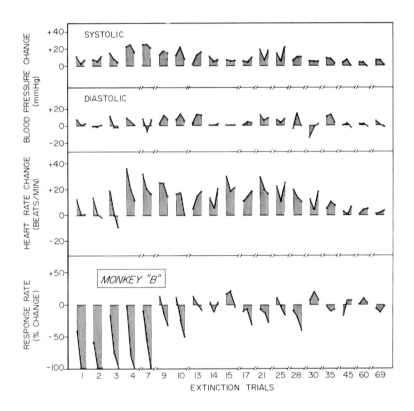

FIGURE 13.   Minute-by-minute changes in blood pressure, heart rate, and lever-pressing rate for Monkey B on successive 3-minute presentations of the clicker alone without shock during extinction of the conditioned emotional response. The zero points represent control values calculated from the 3-minute interval immediately preceding the clicker.

When the conditioned "anxiety" response was extinguished by repeated presentations of clicker alone without shock during daily lever-pressing sessions with such animals following extended exposure to recurrent emotional conditioning of this type, a further divergence between autonomic and behavioral response to emotion was observed. Figure 13 illustrates this characteristic difference in extinction rates for the cardiovascular and instrumental componets of the conditioned emotional response with Monkey B. Although virtually complete recovery of the lever-pressing rate in the presence of the clicker can be seen to have occurred within ten such extinction trials, both heart rate and blood pressure elevations in response to the clicker alone persisted well beyond the

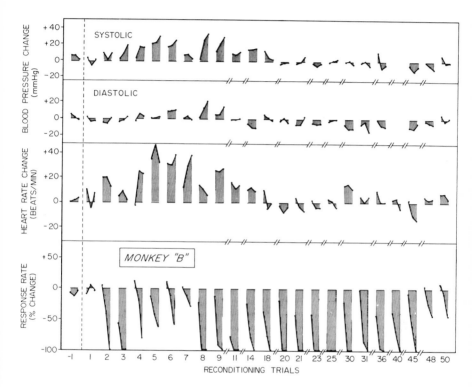

FIGURE 14. Minute-by-minute changes in blood pressure, heart rate, and lever-pressing response rate for Monkey B on the last extinction trial (far left section) and on successive 3-minute clicker-shock trials during reacquisition of the conditioned emotional response. The zero points represent control values calculated from the 3-minute interval immediately preceding the clicker.

fortieth extinction trial. Finally, reconditioning of the "anxiety" response with this same animal, as shown in Fig. 14, rapidly produced behavioral suppression accompanied immediately by the tachycardic and pressor responses. Significantly, the initial cardiac decelerative response characteristic of the early trials, during the original emotional conditioning, failed to appear during reconditioning with any of the animals.

The experimental approaches thus far described to the psychophysiological analysis of emotion have emphasized *suppressive* effects upon behavior. Under other conditions, however, a prominent consequence of exposure to such emotion-producing aversive events is an increase in the frequency of avoidance behavior. The conditioned avoidance model which has provided the basis for extensive experimental analysis in this area has been described in previous reports on the psychophysiology of emotional behavior (Mason *et al.*, 1957;

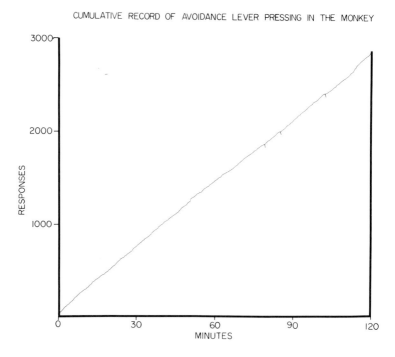

CUMULATIVE RECORD OF AVOIDANCE LEVER PRESSING IN THE MONKEY

FIGURE 15. **Cumulative record of avoidance lever pressing showing high, stable rate of approximately 1500 responses per hour. The three small vertical marks on the cumulative record indicate the occurrence of shocks when 20 seconds elapsed between lever responses.**

Sidman *et al.*, 1962; Sidman, 1953; Brady, 1965). Briefly, the basic procedure involves programming shocks to the feet of the monkey in the primate chair every 20 seconds unless the animal presses the lever within that interval to postpone the shock another 20 seconds. This avoidance requirement generates a stable and durable lever-pressing performance (illustrated in Fig. 15) which has been shown to be consistently associated with twofold to fourfold rises in corticosteroid levels for virtually all animals during two-hour experimental sessions, as shown in Fig. 16, even in the absence of any shock (Mason *et al.*, 1957; Brady, 1962, Brady, 1966). It has also been possible to demonstrate quantitive relations between the rate of avoidance responding in the monkey and the level of pituitary-adrenal cortical activity independently of the shock

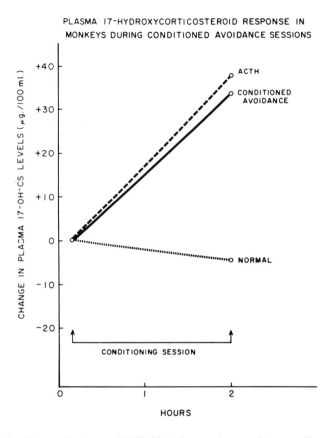

PLASMA 17-HYDROXYCORTICOSTEROID RESPONSE IN
MONKEYS DURING CONDITIONED AVOIDANCE SESSIONS

FIGURE 16. Changes in plasma 17-OH-CS during two-hour avoidance performance. The heavy dotted line labeled "ACTH" shows the rate of steroid rise over a two-hour period following only one I.V. injection of 16 mg/kg ACTH. The heavy solid line labeled "conditioned avoidance" compares the rate of steroid elevation during a two-hour exposure to the shock avoidance contingency with the ACTH response and the "normal" levels for a similar two-hour control period represented by the smaller dotted line in the lower portion of the figure.

frequency (Sidman *et al.*, 1962). Marked differences in the hormone response have been observed, however, when the avoidance procedure includes a discriminable exteroceptive warning signal presented 5 seconds prior to administration of the shock whenever 15 seconds had elapsed since the previous response. Figure 17 compares the 17-OH-CS levels measured during "regular" and "discriminated" avoidance sessions with the monkey and shows the consistently reduced corticosteroid response associated with programming such a warning signal. Conversely, superimposing so-called "free" or unavoidable shocks upon a well-established avoidance baseline without a warning signal has been observed to produce marked elevations in 17-OH-CS. Figure 18, for example, shows that the

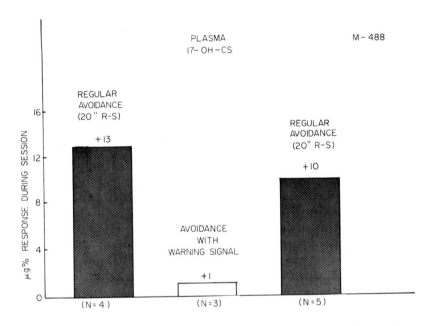

FIGURE 17.   Plasma 17-OH-CS responses during nondiscriminated ("regular") and discriminated ("warning signal") avoidance sessions.

presentation of such "free shocks" during 2-hour avoidance sessions more than doubles the corticosteroid response as compared to the regular nondiscriminated avoidance procedure.

Concurrent biochemical measurements of plasma corticosteroid and catecholamine levels have also been made in the course of several avoidance experiments with the monkey and the results illustrated in Fig. 19 confirm the previously described emotional conditioning pattern of 17-OH-CS and norepinephrine elevations with no significant alteration in epinephrine levels. Two experimental manipulations involving the avoidance procedure, however, have been observed to produce significant variations in this hormone pattern. Figure 20, for example, shows at least a modest epinephrine elevation with no change in norepinephrine accompanying presentation of the avoidance signal to a well-trained avoidance monkey following removal of the response lever from the restraining chair. Significantly, the effect occurred within one minute of the signal presentation and could not be observed following 10 minutes of continued

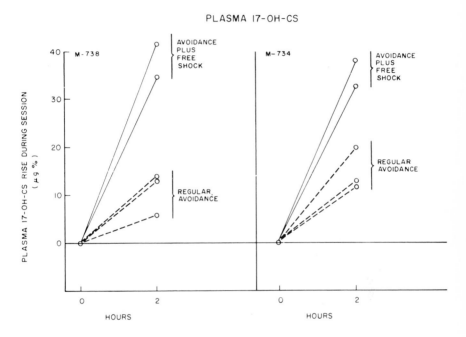

PLASMA 17-OH-CS

FIGURE 18. Plasma 17-OH-CS responses during "regular" nondiscriminated avoidance and during avoidance with "free shocks".

exposure. The results obtained with the second series of experiments involving such variations in catecholamine levels are illustrated in Fig. 21 which shows the effects of "free shock" administration to a monkey at different stages in the course of avoidance training. The mild norepinephrine and epinephrine elevations shown at the left side of Fig. 21 were obtained during an early conditioning session involving more than 100 "free shocks" before the monkey had acquired the avoidance behavior. The middle section of Fig. 21 shows the modest rise in norepinephrine levels with no change in epinephrine which accompanied later experimental sessions involving performance of the well-learned avoidance response. Finally, the right side of Fig. 21 shows the results of a series of experiments in which "free" or unavoidable shocks were programmed at the rate of one per minute (approximately the shock frequency occurring during a typical avoidance session) with this same monkey.

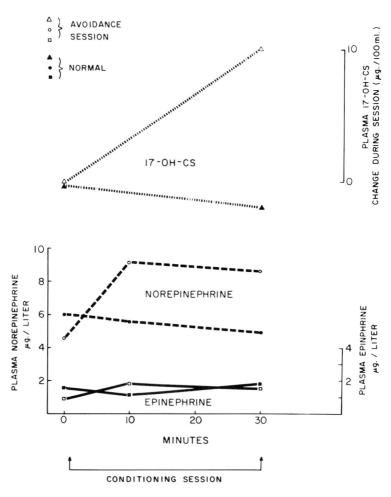

FIGURE 19. Plasma 17-OH-CS, norepinephrine, and epinephrine levels during conditioned avoidance sessions.

Significantly, dramatic elevations in both epinephrine and norepinephrine can be seen to have accompanied this procedural change even though the animal received no more shock than during previous regular avoidance sessions.

In experiments involving more complex sequences of emotional behavior patterns with the monkey as well, it has been possible to observe differential changes in catecholamine levels under specific conditions. Figure 22, for example, summarizes the results obtained in an experiment during which the withdrawal of a blood sample 10 minutes prior to the start of a session produced marked elevations in both epinephrine and norepinephrine. In the course of previous

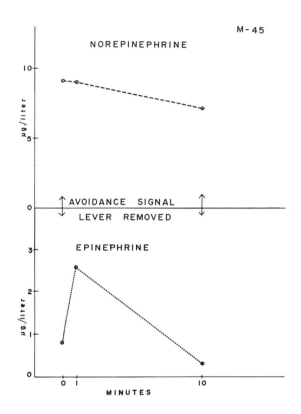

FIGURE 20.   Plasma epinephrine and norepinephrine levels following removal of the lever during an avoidance session.

conditioning trials, several different combinations of lever pressing for food alone, clicker-shock pairing alone, and both lever pressing and clicker-shock pairing concurrently (the conditioned "anxiety" procedure) had been randomly programmed in such a way that the blood-withdrawal signal could not be predictably associated with any specific component of the sequence. Under these somewhat ambiguous circumstances both epinephrine and norepinephrine levels rose significantly during the 10 minutes preceding the programmed session

although epinephrine levels fell precipitously immediately after presentation of
the first specific lever-pressing signal. In a similar experiment, illustrated in Fig.
23 involving randomly programmed 10-minute component segments of "time
out" (S$\triangle$), the shock avoidance procedure described above and a conditioned
"punishment" or "conflict" situation which provided for the production of
shock by each lever response emitted in the presence of a specific auditory
stimulus, extremely large epinephrine and norephinephrineresponses were again
observed during the initial 10-minute "time out" component prior to the

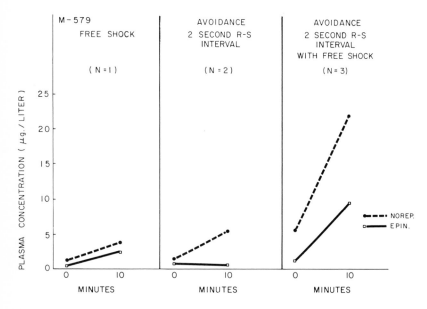

FIGURE 21.   Plasma epinephrine and norepinephrine responses to "free shock" alone,
"regular" nondiscriminated avoidance, and avoidance with "free shock".

unpredictable onset of a specifically conditioned emotional behavior signal.
Interestingly, both epinephrine and norepinephrine levels can be seen to decline
again after presentation of the first specific signal even though in this case it
required participation in a shock avoidance task.

Extended exposure to continuous 72-hour avoidance sessions has recently
provided the setting for an analysis of a broader spectrum of hormonal changes
in relationship to emotional behavior in the Rhesus monkey (Mason *et al.*,
1961a; Mason *et al.* 1961c). The pattern of corticosteroid and pepsinogen
changes observed before, during, and after such a continuous 72-hour avoidance
experiment, for example, is shown in Fig. 24. Although plasma 17-OH-CS levels

showed the expected substantial elevation throughout the 72-hour avoidance session, plasma pepsinogen levels were consistently depressed below baseline values during this same period. The postavoidance recovery period, however, was seen to have been characterized by a marked and prolonged elevation of pepsinogen levels which endured for several days beyond the 48-hour postavoidance interval required for recovery of the preavoidance corticosteroid baseline. The consequences of repeated exposure to such continuous 72-hour avoidance stress over extended periods up to and, in some cases, exceeding one year upon patterns of thyroid, gonadal, and adrenal hormone secretion have most recently been the focus of studies with a series of five chair-restrained

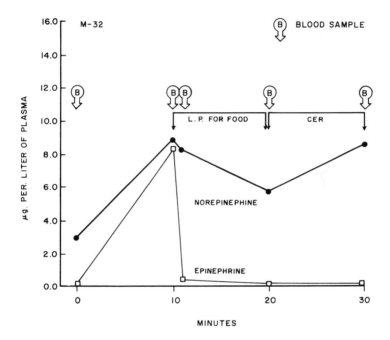

FIGURE 22. Plasma epinephrine and norepinephrine responses to ambiguous blood-withdrawal signal.

Rhesus monkeys. Two of the five monkeys participated in the 72-hour avoidance experiment on six separate occasions over a six-month period with an interval of approximately four weeks intervening between each exposure. The remaining three animals performed on a schedule which repeatedly programmed 72-hour avoidance cycles followed by 96-hour nonavoidance or "rest" cycles (3 days "on" and 4 days "off") for periods up to and exceeding one year.

The two animals exposed to repeated 72-hour avoidance at monthly intervals

for six months showed a progressively increasing lever-pressing response rate
with each of the six successive 72-hour avoidance sessions, as illustrated in Fig.
25. During the initial 72-hour avoidance experiment with these two animals
response rates averaged 16 resp/min and 18 resp/min, respectively. Response rate
values for these same monkeys during the sixth 72-hour avoidance experiment
averaged 28 resp/min and 27 resp/min. In contrast, shock frequencies over this
same period showed a sharp decline within the first-two 72-hour avoidance

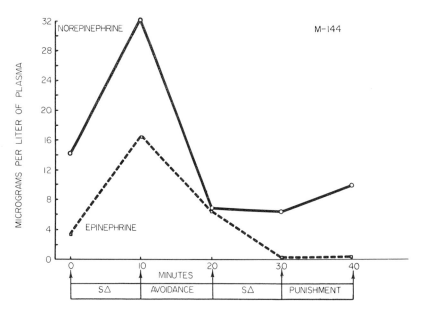

PLASMA EPINEPHRINE AND NOREPINEPHRINE LEVELS IN
MONKEY DURING CONDITIONED EMOTIONAL RESPONSE

FIGURE 23.   **Plasma epinephrine and norepinephrine responses to randomly programmed
components of a multiple schedule conditioning procedure.**

sessions and remained at a stable low level (not exceeding two shocks per hour
for either animal) for the remaining four 72-hour avoidance cycles. Hormone
changes related to the repeated 72-hour avoidance cycles showed consistent and
replicable patterns over the six-month experimental period for both animals.
During the initial experimental sessions, as shown in Fig. 25, both monkeys
showed approximately threefold elevations in 17-OH-CS levels during 72-hour
avoidance and returned to near baseline levels about six days afterwards. The
remaining four monthly experiments were characterized by substantial, though

diminished steroid responses (approximately twofold elevations in 17-OH-CS levels) during avoidance with essentially the same six-day period required for recovery of basal levels. Significant changes related to the extended avoidance performance were also observed in catecholamine, gonadal and thyroid hormone levels with recovery cycles extending in some instances (thyroid) for three weeks following the 72-hour avoidance period (Mason, 1968b).

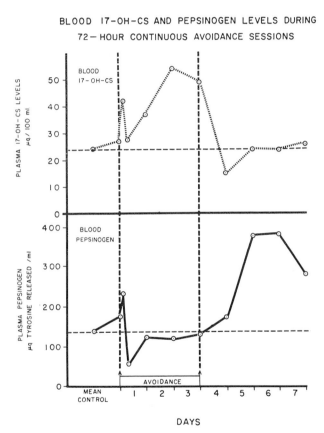

BLOOD 17-OH-CS AND PEPSINOGEN LEVELS DURING
72-HOUR CONTINUOUS AVOIDANCE SESSIONS

FIGURE 24. Mean blood levels of 17-OH-CS and pepsinogen during 72-hour continuous avoidance sessions.

The three remaining monkeys required to perform on the 3 days "on," 4 days "off" avoidance schedule showed an initial increase in lever-pressing response rates for approximately the first ten avoidance sessions similar to that seen with the two animals described above. By approximately the 29th weekly session with these animals, however, lever-pressing response rates during the 72-hour avoidance period had decreased to a value well below that observed during the initial avoidance sessions, and the performance tended to stabilize at this new low level for the ensuing weeks of the experiment. In contrast, shock frequencies for all animals quickly approximated a stable low level within the first two or three exposures to the avoidance schedule and seldom exceeded a rate of two shocks per hour for the remainder of the experiment. Typically, for example,

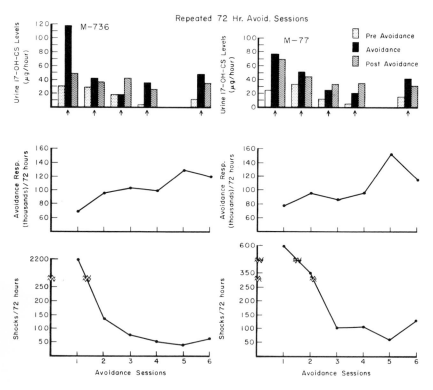

FIGURE 25. Steroid levels, avoidance response rates, and shock frequencies for animals M-736 and M-77 during six monthly 72-hour avoidance sessions.

Monkey M-157 exposed to this program for some 65 weekly sessions, as illustrated in Fig. 26, showed an average response rate of 23 resp/min during the initial 72-hour avoidance session, 32 resp/min during the 10th avoidance session, 19 resp/min during the 20th avoidance session, and 16 resp/min, 20 resp/min, and 19 resp/min during the 30th, 40th, and 50th weekly avoidance sessions respectively. The initial 72-hour avoidance sessions characterized by progressive increases in lever-pressing rate were invariably accompanied by elevations in the

17-OH-CS levels. By the 20th weekly avoidance-rest cycle, however, steroid levels had dropped below initial basal values, and no elevation in response to the 72-hour avoidance performance could be observed. By the 30th weekly session, 17-OH-CS levels had returned to their pre-experimental basal values but continued exposure to the 3-day "on," 4-day "off" schedule failed to produce

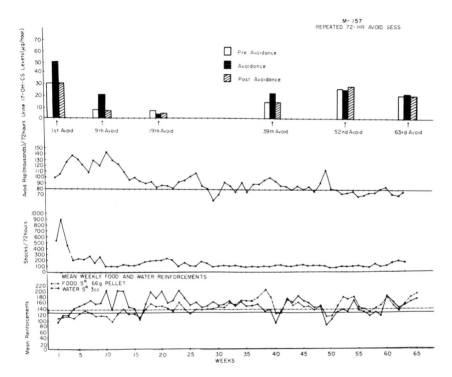

FIGURE 26. Steroid levels, avoidance response rates, shock frequencies, and food and water intake levels for animal M-157 throughout sixty-five weekly 72-hour avoidance sessions.

any further steroid elevation in response to the 72-hour avoidance requirement up through the 65th experimental session. Figure 26 also reflects the fact that following initial adjustments during the early sessions of the program shock frequencies remained at a stable low level and normal food and water intake was maintained essentially unchanged throughout the extended course of the experiment.

The general pattern obtained with M-157 has been replicated with only minor variations in the two additional animals completing 56 and 46 weeks respectively on this same experimental program. The change in responsivity of the pituitary-adrenal system to the avoidance stress with continued exposure to this procedure over extended time periods is perhaps the most consistent and striking observation in all three monkeys and is somewhat at variance with repeated findings in many previous acute studies of a close positive relationship between steroid elevations and avoidance performance. These most recent findings, however, indicate that continued exposure to this repeated performance requirement on the time schedule programmed in this experiment, produces an apparent dissociation between the avoidance performance and the 17-OH-CS response. Although a definitive analysis of such relationships is not possible on the basis of these data alone, a critical role of the temporal parameters (work-rest cycles) is clearly indicated. Certainly, related findings, on the course of recovery for a broad range of hormone measures presently being pursued, provide additional support for this focus upon temporal factors in the measurement of psychophysiological responses to emotional conditioning.

CONCLUSIONS

The results of these experiments establish firm relationships between a broad range of autonomic-endocrine system activity and behavioral interactions involving various aspects of emotion. The initial findings emphasizing changes in absolute levels of selected hormones can be viewed as reflecting relatively undifferentiated consequences of arousal states associated with such emotion-producing situations. The definite temporal course of visceral and steroid changes under such conditions and the quantitative nature of the relationship between degree of behavioral involvement and level of physiological response has been well documented. In addition, the critical role of an organism's behavioral history in determining the nature and extent of autonomic-endocrine response to emotion has been convincingly demonstrated.

Clearly, however, the most meaningful dimension for hormone and visceral analysis in relationship to more chronic emotional interactions would appear to be the broader patterning or balance of secretory and visceral change in many interdependent autonomic and endocrine systems which in concert regulate metabolic events. The extensive and prolonged participation of these fundamental systems in behavioral interactions suggests a relationship between such physiological activity and the more durable aspects of feelings involving generalized mood states and affective dispositions. The evidence for independent variations in the behavioral and physiological response patterns emerging from the present series of psychophysiological studies, however, does provide experimental support for the distinctions between feelings and emotional behavior which characterize the conceptual model of emotion proposed above. Indeed, the differentiation of such autonomic-endocrine and behavioral response patterns in relationship to the historical and situational aspects of environmental interactions could well form the basis for a functional analysis involving distinguishable intraorganismic processes under conditions of both episodic and persistent emotional involvement.

REFERENCES

Brady, J.V. (1962). Psychophysiology of emotional behavior. In A. Backrach (Ed.), *Experimental foundations of clinical psychology*. Basic Books, New York.

Brady, J.V. (1965). Experimental studies of psychophysiological responses to stressful situations. *Symposium on medical aspects of stress in the military climate*. Pp. 271-295. Walter Reed Army Institute of Research, Government Printing Office, Washington.

Brady, J.V. (1966). Operant methodology and the production of altered physiological states. Pp. 609-633 in W. Honig (Ed.), *Operant behavior areas of research and application*. Appleton, New York.

Brady, J.V. (1967). Emotion and the sensitivity of the psychoendocrine systems. Pp. 70-95 in D. Glass (Ed.)., *Neurophysiology and emotion*. Proceedings of a conference on biology and behavior. The Rockefeller Univ. Press and Russell Sage Foundation, New York.

Brady, J.V., Kelly, D. and Plumlee, L. (1969). Autonomic and behavioral responses of the rhesus monkey to emotional conditioning. *Ann. N.Y. Acad. Sci.*, 159, 959-975.

Estes, W.K. and Skinner, B.F. (1941). Some quantitative properties of anxiety. *J. Exp. Psychol.*, 29, 390-400.

Hunt, H.F. and Brady, J.V. (1951). Some effects of electroconvulsive shock on a conditioned emotional response ("anxiety"). *J. Comp. Physiol. Psychol.*, 44, 88-98.

Kantor, J.R. (1966). Feelings and emotions as scientific events. *Psychol. Record*, 16, 377-404.

Katkin, E.S. and Murray, E.N. (1968). Instrumental conditioning of autonomically-mediated behavior. *Psychol. Bull.*, 70, 52-68.

Mason, J.W. (1958). Restraining chair for the experimental study of primates. *J. Appl. Physiol.*, 12, 130-133.

Mason, J.W. (1968). Organization of psychoendocrine mechanisms. *Psychosomat. Med.*, 30, 565-808.

Mason, J.W. and Brady, J.V. (1956). Plasma 17-hydroxycorticosteroid changes related to reserpine effects on emotional behavior. *Science*, 124, 983-984.

Mason, J.W., Brady, J.V. and Sidman, M. (1957). Plasma 17-hydrocorticosteroid levels and conditioned behavior in the rhesus monkey. *J. Endocrinol.*, 6, 741-752.

Mason, J.W., Brady, J.V., Polish, E., Bauer, J.A., Robinson, J.A., Rose, R.M. and Taylor, E.D. (1961a). Patterns of corticosteroid and pepsinogen change related to emotional stress in the monkey. *Science*, 133, 1596-1598.

Mason, J.W., Mangan, G., Brady, J.V., Conrad, D. and Rioch, D. (1961b). Concurrent plasma epinephrine, norepinephrine and 17-hydroxycorticosteroid levels during conditioned emotional disturbances in monkeys. *Psychosomat. Med.*, 23, 344-353.

Mason, J.W., Brady, J.V., Tolson, W.W., Robinson, J.A., Taylor, D.E. and Mougey, E.H. (1961c). Patterns of thyroid, gonadal, and adrenal hormone excretion related to psychological stress in the monkey.*Psychosomat. Med.*, 23, 446.

Mason, J.W., Brady, J.V. and Tolson, W.W. (1966). Behavioral adaptations and endocrine activity. In R. Levine (Ed.), *Proceedings of the Association for research in nervous and mental diseases*. Williams and Wilkins, Baltimore.

Razran, G. (1961). The observable unconscious and the inferable conscious in current Soviet psychophysiology: Interoceptive conditioning, semantic conditioning, and the orienting reflex. *Psychol. Rev.*, 68, 81-147.

Schuster, C.R. and Brady, J.V. (1964). The discriminative control of a food reinforced operant by interoceptive stimulation. *Pavlov J. Higher Nervous Activity*, 14, 448-458.

Sidman, M. (1953). Avoidance conditioning with brief shock and no exteroceptive warning signal. *Science*, 118, 157-158.

Sidman, M., Mason, J. W., Brady, J. V. and Thach, J. (1962). Quantitative relations between avoidance behavior and pituitary-adrenal cortical activity. *J. Exp. Analysis of Behavior*, 5, 353-362.

Slucki, H., Adam, G. and Porter, R. W. (1965). Operant discrimination of an interoceptive stimulus in rhesus monkeys. *J. Exp. Analysis of Behavior*, 8, 405-414.

Chapter 6

Affect as the Primary Motivational System*

Silvan S. Tomkins†

What do human beings really want? The answer to this fundamental question has not changed radically from that first time, in a dimly lit cave one night after the days work had been done, when one of our more reflective forebearers wrinkled his forehead, scratched his beard, and, in wonder and perplexity, began the study of human motivation. His answer to the fundamental question — what do human beings really want — was the same answer that was to be given for some few thousand years, up to and including Hull and Freud. That answer was, and for not a few still is, that the human animal is driven to breathe, to eat, to drink, and to engage in sex — that the biological drives are the primary sources of motivation of all animals, not excluding man. The clarity and urgency of hunger, of thirst, of anoxia, and of lust provided the basic paradigm that captured the imaginations of all theorists. Protests against this paradigm have been perennial, but none of its competitors has had its hardiness.

This is a radical error. The intensity, the urgency, the imperiousness, the "umph" of drives is an illusion. The illusion is created by the misidentification of the drive "signal" with its "amplifier." Its amplifier is the affective response which is ordinarily recruited to "boost the gain" of the drive signal.

Consider anoxic deprivation. Almost any interference with normal breathing will immediately arouse the most desperate gasping for breath. Is there any motivational claim more urgent than the demand of one who is drowning or choking to death for want of air? Yet it is not simply the imperious demand for oxygen that we observe under such circumstances. We are also observing the

*This work was supported in whole by a Public Health Research Career Award from the National Institute of Mental Health, 1-K6-MH-23, 797-01.

†Livingston College, Rutgers University, New Jersey.

rapidly mounting panic ordinarily recruited whenever the air supply is suddenly jeopardized. The panic amplifies the drive signal, and it is the combination of drive signal and panic which we have mistakenly identified as the drive signal. We have only to change the rate of anoxic deprivation to change the nature of the recruited affect which accompanies the anoxic drive signal. Thus, in the Second World War, those pilots who refused to wear their oxygen masks at 30,000 feet suffered a more gradual anoxic deprivation. They did not panic for want of oxygen. They became euphoric. It was the affect of enjoyment which the more slowly developing anoxic signal recruited. Some of these men, therefore, met their deaths with smiles on their lips.

Consider next that most imperious, primary drive of sex. Surely the tumescent, erect male is driven. Surely the tumescent sexual organ is the site of both the sexual urge and sexual pleasure. So it is, but just as we misidentify panic and the anoxic signal, so here we have misidentified the tumescence of the sexual drive with the affect of excitement. Excitement is ordinarily recruited as an amplifier of the sexual drive signal. Still, no one has ever observed an excited penis. It is a man who is excited and who breathes hard, not in the penis, but in the chest, the esophagus, the face, and the nose and nostrils. Both the sexual urge and the sexual pleasure of intercourse are ordinarily as amplified by excitement as anoxia is amplified by panic.

The potency of the sexual drive is notoriously vulnerable to the learned recruitment of affect which inhibits sexual satisfaction. If one learns to feel ashamed or afraid of sexuality, tumescence may become impossible, and the potent primary drive becomes impotent. To be fully sexually aroused and satisfied, one must be capable of excitement as well as tumescence. The contribution of affect to complete sexual satisfaction is nowhere clearer than in those who report unimpaired sexual pleasure and even orgasm but who, nonetheless, complain of lack of sexual satisfaction. What can it mean when the genitals are tumescent and yield sexual pleasure from mutual stimulation, which produces mutual orgasm, and yet both partners report that they are sexually unfulfilled and dissatisfied? Sexual intercourse repeated with the same partner is vulnerable to such attenuation of satisfaction whenever the decline in novelty of the interpersonal relationship is such that excitement can no longer be sustained. Those who are generally bored with each other may also be unable to become sexually excited even when they are capable of stimulating tumescence and orgasm. Excitement is no more a peculiarly sexual phenomenon than panic is unique to anoxic deprivation.

The relationship we have postulated between drive system and the affect system must also be postulated between both of these and nonspecific amplifying systems, such as the reticular formation. This and other amplifier circuits serve both motivational and nonmotivational systems. The words "activation" and "arousal" have tended to confound the distinction between amplification from affects and the nonspecific amplification of any neural message, be it a sensory, a motor, a drive, or an affect message.

Amplification is the preferable, more generic term, since it describes equally well the increase or decrease in gain for any and every kind of message or structure. The terms "activation" and "arousal" should be abandoned because of their affective connotations.

It is now clear from the work of Sprague *et al.* (1961) that it is possible by appropriate anatomical lesion to produce a cat who is active by virtue of intact amplifier structures but who shows little affect and, conversely, to produce a cat who is inactive and drowsy but who responds readily with affect to mild stimulation.

"Thus it appears that after interruption of much of the classical, lemniscal paths at the rostral midbrain, the cat shows. . .little attention and affect, despite the fact that the animal is wakeful and active and has good motor capacity. . . . These cats are characterized by a lack of affect, showing little or no defensive and aggressive reaction to noxious and aversive situations and no response to pleasurable stimulation or solicitation of affection by petting. The animals are mute, lack facial expression, and show minimal autonomic responses. . . . Without a patterned afferent input to the forebrain via the lemnisci, the remaining portions of the central nervous system, which include a virtually intact reticular formation, seem incapable of elaborating a large part of the animal's repertoire of adaptive behavior. . . . In contrast to this picture, a large reticular lesion sparing the lemnisci results in an animal whose general behavior is much like that of a normal cat except for chronic hypokinesia or drowsiness and for strong and easily aroused affect to mild stimulation." (Sprague *et. al.*, 1961, pp. 172-173.)

Both drives and affects require nonspecific amplification, but the drives have insufficient strength as motives without concurrent amplification by both the affects and the nonspecific amplifiers. Their critical role is to provide vital information of time, of place, and of response — where and when to do what — when the body does not know how to help itself otherwise. When the drive signal is activated, we learn first when we must start and stop consummatory activity. We become hungry long before our tissues are in an emergency state of deficit, and we stop eating, because of satiety, long before the tissue deficit has been remedied.

But there is also information of place and of response — where to do what. When the drive is activated, it tells us a very specific story — that the "problem" is in the mouth in the case of hunger, farther back in the nose and throat and chest if it is an oxygen drive, in the urethra if it is the urination drive, at the anal sphincter if it is the defecation drive. This information has been built into the site of consummation, so the probability of finding the correct consummatory response is very high. That this information is as vital as the message when to eat can be easily demonstrated.

Let us suppose that the hunger drive were "rewired" to be localized in the urethra, and the sex drive localized in the palm of the hand. For sexual satisfaction, the individual would first open and close his hand and then reach for a wide variety of "objects" as possible satisfiers, cupping and rubbing his hand until orgasm. When he became hungry he might first release the urethra and urinate to relieve his hunger. If this did not relieve it, he might use his hands to find objects which could be put inside the urethra, depending on just how we had rewired the apparatus. Such an organism would be neither viable nor reproductive. Such specificity of time and place of the drive system, critical though it is for viability, is nevertheless a limitation of its general significance for the human being.

It is the affects, rather than the drives, which are the primary human motives. This primacy is demonstrated first in that the drives require amplification from the affects, whereas the affects are sufficient motivators in the absence of drives. One must be excited to be sexually aroused, but one need not be sexually aroused to be excited. To motivate any man, it is quite sufficient to arouse either excitement or joy or terror or anger or shame or contempt or distress or surprise.

Second, in contrast to the specificity of the space-time information of the drive system, the affect system has those more general properties which permit it to assume a central position in the motivation of man. Thus, the affect system has generality of time rather than the rhythmic specificity of the drive system. Because the drive system is essentially a transport system, taking material in and out of the body, it must impose its specific temporal rhythms strictly. One cannot breathe only on Tuesday, Thursday, and Saturday, but one could be happy on Tuesday, Thursday, and Saturday and sad on Monday, Wednesday, and Friday.

In contrast to the necessary constraints of a system which enjoys few degrees of freedom in transporting material in and out of the body, there is nothing inherent in the structure of the affect mechanism which limits its activation with respect to time. One can be anxious for just a moment or for half an hour, for a day, for a year, for a lifetime, or never; one can be anxious only occasionally now, though much more frequently some time ago, or conversely.

There are structures in the body which are midway between the drive and affect mechanisms. Thus the pain receptors on the back of my hand are as site-specific as any drive. If I were to place a lit cigarette on the skin of my hand, I would experience pain. But the pain mechanism is similar to the affect mechanism in its time generality. There is nothing in the nature of the pain receptors which requires that they be stimulated rhythmically or that they ever be stimulated, and there is nothing which will prevent them from being stimulated whenever I happen to have an accident.

The affect system permits generality of object. Although one may satisfy hunger with Chinese, American, or Italian food, it must be some variety of edible object. Not so with any affect. There is literally no kind of object which has not been linked to one or another of the affects. In masochism, man has even learned to love pain and death. In Puritanism, he has learned to hate pleasure and life. He can invest any and every aspect of existence with the magic of excitement and joy or with the dread of fear or shame or distress.

Affects are also capable of much greater generality of intensity than drives. If I do not eat, I become more and more hungry. As I eat, I become less hungry. But I may wake mildly irritable in the morning and remain so for the rest of the day, or one day I may not be at all angry until quite suddenly something makes me explode in a rage. I may start the day moderately angry and quickly become interested in some other matter and so dissipate my anger.

Not only are both the intensity and duration of affects capable of greater modulation than is possible for drives, but so is their density. By "affect density," I mean the product of intensity times duration. Most of the drives operate within relatively narrow density tolerances. The consequences of too much variation of density of intake of air is loss of consciousness and possible death. Compared with drives, affects may be either much more casual and low in density or much more monopolistic and high in density. By virtue of the flexibility of this system, man is enabled to oscillate between affect fickleness and obsessive possession by the object of his affective investments.

Not only may affects be widely invested and variously invested, but they may also be invested in other affects, combine with other affects, intensify or modulate them, and suppress or reduce them. Neither hunger nor thirst can be used to reduce the need for air, as a child may be shamed into crying or may be shamed into stopping his crying.

The basic power of the affect system is a consequence of its freedom to combine with a variety of other components in what may be called a central assembly. This is an executive mechanism upon which messages converge from all sources, competing from moment to moment for inclusion in this governing central assembly. The affect system can be evoked by central and peripheral messages from any source, and in turn it can control the disposition of such messages and their sources.

If the affects are our primary motives, what are they and where are they? Affects are sets of muscle, vascular, and glandular responses located in the face and also widely distributed through the body, which generate sensory feedback which is inherently either "acceptable" or "unacceptable." These organized sets of responses are triggered at subcortical centers where specific "programs" for each distinct affect are stored. These programs are innately endowed and have been genetically inherited. They are capable, when activated, of simultaneously capturing such widely distributed organs as the face, the heart, and the endocrines and imposing on them a specific pattern of correlated responses. One does not learn to be afraid or to cry or to be startled, any more than one learns to feel pain or to gasp for air.

Most contemporary investigators have pursued the inner bodily responses after the James-Lange theory had focused attention on their significance. Important as these undoubtedly are, I regard them as of secondary importance to the expression of emotion through the face. The face motivates in the same way as the penis motivates. The penis does not motivate when it is in a flaccid state, because the receptors are then enclosed and relatively insensitive. When, however, the organ becomes engorged with blood these receptors are moved and become exquisitely sensitive to stimulation of the skin. It is my belief that the face also possesses potentially sensitive receptors which require changes in blood flow to move them into positions in which they become extremely sensitive to muscle and skin stimulation which is provided by the facial muscular affective responses. To pursue the analogy, the facial affect system is automasturbatory in nature. The innate affect program therefore consists of simultaneous changes in breathing, in a vocal cry, in changes in blood flow to the face, and in a patterned set of muscular responses on the face which stimulates the receptors rendered sensitive by vascular changes. The awareness of this set of responses is the awareness of affect.

The relationship between the face and the viscera is analogous to that between the fingers and the forearm, upper arm, shoulders, and body. The fingers do not "express" what is in the forearm or shoulder or trunk. They lead rather than follow the movements in these organs to which they are an extension. Just as the fingers respond both more rapidly and with more precision and complexity than the grosser and slower-moving arm to which they are attached, so the face expresses affect, both to others and to the self via feedback, which is more rapid and more complex than any stimulation of which the slower-moving visceral organs are capable. There is, further, a division of labor between the face and the inner organs of affective expression similar to that which exists between the fingers and the arm. It is the very gross and slower-moving characteristic of the inner organ system which provides the counterpoint for the melody expressed by the facial solo. In short, affect is primarily facial behavior. Secondarily it is bodily behavior, outer skeletal and inner visceral behavior. When we become aware of these facial and/or visceral responses, we are aware of our affects. We may respond with these affects, however, without becoming aware of the feedback from them. Finally, we learn to generate, from memory, images of these same responses which we can become aware of with or without repetition of facial, skeletal, or visceral responses.

If we are happy when we smile and sad when we cry, why are we reluctant to agree that smiling or crying is primarily what it means to be happy or sad? Why should these be regarded as "expressions" of some other, inner state? The reasons are numerous, but not the least of them is a general taboo on sharing this knowledge in eye-to-eye intimacy.

The significance of the face in interpersonal relations cannot be exaggerated. Not only is it a communication center for the sending and receiving of information of all kinds, but because it is the organ of affect expression and communication, it is also necessarily brought under strict social control. There are universal taboos on looking too directly into the eyes of the other because of the likelihood of affect contagion, as well as escalation; because of the unwillingness to express affect promiscuously; and because of concern lest others achieve control through knowledge of one's otherwise private feelings. Man is primarily a voyeuristic animal, not only because vision is his most informative sense, but also because the shared eye-to-eye interaction is the most intimate relationship possible between human beings. There is in this way complete mutuality between two selves, each of which is simultaneously aware of the self and the other. Indeed, the intimacy of sexual intercourse is ordinarily attenuated, lest it become too intimate, by being performed in the dark. In the psychoanalytic myth, the crime of the son in witnessing the "primal scene " is voyeuristic, and Oedipus is punished, in kind, by blindness.

The taboo on the shared interocular experience is easily exposed. If I were to ask you to turn to another person and stare directly into his eyes while permitting him to stare directly into your eyes, you would become aware of the taboo. Ordinarily we confront each other by my looking at the bridge of your nose and your looking at my cheekbone. If our eyes should happen to meet directly, the confrontation is minimized by glancing down or away, by letting the eyes go slightly out of focus, or by attenuating the visual datum by making it ground to the sound of the other's voice, which is made more figural. The taboo is not only on looking too intimately but also on exposing the taboo by too obviously avoiding direct confrontation. These two strategies are taught by shaming the child for staring into the eyes of visitors and then shaming him a second time for hanging his head in shame before the guest.

Only the young or the young in heart are entirely free of the taboo. Those adults whose eyes are caught by the eyes of another in the shared interocular intimacy may fall in love on such an occasion or, having fallen in love, thereby express the special intimacy they have recaptured from childhood.

If the affects are primarily facial responses, what are the major affects? I and my colleagues have distinguished nine innate affects. The positive affects are (a) interest or excitement, with eyebrows down, stare fixed or tracking an object; (b) enjoyment or joy, the smiling response; and (c) surprise or startle, with eyebrows raised and eye blink. The negative affects are (a) distress or anguish, the crying response; (b) fear or terror, with eyes frozen open in fixed stare or moving away from the dreaded object to the side and with skin pale, cold, and sweating and with trembling and hair erect; (c) shame or humiliation, with eyes and head lowered; (d) contempt with the upper lip raised in a sneer; (e) disgust or a deep nausea response and (f) anger or rage, with a frown, clenched jaw, and red face.

Viewing these as innately patterned responses, are there also innate activators of each affect? Inasmuch as we have argued that the affect system is the primary motivational system, it becomes critical to provide a theory of the innate activators of the affect system. Consider the nature of the problem. The innate activators had to include the drives as innate activators but not to be limited to drives as exclusive activators. The neonate, for example, must respond with innate fear to any difficulty in breathing, but must also be afraid of other objects. Each affect had to be capable of being activated by a variety of unlearned stimuli. The child must be able to cry at hunger or loud sounds as well as at a diaper pin stuck in his flesh. Each affect had, therefore, to be activated by some general characteristic of neural stimulation, common to both internal and external stimuli, and not too stimulus-specific like a releaser. Next the activator had to be correlated with biologically useful information. The young child must fear what is dangerous and smile at what is safe. Next the activator had to "know the address" of the subcortical center at which the appropriate affect program is stored — not unlike the problem of how the ear responds correctly to each tone. Next, some of the activators had not to whereas others had to be capable of habituation; otherwise a painful stimulus might too soon cease to be distressing and an exciting stimulus never be let go — like a deer caught by a bright light. These are some of the characteristics which had to be built into the affect mechanism's activation sensitivity. The most economical assumption on which to proceed is to look for communalities among these varieties of characteristics of the innate alternative activators of each affect. This I and my associates have done, and we believe it is possible to account for the major phenomena with a few relatively simple assumptions about the general characteristics of the stimuli which innately activate affect.

We would account for the differences in affect activation by three general variants of a single principle — the density of neural firing or stimulation. By "density" we mean the number of neural firings per unit time. Our theory posits three discrete classes of activators of affect, each of which further amplifies the sources which activate them. These are stimulation increase, stimulation level, and stimulation decrease. Thus, there is provision for three distinct classes of motives — affects about stimulation which is on the increase, about stimulation which maintains a steady level of density, and about stimulation which is on the decrease. With respect to density of neural firing or stimulation, then, the human being is equipped for affective arousal for every major contingency. If internal or external sources of neural firing suddenly increase, he will startle or become afraid, or he will become interested, depending on the suddenness of increase of stimulation. If internal or external sources of neural firing reach and maintain a high, constant level of stimulation, which deviates in excess of an optimal level of neural firing, he will respond with anger or distress, depending on the level of stimulation. If internal or external sources of neural firing suddenly decrease, he will laugh or smile with enjoyment, depending on the suddenness of decrease of stimulation.

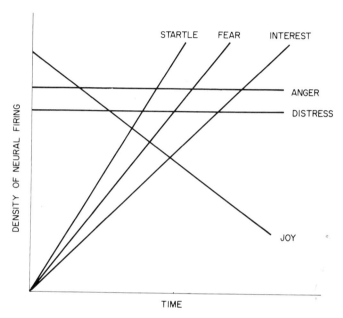

FIGURE 1.   Graphical representation of a theory of innate activators of affect.

The general advantage of affective arousal to such a broad spectrum of levels and changes of level of neural firing is to make the individual care about quite different states of affairs in different ways. It should be noted that, according to our views, there are both positive and negative affects (startle, fear, interest) activated by stimulation increase but that only negative affects are activated by a continuing unrelieved level of stimulation (distress, anger) and only positive affects are activated by stimulation decrease (laughter, joy). The latter, in our theory, is the only remnant of the tension-reduction theory of reinforcement. Stimulation increase may, in our view, result in punishing or rewarding affect, depending on whether it is a more or less steep gradient and therefore activates fear or interest. A constantly maintained high level of neural stimulation is invariably punishing inasmuch as it activates the cry of distress or anger, depending on how high above optimal levels of stimulation the particular density of neural firing is. A suddenly reduced density of stimulation is invariably rewarding, whether, it should be noted, the stimulation which is reduced is itself positive or negative in quality. Stated another way, such a set of mechanisms guarantees sensitivity to whatever is new, to whatever continues for any extended period of time, and to whatever is ceasing to happen. In Fig. 1, I have graphically represented this theory.

Thus any stimulus with a relatively sudden onset and a steep increase in the rate of neural firing will innately activate a startle response. As shown also in Fig. 1, if the rate of neural firing increases less rapidly, fear is activated, and if still less rapidly, interest is innately activated. In contrast, any sustained increase in the level of neural firing, as with a continuing loud noise, would innately activate the cry of distress. If it were sustained and still louder, it would innately activate the anger response. Finally, any sudden decrease in stimulation which reduced the rate of neural firing, as in the sudden reduction of excessive noise, would innately activate the rewarding smile of enjoyment.

In conclusion, the affect system provides the primary blueprints for cognition, decision, and action. Man is responsive to whatever circumstances activate positive and negative affects. Some of these circumstances innately activate the affects. At the same time, the affect system is also capable of being instigated by learned stimuli. The human being is thus urged by nature and by nurture to explore and to attempt to control the circumstances which evoke his positive and negative affective responses. It is the freedom of the affect system which makes it possible for the human being to begin to implement and to progress toward what he regards as an ideal state — one which, however else he may describe it, implicitly or explicitly entails the maximizing of positive affect and the minimizing of negative affect.

REFERENCE

Sprague, J.M., Chambers, W. W., and Stellar, E. (1961). Attentive, affective and adaptive behavior in the cat. *Science*, <u>133</u>, 165-173.

Chapter 7

The Assumption of Identity and Peripheralist-Centralist Controversies in Motivation and Emotion

Stanley Schachter*

Though we rarely bother to make the matter explicit, the assumption of an identity between a physiological state and psychological or behavioral event is implicit in much contemporary work in such areas as motivation, psychophysiology, psychopharmacology or any domain concerned with the relationship of bodily state to emotion or to behavior. Simply put, much of this work seems to proceed on the assumption that there is a simple, one-to-one relationship between a biochemical change or a physiological process and a specific behavior. It is as if we assumed that the physiological state is an "unconditionally sufficient condition" to account for a psychological event.

Stated this baldly, I suspect that you may feel that I overstate the point and construct a straw man. And certainly one could maintain that I exaggerate the case if one considers, for example, the abundant work in an area such as psychopharmacology which has demonstrated again and again the effects of social context, set and expectation on drug action. Though a specific drug may have identical physiological effects on most subjects, its behavioral and affective consequences seem variable and astonishingly manipulable by essentially cognitive or situational factors. All of us *know* this to be fact, but I suspect that it is a fact that we compartmentalize. It may be true for something as exotic and poorly understood as the effects of a psychotropic drug; it is not true for behaviors such as eating, drinking and urinating, the biological bases of which we presumably understand quite well. Let me illustrate the point by considering

*Columbia University, New York.

hunger – a motivational state whose biological basis has probably been more thoroughly researched and is better understood than any of the other drive states.

The gist of the immense body of research on hunger can be quickly summarized as follows:

1. Food deprivation leads to various peripheral physiological changes such as modification of blood constituents, increase in gastric motility, changes in body temperature and the like.

2. By means of some still debated mechanism, these peripheral changes are detected by a hypothalamic feeding center.

3. Directly manipulating hypothalamic structures, by lesion or electric stimulation techniques, directly manipulates the amount eaten.

Presumably some or all facets of this activated peripheral-central physiological machinery lead the organism to search out and consume food. Acknowledging the inevitable scientific controversy about details, these facts appear to be as well established as any in the motivational field. From individual to individual, from species to species, these appear to be the inevitable physiological consequences of food deprivation. On the basis of current knowledge, however, one may ask, when this biological machinery is activated, do we necessarily describe ourselves as hungry and eat?

For most of us raised on the notion that hunger is the most primitive of motives, wired into the animal and unmistakable in its cues, the question may seem farfetched, but there is increasing reason to suspect that there are major individual differences in the extent to which these physiological changes are associated with the desire to eat.

On the clinical level, the analyst Hilda Bruch (1961) has observed that her obese patients literally do not know when they are physiologically hungry. To account for this observation she suggests that, during childhood, these patients were not taught to discriminate between hunger and such states as fear, anger, and anxiety. If this is so, these people may be labeling almost any state of arousal "hunger" or, alternatively, labeling no internal state "hunger."

If Bruch's speculations are correct, it should be anticipated that the set of physiological symptoms which are considered characteristic of food deprivation are not labeled "hunger" by the obese. In other words, the obese literally may not know when they are physiologically hungry. For at least one of the presumed physiological correlates of food deprivation, this does appear to be the case. In an absorbing study, Stunkard (1959) and Stunkard and Koch (1964) have related gastric motility to self-reports of hunger in 37 obese subjects and 37 subjects of normal size. A subject who had eaten no breakfast, came to the laboratory at 9 a.m. He swallowed a gastric balloon, and for 4 hours Stunkard continuously recorded gastric motility. Every 15 minutes the subject was asked if he was hungry. He answered "yes" or "no," and that is all there was to the study. We have, then, a record of the extent to which a subject's self-report of hunger corresponds to his gastric motility. The results show that (a) obese and normal subjects do not differ significantly in degree of gastric motility, and (b) that, when the stomach is not contracting, the reports of obese and normal subjects are quite similar, both groups reporting hunger roughly 38 percent of the time. However, when the stomach is contracting, the reports of the two groups differ markedly. For normal subjects, self-report of hunger coincides with gastric motility 71 percent of the time. The percentage is only 47.6 for the obese. Stunkard's work seems to indicate that obese and normal subjects do not refer to the same bodily state when they use the term *hunger*.

If this inference is correct, we should anticipate that, if we were to directly manipulate gastric motility and the other symptoms that we associate with hunger, we would, for normal subjects, be directly manipulating feelings of hunger and eating behavior. For the obese, there would be no correspondence between manipulated internal state and eating behavior. To test these expectations, Schachter *et al.* (1968) performed an experiment in which bodily state was manipulated by the obvious technique of manipulating food deprivation, so that some subjects had empty stomachs and others had full stomachs before eating.

Our experiment was conducted under the guise of a study of taste. A subject came to the laboratory in midafternoon or evening. He had been called the previous evening and asked not to eat the meal (lunch or dinner) preceding his appointment at the laboratory.

It was explained that all subjects had been asked not to eat a meal before coming to the laboratory because "in any scientific experiment it is necessary that the subjects be as similar as possible in all relevant ways. As you probably know from your own experience," the experimenter continued, "an important factor in determining how things taste is what you have recently eaten." The introduction over, the experimenter then proceeded as follows. For the "full stomach" condition he said to the subject, "In order to guarantee that your recent taste experiences are similar to those of other subjects who have taken part in this experiment, we should now like you to eat exactly the same thing they did. Just help yourself to the roast beef sandwiches on the table. Eat as much as you want — till you're full."

For the "empty stomach" condition, the subjects, of course, were not fed.

Next, the subject was seated in front of five bowls of crackers and told, "We want you to taste these different kinds of crackers and tell us how they taste to you." The experimenter then gave the subject a long set of rating scales and said, "we want you to judge each cracker on the dimensions (salty, cheesy, garlicky, and so on) listed on this sheet. Taste as many or as few of the crackers of each type as you want in making your judgments; the important thing is that your ratings be as accurate as possible."

The subject then proceeded to taste and rate crackers for 15 minutes, under the impression that this was a taste test; meanwhile, we were simply counting the number of crackers he ate. There were, of course, two types of subjects: obese subjects (from 14 percent to 75 percent overweight) and normal subjects (from 8 percent underweight to 9 percent overweight).

To review expectations: if it is correct that the obese do not label as hunger the bodily states associated with food deprivation, then our manipulation should have had no effect on the amount eaten by obese subjects; on the other hand, the eating behavior of normal subjects should directly parallel the effects of the manipulation on bodily state.

It will be a surprise to no one to learn, from Fig. 1, that the normal subjects ate considerably fewer crackers when their stomachs were full of roast beef sandwiches than when their stomachs were empty. The results for obese subjects stand in fascinating contrast. They ate as much — in fact slightly more — when their stomachs were full as when they were empty. Obviously the actual state of the stomach had nothing to do with the eating behavior of the obese.

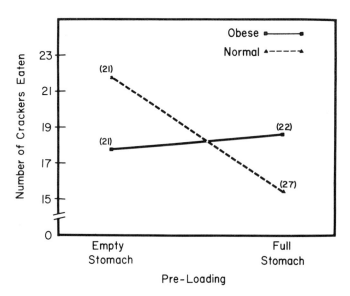

FIGURE 1.   Effects of preliminary eating on the amounts eaten during the experiment by normal and obese subjects. Numbers in parentheses are numbers of subjects.

It seems clear that the set of bodily symptoms the subject labels "hunger" differs for obese and normal subjects. Whether one measures gastric motility as Stunkard did, or manipulates motility and the other physiological correlates of food deprivation, as I assume my co-workers and I have done, one finds, for normal subjects, a high degree of correspondence between the state of the stomach and eating behavior and, for obese subjects, virtually no correspondence.

Though all of this is irrelevant to "emotion," I have dwelt on these studies at some length in order to illustrate that the assumption of identity is not necessarily valid even in a behavioral domain such as eating where most of us have unquestioningly accepted the assumption.

EMOTION AND THE ASSUMPTION OF IDENTITY

Let us turn now to the field of emotion where I believe that the identity assumption has been at the heart of the major controversies in the area and has guided much of the research of the past 75 years. This is undoubtedly due to William James whose formulation of emotion virtually embodies what I have called the assumption of identity. James (1890) wrote, "the bodily changes follow directly the perception of the exciting fact, and our feeling of the same changes as they occur *is* the emotion." James directly equates emotion with bodily changes and visceral feelings. From this it must follow, first, that the different emotions will be accompanied by recognizably different bodily states, and second, that the manipulation of bodily state, by drugs or surgery, will also manipulate emotional state. These implications have, directly or indirectly, guided much of the research on emotion since James' day. The results of this research, which is still going on by the way, provided little support for a purely visceral formulation of emotion, and led Cannon (1929) to his brilliant and devastating critique of the James-Lange theory — a critique based on the following points, each of which is an attack on the "identity" implications of James' view of matters: (a) the total separation of the viscera from the central nervous system does not alter emotional behavior; (b) the same visceral changes occur in very different emotional states and in nonemotional states; (c) the viscera are relatively insensitive structures; (d) visceral changes are too slow to be a source of emotional feeling; and (e) the artificial induction of visceral changes that are typical of strong emotions does not produce the emotions.

Though new data have weakened the cogency of some of these points, Cannon's logic and findings make it inescapably clear that, as with hunger, a formulation of emotion that rests on the assumption of identity is simply inadequate to cope with the facts. In an effort to cope with the obvious inadequacies of a purely visceral or peripheral formulation, I suggested several years ago that cognitive factors may have major effects on emotional states, and my colleagues and I undertook a program of research on the interaction of physiological and cognitive determinants of emotional state. This program was based on speculation about what was, at that time, a hypothetical event. Imagine a subject who was covertly injected with adrenalin, or was fed a sympatho-mimetic agent, such as ephedrine. Such a subject would become aware of palpitations, tremor, etc., and at the same time would be utterly unaware of why he felt this way. What would be the consequences of such a state?

In other contexts, I have suggested that precisely this condition would lead to the arousal of evaluative needs; that is, pressures would operate on such an individual to understand and evaluate his bodily feelings. His bodily state roughly resembles the condition in which it has been at times of emotional excitement. How would he label his present feelings? I would suggest that such an individual would label his bodily feelings in terms of the situation in which he finds himself. Should he at the time be watching a horror film, he would probably decide that he was badly frightened. Should he be with a beautiful woman, he might decide that he was wildly in love or sexually excited. Should he be in an argument, he might explode in fury and hatred. Or, should the situation be completely inappropriate, he could decide that he was excited or upset by something that had recently happened. In any case, it is my basic assumption that the labels one attaches to a bodily state, how one describes his feelings, are a joint function of such cognitive factors and of a state of physiological arousal.

This line of thought, then, leads to the following propositions. (a) Given a state of physiological arousal for which an individual has no immediate explanation, he will "label" this state and describe his feelings in terms of the cognitions available to him. To the extent that cognitive factors are potent determiners of emotional states, it could be anticipated that precisely the same state of physiological arousal could be called "joy" or "fury" or any of a great diversity of emotional labels, depending on the cognitive aspects of the situation. (b) Given a state of physiological arousal for which an individual has a completely appropriate explanation (e.g., "I feel this way because I have just received an injection of adrenalin"), no evaluative needs will arise and the individual is unlikely to label his feelings in terms of the alternative cognitions available. (c) Given the same cognitive circumstances, the individual will react emotionally or describe his feelings as emotions only to the extent that he experiences a state of physiological arousal.

The experimental test of these propositions requires, first, the experimental manipulation of a state of physiological arousal or sympathetic activation; second, the manipulation of the extent to which the subject has an appropriate or proper explanation of his bodily state; and third, the creation of situations from which explanatory cognitions may be derived.

In order to satisfy these requirements, Jerome Singer and I constructed an experiment that was cast in the framework of a study of the effects of vitamin supplements on vision. As soon as a subject arrived, he was told: "In this experiment we would like to make various tests of your vision. We are particularly interested in how a vitamin compound called Suproxin affects the visual skills. If you agree to take part in the experiment we would like to give you an injection of Suproxin."

If a subject agreed (and all but one of the 185 subjects did), he received an injection of one of two forms of "Suproxin" — placebo or epinephrine. We have, then, two groups of subjects — placebo subjects on whom the injection can have no possible effects, and epinephrine or adrenalin subjects who, within a few minutes after injection, will become aware of the full battery of sympathomimetic symptoms. In order to manipulate the extent to which subjects had a proper explanation of their bodily state, those who received epinephrine received one of two types of instructions.

Before receiving the injections, the *informed* subjects are told, "I should also tell you that some of our subjects have experienced side effects from the Suproxin. These side effects will only last for 15 or 20 minutes. Probably your hands will start to shake, your heart will start to pound, and your face may get warm and flushed." These subjects, then, are told precisely what they will feel and why they will feel it. For such subjects, the evaluative needs are low. They have an exact explanation for their bodily feelings and cognitive or situational factors should have no effects on how the subject labels his feelings.

The *uninformed* subjects are told that the injection will have no side effects at all. These subjects, then, will experience a state of sympathetic arousal, but the experimenter has given them no explanation why they feel as they do. Evaluative needs, then, should be high, and the cognitive-situational factors should have maximal effect on the way such a subject labels his bodily state.

Finally, in order to expose subjects to situations from which they might derive explanatory cognitions relevant to their bodily state, they are placed in one of two situations immediately after injection.

Euphoria. A subject was placed alone in a room with a stooge who had been introduced as a fellow subject and who, following a completely standardized routine, acted in a euphoric-manic fashion, doing such things as flying paper airplanes, hula-hooping, and the like, all the while keeping up a standard patter and occasionally attempting to induce the subject to join in.

Anger. A subject was asked to fill out a long, infuriatingly personal questionnaire that asked such questions as: "With how many men (other than your father) has your mother had extramarital relationships?" 4 and under: — — —; 5-9: — — —; 10 and over: — — —.

Filling in the questionnaire alongside the subject was a stooge, again presumably a fellow subject, who openly grew more and more irritated at the questionnaire and who finally ripped the thing up in a rage, slammed it to the floor while biting out: "I'm not wasting any more time; I'm getting my books and leaving," and stamped out of the room.

In both situations, an observer, watching through a one-way mirror, systematically recorded the behavior of the subject in order to provide indices of the extent to which the subject joined in the stooge's mood. Once these rigged situations had run their course, the experimenter returned and, with a plausible pretext, asked the subject to fill out a series of standardized scales to measure the intensity of anger or euphoria.*

We have, then, a set of experimental conditions in which we are simultaneously manipulating the degree of sympathetic arousal and the extent to which subjects understand why they feel as they do, and measuring the impact of these variations on the extent to which the subject catches the mood of a situation rigged to induce euphoria in one set of conditions and to induce anger in another. From the line of thought that generated this study, it should be anticipated that subjects, injected with epinephrine and told that there would be no side effects, should catch the mood of the rigged situation to a greater extent than subjects who had been injected with a placebo or those who had been injected with epinephrine and given a completely appropriate explanation of what they would feel and why.

Examining first the results of the euphoria conditions, we find that this is exactly the case. The uninformed epinephrine subjects — those who had been told that there would be no side effects — tend to catch the stooge's mood with alacrity; they join the stooge's whirl of activity and invent new manic activities of their own. In marked contrast, the informed epinephrine subjects and the placebo subjects who give no indication of autonomic arousal tend simply to sit and stare at the stooge in mild disbelief. The relevant data are reported in detail elsewhere. For present purposes it should suffice to note that these differences between conditions are large and statistically significant on both observational and self-report measures of mood.

In the anger conditions, the pattern of results is precisely the same. Uninformed epinephrine subjects grow openly annoyed and irritated, while placebo and informed epinephrine subjects maintain their equanimity.

The evidence is good, then, in support of our basic proposition. Given a state of physiological arousal for which a subject has no easy explanation, he proves readily manipulable into the disparate states of euphoria and anger. Given an identical physiological state for which the subject has an appropriate explanation, his mood is almost untouched by the rigged situation.

Such results are not limited to the states of anger and euphoria. In still other experiments in which similar techniques and comparisons were employed, we have been readily able to manipulate uninformed epinephrine subjects into amusement, as measured by laughter at a slapstick movie, and into fearful or anxious states.

---

*For purposes of brevity, the description of this experiment does not include details of all the conditions in this study. The chief omission is a description of a control condition introduced to evaluate alternative interpretations of the data. The interested reader is referred to the original paper by Schachter and Singer (1962).

In sum, precisely the same physiological state — an epinephrine-induced state of sympathetic arousal — can be manifested as anger, euphoria, amusement, fear, or, as in the informed subjects, as no mood or emotion at all. Such results are virtually incomprehensible if we persist in the assumption of an identity between physiological and psychological states, but they fall neatly into place if we specify the fashion in which cognitive and physiological factors interact. With the addition of cognitive propositions, we are able to specify and manipulate the conditions under which an injection of epinephrine will or will not lead to an emotional state and to predict what emotion will result.

It seems clear that specifying the action of cognitive factors does allow us to cope with many of the difficulties imposed on peripheral theories by acceptance of the assumption of identity. What about the central theories — that variety of theory that from Cannon's day on has involved one or another of the brain stem structures as crucial to emotion and motivation? I suspect that the assumption of identity has led the central theorists into as many and similar difficulties as William James ever had. A *purely* central theory of emotion or motivation seems as inadequate at coping with all of the facts as a purely peripheral theory. In the field of hunger, for example, we know that there is a feeding control center in the ventromedial area of the hypothalamus. Experimentally produce ¹ lesions in this area lead to hyperphagia and immensely obese animals. This is one of a large number of related findings which has led many scholars (e.g., Rosenzweig, 1962) to the conclusion that feeding behavior is entirely under central control. However, as both Miller *et al.* (1950) and Teitelbaum (1955) have demonstrated, such lesions lead to overeating and obesity *only* when the available food is palatable. When the food is unpleasant (coarse in texture or adulterated with quinine) the experimental animals eat considerably less and grow thinner than control animals presented with the same diet. It would appear that this feeding control center operates in intimate interaction with environmental stimuli.

Though I don't know of many experiments directly dealing with the problem, I suspect that in the field of emotion there are strong parallels to these findings on eating behavior. Among the chief experimental supports for central theories of emotion are, of course, the results of the numerous demonstrations of the effects of direct brain stimulation in the production of an intense emotional state such as rage. Whether or not such states can be induced in the absence of appropriate external stimuli is, in the present context, the crucial question. Though I claim absolutely no expertise, my talks with researchers in this area and my reading of the publications to which they have directed me have just about convinced me that the external circumstances surrounding the stimulated animal play an extraordinary role in determining whether or not electric brain stimulation leads to emotional display. Experiments directly dealing with this point seem rare but what I have found so far certainly supports the suspicion. The studies of von Holst and von Saint Paul (1967) of aggression in the rooster neatly illustrate the point. When presented with a stuffed weasel (a natural enemy) an unstimulated rooster ignores the stuffed animal. When electrically stimulated, the rooster attacks the statue. If the stuffed animal is absent, the rooster will attack its keeper's face after sustained stimulation. However, in von Holst's words, "if all substitutes for an enemy are lacking — when there is, so to speak, no hook on which to hang an illusion — the rooster exhibits only motor restlessness. Moreover, the same motor restlessness is observed if one stimulates brain areas associated with hunger, thirst, courtship, or fighting* under conditions in which the environment does not permit the unreeling of the entire behavior sequence. For this reason it is often necessary to vary the external conditions to be sure which behavior sequence — which complex drive — has in fact been activated."

It would appear, then, that the central theorists of emotion are faced with many of the same problems as are the peripheralists. Direct stimulation of the brain stem structures does produce emotional behavior — but only in the presence of appropriate external stimuli. The experimental production of the peripheral correlates of emotion also produces emotional behavior — but again, only in the presence of appropriate external stimuli. A bewildering state of affairs so long as one persists in the assumption of identity; no problem at all if one abandons the assumption.

If we are eventually to make sense of this area, I believe we will be forced to adopt a set of concepts with which most physiologically inclined scientists feel somewhat uncomfortable and ill-at-ease, for they are concepts which are difficult to reify, and about which it is, at present, difficult to physiologize. We will be forced to examine a subject's perception of his bodily state and his interpretation of it in terms of his immediate situation and his past experience. We will be forced to deal with concepts about perception, about cognition, about learning, and about the social situation.

In order to avoid any misunderstanding, let me make completely explicit that I am most certainly not suggesting that such notions as perception and cognition do not have physiological correlates. I am suggesting that at present we know little about these physiological correlates, but that we can and must use nonphysiologically anchored concepts if we are to make headway in understanding the relations of complex behavior patterns to physiological and biochemical processes. If we don't, my guess is that we will be just about as successful at deriving predictions about emotion or any other complex behavior from a knowledge of biochemical and physiological conditions as we would be at predicting the destination of a moving automobile from an exquisite knowledge of the workings of the internal combustion engine and of petroleum chemistry.

---

* The one exception noted by von Holst is escape behavior which "can be evoked in the absence of the appropriate external object (or its substitute) when the brain stimulation is sufficiently intense." Von Holst seems so convinced of the importance of external circumstances that he suggests for his exception, "it is probable that the absent object of fear is being hallucinated."

REFERENCES

Bruch, Hilda. (1961). Transformation of oral impulses in eating disorders: A conceptual approach. *Psychiat. Q.*, 35, 458-481.

Cannon, W.B. (1929). *Bodily changes in pain, hunger, fear and rage; an account of recent researches into the function of emotional excitement* (2nd ed.). Appleton, New York.

James, W. (1890). *The principles of psychology*. Holt, New York.

Miller, N.E., Bailey, C.J., and Stevenson, J.A.F. (1950). Decreased "hunger" but increased food intake resulting from hypothalamic lesions. *Science*, 112, 256-259.

Rosenzweig, M.R. (1962). The mechanisms of hunger and thirst. In L. Postman (Ed.), *Psychology in the making*. Knopf, New York.

Schachter, S. and Singer, J.E. (1962). Cognitive, social, and physiological determinants of emotional state. *Psychol. Rev.*, 69, 379-399.

Schachter, S., Goldman, R., and Gordon, A. (1968). Effects of fear, food deprivation, and obesity on eating. *J. Personality and Social Psychol.*, 10, 91-97.

Stunkard, A. (1959). Obesity and the denial of hunger. *Psychosomat. Med.*, 21, 281-289.

Stunkard, A. and Koch, C. (1964). The interpretation of gastric motility: I. Apparent bias in the reports of hunger by obese persons. *Arch. Genet. Psychiat.*, 11, 74-82.

Teitelbaum, P. (1955). Sensory control of hypothalamic hyperphagia. *J. Comp. Physiol. Psychol.*, 48, 156-163.

Von Holst, E. and von Saint Paul, U. (1967). Electrically controlled behavior. In J.L. McGaugh, N.M. Weinberger, and R.E. Whalen (Eds.), *Psychobiology*. Freeman, San Francisco.

Part III

Cognitive Theories
of Feeling and Emotion

INTRODUCTION

This largest section is devoted to cognitive theories. While behavior theory is still supreme in such fields as learning, where at first glance cognition seems equally important, there is hardly a rival in sight for cognitive theory in the field of emotion. This may be at least partly the result of the early ascendancy of behavior theory which identified emotion with emotional behavior and saw the origin of emotion in the stimulus situation. On that assumption, all that was needed was to apply the appropriate stimulus and record the responses. There was no need to accord special status to emotional behavior.

In time, theorists came to realize that the same stimulus situation does not always produce the same emotional responses, except for the most harrowing situations as exemplified by the popular stress experiments. At long last, the origin of emotion was seriously considered. Today, most of the newer theories of feeling and emotion assume that these experiences depend on the interpretation and evaluation of the situation.

Earliest in time came Jung's concept of the "feeling function" (as presented by Hillman) which evaluates everything that is encountered. For Jung, feeling is one of several possible approaches to the world. It may be a preferred (dominant) function or it may be accessory, and even unconscious; it may be introverted or extraverted. For Arieti, coming from the Freudian tradition, there are three types of cognition determining emotion. These cognitions range from the most primitive to the most advanced symbolic level. Accordingly, they give rise to three orders of emotions: protoemotions (or first order emotions), second order and third order emotions, of which the last two occur only in man.

Among psychologists, theories of emotion reveal the preoccupation of each theorist. Simonov draws on information theory to suggest that emotion is equal to need, multiplied by the difference between necessary and available information; while Leeper insists that emotions or emotional motives are part of the (motivating) perceptual process. Both theorists assume cognitive processes in emotion, but Simonov does not consider that information has to be processed and evaluated, and Leeper includes emotion in the perceptual (cognitive) process. All four theorists stipulate or at least imply neural correlates for emotion but do not spell them out.

While for Leeper the perceptual process includes all psychological activities from sense experience on, excluding only overt action, Arnold analyzes this process into repeated rounds of sense experience, appraisal, tendency to action (which may be either the desire to know more about the situation or the attraction and repulsion produced by the appraisal). Instead of saying, as Leeper does, that the process of perception in many instances is a motivational process, Arnold sees the motivational factor in the subject's appraisal of the situation (in man, both intuitive and reflective) as good or bad here and now. The sequence and complex of psychological activities from perception to emotion and action then leads to the identification of brain structures and circuits mediating these activities.

Peters' paper, the last in the section, represents a philosopher's critique of psychological theories. For Peters, emotion is aroused by appraisal but is connected with wishing rather than action. Only a motive, also aroused by an appraisal, can lead to action.

Knowing, interpreting, evaluating the situation is necessary for emotion in all these theories; they differ only in the way in which this cognition is defined, and in the relation of emotion to action.

Chapter 8

C. G. Jung's Contributions to "Feelings and Emotions": Synopsis and Implications

James Hillman*

At the turn of the century, when Jung began to write on psychology, there were no clear distinctions among the various components which had been grouped, or discarded, in that bag called "the affective faculty." From the time of the Enlightenment in Germany (eighteenth-century writers such as Moses Mendelssohn, J. N. Tetens, and Kant) the soul was divided into three parts: thinking, willing, and feeling; the cognitive, conative, and affective faculties. Into the affective faculty was thrown everything that did not fit into thinking or willing. Thus it embraced desires, drives, and impulses as well as intuitions, instincts, moods, sensations, and of course, feelings, emotions, affects, and passions. Different psychologists at different times would rescue this or that piece of the affective faculty, such as sensation or impulse, and incorporate it into their system of thinking or willing. But fundamentally, this third region of the psyche, like Plato's third class of men, was inferior; the model on which it was conceived echoed the ancient trinitarian division of the soul, the lowest aspect of which was associated with what was below the diaphragm, especially the liver. Furthermore, this bag of feelings was always in opposition to thinking, or, as Moses Mendelssohn said at the beginning of the modern tripartite division, "We no longer feel as soon as we think." By the way, the opposition between thinking and feeling is still found in the scientistic psychology without heart and the romantic psychology without head. Jung, too, as we shall see, presents thinking and feeling as opposed functions; but his psychology, having for its over-all aim the union of opposites in the soul, does not rest in this split between head and heart.

*In private practice, Zurich, Switzerland.

MODERN THEORIES OF FEELING

The lack of differentiation in conceptualizing the affective faculty and its functions betrays a lack of differentiated experience of these processes themselves in the collective psyche of Western nineteenth-century man, who after all is simply describing himself, painting his own portrait, in his theories. It was as if feeling and emotion had lost touch with consciousness, or had fallen into the unconscious. Therefore, it is no surprise that the most acute differentiation of feeling and emotion was made by psychiatrists in their investigations of the unconscious and their descriptions of psychopathology. The invention of that language, mainly in clinics and asylums throughout the nineteenth century, encompassed a wide range of the passions of the soul, but from their obverse, abnormal, unconscious side. While nineteenth-century academic psychology was making acute observations in regard to thinking processes, sensation, perception, and memory – feeling and emotion were still largely in a bag. Some psychologists, mainly German (Lersch, Bollnow, Krueger – see Hillman, 1961, Ch. 9 for examples) believed that this bag must be kept closed. The affective realm belonged inside, in the depths of the person. To open it to thought would kill the very object under observation. "We no longer feel as soon as we think." In other words, in the nineteenth century there was a problem of feeling and emotion, not only academically but conceptually. The conceptual problem expresses a psychological problem, a feeling problem of the human soul. It is a problem we are not done with even today.

JUNG'S FEELING FUNCTION

Jung clearly separated feeling from the other affective processes and so helped to reinstate it. In his *Psychological Types* (1921), he defined feeling as a distinct function of consciousness, placing it on a par with thinking. We shall return to his definition of feeling.

Jung came upon the role of feeling also experimentally. His earliest descriptions of feeling stem from his association experiments which he devised and performed during the first decade of the century. In these experiments he sometimes found affective reactions to stimulus words, such as "yes," "bad," "I like," rather than ideational associations in the stricter sense. These affective reactions judged the stimulus word, qualified it with a subjective appreciation, and established a connection between the individual and the stimulus by means of this subjective appreciation.

In attempting to give full recognition to these affective reactions, he began to formulate his theory of types in a paper read in 1913 at the Psychoanalytical Congress in Munich. This first formulation made one basic division between thinking, introversion, and dementia praecox on the one hand, and feeling, extraversion, and hysteria on the other. (Jung, 1923, pp. 273-74n. and 1916, p. 403.) This simplification was transformed in his final elaboration of feeling as it appears in his 1921 major work, published in English in 1923 as *Psychological Types*. I quote now (pp. 543-46) from that work the essence of Jung's definition of feeling:

"Feeling is primarily a process that takes place between the ego and a given content, a process, moreover, that imparts to the content a definite *value* in the sense of acceptance or rejection ('like' or 'dislike'); but it can also appear, as it were, isolated in the form of mood, quite apart from the momentary content of consciousness or momentary sensations.

" . . . feeling is also a kind of *judging*, differing, however, from an intellectual judgment, in that it does not aim at establishing an intellectual connection but is solely concerned with the setting up of a subjective criterion of acceptance or rejection. The valuation by feeling extends to *every* content of consciousness, of whatever kind it may be. When the intensity of feeling is increased, an *affect* results, which is a state of feeling accompanied by appreciable bodily innervations.

" . . . feeling like thinking is a *rational* function, since, as is shown by experience, values in general are bestowed according to the laws of reason, just as concepts in general are framed after the laws of reason.

"Naturally the essence of feeling is not characterized by the foregoing definitions: they only serve to convey its external manifestations. The conceptual capacity of the intellect proves incapable of formulating the real nature of feeling in abstract terms, since thinking belongs to a category quite incommensurable with feeling. (Compare Mendelssohn, 1843-55.)

"When the total attitude of the individual is oriented by the function of feeling, we speak of a *feeling-type*."

The feeling function is that psychological process that evaluates. Through the feeling function we appreciate a situation, a person, an object, a moment, in terms of value. A prerequisite for feeling is therefore a structure of feeling memory, a set of values, to which the event can be related. As a process that is always going on and that gives or receives feeling-tones — even the feeling-tone of indifference — the feeling function connects both the subjective "me" to the object by imparting value or "importance" (cf. Whitehead, 1938), and the object to the subjective "me" by receiving it within the subjective value system. Feeling, therefore, functions as a relation, and is often called "the function of relationship." Because it relates us, it has to do with adaptation — extravertedly to an environment, or introvertedly to our subjective *milieu interne*. Through feeling, subject is related to object, to the contents of his own psyche as values, and to his own subjectivity as general feeling-tone or mood.

As a process feeling requires time, more time than is needed for perception. It behaves in the same way as thinking, rationally organizing perceptions. It is coherent, if not systematic. The ability to handle a problem or talk with a person in the right way shows a rational discrimination, and an adaptation to what is needed leading to correct conclusions. Yet, the entire operation may not be intellectual. One says different things to different people according to the values of the situation, and according to the requirements of the other person and one's own objective psyche as subjectively felt. These answers to questions may not be either truthful or correct in the logical sense, but from the point of view of feeling they may be exactly right. When a child asks for an explanation, an answer may be given from thinking or from feeling; at times, a story which answers to the anxiety in the child may be "truer" than an intellectual explanation of causes. To hit the mark truly does not mean always to tell the factual or logical truth. In therapy a problem may often be relieved by absurdities of anecdote or parable rather than by relentless analytical pursuit. Often the whole picture of harmony is more important in resolving a conflict than either logic or facts. The function of feeling then creates a situation in which viewpoints may reasonably blend even though the opposing logical and factual issues have not been settled and may even have been compromised. One may be irrationally at odds with an appointment or an outer obligation, yet in tune with one's own values and mood. To do something when you "don't feel right" may be more irresponsible and destructive than failing the commitment. On waking in the morning, feeling tells us how things are with us regardless of the outer rationality of weather, time on the clock, duties of the day, state of the body. And above all, feeling provides the order and logic for love. Let us now look at some implications.

First, in Jung's use the term *feeling* differs sharply from other ways in which the word "feeling" is used, such as feeling certain, feeling something is in the air, feeling something is fishy, rotten — all of which belong to what Jung calls the function of intuition. So, too, feeling comfortable, exhausted, or feeling the texture of cloth, refer to the function of sensation. In this or that individual at this or that moment, feeling may be muddled with intuition or sensation, but by definition feeling is distinctly other than sensation and intuition.

Second, feeling is a *function*. A function (from *fungor*) acts, performs, operates. A function is an activity, a process that goes on during a period of time. It has consistency, continuity, and identity. As such, it can be a function of the ego-personality. Feeling is an instrument by which events are shaped and colored and with which we evaluate experiences. We have it in our hands to use; by means of the feeling function we make ethical and aesthetic judgments, develop a hierarchy of values, elaborate manners and taste, carry out intimate and social relationships, and experience religious life.

Third, feeling as a function differs from *feelings as contents*. This distinction between the feeling function and feelings is of major importance in Jung's work and has major implications. The feeling function may evaluate thoughts, objects, psychic contents, or events of any kind. It is not restricted to feelings. The feeling function feels (appreciates and relates to) not only feelings. Feeling is not limited to feelings any more than thinking is limited only to thoughts. We may feel our thoughts, discover their value, their importance. So, too, may we think feeling and about feelings — as we are doing, for instance, in this symposium. Feelings themselves — irritation, enjoyment, boredom — may be handled adequately or inadequately, valued positively or negatively by the feeling function. We may be fittingly bored or wrongly and badly bored; we may be well irritated or poorly irritated. The organization of feelings depends less on the feelings than it does upon the function.

Fourth, in Jungian psychology a great deal is made both in theory and in practical work of *inferior functioning.* The feeling function may be dominant as in the feeling-type, or it may be less developed and inferior. It may be a typical way in which the ego-personality functions, or the feeling function may be affect-charged and rather ego-alien. Inferior feeling refers to the inadequacy of the function. Inferior feeling botches up values and makes the wrong feeling-judgments. It performs wrongly, or rightly at the wrong time. Its timing is off. It does not inform the person how he feels about this or that, whether he likes or loves, whether he is adaptively related to what is taking place outside or inside. He can feel sad only when he falls ill, or feel happy only when given recognition. His feeling depends on the performances of his body, or the actions of others. His own function seems not to be present. His work-world has no feeling (moral or social) consequences. Even such positive feelings as love, joy, or giving, may be handled inadequately by an inferior feeling function so that they are misplaced, inappropriate, and destructive. Our love is autoerotic, our joy unenthusiastic, our giving inconsiderate. An analogy may be made with thinking: inferior thinking may be reflecting on such major ideas as God, the nature of matter or energy, or the inter-relationship of cells. But these ideas, in themselves positive and significant, may be handled in a mystifying, confused, even archaic way, revealing the inappropriateness and inadequacy of inferior thinking, even if that is at times originally creative.

But, *fifth*, inferior feeling is not to be confused with *negative* feelings. Negative feelings are those either inwardly experienced as bad and painful, such as guilt, boredom, fear, or as socially condemned, such as hatred and envy. Just as positive feelings can be mishandled by an inferior feeling function, so can these so-called negative feelings be expressed appropriately and adequately. Think of Jonathan Swift and what he did with his negative feelings of hatred and misanthropy. Therefore, from this point of view, we might say that there is no feeling which in itself is negative. Much depends on the way in which feeling functions with it. The psychotherapeutic, even cultural, problem is not the problem of negative feelings — hatred, aggression, envy, and the seven deadly sins which we bring originally with us into life. Rather, the therapeutic and cultural problem concerns the development of the feeling function so that it becomes an adequate container, or channel, or mode of operation for these feelings. The general inferiority of this function in our society has many sources: our emphasis upon intellect, our competitive educational system, the lack of cultivation of the feminine virtues in man and woman, the decline of feeling systems such as religion, morals, aesthetics, manners, friendships; loss of interest in personal essays, letter-writing and diaries, and in loving rather than its technics and legal programmatics.

Sixth, an *education* of the feeling function is possible. Because the education of feeling is largely absent in our usual education, it has become a main theme in therapy, whether in groups, in sensitivity training or individual analysis. This education begins with the function of feeling itself, just where it is. If you permit, it is an education through faith, faith in the function itself which can develop if allowed to be exercised. Therefore, the education of feeling means foregoing the familiar condemnations of its inferiorities from above by our superior thinking. It begins with the courage of the heart: to like what one likes, to feel what one feels, to refuse what one truly cannot abide. It requires admission into consciousness and the re-evaluation of so-called negative feelings. Although the education of feeling may begin on this level of highly personal feeling reactions, eventually discrimination becomes more objective and the personal factor recedes.

Seventh, and finally, feeling plays a *central role in Jung's psychology*. We cannot read Jung with the intellect alone. Conscious comprehension of Jungian psychology means feeling comprehension as well. All the principal conceptual symbols – introversion, complex, shadow, self, synchronicity, for example – are experiences of feeling. A complex is a felt-reality. A symbol is not only a sense image with intuitional and intellectual content; it presents itself as value and as a living relationship, evoking feeling.

EMOTION AND AFFECT

We come now to emotion. Jung uses the term more or less interchangably with affect. A distinction between emotion and affect, partly based on Jung, was made by Ernst Harms at the 1948 Mooseheart Symposium. I, too, differentiate emotion and affect. In my book *Emotion* (1961) emotion and effect are differentiated. I conceived emotion as a total event of the personality, activating all levels and therefore a symbolic kind of transformed consciousness with "body" in it. Emotion is thus less than normal unemotional consciousness because it has levels of affect which narrowly intensify awareness, and yet more than normal unemotional consciousness because it is a heightened total condition. Affects, on the other hand, I conceived as not total, but partial, primitive, and relatively unconscious. Simply: affect lowers the mental level to what Janet would call *la partie inférieure d'un fonction*, whereas emotion raises, transforms, and symbolizes. Emotion is essentially a purposive creative state which has affect within it.

The image of the centaur expresses what I mean. In Greek myth, the centaur, half-man, half-animal, instructor of Achilles, Jason and Hercules, i.e., heroic consciousness, as well as Asklepios, i.e., therepeutic consciousness, and an inventor of music and medicine — indeed a high state of emotional awareness — is also the creature used for capturing wild bulls, or the blind impulse of affect. The whole man, at one with body consciousness, or in a state of emotional being, overcomes the affects.

Jung does not distinguish in his definitions between affect and emotion (1923, p. 541). His distinction between feeling and emotion/affect is mainly quantitative (1923, p. 522). Feelings become affects when they release physical innervations.

These physical innervations which characterize affect in distinction to feeling are important in Jung's thought in two ways. First, the physical component of affect makes possible the measurement of the complex with physical methods (psychogalvanic phenomenon). Secondly, Jung's view of schizophrenia, which goes back to the early years of the century, also requires this physical quantitative view of affect. Jung suggested that the physical innervations or affective charges bound up with the psychic factors in a repressed complex could ultimately act as a toxin inducing physiological changes resulting in schizophrenia.

JUNG'S CONCEPT OF THE COMPLEX

Clearly, Jung's theory of affect cannot be separated from his theory of the complex. And his psychology was called at the beginning not analytical psychology but complex psychology, attesting to the central role which in his view the complex plays in the human psyche. A complex may be defined as a group of psychic contents intertwined in a specific pattern and cohesively united by a similar and ambivalent affective tone. They are affect-laden. The ambivalence is experienced as compulsion and inhibition, as desire and anxiety. Complexes, like affects, are ego-alien; we experience them as intruders. We not only have them, but they have us, dominating us, driving us, inhibiting us. The personal aspect of the complex consists of events of my personal life — associations, memories, habits, and the like. The archetypal core of the complex is both an instinctual pattern of behavior and an image-idea. For example, the mother-complex affects the ego with desires for incest, with bad-tempered, demanding, indecisive moods of lameness, with omnipotence urges and desires for sexual prowess, and with longings for liberation and transcendence. These affects are presented on a fantasy level by symbolic ideas and images such as the dragon-hero fight, the wounded hero, the mighty phallic lover, Jesus the truthbringer, etc.

PERRY'S "AFFECT-EGO"

The latest Jungian contribution to the theory of emotion was made quite recently by John Weir Perry (1968). His ideas are relevant here. The complex always constellates the ego in a specific way; by affecting the ego it gives us an "affect-ego." For example, when the mother-complex has me, my ego may act the weak and wounded son-lover. When the father-complex has me, the ego is caught by the image and affects of the son in one of its forms: dutiful prince and successor, rebellious father-killer, tricky Tom Thumb who will not grow up. The generation struggle today is loaded with affect-ego problems, the sons constellating the fathers, the fathers constellating the sons through these archetypal complexes so that perception of each other is affected and distorted into pre-existent archetypal images. The patterns of affect in suppression and in rebellion going on around us are so universally similar — both in behavior and in ideational image — that they seem stamped from one typical, or archetypal, pattern.

Thus the complex is paramount in Jungian practice. An affect is always presumed to contain an archetypal core which reveals itself in specific patterns of behavior and specific images of fantasy. We go avidly after these fantasies and images (via dreams, say) in order to discover what complex is constellated, what archetypal pattern is being enacted. Then we compare the motifs of the complex with objective psychological material; that is, we amplify the motif beyond its personal associations, seeing the personal family fights also in view of the specific symbolic patterns of the Mother and Son-lover or Father and Son struggles, etc. So, we look at affects with a mythic eye, as fantastic symbolic role-playings of the person, which are necessary to the personality as a whole, and purposive even if ego-alien at the moment of occurrence. We regard the stimuli which discharge an affect, even if coming from without and seemingly trivial and incidental, as necessary to a person's mythic pattern of life, else they would not affect him. Thus affects have a survival value. Furthermore, we consider changes of mood and expressions of affect as belonging to personality transformation, and that this process of transformation could not take place without mood and affect. Thus, important for our approach is the intrapsychic origin of mood and affect; and the question of how mood and affect arise from wholly inner self-steering fantasies.

There are other aspects of Jung's theory of emotion which we shall have to leave aside, such as the Shadow or the Anima. The "Anima" in particular (the feminine aspect of the man) is the archetype involved with the irrational and moody complexes of the male personality. (I have taken this up in some detail in relation to affect in the last chapter of my book *Insearch*, 1967.) We must also leave aside the implications for parapsychology of Jung's view of emotion. His theory of synchronicity, an acausal connecting principle for the explanation of meaningful coincidences, also involves his theory of emotion.

IMPLICATIONS FOR THERAPY

We can, however, discuss the practical implications for therapy which Jung's view offers. This seems most relevant, since therapy involves everyone dealing with the problem of his own emotional life. We are all in therapy with ourselves, interminably. The perennial problem of emotion — to use the phrase of Magda Arnold — is not theory-forming, but "how to live," or "how to be" in Joseph Conrad's words. How can we survive, and how can the world around us survive, our affective attacks; how can affect become emotion, without which we cannot survive? The great conundrum of affect is the double-bind: "Thou shalt not repress," and on the other hand, "Thou shalt not act out." So what are we to do with our affects? I may get rid of them neither by repressing them within nor acting them out.

This leaves but one choice: living affects in, keeping them, holding onto them with all the intensity they bring with them, in order to gain their secret, their image, their fantasy, their purpose in my life. If held and watched and felt, the affect will ultimately reveal its image, i.e., the other side of the complex (on the hypothesis that the image and the affect are aspects of one complex). By living-in the affect, by concentrating upon it, by fantasying the terror, the hatred, the lust right through to the end — neither repressing nor acting out — by dreaming the dream along in the phrase of Jung, one does answer Conrad's question "how to be" with Conrad's own answer: "Immerse yourself in the destructive element." For then, experience shows that the affect will, with grace, transform itself into emotion; through the vigil one has kept with it, there has been added consciousness to what was hitherto blind. By having lived close to it, one has joined with it. No longer man wrestling with wild bull, we have a new kind of emotional awareness, man and animal-nature joined, the Centaur. Thus can affect transform us, rather than we it; it transforms our life and our awareness into emotional and symbolic experience. What hitherto was a symptom in our case history, to be dealt with or explained, now, with grace, is psychologically integrated, part of experience, and built into our soul-history.

In Hindu esoteric psychology (Tantra), in that system called the Kundalini Yoga, the place of affect is the imaginal belly, between the navel and the solar plexus. The area would include the liver of Greek antiquity, and the upper colon of eighteenth century psychiatry, so long considered the "locus of insanity."

This region is described in the Kundalini system as a seething cauldron, a place of fire, and there the God, Rudra the "howler," abides. But this place is also called "filled with jewels." Affects, much as they may howl, burn and stew, are nothing to "get rid of" with abreaction, behavior therapy or tranquilizers, for that would be to get rid of the potential jewels. If contained psychologically — held, kept, lived-in, and above all *valued with feeling* — the passion can transform into valuable psychological treasures, those diamond bodies of indestructible psychic experiences.

REFERENCES

Harms, E. (1950). A differential concept of feelings and emotions. In M. L. Reymert (Ed.), *Feelings and emotions*, McGraw-Hill, New York.
Hillman, J. (1961). *Emotion*. Northwestern Univ. Press, Evanston, Illinois.
Hillman, J. (1967). *Insearch*. Scribners, New York.
Jung, C.G. (1916). *Collected papers on analytical psychology*. Bailliere, London.
Jung, C.G. (1923). *Psychological types*. Harcourt, Brace, New York.
Jung, C.G. (1953-). Two essays on analytical psychology. In *Collected works*, Vol. 7. Pantheon, New York.
Mendelssohn, M. (1843-55). Philosophische Schriften. In *Moses Mendelssohn's Gesammelte Schriften*. Brockhaus, Leipzig.
Perry, J.W. (1968). Emotions and object relations. Paper read at the *Fourth International Congress of Analytical Psychology*, Zurich.
Whitehead, A.N. (1958). *Modes of thought*. Putnam, New York.

Chapter 9

Cognition and Feeling

Silvano Arieti*

As a psychiatrist, I must preface my paper with the statement that emotions and feelings have played a very ambiguous role in psychiatric theory. It is true that the psychiatric literature has constantly reaffirmed the importance of emotion, motivation and feeling. As a matter of fact, in psychodynamic interpretations it is assumed that we discuss the emotional forces which consciously or unconsciously determine the individual's overt or hidden behavior. However, when we deal with a theoretical presentation of this matter, we promptly discover a state of utter confusion. In my opinion, one of the reasons for this lack of clearness can be found in the fact that most psychiatrists, classical psychoanalysts as well as experimental psychologists, have tried to pattern all levels of psychological organization in accordance with what they have learned from the study of the simplest physiological and emotional levels. Undoubtedly, the states of hunger, thirst, fatigue, the need for sleep, the sexual urges, the fear about one's physical survival, are powerful dynamic forces and require much additional study. However, they do not include all the psychological factors that affect man favorably or unfavorably.

Modern civilization has in many countries increased the opportunities for physical comfort, adequate nourishment, and sexual gratification. And yet, clinical evidence — although not yet validated by reliable statistical analysis — seems to indicate that mental illness and psychological malaise have increased and not decreased in these countries. It should thus be relatively easy to infer that problems belonging to the higher levels of the psyche are to a large extent responsible for man's psychological difficulties. For this reason, comparative studies of animals, although elucidating basic psychological mechanisms, do not enlighten us on many aspects of human psychopathology.

In my opinion, the factors responsible for these difficulties have to do directly or indirectly with cognition; and cognition has not received adequate consideration in psychiatric and psychoanalytic studies. Perhaps historians of science will find deeply rooted cultural reasons for this neglect. They may interpret it as part of an overall anti-intellectual cultural climate which started toward the end of the nineteenth century and continued into the twentieth. More specifically, psychologists and psychiatrists may justifiably be inclined to believe that the behavioral school, with its emphasis on overt behavior, and classical psychoanalysis with its emphasis on psychic energy or libido, have not been well-disposed, and perhaps even intolerant of studies of cognition. In my opinion, this neglect of cognition has hindered the study of human feelings and emotions.

FIRST-ORDER EMOTIONS OR PROTOEMOTIONS

In other writings I have described what I think are the relations between simple feelings like pain, hunger, etc., and emotions (1967). All of them are "felt experiences" or experiences of the inner status of the organism. The main characteristic which justifies the inclusion of feelings and emotions in the category of experiences of inner status is the fact that they occur when an intraorganismic state is subjectively experienced. It is thus not without reason that in English the word *feeling* has a connotation so vast as to include simple sensation as well as high-level affects. It refers to all experiences of inner status. From all of these experiences we can abstract the subjective qualities of pleasantness and unpleasantness. These experiences become motivational factors because the awareness of what is pleasant elicits behavior aimed at searching for or retaining of pleasure. On the other hand, the awareness of what is unpleasant elicits behavior which tends to avoid or discontinue the experience.

Such awareness of pleasantness and unpleasantness is an experience which may not be accompanied by higher cognitive processes. Let us see, however, what happens in emotional experience. In previous writings I have divided emotions into three orders. The first order includes the simplest, which I have called protoemotions or first-order emotions. They are of at least five types: (a) *tension* — a feeling of discomfort caused by different situations, like excessive stimulation and obstructed physiological or instinctual response; (b) *appetite* — a feeling of expectancy which accompanies a tendency to move toward, contact, grab, or incorporate an almost immediately attainable goal; (c) *fear* — an unpleasant, subjective state, which follows the perception of danger and elicits a readiness to flee; (d) *rage* — an emotion which follows the perception of danger to be overcome by fight; that is by aggressive behavior, not by flight; and (e) *satisfaction* — an emotional state resulting from the gratification of physical needs and relief from other emotions.

In a general sense we can say that protoemotions: (a) are experiences of inner status which cannot be sharply localized and which involve the whole or a large part of the organism; (b) either include a set of bodily changes, mostly muscular and humoral, or retain some bodily characteristics; (c) are elicited by the presence or absence of specific stimuli, which are perceived by the subject as related in a positive or negative way to its safety and comfort; (d) become important motivational factors and to a large extent determine the subject's type of external behavior; (e) have an almost immediate effect; if they unchain a delayed reaction, the delay ranges from a fraction of a second to a few minutes; (f) require a minimum of cognitive work in order to be experienced. For instance, in fear or rage a stimulus must be promptly recognized as a sign of present or imminent danger.

The last two characteristics require further discussion. Protoemotions are not experienced instantaneously like simple sensations. They presuppose some cognitive work. However, this cognitive work is of very short duration, presymbolic, or in some cases, symbolic to a rudimentary degree. Presymbolic cognition includes perception and some learning. It also includes the sensorimotor intelligence described by Piaget (1936) in the first year and a half of life. The learning required at this level is very simple. It deals with the immediately given, that is, with either direct stimuli or with signals and not symbols. Signals (or signs) indicate things. Some of them may actually be parts of the things they indicate, though that is not always the case. Like the ringing of the bell for the conditioned dog, signals announce something that is about to occur.

An organization at the protoemotional level is very simple. It is, indeed, extremely important from the point of view of man, but does not include what is most pertinent to the field of psychiatry. In fact, we must go to the second-order emotions to find such psychological experiences as anxiety, anger, wish, security.

SECOND-ORDER EMOTIONS

Second-order emotions are not elicited by a direct or impending attack on the organism or by a threatened immediate change in homeostasis, but by cognitive symbolic processes. The prerequisite learning does not deal only with immediate stimuli, or with signals, but also with symbols; that is, with something that represents stimuli, something that stands for the direct sense-data.

These symbols may vary from very simple forms to the most complicated and abstract cognitive representations. I shall start with considering the simplest: the image, that psychological phenomenon which has been so badly neglected in psychology and psychiatry. We know that an image is a memory trace which assumes the form of a representation. It is an internal quasi-reproduction of a perception which does not require the corresponding external stimulus in order to be evoked. Although we cannot deny that at least rudimentary images occur in animals, there seems to be no doubt that images are predominantly a human characteristic. The child closes his eyes and visualizes his mother. The mother may not be present, but her image is with him; it stands for her. He may lie peacefully in bed and that image will be with him until he falls asleep. By being represented by her image, the mother acquires a psychic reality not tied to her physical presence. Image formation is actually the basis for all higher mental processes. It enables the human being not only to recall what is not present, but to retain an affective disposition for the absent object. The image thus becomes a substitute for the external object. It is actually an *inner object*, although it is not well organized. When the affective associations to the image are pleasant, it reinforces our longing or appetite for the corresponding external object. The image thus has a motivational influence in leading us to search out the actual object, which in its external reality is still more gratifying than the image. The opposite is true when the affective associations to the image are unpleasant: we are now motivated to keep from exchanging the unpleasant inner object for the corresponding external one, because that is even more unpleasant.

Now, let us see how images may increase the emotional gamut. Anxiety is the emotional reaction to the expectation of danger. The danger is not immediate, nor is it always well defined. Its expectation is not the result of a simple perception or signal, as it is in the case of fear. Images may enable a man to anticipate a future danger and its dreaded consequences, even though he does not expect it to materialize for some time. In its simplest forms, anxiety is fear mediated by images, it is image-determined fear. However, as we shall see shortly, the danger is often represented by sets of symbols that are more complicated than sequences of images.

The same remarks apply to another second-order emotion: anger. In its simplest form, anger is image-determined rage, that is, rage elicited by the images of the stimuli which generally elicit rage. While rage usually leads to immediate motor discharge, generally directed against the stimulus which elicits it, anger tends to last longer, although it retains an impelling character. The prolongation of anger is possible because it is mediated by symbolic forms, just as anxiety is. If rage is useful for survival in the jungle, anger was useful within the first human communities to maintain a hostile-defensive attitude toward the enemy, whether the latter was present or not.

Wishing is an emotional state that has received little consideration in the literature, except when it has been confused with appetite. While appetite is a feeling accompanied by a preparation of the body for approach and incorporation, wishing means a pleasant attraction toward something or somebody, or toward doing something. Contrary to appetite, wishing is made possible by the recall of the image or other symbols of an object whose presence is pleasant. The mnemic image of an earlier pleasant experience — for instance, of the satisfaction of a need — evokes an emotional disposition which motivates the individual to replace the image with the real object of satisfaction. A search for the real object is thus initiated, or at least contemplated. This search may require detours, since a direct approach is often not possible.

Security is the last second-order emotion. It has played an important role in the theoretical framework of the psychiatrist, Harry Stack Sullivan (1953). It is debatable whether such an emotion really exists or whether the term indicates only the absence of unpleasant emotions or else a purely hypothetical concept. We may visualize the simplest form of security, an image-determined satisfaction. That is, images permit the individual to visualize a state of satisfaction not only for today but also for tomorrow.

Much could be said about the somatic processes that accompany these second-order emotions and how they have changed to adapt to less immediate situations; for instance, how anxiety differs somatically from fear. But in this paper I must limit myself to deal with the connection of feelings and emotions with cognition. Thus far, I have discussed second-order emotions in their relation to images. Images are analogous symbols — a relation of likeness between the image and the represented thing is established. The brain can be compared to an analog computer in its use of images. With the advent of language, however, the nervous system becomes more like a digital computer. A system of arbitrary signs is now capable of eliciting the emotions which before could be aroused only by external stimuli or images.

Up to this level of development, emotions seem to be experiences of inner status which are involved only with the organism itself, its immediate surroundings, or the image of the immediate surroundings. Emotions, *qua* emotions, *qua* experiences of inner status, are not symbolic. They stand only for themselves. They do not go beyond the boundaries of the organism. However, when they become connected with symbols, they partake of the infinity of the universe. I shall come back to this point later. Here, however, I want to emphasize that second-order emotions can be elicited by a preconceptual type of cognition. Phylogenetic, ontogenetic and microgenetic studies by Werner (1948) and many other authors, including myself, have revealed that before reaching a mature intellectual level (what in psychoanalysis is called secondary process thinking, and in logic Aristotelean thought) the psyche goes through various levels of symbolic prelogical thinking variously designated as primary process, paleologic, paralogic, etc.

I cannot go into this matter now; but what I want to say is that at a developmental level where only first-order emotions are possible, the animal remains within the boundaries of a limited psychological reality, but is indeed a realist. The animal is capable of a nonsymbolic reality-bound type of learning.

He interprets signs in the light of past experience. When man starts to use symbols, especially preconceptual symbols, he opens his eyes toward the infinity of the universe, but also toward an infinity of errors and toward the realm of unreality. For instance, anxiety may be inappropriate because it is based, not on a realistic appreciation of danger, but on danger which is based on inaccurate or arbitrary symbolization. Psychiatry offers numerous examples of this possibility. For instance, some psychiatric patients tend to revert to the level of first-order emotions, as in developing a phobia, which is an abnormal fear. The patient changes his anxiety into fear, though the fear is groundless. Thus a patient, who is anxious about serious psychological problems he has to face in life, becomes afraid of dogs or horses. He goes into a state of panic at the sight of them.

THIRD-ORDER EMOTIONS

With the development of language, the gradual abandonment of preconceptual levels and the development of conceptual levels, third-order emotions occur, as I have described in other writings. In conjunction with first- and second-order emotions, these offer to the human being a very complex and diversified emotional repertory. In third-order emotions, language plays a greater role. The temporal representation is enlarged both toward the past and toward the future. Emotional experience has only one temporal dimension: the present. When it becomes connected with cognitive structures, it remains an experience in the present, but an experience which may be involved with a distant past or a distance future. A person may be disturbed now by what happened long ago or may happen in the future.

Third-order emotions, although capable of existing even before the advent of the conceptual level, expand and are followed by even more complex emotions at the conceptual level. Important third-order emotions are depression, hate, love and joy. To discuss adequately even what we know about them – which is little in comparison to what remains to be known – would fill many books. In the remaining time I shall make some comments about depression, and finally, I shall say a few words about hate.

Before the psychoanalytic era, depression received even more consideration by psychiatrists than anxiety. For the purpose of this paper, I shall make no distinction between depression, melancholia, sadness, anguish, mental pain, etc.

As a subjective experience, depression is difficult to define or even describe. It is a pervading feeling of unpleasantness, often accompanied by bodily symptoms. In depression, contrary to what happens in anxiety, there is no thought that a dangerous situation is about to occur. The dangerous event has already taken place; the loss has been sustained. Indeed, not only the present but the future seems affected by this loss. Whatever happened to make the individual feel depressed seems to him to have an impact on the future, too.

Thus it is evident that depression follows cognitive processes, such as evaluations and appraisals which require verbal expression. For example, a person is told of the sudden death of a friend. He evaluates the news and understands what it means to his dead friend and to him, too, as the survivor, who will be deprived of his friend's company. All these processes would not be possible without language. Linguistic forms evoke surprise, evaluation and an unpleasant feeling called sadness or depression. This feeling tends to linger. Some people may compare this feeling to apparently similar ones which occur in the newborn when the mother leaves, or even in animals, like dogs, when the master leaves and they are left alone. These feelings in newborn babies and in animals are unpleasant, but should more properly be called deprivation, discomfort, tension, because they are not based upon anticipation of the future. Depression seems to me to be accompanied by complex and elaborate cognitive processes. However, in many cases, particularly in psychiatric conditions, the feeling of depression is so powerful that it drowns out the idea that actually aroused the depression — which then is said to have been produced by unconscious causes. At times, the idea has an inappropriate symbolic value and so engenders a depression that seems incongruous.

Although at first sight depression appears to have no purpose it has protective value, just as anxiety has. Like other unpleasant sensations and emotions, it is useful because it stimulates the person to nonacceptance of the emotion, that is, to its removal. How can depression be removed; Let us take again the person saddened by the death of someone close to him. For a few days, all thoughts connected with the beloved departed will bring about a painful, almost unbearable feeling. Any thought even remotely related to him will arouse depression. The survivor cannot adjust to the idea that the deceased is no longer alive. But since the deceased was so important to him, many of the survivor's thoughts or actions are directly or indirectly connected with the deceased and so elicit an unpleasant reaction.

Nevertheless, after a certain period of time, the survivor becomes adjusted to the idea that the deceased is no longer present. The unpleasant, unacceptable sadness is removed because it has forced the survivor to reorganize his thinking, to regroup his thoughts into different constellations, to search for new directions. He especially had to rearrange the ideas connected with the departed. This rearrangement can be carried out in several ways, according to a person's mental predisposition. He may no longer consider the deceased indispensable; he may associate the image of the beloved dead mainly with the qualities he had that brought joy, so that the memory no longer brings mental pain; or he may think of his friend's life as not really ended but as being continued either in another world, or in this world through the lasting effects of his actions. Those who try to console the survivor do so by helping him to rearrange his thoughts.

Whatever the ideational rearrangement, it does not mean moving away from a physical source of discomfort, as in pain, or from the source of threat, as in fear and some forms of anxiety. The moving away is only from depressive thoughts. The escape from depression can only occur through cognitive means.

The cognitive means I have mentioned above are very common, but they are not the only ones. A few people make different cognitive rearrangements. They do not try to change their thought pattern nor do they try to persuade themselves that the unacceptable is acceptable. They end up by accepting the unacceptable. This acceptance of mental pain or sadness as a fact of life adds a new dimension to experience, for the enigma of man's position in the universe and the mysterious order of things is forcibly brought to his attention. Such acceptance of pain may actually decrease or even dissolve the depression.

These remarks should not be interpreted as meaning that man should make no effort to remove or change the sources of pain. But when he is faced with the immutable, he may learn to accept it; and he can do this only through the media of cognitive processes. As a matter of fact, we know of cultural trends toward making an apotheosis of melancholia. One such trend started in the Italian Renaissance with Marsilio Ficino (1433-1499), Lorenzo the Magnificent (1449-1492), and Iacopo Sannazzaro (1456-1530). As we know, this trend expanded to other countries and to other media, as seen, for instance, in the art of Albrecht Dürer (1471-1528).

I must resist the urge to go deeper into these cultural trends, and mention instead that *hate* is the third-order emotion which corresponds to the second-order emotion *anger* and to the first-order emotion *rage*. The three together constitute hostility, but hate is the only one among the three which has the tendency to become a chronic emotional state sustained by special thoughts. Thus a feed-back mechanism is established between these sustaining thoughts and the emotion. Hate leads to calculated action, and at times to premeditated crimes. Some authors in the fields of psychology and ethology have a tendency to reduce every form of hostility to rage and aggression, as is the case in animals. This can be done only when the role of cognition is minimized.

The emotions I have mentioned (as well as others I have not mentioned) may combine in many ways. With the ontogenetic and cultural development of man, cognition and affect have an increasing reciprocal influence. Cognitive processes create more and more motivational and therefore emotional factors, and emotions become the propelling drives toward further cognitive processes. By accompanying any cognitive process, emotions transcend the boundaries of the organism and, like human symbolic processes, may become involved with the whole universe known to man. If man studies complicated mathematical problems or looks at the distant stars, or thinks of things that occurred in the remote past or are expected to occur in the distant future, not only does he attempt to reflect on events regardless of space and time, not only does he search for a coherent relationship among the apparently unrelated parts of nature, but his inner self, his inner status, his highest level homeostasis is altered as a result of endeavors. Thus every cognitive process becomes an inner experience. He who looks on all time and all existences is touched in his inner being by every time and every existence. Whatever is conceived touches the core of man. The process called internalization in psychoanalysis comes about not just because a portion of the ordered external world has become an enduring part of the knower but rather because it has been transformed into an emotional experience.

REFERENCES

Arieti, S. (1967). *The intrapsychic self: feeling, cognition and creativity in health and mental illness.* Basic Books, New York.

Piaget, J. (1936). *La naissance de l'intelligence chez l'enfant.* Delachaux and Niestle, Neuchatel.

Sullivan, H.S. (1953). *The interpersonal theory of psychiatry.* Norton, New York.

Werner, H. (1948). *Comparative psychology of mental development* (rev. ed.). Follett, New York.

Chapter 10

The Information Theory of Emotion*

Pavel V. Simonov†

Recent achievements of neurophysiology have substantially widened our knowledge about the central nervous structures responsible for the occurrence of positive and negative emotions. These structures are located in the archicortex, subcortical nuclei and the midbrain. However, the question of which specific attributes of conditioned regulation give rise to the excitation of specialized emotional centers still remains obscure. It is clear that animal and human emotions should not be identified with the occurrence and satisfaction of the need of a living organism for food, water, avoidance of harmful influences and the like. First of all, with motor habits acquired and stabilized, the satisfaction of a need may be achieved without any obvious sign of emotional strain. Secondly, one and the same need may lead to the arousal of different emotions, depending on the situation.

Our own experiments and the analysis of published data have led us to the view that negative emotions constitute a special nervous mechanism thrown into action when a living being lacks the information necessary and sufficient for organizing the actions that will satisfy a need — as Pavlov says when a dynamic habit of adaptive reactions does not take shape. Quantitatively, these relations may be expressed by the formula: $E = -N(I_n - I_a)$, where emotion is equal to need multiplied by the difference between the prognostically necessary and available information. The value of the term "information" is determined by the growing possibility of reaching the goal as a result of receiving a given communication.

*This paper is part of a report presented at the Congress of Psychology, Moscow, 1966.

†Institute of Higher Nervous Activity and Neurophysiology of the Soviet Academy of Sciences, Moscow, USSR.

The compensatory involvement of the nervous mechanism of emotion has several important consequences: (a) the living system passes over to dominant types of reaction, as a result of which some indifferent stimuli or signals (which previously had a different significance) begin to evoke orienting, defensive, sexual and other reactions. The manifest inertia of emotional dominants ensures the prolongation of activity even when there is scant possibility of reaching the goal so that motor reactions are usually not effective; (b) the wastefulness of hypercompensatory dominant behavior leads to intensification of the activity of the circulatory and respiratory systems, and the glands of internal secretion, all changes typical for emotions; (c) emotions exert a powerful activating influence on the higher levels of the brain, increase alertness, and apparently facilitate the activation of the conditioned reflex connections in the cortex of the cerebral hemispheres which represent the registration of experience.

But the above-mentioned characteristics of emotional reactions are effective and expedient only under conditions of information deficiency. To the extent that this deficiency is eliminated and a new dynamic habit is formed, the advantages of the emotional mechanism turn into disadvantages. Reactions that correspond exactly and subtly to external signals are far more effective than dominant (emotional) behavior. Negative effects of emotion are also demonstrated in the sportsman's "prestart nervousness," in the imitative behavior of crowds, and in mass panic and human neuroses. Indeed, neurosis is a classical "information disease." It is no accident that psychotherapy is aimed primarily at eliminating the information deficiency in neurosis.

EMOTION AND THE GENERALIZATION
OF CONDITIONED REFLEXES

It is well known that the building up of a new conditioned reflex is accompanied by strong and widely generalized changes in the electrical activity of the brain and by clear-cut changes in the vegetative nervous system. As soon as the conditioned reflex is consolidated, these symptoms disappear almost completely, and the electrical changes in the brain together with autonomic nervous system changes begin to correspond to the specific motor components of the conditioned reflex. As far back as 1924, the Soviet psychiatrist V.P. Osipov called the first stage of reflex formation "the emotional stage," and the second "the cognitive, intellectual, stage." In the opinion of Morrell *et al.* (1960), an early stage of conditioned reflex formation (or a new system of conditioned reflex connections) requires the participation of the limbic and hippocampal system, while the neocortex is dominant in the later stages. In the face of the general uncertainty as to the exact mechanism, it seems legitimate to postulate the nervous mechanism of the emotions as instrumental in the formation of the conditioned reflex, particularly in its initial stage. At any rate, this stage cannot be reduced merely to the orienting reflex because generalization phenomena will vary according to the character of reinforcement: food, mate, or pain.

EMOTION AND THE ORIENTING REFLEX

If we regard the orienting reaction as a specific activity aimed at identifying the stimulus and determining its significance for the organism, the activation of the emotional nervous mechanism is an example of the disruption of the habitual response. When a new response habit is formed (which at the same time changes perception but does not become a mere "model of the stimulus" as E. N. Sokolov believes) the electrophysiological and vegetative signs of emotional stress disappear, while those components of the orienting reactions that are necessary for perceiving a repetitive signal are firmly retained.

POSITIVE EMOTIONS

We have already mentioned the impossibility of equating positive emotions with the satisfaction of need. When such satisfaction is achieved, all emotional stress disappears and is replaced by rest, indifference and drowsiness. According to the above formula, emotion becomes positive when $I_a > I_n$ — that is, there is a surplus of information available as compared with the information necessary to satisfy a sufficiently strong need. If a man feels positive emotions even after the need is satisfied, it is only because the memory apparatus retains some traces of the former situation in which the need had not yet been satisfied.

Because of the inertia of emotion, positive emotions endure and thus facilitate behavior though there may again be a deficiency of information. Minor successes that occur from time to time help us to persevere in a difficult project. Positive emotions serve as compensatory mechanisms but this function is not revealed at the moment of their arousal (as in the case of negative emotions) but at further stages of activity. Positive emotions help create a new goal and help us in pursuing it.

CLASSIFICATION OF EMOTIONS

The different emotions depend on the strength of the need, the extent of the information deficiency (or redundancy), and the specificity of action aimed at satisfying a need. Contact interaction with the object (in which the living being is able to interrupt or to prolong contact, but is unable to prevent or initiate it) is accompanied by an emotional tone (pleasure, displeasure, aversion, suffering). When action at a distance is required (attaining possession; defense, struggle), there will be emotions in the proper sense of the term. Table I illustrates the dependence of emotions on the character of the action.

TABLE I
THE DEPENDENCE OF EMOTIONS ON THE CHARACTER OF ACTIONS

Need [a]	Information	Contact action	Action at a distance		
			Possession	Avoidance Defense	Overcoming obstacles
intense	surplus	enjoyment pleasure	delight happiness gladness	fearlessness boldness confidence	exultation inspiration cheerfulness
less intense	as required	comfort Homeostasis	tranquility	slackness	imperturbability
intense	deficiency	displeasure aversion suffering	uneasiness sorrow grief despair	watchfulness anxiety fear horror	impatience indignation anger fury, rage

[a] inherited or acquired

The above emotions are often combined in very different ways. The quality of need also leaves its imprint on the emotions. In this context, however, it was important to emphasize action as a factor which determines the group to which an emotion belongs.

THE NEUROPHYSIOLOGICAL BASIS OF EMOTION

The needs and emotions of higher living beings are chiefly represented in the limbic system. On the one hand, there are "centers of needs" — hunger, thirst, satiation, pain, sexual attraction, and the like; on the other hand, executive "centers of emotion" — fear, aggression, joy, and so on. However, under normal conditions, the activation of these executive centers is apparently initiated by the cerebral cortex where the subject's individual experience is registered as a system of conditioned reflex connections. Data secured by Luria (1966) and Pribram (1961) give grounds for assuming that the frontal, parietal, and temporal cortex play a special part in the process of collating prognostically necessary and available information. The hippocampus also seems to be directly related to this process (Adey, 1961).

CONCLUSION

From the physiological point of view, emotions constitute a special nervous mechanism which ensures the adaptive behavior of higher living beings in situations which disrupt their habit system, that is, when there is a lack of the information required for reaching a goal and satisfying a need. Although positive emotions are aroused whenever the newly acquired information exceeds the previously existing need for it, positive emotions also impel living beings to strive for their goals despite an "information vacuum." In this way, positive emotions also serve as a means of overcoming the deficiency of information experienced by the individual. In a sense, emotions are opposed to rational experience because logic alone is insufficient for the success of adaptive actions in a changing environment.

REFERENCES

Adey, W.R., Walter, D.O. and Hendrix, C.E. (1961). Computer techniques in correlation and spectral analyses of cerebral slow waves during discriminative behavior. *Exp. Neurol.*, 3, 501-524.

Luria, A.R. (1966). Frontal cortex and the control of behavior. In *Frontal cortex and the control of psychic processes*. Moscow Univ. Press (Russ.).

Morrell, F., Barlow, J. and Brazier, M. (1960). Analysis of conditioned repetitive response by means of the average response computer. In *Recent advances in biology and psychiatry*. Grune and Stratton, New York.

Pribram, K. (1961). To the theory of physiological psychology. In *Problems of psychology*, 2, 133-156. (Russ.).

Chapter 11

The Motivational and Perceptual Properties of Emotions as Indicating Their Fundamental Character and Role

Robert Ward Leeper*

I want to start with the proposition that our reasons for interest in feelings and emotions are not merely theoretical or scientific interests, strong though these might be. The sources of our interest, I believe, exist also in the fact that the most important problems of modern society are, in many respects, emotional problems. Both directly and indirectly is this so. Directly because of the fact that, in our modern world, there are such powerful and widespread feelings of aloneness, rejection, insecurity, discouragement, alienation, and resentment, rather than the positive emotions which people might well prefer to have. Indirectly in that, if it be protested that the crucial problems of modern society are problems of international conflict, economic waste and exploitation, racial discrimination, population explosions, and the like, the answer that might well be made is this: what underlies these other problems, in considerable degree, are emotional factors such as fears of other nations with different ideological orientations, difficulties in making emotional readjustments regarding what constitutes a satisfying, heart-warming size of family, and emotional commitments to special privileges on the part of far too many groups within society.

Implicit in any such proposal is necessarily some view of the nature of the emotional aspects of human life. Thus, it might seem that I must be assuming that emotions are basically disruptive or disorganizing processes, much as Piéron (1928), P.T. Young (1943, 1961), and many other psychologists have assumed.

*University of Oregon, Eugene.

But this is not my assumption. If emotions were intrinsically disruptive, they would produce various difficulties. But their practical significance would be by no means as great as I have suggested. On the other hand, I am not picturing emotions as having solely constructive or adaptive values which our society is failing to use. Whether the organizing influences from any emotion are adaptive or maladaptive depends on circumstances, as is the case with any motive. A wild animal, for example, pays with its life if its motive of hunger leads it to take the bait from a trap. Emotions can have analogous influences.

The basic view that I am assuming regarding emotions gives them a much more pervasive and responsible role in the lives of human beings and other higher animals than most of the older theories about emotions have suggested. Their nature, it seems to me, calls for a kind of reinterpretation which has been recommended by a few psychologists, but only a few, so that this type of approach – if indeed it is consistent with what we now know – calls for some much more extended examination. The two main aspects of the view which I will propose will be dealt with in separate sections of this paper.

THE CONCEPT OF EMOTIONS AS MOTIVES

In brief, what I am proposing under this first heading is that one of the most fundamental points that can be made about emotions is that they are *motives*. They are distinguishable in some ways from the more traditionally recognized motives such as hunger, thirst, and fatigue – what might be called the physiologically-based motives – but they are part of the same continuum which includes such other motives toward the other pole. They are part of a larger category or class, in other words, which is defined by certain basic kinds of functions, by certain basic influences on the psychological life of the organism.

In fact, what I am proposing is that emotions are not merely motives, but in the higher animals (including man) are especially important motives. Furthermore, they are not just rare events, of intense sorts, as the traditional ideas about emotions portray them as being, but are more or less perpetually active motives and do most of their work at moderate or weak intensities, just as the motive of thirst, for example, under ordinary circumstances produces what drinking is needed without its ever getting beyond a rather low level. At such lower levels, emotions do most of their work without the individual's having any notable thought of being motivated, because the emotional processes tend to be experienced as objectified or projected as perceptions of the situation. They are usually not experienced as something special within oneself. The higher the development of the brain, the more it is true that a great part of the constructive influences in the life of the organism need to come from emotional sources. The greater are the dangers too, of course, when emotions go wrong, but the greater are the possibilities of constructive contributions which the physiologically-based motives could not provide.

If all this is true, the most fundamental type of research on emotions which needs to be conducted is research on their role as motives — their role, that is, in arousing and sustaining activity, in producing exploratory reactions, in facilitating learning in situations in which no adequate means of serving such emotional motives has been acquired previously, in governing performance or habit-use, in helping produce problem-solving learning, in helping govern choices between alternatives, in producing willingness to endure penalties to reach some goal or a willingness to forego some reward, and in influencing thought-content and sensory perceptions. These are the influences that we have already learned that we must recognize and measure when we want to work with the simpler and more easily-studied motives of a physiologically-based sort, such as hunger, thirst, and pain. The fact that there is a physiological need that ought to be served is no sufficient reason for assuming that a corresponding motive will exist. In high-altitude flying, it was learned that there is no physiological motive that would pressure a flier to don an oxygen mask; similarly, dangerous levels of carbon monoxide produce no related motive. Only indirectly is it known what strength of motive would be associated with different deprivation-periods in different species. These various and primarily behavioral criteria are our necessary reliance in work on the traditionally-recognized motives.

Historically, most of the psychological research on emotions has not explicitly concerned any such motivational effects or recognized any reliance on them. Instead, emphasis has been placed on facial and postural expression of emotions, on questions of whether different emotions are distinguished by related physiological effects, and on questions of the neurological mechanisms of emotions. In all of these cases, however, the research worker has had to depend on the motivational effects of emotions to know which emotion he was dealing with in each case.

The same is the case in everyday life. When a parent judges a child's emotional response and uses the words that teach the child the names of different emotional experiences, the parent does not identify the child's emotion by testing his pulse, or his galvanic skin reaction, or by learning what subcortical neural centers are operating. It is fundamentally from the types of motivational influences mentioned above that the parent says, "You don't need to be afraid of that," or "What makes you so angry with him?" or "You like Tommy, don't you?"

To put all this more briefly, we might say that motives of all kinds are main factors in producing the *goal-directedness* of behavior and mental activity. This is the crucial distinguishing property of emotions.

However, if emotions are thus fundamentally motives, it might well be asked why it took so long before we explicitly viewed emotions in these terms. As I have proposed elsewhere in more detail (Leeper, 1965, pp. 27-47), I believe that our explanation of this delay must be sought in certain general hypotheses about how knowledge develops in any new scientific area (or within human culture more generally, for that matter). In many different fields, the records suggest that the growth of systematic knowledge very commonly does not start with what is most urgent from a practical point of view, nor with what will ultimately prove of greatest theoretical interest. The growth of systematic knowledge starts, instead, with what has these three properties: (a) What gets recognized and comes to be understood first are those things that are relatively highly tangible in the sense of being directly perceptible and even attention-commanding; (b) what gets worked on first are those phenomena where both the decisive causes and the effects have close time relations; and (c) what gets worked on first are those phenomena where the cause-and-effect relationships are relatively invariable.

Because of these tendencies — ones that operated also in the history of medicine, physics, anthropology, and every other field, as far as I know — the ideas about emotions that developed in everyday life, and subsequently the ideas about emotions and the research on emotions by psychologists, started with the more sensational and easily perceived emotions — namely, the intense and dramatic cases of fear, rage, extreme depression, and so on. The work started with relatively simple causal factors, such as the training with electric shocks in the classic experiments on fear by Neal Miller (1948) with rats and by Solomon and Wynne (1953, 1954) with dogs. In both of those studies, the effects recorded were *motivational* effects. But with human subjects, the commonly studied effects have been such things as galvanic skin responses, changes of heartbeat, and other autonomic effects. An exception to this statement would be the extensive work in recent years on the effects of "need for achievement" on interpretations of Thematic Apperception Test cards (see Atkinson and Feather, 1966); but this work usually has been discussed without any suggestion that phenomena of emotion are involved in it.

Another question that might well be asked would be the question as to why emotional functioning is so apparent a characteristic of the higher species. It seems to me that, from the standpoint of the older ideas of emotions as disruptive processes, this question is rather hard to answer, because that portrayal is hard to reconcile with the principle that what is retained and widely exhibited must generally have had some biological survival-value or some adaptive value, rather than the reverse. From a motivational standpoint, however, it seems more understandable that the higher vertebrates would have developed some type of motivation of this sort. In such higher vertebrates, three very notable developments were the developments of very excellent distance receptors, great learning ability, and complex sensory-perceptual capacities. By means of these, the higher animals became able to use a greatly enlarged environment. They became able to respond, not merely to those things with which they had direct physical contact, but to objects remote from them and yet significant as potential sources of danger or food or the like. It became possible for such animals to distinguish on the basis of fine differences of pattern, and on the basis of qualities that could be used appropriately only on the basis of past experience.

If these increased aids for perceiving the environment were to be useful, however, the organism in each case had to do more than just receive information and take factual note of things. It was not enough for a baboon, for instance, to note, in good information-processing terms, "Yes, yes, I see that a lion is creeping toward me through the bushes, but I've finally reached this water hole after a long hot day and I'm just starting to satisfy a basic physiological drive." In such situations, the splendid distance receptors, the great learning ability, and the unusual perceptual resources would have had little biological value if they had not involved some motivational qualities as well. What was required was a kind of motivation that would have the same basic types of influences as the older physiologically-based motives, but that would be based on finely structured constellations of stimulation and that, in many cases, would be sufficiently powerful even to override strong physiological drives and govern the main behavior of the animal.

After all the insults thrown at emotional processes in the older psychological literature — all the accusations that emotions were either disorganizing processes or at least primitivizing processes — it might seem rather odd to suggest that the additional sort of motivation thus developed in the higher animals, to care for such requirements as noted above, were the emotional processes in such higher animals.

By now, however, except among the Skinnerians, who somewhat are recapitulating the phylogeny of psychological thought about emotions, it is becoming somewhat commonplace, even, for psychologists to recognize this motivational role of emotions. Sometimes, as with the neo-Hullians, there seem to be difficulties in attributing this role to anything except anxiety or fear; but even this is passing, and we are pretty well on the road to recognizing that emotional processes are not mainly the spectacular excesses discussed in the older literature, but also the quiet, long-sustained emotional motives of enjoyment of one's work, pride in what one is doing, affection for one's family and enjoyment of serving them, enjoyment of the esthetic side of the world, and so on. It naturally has been taking more time to appreciate theoretically the importance of these, just as it has taken time to appreciate the importance, in nutritional matters, of such minor elements as iodine, cobalt, sulfur, phosphorus, the various vitamins and enzymes, and fatty materials of some sorts rather than others. It is the old story. The more tangible things get recognized first, along with those things that have more immediate and invariable effects. But the things that get recognized first, though they remain part of the total picture, are not necessarily the most important things.

THE CONCEPT OF EMOTIONS AS PERCEPTIONS

Because of the increasing readiness to recognize motivational contributions of emotions, the main question in this field has changed. Now it is more the question: "What is the basic nature of these processes — these emotions — that play this motivating role? If we peer into the black box and try to learn more about emotions, not merely in terms of what they arise from and what they do, but in terms of what sorts of processes they are, what would we learn?"

On this question, what I want to propose is, in brief, that emotions are perceptual processes. I mean this, furthermore, not in some odd and marginal sense, but in the full sense of processes that have definite cognitive content, or are rich in informational terms as well as in terms of their motivational properties. In fact, just to turn things around a bit, I would like to propose that emotional processes are a more authentic paradigm of perceptual processes than are those simpler examples that usually are cited in chapters and textbooks on perception. To avoid misunderstandings, let me make clear that I am not proposing that emotions are ever, except in incidental ways, perceptions of unusual physiological effects such as a James-Lange type of theory would emphasize. Instead, I am proposing that emotions are basically *perceptions of situations* and that, commonly, they are *long-sustained perceptions of the more enduring and significant aspects of such situations.*

Any such proposal is of course at odds with traditional ideas of perceptions and emotions. Traditional psychological theory placed emotions and perceptions in separate and mutually exclusive categories. Indeed, this older psychological thought assumed also that emotions are lower-order processes, partly because emotions were pictured as dependent on subcortical mechanisms and the autonomic nervous system, whereas perceptions and cognitive activities generally in the higher vertebrates were pictured as dependent on the neocortex and on the somatic nervous system.

However, any such neurological dichotomy can be dismissed fairly surely. The new discoveries about the influences of the brainstem reticular formation were merely part of the evidence showing the interdependence of cortical and subcortical functioning both in cognitive activities and in emotional processes (see McCleary and Moore, 1965, for a simple and clear summary of some main evidence). It doubtless is true that the neocortex must make some special contributions to certain types or aspects of cognitive activities, but it must be remembered that the full gamut of basic psychological functions was developed in biological evolution before there was such a thing as neocortical tissue; and this recent "invention" must be a sort of supplementary device, rather than something that distinguishes two such basic sorts of functioning as perceptual processes and emotional processes. Indeed, since emotional functioning is most developed in creatures like man and chimpanzees, less in dogs, and still less in chickens, it may even be that the neocortical part of the brain has been as crucial for emotional characteristics as for traditionally recognized sorts of perception, learning, and thinking.

Even aside from such neurological issues, however, the fact still remains that any proposal that emotions (and other motives too, for that matter) are perceptions is seriously at odds with traditional ideas about perceptions. From a historical standpoint, this is not very surprising. The psychology of perception was the first major field of experimental psychology to develop. It necessarily worked with phenomena that were relatively feasible to explore by laboratory methods. In keeping with the hypothesis that I sketched earlier about differential rates of development of knowledge on different sorts of problems, we should expect, in fact, that such perceptual research originally would deal mostly with unusually tangible factors and with phenomena in which causes and effects were close in time and rather highly correlated. The work on negative after-images was such a case, or work on spatial perception or apparent movement. Out of such work, certain broad conceptions developed that portrayed perception in terms of such convenient paradigms. It would be unjust to criticize earlier workers for starting with the phenomena that they used. Any science has to start with what is relatively simple. Even at that, the task of pioneer workers is terrifically difficult. But, the question still remains as to whether, with the much richer body of empirical material that we now can draw on, we still will find the old basic conceptions the most profitable for ourselves.

Main Features of Traditional Perceptual Orientations

Let me sketch what I mean by the traditional view regarding perceptions. In this older view, it was taken for granted that perceptions are always conscious experiences and that virtually the only appropriate method for studying them would be subjective observation, whether in an older structuralist sense or in a larger-unit phenomenological sense. Perceptions were thought of as only those experiences primarily under the control of, or mainly predictable from, properties of the more or less immediately preceding physical stimulation. Accordingly, even when some perceptual psychologists confined most of their work to visual perception, they still did not take an interest in the visual experiences aroused by Rorschach inkblots or by the pictures used in the Thematic Apperception Test or TAT. The experiences aroused by these two materials were so variable from person to person and were accordingly so unpredictable from stimulus properties that perceptual psychologists did not feel tempted to include them in their research field. They did not exclude phenomena in which there were significant contributions by variables within the organism. Thus they worked with reversible figures, with refinements of sensory organization from learning, and with figural aftereffects. But, for the sake of convenience, they dealt only with relatively simple stimulus materials, rather than with stimulus materials that were less structured and that would evoke more complex processes. Most of their work, furthermore, was confined not merely to visual materials, but to *static* visual stimulus materials, even as shown by brief tachistoscopic exposures, rather than focusing also on temporally extended materials like rhythms, melodies, and speech.

What the psychology of perception has dealt with has mostly been motivationally-neutral or motivationally-colorless experiences. In consequence, the experiences that were studied were relatively temporary or transient experiences, and not experiences that tended to translate themselves into any overt behavior except to oblige the experimenter. Because of this fact, and because of the subjectivist tradition in the field of perception, the perceptions that were studied were viewed essentially as though they were *terminal* processes — not as phases of biological processes that called for study in terms of their further influences.

Changes of These Traditions from within Perceptual Psychology as Such

It may seem that I have given a sort of caricature of perceptual psychology. I think not, but I would like to hasten to add that some rather significant changes in those older lines of thought have been coming from within the psychology of perception itself. Thus, many perceptual psychologists would now insist that perceptions can be either conscious or unconscious, just as processes of mental set or concept-formation may be conscious or unconscious. They also insist that much of perceptual research needs to depend on inferences from behavioral data. Many of them would insist that tachistoscopic exposures are a very special type of stimulus situation. Even with ordinary "still" pictures, a perception, they would say, has to be developed by integrative brain activity from a series of fixations. Many perceptual psychologists would agree with the point that James Gibson (1966) has recently been emphasizing, particularly as a consequence of his research with tactual form perception, that perceptual experience not only usually comes from a sequence of stimulations, but often involves an active *search* from which a more adequate perception can be developed.

Some perceptual psychologists have been inclined to emphasize functional similarities between traditional examples of perception and, on the other hand, the more complex phenomena that commonly are spoken of as matters of thought or reasoning. Thus, as Wolfgang Köhler (1944, p. 144) said in his obituary for Max Wertheimer: " . . . he never tired of demonstrating to himself and to his students that the same basic concepts apply to both topics."

Some other perceptual psychologists have been urging that perceptual experiences are not in all cases motivationally neutral processes. Thus, Pfaffmann (1964) and P. T. Young (1967) have been emphasizing that gustatory and olfactory perceptions usually have a significant affective quality and consequently tend to be important in the behavior of animals and humans. Helson (1967, pp. 314-315) too, in his recent major chapter on perception, has said, "That perception is more or less tinged with affect is generally recognized, yet psychologists have been slow to include affect as a dimension of perception. . . . Wherever there is affect we can presume there is also motivation. The fact that tastes and odors are so heavily affectively loaded leads us to expect them to be strong motivators also, and this point has been stressed by Pfaffmann. . . ."

More and more emphasis is being placed on the principle that perceptual organizations rather commonly cannot be predicted just from present stimulus qualities, but must be understood also in terms of past learning (Neisser, 1967; Eleanor Gibson, 1969), including even the learning of abstract concepts of "conservation of volume" and the like, as per Piaget's research with children.

The Still Further Changes That Need To Be Made in the Conception of Perception

The above-mentioned changes in perceptual psychology have created more possibility of dealing with emotions as part of a whole domain of perceptual functioning. However, there is still a very sizeable difference between even the "thus up-dated" portrayal of perceptions and, on the other hand, the conception of perceptions that we would have to use to justify speaking of emotions as authentic, full-bodied perceptual processes. What I need to do, therefore, is to go back to the phenemena that are accepted by perceptual psychologists as their paradigms, and try to define what I understand to be the fundamental functional properties that those examples possess.

The crucial properties that have been demonstrated in traditional perceptual research, I submit, are the following: (a) Perceptions are complex brain processes that "represent" or "portray" or "stand for" different objects, situations, events, relationships, and so on. Sometimes they are representations merely of things or events within the environment or within the organism, but frequently they represent the environment and organisms as interacting with each other. (b) These complex representations, because of how they are dynamically organized, constitute new *functional units* in the brain activities. The properties of these functional units generally do not exist in the parts, but exist only in the larger processes as integrations from neural contributions from different sources, as in the case of experience of a melody from a series of notes of different pitch.

These functional units are what are then significant in the further activity of the individual, rather than the organism's living in terms of the parts that went into the integrated product. (c) Perceptions are dynamically organized in the further sense that the total process tends to govern the properties of perceived parts within such larger wholes. A word like "run," for example, can have any of a dozen or more instant meanings in different sentences. (d) Perceptions tend to obey a "best-form" or "minimum" principle (Hochberg, 1957). (e) Perceptions from a given stimulus-situation are in many cases subject to drastic reorganization into markedly different perceptual experiences, as with the Rubin vase or the Boring "My wife and my mother-in-law" figure. (f) Perceptual organizations commonly are more or less modified by learning – slightly in some cases, profoundly in other cases, as in incomplete or fragmentary pictures where the individual at first may have great difficulty. (g) Perceptual processes are highly veridical in some cases, as with accurate spatial perceptions, and compellingly false in other cases, as with a trapezoidal window which one knows is rotating, but which, simultaneously, he perceives as though it were oscillating back and forth. (h) Many perceptual activities do not have merely a single phase, but go through a series of transformations or developments within the same stimulus situation. Thus, the rotating trapezoidal window tends to be perceived in authentic terms at first, and shifts to the oscillating effect only with sustained inspection. Some other perceptions go through still more complex sequences of development.

This is a considerable set of properties. Of course, in this list, I have said nothing about any dependence on immediately preceding receptor stimulations, nor on whether these processes are all motivationally neutral, nor on whether the representation might be some complex one that required a great deal of development through prior learning, as in the case of the perceptions of discrimination situations that Harlow's monkeys achieved in his research on "learning sets." I have said nothing as to whether perceptions are necessarily transient affairs, rather than such long-sustained processes as those that are involved when a person in a theater, watching a very compelling and powerful drama, still continues to *perceive* it as a play rather than as real life.

The reason I have omitted such features that traditionally were included in older ideas of "perceptions" is that these eight properties which I listed above are very important ones, significant enough to define a theoretically very important category of psychological processes which would include many examples that would not come under the traditional definition of perception because of their lack of those special properties I passed over without mentioning. Let me give one important illustration. A point that has been emphasized in three outstanding discussions of the basic nature of scientific work (Conant, 1947; Hanson, 1958; Kuhn, 1962) is that scientific thinking often encounters great difficulties in developing some new conception that would account more efficiently for new empirical findings. Such scientific discoveries often call for drastic reorganizations of old formulations, as with the shift from the Ptolemaic to the Copernican conception of the solar system; or as the shift from the older phlogiston theory in chemistry to the theory of oxygen which Lavoisier developed; or as the shift from the theory that lift-pumps "pull" the water up from a well, as even Galileo assumed, to the theory that the water rises partly because of the pressure of air on the water in the well and partly from the reduced pressure in the pump itself. In such cases, as Wertheimer emphasized, there are difficulties of reorganization of complex thought which seem to exhibit basically the same property in thought that also can be demonstrated with many traditional perceptual materials.

This illustration of common properties over a much enlarged category of perceptual processes is of course no more than a suggestion. There is no space for me to attempt an adequate job on this matter. But, from the reader's standpoint, this may not be too crucial anyway. The question the reader may well have in mind is this: "Let's waive that problem for a while. Suppose we did have reasons for saying that there would be some gains in expanding the term perceptions so that it would cover all sorts of representations, rather than merely those dealt with in traditional perceptual psychology. If we did, where would you go from there? What use would you make of this conclusion that 'perceptions' are sometimes very long-sustained processes, sometimes very complex representations, and so on? What, then, would you make of this with reference to our theoretical understanding of emotions?"

To answer this question, I feel that we might do well to go back and remind ourselves of some things that have been learned about reflexes. This may seem like an odd thing for a cognitive psychologist to.be saying, but my conviction is that reflexes have been vastly underestimated. Far better would it be for psychology if such a thing as the knee jerk had never been invented. It is a very poor prototype of reflex activities.

If we study a more adequate sampling of reflexes, we find a number of properties: (a) A reflex response does not necessarily occur merely because the normal stimulus for that reflex was presented. Each reflex does not live in a world by itself, but may either be facilitated or suppressed because of other reflexes that currently were activated. The sneezing reflex, for example, momentarily excludes breathing. (b) In the absence of other prepotent reflex tendencies, however, the function of reflex mechanisms is to transmit neural excitations in some coordinated way so that sensing mechanisms of more or less delicate sorts can bring changes through effector responses. (c) In the production of their effects, reflexes in at least many cases operate as cybernetic, goal-directed mechanisms. Thus, when a person's gaze shifts to another object at a different distance, there are no predetermined means for producing the required convergence of the eyes and focusing of each lens. There has to be sensory feedback and adjustment of muscular reactions until these achieve the clearest visual effects possible under the given conditions. (d) Reflex mechanisms are typically means of amplification or magnification of the initial phases of the nervous process. The intensity of a reflex response does not depend on the intensity of the stimulus. For example, when a person sneezes, the physical stimulation in the nostrils can be very slight and yet the reflex mechanism can produce a massive efferent discharge and massive muscular reaction. As Dr. Stanley-Jones (1965, p. 158) has said: "Nervous tissue, in general, possesses the power of almost unlimited multiplication and distribution of neural impulses."

Even though these reflex mechanisms are fairly remarkable evolutionary achievements, however, they still have their deficiencies. They cannot provide for differential responses to slightly differently-patterned constellations of stimulation. They are little subject to modification by learning. And — perhaps most significantly of all — they have little capacity for long-sustained operation after the arousing stimulus has been removed. Thus, if a cuttlefish (close relative of the octopus) sees a prawn disappear behind a rock, it can still pursue this heaven-sent morsel if the brain of the cuttlefish is intact. However, if the lobe of the brain has been removed that deals with relatively complex visual functioning, the cuttlefish's pursuit stops when the prey leaves the field of vision. Part of the function of perceptual processes, therefore, even in such an invertebrate, is to keep the representational process going in a way that the lower, more nearly reflex-type mechanisms cannot.

It seems reasonable to assume that, as evolutionary development added more complicated neural mechanisms to the phylogenetically older reflex mechanisms, these new neural mechanisms were not merely devices for sensing and experiencing things, but were full biological mechanisms — mechanisms that would be able to sense things that might be significant to the organism, that might be able to amplify the sensory input to the brain in some cases and produce a strongly dominant process, that might use this process to produce some effector activities and to direct these cybernetically toward the achievement of some goal, and that might interact with other perceptual processes to determine which ones should be deferred from immediate overt expression or which ones should even be entirely inhibited. Many of such perceptual processes actually would have a terminal character because they would have no sufficient motivational significance or value in comparison with other perceptual processes occurring at the same time. Indeed, since the development particularly of the visual and auditory mechanisms has been so elaborate, the number of perceptual processes that end "without going any farther" is probably vastly greater than the number of reflex responses that "do not get anywhere." Hence, statistically speaking, the motivationally neutral perceptions that have been studied in traditional perceptual psychology are probably the most typical perceptual processes. But, from a broader biological standpoint, the perceptual processes that ought to be providing our paradigms of perceptual functioning are the smaller group that possess some motivational quality and that consequently tend to translate themselves into biologically significant effects — either in behavior or in further central processes of planning or preparing for subsequent behavior.

A great deal of the work in physiological psychology is consistent with this sort of suggestion. It used to be that psychologists and physiologists spoke about physiologically-based motives as products of "strong stimuli" — as from burns, blows, electric shocks, unusual bladder distention, and so on. Reinforcements were interpreted as coming from reductions in these "strong stimuli." However, more recent neuropsychological research suggests a basically different picture. In the course of evolution, motivational mechanisms were worked out that are touched off more by slight warning factors, and the reduction of the motive comes from getting some other signals that the requisite steps probably have been taken. Thus, a dog with a fistula from its throat to the outside of the body will drink the appropriate amount of water to meet its bodily need, and then will stop drinking even though none of the water has gone down into the stomach and could do any good. Hunger starts long before the body is in serious deficit condition, and after food is found the animal stops eating long before the food has been digested and the necessary nutriment carried out to the cells where it is to be used. Through a control by "signals," the physiologically-based motives are a much more sensitive, "before-handed," and usually biologically advantageous type of process.

Emotional motives depend on basically this same sort of mechanism, except that the "sensing mechanism" here is not activated by some relatively simple feature of external stimulation or internal chemical condition. Nevertheless, the sensing mechanism in an emotional motive picks up something that is merely a signal of something else which is likely to be biologically important. Thus, the day-old baby goat will resist being pushed out onto the glass surface over the lower part of a "visual cliff" apparatus. A duckling within some hours after hatching will be sounding distress calls because there is nothing that is moving in its environment that looks and sounds somewhat like a mother duck, but will persistently, energetically, and (one might say) "happily" follow something that does resemble a mother duck. The duckling has not learned from experience that it would suffer cold or hunger or dangerous attacks if it did not have this signaling object; it has emotional mechanisms that are touched off merely by signals which, statistically speaking, are fair indicators of less favorable or more favorable circumstances. Because such mechanisms had species-survival value in the course of evolution, the duckling now has emotional motives that are related to *symbols* of realities, rather than to the realities as such. The same would be true for other emotional motives that apparently are involved in parental behavior, territoriality, herd tendencies in some species, intraspecies conflicts, and so on.

In some other cases, it seems that what has been provided by evolutionary development has been, not some such specifically shaped motivational mechanism, but more a motivational basis for some much wider range of possible activities. The exploratory motive would be such a case, or the interest in "producing effects in the environment" that Robert White (1959) has written about so convincingly. Considerable development might be required with some of these. Few persons are devotees of Bach, for instance, after having heard only a little of his music, but prolonged exposure seems to have some insidious addictive influences.

We have a vast amount to learn to determine the means by which we can predict what perceptual processes will be strong in emotional value and what ones will not, and regarding what types of emotional value. But, if the thesis presented in this paper is correct, what we are working with, when we try to understand the problems of emotions, are problems regarding processes that have a full perceptual character, rather than some simpler or more primitive character. Emotions, we might say, are the individual's perceptions or representations of what he regards as the most significant realities in his life.

IMPLICATIONS OF A
MOTIVATIONAL-PERCEPTUAL THEORY OF EMOTIONS

Many different theoretical and practical implications come from the sort of theory I have sketched. I will confine my comments to only three of them.

I mentioned that one of the fundamental properties of perceptions is that they provide *functional units*, more or less modifiable by learning, in terms of which the brain operates. This is a quite different interpretation of emotions than the proposal in Plutchik's paper that there is merely a limited number of innate emotional components and that learning will influence emotions only by changing what stimuli will arouse what emotional components or by combining emotional components in some new association in particular cases. According to a perceptual-motivational theory of emotions, our emotional life should become vastly more diversified in different cases, I believe, than Plutchik's formulation could account for. This is the first implication of a motivational-perceptual theory of emotion. The second implication is as follows.

If emotions are perceptions of life situations, it then to some extent follows that the achievement of a satisfactory emotional life for modern man will have to come through the creation of some appropriate objective realities, because our perceptual processes, though subject to some errors and distortions, are to some considerable degree a means for recognizing objective realities. In some degree, therefore, they cannot be changed without changing the external realities that they are the means of experiencing.

This is relevant to the fact that we are currently seeing a great deal of restlessness, feeling of disillusionment and insecurity, and feeling of alienation from their society on the part of young people of our country. This is not so surprising. The objective realities provide too much that supports the emotional-perceptual processes of a young person when he says, "Why shouldn't I feel that I am relatively powerless in a society which is showing no sufficient respect for fine human values? I am in a country that is waging a terribly cruel and destructive war on the pretext that we are supporting a democratic government, when actually the great majority of well-informed and highly intelligent persons in this and other countries are convinced that we are supporting a puppet government for our own selfish interests. I am told that I must go out and kill and perhaps be killed — and I am told all this by an older society that won't even tax itself realistically to restrict war-time profits and prevent a continuing inflation. Why shouldn't I feel I live in a world that cannot be trusted?"

In the third place, I would like to make the very sweeping proposal that mankind has gone through two great ages and now needs to start a third if it can possibly find the means for this. In the first great age (Howell, 1968), mankind learned by terribly slow, groping processes to handle the simpler problems of physical existence — to use fire, to make tools and weapons of wood and stone and eventually bronze, and also to learn the techniques of agriculture. The second great age, growing at first only gradually out of the first, but then accelerating more and more rapidly, has been an age of learning, technological development, and great scientific accomplishment. In this second great age, because of the evidence of the values of objectively valid knowledge, the idea that has come to be emphasized is that the crucial consideration in the education of the individual is to help him subordinate all else to objective realities. In pursuit of this ideal, as Hillman (1961) has said, we have developed the belief that emotions are basically antithetical to such disciplined, objectively-oriented cognitive activity and interests. Our striving in education and in our individual lives, therefore, has been to accentuate intellectual functioning and to keep emotional functioning within some very limited areas.

What this has meant, however, has not been that emotions have been eliminated in education or in other phases of our lives. Persistent, goal-directed activity has to be motivated somehow. Hence, what has happened is that, rather than avoiding emotions, our objectively-oriented culture has led to a very heavy use of negative emotional motives (fear of punishment, sense of shame, feelings of insecurity, and so on) and to a use of positive emotional motives of only very crude or cheap sorts, such as cravings for luxuries and special status. Our present cultural crisis illustrates the costly consequences of this.

It remains to be seen whether we can develop a third great age in which we will realize that a child or adult always experiences situations by means of processes that are partly intellectual or cognitive in character and partly emotional. It remains to be seen whether we can learn to recognize these more subtle aspects of human life and find some adequate means whereby the necessary emotional-motivational basis of education, scientific work, industrial activity, home-making, artistic activity, and all the rest of modern life can be put on a basis of preponderantly positive emotional motives, long so neglected by psychologists.

This is a very complex task. The first step in coping with such a program, however, is perhaps the step of coming to realize how fundamental a role is played in human life by emotional processes, which mostly have been viewed merely as a burden or a curse.

SUMMARY

Instead of being relatively rare events in human life, and instead of having basically disruptive influences, emotional processes operate as virtually perpetually active and generally constructive motives in man and other higher animals. However, both in popular thought and in older psychological interpretations, the kinds of emotional experience and the kinds of emotional influences that have been explicitly recognized have been merely the more tangible and attention-commanding instances, as is naturally the case in any relatively new field of knowledge and investigation. Even at that, both laymen and research psychologists have actually relied on the motivational effects of emotions to identify what particular emotion was present in each given situation and to assess its strength. An adequate theory of emotion requires that we take seriously what was thus used merely in unformulated and more or less intuitive terms. Emotions basically are motives, and most of their work is done in quiet and generally constructive ways at relatively low levels of intensity.

To understand more thoroughly the nature of these emotions, we need first to make some considerable revisions in our conceptions of perceptual processes, going far beyond what tends to be carried over from the old days of merely subjectivist investigations of relatively simple perceptual phenomena. In a broadened and enriched sense of perceptual processes, emotions need to be understood as perceptions. Several important implications are mentioned which flow from such a perceptual-motivational theory of emotions.

In conclusion, I might indicate some other sources related to the present interpretation of emotions. My own ideas have developed in a series of papers (Leeper, 1932, 1948, 1963a, 1963b, 1965; Leeper and Madison, 1959). Three other perceptual psychologists who have proposed essentially the same interpretation in recent years have been George Klein (1958), W. C. H. Prentice (1961), and, if I understand correctly his intent, Wolfgang Köhler (1959) in his presidential address before the American Psychological Association. A splendid early statement by Felix E. Krueger (1928) was not available in intelligible terms until Magda Arnold (1968) recently retranslated the paper he presented to the first of these International Symposia on Feelings and Emotions. Except for some features resulting from his primarily subjectivist approach, it seems to me that Krueger was presenting, a bit over forty years ago, an interpretation of feelings and emotions that is basically consonant with what I have tried to propose in the present paper.

REFERENCES

Arnold, Magda (Ed.) (1968). *The nature of emotion: selected readings*. Penguin, Baltimore.

Atkinson, J.W. and Feather, N.T. (Eds.) (1966). *A theory of achievement motivation*. Wiley, New York.

Conant, J.B. (1947). *On understanding science*. Yale Univ. Press, New Haven.

Gibson, Eleanor J. (1969). *Principles of perceptual learning and development*. Appleton, New York.

Gibson, J.J. (1966). *The senses considered as perceptual systems*. Houghton, Boston.

Hanson, N.R. (1958). *Patterns of discovery*. Cambridge Univ. Press, England.

Helson, H. (1967). Perception. Pp. 311-343 in H. Helson and W. Bevan (Eds.), *Contemporary approaches to psychology*. Van Nostrand, Princeton, New Jersey.

Hillman, James. (1961). *Emotion*. Northwestern Univ. Press, Evanston, Illinois.

Hochberg, J.E. (1957). Effects of the Gestalt revolution: the Cornell symposium on perception. *Psychol. Rev.*, 64, 73-84.

Howell, F.C. (1968). *Early man*. Time-Life Books, New York.

Klein, G.S. (1958). Cognitive control and motivation. Pp. 87-118 in G. Lindzey (Ed.), *Assessment of human motives*. Rinehart, New York.

Köhler, W. (1944). Max Wertheimer, 1880-1943. *Psychol. Rev.*, 51, 143-146.

Köhler, W. (1959). Gestalt psychology today. *Am. Psychologist*, 14, 727-734.

Krueger, F.E. (1928). The essence of feeling. Pp. 97-108 in Magda Arnold (Ed.), *The nature of emotion: selected readings*. Penguin, Baltimore.

Kuhn, T.S. (1962). *The structure of scientific revolutions*. Univ. of Chicago Press, Chicago, Illinois.

Leeper, R.W. (1932). The evidence for a theory of neurological maintenance of states of emotional motivation. *Psychol. Bull.*, 29, 571 (abstract).

Leeper, R.W. (1948). A motivational theory of emotion to replace "emotion as disorganized response." *Psychol. Rev.*, 55, 5-21.

Leeper, R.W. (1963a). The motivational theory of emotion. Pp. 657-665 in C. L. Stacey and M. F. DeMartino (Eds.), *Understanding human motivation*. Howard Allen, Cleveland, Ohio.

Leeper, R.W. (1963b). Learning and the fields of perception, motivation, and personality. Pp. 365-487 in Vol. 5 in S. Koch (Ed.), *Psychology: a study of a science*. McGraw-Hill, New York.

Leeper, R.W. (1965). Some needed developments in the motivational theory of emotions. Pp. 25-122 in D. Levine (Ed.), *Nebraska symposium on motivation*, Univ. of Nebraska Press, Lincoln, Nebraska.

Leeper, R.W. and Madison, P. (1959). *Toward understanding human personalities*. Appleton, New York.

McCleary, R.A. and Moore, R.Y. (1965). *Subcortical mechanisms of behavior.* Basic Books, New York.
Miller, N.E. (1948). Studies of fear as an acquirable drive: I. Fear as motivation and fear-reduction as reinforcement in the learning of new responses. *J. Exp. Psychol.*, 38, 89-101.
Neisser, U. (1967). *Cognitive psychology.* Appleton, New York.
Pfaffmann, C. (1964), Taste, its sensory and motivating properties. *Am. Sci.*, 52, 187-206.
Piéron, H. (1928). Emotion in animals and man. In M. L. Reymert (Ed.), *Feelings and emotions: The Wittenberg symposium.* Clark Univ. Press, Worcester, Massachusetts.
Prentice, W.C.H. (1961). Some cognitive aspects of motivation. *Am. Psychologist*, 16, 503-511.
Solomon, R.L. and Wynne, L.C. (1953). Traumatic avoidance learning: acquisition in normal dogs. *Psychol. Monographs*, 67, No. 4 (whole No. 354).
Solomon, R.L. and Wynne, L.C. (1954). Traumatic avoidance learning: the principles of anxiety conservation and partial irreversibility. *Psychol. Rev.*, 61, 353-385.
Stanley-Jones, D. (1965). The kybernetics of cyclothymia. In N. Wiener and J. P. Schade (Eds.), *Progress in brain research, Vol. 17, Cybernetics of the nervous system.* Elsevier, Amsterdam.
White, R.W. (1959). Motivation reconsidered: the concept of competence. *Psychol. Rev.*, 66, 297-333.
Young, P.T. (1943). *Emotion in man and animal.* Wiley, New York.
Young, P.T. (1961). *Motivation and emotion.* Wiley, New York.
Young, P.T. (1967). Affective arousal: some implications. *Am. Psychologist*, 22, 32-40.

Chapter 12

Perennial Problems in the Field of Emotion

Magda B. Arnold*

In the field of emotion, one of the persistent problems has been the question how the bodily symptoms and the psychological experience are correlated; and even more, whether the one arouses the other or whether they are both aroused together by a common cause.

ORIGIN OF EMOTION

Throughout history, most thinkers have assumed that the bodily aspect is the expression of an experienced emotion; that is, that the emotion is the main, if not the basic, element of the complex experience that gives rise to bodily changes. But the young science of psychology, eager to establish its status as a science, soon began to question long-established assumptions. While Wundt and Titchener merely attempted to analyze emotion into its elements, James, the physiologist turned psychologist, and Lange, the physiologist, questioned the very basis of emotional experience. Not the emotional experience but the physical changes come first, they insisted; thus emotion became the sensation of organic changes. Just how these organic changes are produced in the first place is a problem they did not tackle. The association of ideas seemed to account for most emotional experiences, the "connate adaptation of the nervous system" for the rest. At least part of the reason for James' solution was the notion that the cortex of the brain has been mapped sufficiently so that we could be certain that it is nothing more than "the surface of 'projection' for every sensitive spot and every muscle in the body" (James, 1884, p. 188). Compared to this certainty, it seemed idle to look for any "mind stuff" that would constitute the emotion.

*Loyola University, Chicago.

However, true though it might be that we cannot think away all bodily feelings without losing the emotion, it is no less true that not every object arouses an emotion, and even an object that affects most people emotionally may fail to do so in a particular case. The "connate adaptation of the nervous system" is not an explanation for the arousal of a particular emotion in a particular individual.

One way out of this dilemma was to assume, as did Shand (1914) and others, that there are inherent systems in the mind that are connected with bodily systems, and that emotion is such a psychophysical system stimulated by certain objects and situations. In this way, the importance of physical changes in emotion was preserved while the mental part of the system took care of the fact that the situation has to be interpreted by the individual before an emotion can be aroused.

From that time on, either one or the other facet of emotion was emphasized, either the bodily changes, or the psychological experience. Accordingly, variants of the peripheral theory or various versions of the central theory were offered as the exclusive explanation of emotional phenomena. McDougall (1928), for instance, followed Shand in assuming that emotion is the experienced counterpart of an instinctive impulse; but he added that derived emotions or complex feelings stem from the degree of success or failure of our striving. Thus he distinguished quite clearly between emotions (desires) that have as counterpart an impulse aiming at particular ends, and emotions such as hope, anxiety, regret, which are reactions to experienced success or failure of any desire or striving. Like Shand, McDougall assumed that the instinctive impulse takes care of the bodily changes while the psychological experience specifies the particular goal pursued (in true emotions), or indicates the degree of difficulty such striving encounters (in derived emotions).

In Freudian psychoanalysis, there is again a division of emotions into those that have instinctive roots (love and aggression) and those that arise from immediate threats (anxiety, guilt feelings). While the former were explained by referring them to the instinct they accompany, the latter were thought to originate in the ego, with their physiological aspects shrouded in mystery. To explain the origin of anxiety as the conversion of libido, or the remnant of the birth trauma, has never been particularly convincing. Later psychoanalysts sometimes treated emotions as tension phenomena (Brierley, 1937; Jelgersma, 1921), or as the result of conflict between libidinal drives (Federn, 1936), though it was never made clear that the former explanation can refer only to instinct-connected emotions, and the latter only to those affecting the ego.

For Jung also, emotion or affectivity rests on an instinctual basis. It has archetypal content, that is, it forms complexes "whose ultimate basis is the archetype, the 'instinctual pattern' " (Jung, 1955, p. 43).

Finally, academic psychologists found themselves unable to continue accepting instincts as valid psychological categories. Influenced by Learning

Theory, most psychologists refused to recognize instinctual patterns that owed nothing to learning. They acknowledged the driving force of instinct but denied that it was a vital force producing inherent patterning. Thus instincts became drives that provided the push for any motivated action, and emotion became the bodily upset or excitement produced by the collision of drives. The conflict theory of emotion came into vogue — which focused attention on the emotions of fear and anger but failed to account for positive emotions like joy and love, or even negative emotions like hate. No attention at all was paid to the distinction between an emotion that urges toward a particular goal, and an emotion that is experienced when the pursuit of a goal becomes difficult, a distinction recognized by the early Greeks, medieval Arabs and Schoolmen among prescientific theorists, and by McDougall comparatively recently.

In an attempt to look at the problem from a fresh angle, Krueger (1928) and Klages, (1950) from the point of view of the Gestalt school, emphasized that feelings and emotions are integral parts of perception. For Krueger, they are the experience qualities of the total-whole; for Klages, they represent the intimacy of experience linking perception and action, so that all expression becomes emotional expression. Accordingly, Klages emphasized the impulse quality of emotion that links it with action, but also the emotional quality of perception stamping it as subjective. Krueger, on the other hand, insisted that every kind of activity, even the most abstract intellectual judgment, grows out of a background of feeling. For him also, feeling provides the matrix connecting all other experiences. For both theorists, such a view dispenses them from explaining in detail how emotion is aroused or how the various physiological changes are produced. While such a theory makes it difficult if not impossible to guess at the brain circuits, for instance, that might mediate emotion, it does offer a valuable contribution to our thinking because of the insistence that emotion is indispensable for every type of activity, from perception to action.

While German psychologists emphasized the emotional quality of experience, Dumas in France tried to make a distinction between the first "shock" on realizing the emotional significance of an object, and the enduring attitude that develops eventually. For him, emotion has no impulsion of any kind, it is purely a state of mind, a quality of experience. Consequently, he finds it easy to fit into his theory emotions like joy and sorrow. But fear "is an emotion because it is not a tendency to flee; and anger, because it is not an aggressive tendency" (Dumas, 1968, p. 113) — a statement that is not immediately convincing. Emotional behavior, including physiological changes, he ascribes entirely to the introductory shock that is accompanied by "a more or less rapid interpretation of its cause." Accordingly, the physiological and psychological shock together with the interpretation, both causes the emotion and determines the appropriate action. The emotion proper, he thinks, is a mental state accompanied by physiological excitation or depression. This theory also makes a valuable contribution by insisting that a psychological interpretation of the situation is necessary, and by distinguishing between the first realization of its personal significance, and the later emotion. But to separate the emotion proper from the impulse that goes with it (e.g., in fear or anger) requires an artificial ripping apart of mental state and behavior that allows of no further investigation or explanation.

Within the French tradition, Pradines takes an entirely different stand. For him, the power to act is inherent in emotion; and emotion expresses our reaction to a particular situation. Emotions are dynamic, even though Pradines distinguishes them sharply from *tendencies* which are "dispositions independent of circumstances and without precise orientation" (Pradines, 1968, p.191).

Recent American writers also regard emotions as dynamic, though they preferably term them affective *processes*, which leaves it uncertain whether anything more than a biological dynamism is intended. For P.T. Young (1961), for instance, affective processes are motivational in nature while Leeper (1963) calls them perceptual-motivational, and Lazarus (1966) considers emotions as coping processes. In all these theories, emotions have at least the impulsion inherent in biological processes.

EFFECTS OF EMOTION

Another problem that has been treated in a variety of ways is the question whether emotions are useful, organized and organizing, or whether they constitute a useless interference with goal-directed action. For a long time, the latter view prevailed in the conflict theory of emotion – until Leeper (1948), as the first in the United States, protested that emotion could not be recognized as such unless it were itself organized and organizing. He pointed to the fact that emotion does lead to certain behavior patterns and accompanies much goal-directed behavior. However, Leeper's spirited apology to the contrary, there is no doubt that emotion can also disorganize behavior when it interferes with rather than facilitates a personal goal.

PERENNIAL PROBLEMS

There are some perennial problems, apparently, that still require solution: first, the question of how emotion is related to action. Does it have a dynamic component, is it inevitably connected with an *instinctive* impulse that provides the dynamics, or is it separable from any kind of activity, remaining either a purely mental state, as Dumas has it, or a purely physiological upset? Secondly, how is emotion aroused; directly, by way of perception which produces a "connate adaptation of the nervous system" resulting in activity, including physiological changes which are then sensed; or is it the personal reaction to a particular situation, as Pradines suggests; or, finally, is it the matrix of all experience and action, as Klages and Krueger claim? Thirdly, what is the difference between an emotion that accompanies goal-directed striving, and an emotion that interferes with it? And, finally, how are the physiological changes that go with emotion really produced?

EMOTION: STATIC OR DYNAMIC?

Either emotion itself is a dynamic impulse, or it is a passive state. If the latter, there must be a separate impulsion of some sort (a drive or instinct) to account for action. Then emotion becomes a strictly psychological reaction to a perceived situation which somehow arouses the appropriate drive, and the drive produces the physiological changes and constitutes the impulse to action. Shand, McDougall and Dumas all seem to have chosen this alternative

Now what can such a "static" experience represent? According to Dumas, "the origin of the (mental state in) emotion is not only the shock but also a more or less rapid interpretation of its cause" (1968, p.110). The interpretation, apparently, is a cognitive act. For James and other peripheralists, emotion also is static and is the experience of the physiological changes brought about directly by the "cold" perception of an (emotional) situation. But in fact, only a few stimuli, for instance, a sudden loud noise, an electric shock, etc., can directly produce extensive physiological changes. All other "emotional" stimuli, according to these theorists, achieve this effect via association.

However, association is not a mechanical linkage of conditioned and unconditioned stimuli, conditioned and unconditioned responses. If we take the trouble to sort out what happens between stimulus and response, we find that such linkages depend on memory. Every new situation recalls similar situations experienced in the past, and their effect on us. When we recall similar situations, we re-experience them in visual, auditory, tactual, motor, even olfactory modalities. We recall a picture we have seen, a tune we have heard, a scent we have cherished; we remember a dance step we have learned, in dancing it. When we speak of memory, we usually refer to this modality-specific type. But we also re-live the pain, the joy, the sorrow, the delight, we have felt in the past. Of course, this is not the same experience we have had the first time (but a memory picture after all, is different from an actual visual experience, also), but is, like the original appraisal, a positive or negative reaction. The sight of a friend in the distance (or even of someone who resembles him) immediately gives us a lift, brings a joyful expectation. The sight of a horse that has thrown him causes immediate apprehension in the unlucky rider. These reactions can only be based on the remembered joy or pain; I would like to call this kind of memory "affective memory." We can recognize something on the basis of modality-specific memory, but only on the basis of affective memory can we estimate whether it is going to harm or benefit us. The "interpretation of the situation" mentioned by Dumas and many other psychologists includes both modality-specific and affective memory. In interpreting a situation, we do not merely know it as it is here and now, for instance, when we are still at a safe distance from some danger; nor do we ascribe a vague cognitive "meaning" to it. We *remember* what has happened to us in the past, how this thing has affected us and what we did about it. Then we *imagine* how it will affect us this time and *estimate* whether it will be harmful.

This estimate or evaluation may be reflective but need not be. In emotional reactions, it rarely is. Even when there is a reflective appraisal, there is also an immediate intuitive estimate which inevitably produces an impulse to action unless something is appraised as indifferent and left aside. This appraisal seems to be identical with Dumas' static emotions produced by "interpretation" because it is a state of mind, as yet without any motor tendency, a sheer acceptance or refusal of the expected effect.

At the same time, the appraisal of "good or bad for me" does produce an impulse toward or away from the thing so appraised. This is a motor tendency toward something or away from it, consciously felt in emotion,* which results in muscle contractions and various physiological changes. If no other appraisal intervenes so that no other action impulse is produced, this tendency will lead to action. Now the question is: does this account correspond to fact? Can a "mere" appraisal initiate an impulse to action? Or is it only an instinct that can produce an action tendency?

The notion of instinct, and later drive, was used to explain animal and human behavior that seemed to tend toward certain goals. To avoid the notion of purpose, human behavior was explained in the same way animal behavior was — as the result of a natural tendency to obtain things that can satisfy physiological drives. The most obvious instances are food-seeking and mating. Since there is a clear connection with physiological systems (digestion and reproduction), it seemed reasonable to think that the impulsion toward food and mate is based on physiological changes connected with these systems. Indeed, it has been found in recent years that there are hormonal changes activating hypothalamic nuclei that make the female receptive to the male; and there may be other hormonal changes that activate other hypothalamic nuclei, leading to hunger and food-seeking.

---

*Psychologists who insist that emotion is static usually point to joy and sorrow as examples of emotions that do not have a definite impulse to action. However, in joy, it is the person who is enjoying himself, and doing it quite actively. Being overwhelmed by grief does not mean that the person is passive; he is actively grieving, even though he is not doing anything muscular about it. He has not induced his joy or sorrow deliberately, but even though he may "undergo" emotion, he is the one who is grieving, loving, hating, fearing, despairing; he is never purely passive, he is the one who is doing the "emoting."

While instinct or drive may explain the experienced impulsion, it does not explain individual choice in man or animal. Such choice of action as is implicit in every emotion becomes intelligible only when we attempt to analyze the sequence of activities that lead from perception to action. Instinct and drive psychologists have never spelled out the mechanism by which a drive leads to a particular action.

Hormonal changes may lead to action impulses that activate the appropriate physiological system and so produce hunger or sexual desire. But unless they also activate memory (and imagination) so that men and animals are aware of what it is they are lacking, recall how they have gone about satisfying their desire in the past, and organize their action accordingly, they are reduced to random activity which only by sheer chance could lead them to food or mate. Moreover, the object imagined and remembered must be evaluated as good here and now, to give direction to their activity and a focus for their speech. Instinct or drive can only explain the random impulsion to a specific activity, not the search for a particular goal. Consequently, the great instinct psychologist Freud postulated that the goal of the instinct is discharge. For Freud, the instinct does not have a natural object but can "cathect" any object at all.

In contrast, we know from experience that we prefer particular kinds of food and that we choose a given individual as a friend or mate. Even among animals, there are some individual preferences in addition to the species preference for certain types of food, and for animals of the same species as mate. There is no random impulsion but a directed search. Surely an animal is not a machine that is turned on and off by something outside itself — nor is man. The animal has the same sensory apparatus as the human being, it avoids what is harmful and approaches what is beneficial. Instinct may dispose it to certain actions. But because the animal has to approach the instinctive goal in an environment that is sometimes hostile, it has to evaluate objects and situations directly, intuitively, just as the human being does before he has a chance to use reflective judgment. To be sure, the intuitive appraisal is not experienced as such. It is felt merely as a favorable or unfavorable disposition toward object or situation, as an attraction or repulsion — which is a felt tendency to action.

Hormonal changes may bias this appraisal but do not make it unnecessary. As soon as eggs are developing in the mother bird's body, it begins to pick up pieces of hay or straw to build a nest. Though it is the hormonal change that accounts for the attractiveness of such materials (just as adrenal insufficiency, for instance, accounts for the excessive desire for salt) they must still be evaluated or appraised as good for picking up. A particular place in a tree or under the eaves must be appraised as good for nesting, which arouses an impulse to carry the grass to the selected place and arrange it in a particular pattern. Accordingly, even instinctive actions demand appraisal and the action tendency that depends on it.

There are many actions that are not instinctive in this sense yet are undertaken because of an emotional urge. The dog or child runs because it is fun to do so at this particular time. They rest after a good run because resting feels good now. Anything that is appraised as good here and now will result in an impulse toward it. And what is so appraised depends as much on memory and imagination as it does on the here-and-now experience. This relieves us of the necessity of having to reduce all actions to a few physiologically based drives, and accounts for the widely differing goals of different individuals. Every man has discovered different kinds of satisfactions in the course of his life and will assign different values to objects he wants to attain or avoid.

We have now isolated two components of emotion: one static, the appraisal, which is a mere acceptance or refusal of the expected effect of the situation on us; another dynamic, the impulse toward what is appraised as good, and away from anything appraised as bad. Accordingly, the emotion becomes *a felt tendency toward anything appraised as good, and away from anything appraised as bad*. This definition allows us to specify how emotion is related to action: if nothing interferes, the felt tendency will lead to action. It also allows us to state how emotion is aroused: whatever is perceived, remembered, imagined, will be appraised; if it is appraised as desirable or harmful, an action tendency is aroused. And as we appraise the situation as more desirable or more harmful, we become aware not only that we tend toward or away from it, but also that this is an emotional tendency.

EMOTION AS MATRIX OF EXPERIENCE AND AS A PERSONAL REACTION

Intuitive appraisal is greatly influenced and on occasion even determined by affective memory. This is particularly striking when the original experience has been very intense. A child that has been bitten by a dog may avoid dogs for a long time, whether he remembers the incident later or not. But even if the original experience has not been so intense but child or adult has had many similar experiences, his appraisal of such situations is biased more and more because affective memory gradually hardens into an attitude of acceptance or rejection. Such attitudes, based on affective memory, are indispensable for our daily living: if we had to wait until something actually harmed us before we could appraise it as bad and avoid it, the survival rate of man and animal would drop alarmingly.

Since affective memory is a reliving of the original acceptance or rejection in a new though similar situation, the resulting feeling carries no date line so that we are completely unaware that our here-and-now appraisal is really a prejudgment (literally, a prejudice) dictated by affective memory. For this reason, we rarely make any effort to remember the earlier situations that have given rise to it — and the (modality-specific) memory of the original experience is soon lost to us. It may well be that unconscious repression in the Freudian sense is involved in some instances. But since pleasant experiences are forgotten as easily as unpleasant ones, though their positive or negative affect is relived over and over, it is doubtful that repression is the mechanism that ensures the preservation of the effect of such experiences. Freud himself speaks only of the repression of traumatic memories. But other (modality-specific) memories are also forgotten; indeed, such forgetting is the normal course of events while affective memory remains to guide our appraisals. Hence it seems safe to conclude that it is affective memory as such that has the effects Freud ascribed to repression.

Indeed, affective memory is ubiquitous yet intensely personal because it is the living record of the emotional life history of each person. Being always at our disposal, playing an important role in the appraisal and interpretation of everything around us, it can be called the matrix of all experience and action, as Klages and Krueger have seen. But it is also the intensely personal reaction to a particular situation, based on an individual's unique experiences and biases, as Pradines has suggested.

EMOTION AS ORGANIZING AND AS DISTURBING

Since the appraisal of the situation produces the emotion, and emotion can lead to action, the emotion will be organized according to the evaluation that produced it. It foreshadows a definite pattern of action, and organizes the action to which it urges. However, the appraisal leading to a strong desire is not necessarily final. The diabetic may crave sweets yet refrain from giving in to his desire because he knows what the consequences of an indulgence will be. The smoker knows the dangers of smoking but hopes that he will be lucky — and goes on smoking. In both cases, there is reflection, a weighing of alternatives, in which the intuitive appraisal leading to desire is either counterbalanced or reinforced by deliberate judgment. The final decision may not be the most attractive alternative nor is it always the most prudent choice.

When the deliberate judgment goes against the intuitive appraisal and prevails, there is no conflict, though the decision may be difficult to carry out because the emotional attraction diverts attention from the planned course of action and forces us to make the decision over and over again. Or we may be engaged in a difficult task and have our attention drawn to something appraised as most desirable or intensely threatening. As a result, the deliberate intention may lose out because the emotion interferes with the execution of our plan. Clearly, emotion interferes and disturbs if it urges us in a direction different from that indicated by deliberate judgment.

EMOTION AND PHYSIOLOGICAL CHANGES

If emotion is a felt action tendency based on appraisal, it seems reasonable to assume that the physiological changes so impressive in emotion are ancillary to this tendency. Just as the appraisal results in a felt impulse to action, expressed in muscular tensions in various parts of the body, so there will be hormonal and various other physiological changes. Both the emotion and the physiological changes originate from the same appraisal, though time relations may differ. It takes very little time for nerve impulses relayed from the limbic cortex to arrive in the premotor area, giving rise to the experience of emotion, and even less time to arrive in the hypothalamus, activating neurosecretory cells and the pituitary gland. It takes much longer for the relays from the motor cortex to activate muscles, and still longer for the pituitary hormones to arrive at their target organs.

Emotion and the Brain

Once we have succeeded in identifying the structures that are involved in appraisal, it should be possible to describe the circuits that are involved in mediating the experience of emotion and its characteristic pattern of action, as well as the hormonal changes that go with it. This I have tried to do in my theory of brain function in emotion (Arnold, 1960, vol. 2). This scheme (which I can sketch here only briefly) is not just unsupported speculation but is based on hundreds of actual research reports and guided by a phenomenological analysis of psychological activities from perception to action.

Before sketching the proposed neural connections, it might be profitable to discuss the relation of emotion to brain. The brain is not just a web of electrical relays, it is an integral part of the living person, and has a special function in making psychological activities possible. The brain does not *produce* appraisal and emotion, it *mediates* these functions. It would be even better to say that particular brain structures and circuits are active when we see, appraise, and feel an emotion. It is not the eye, the optic tract or the visual cortex that sees: *we* see because we have a visual sense, the organ of which is the visual apparatus and its neural connections. We can appraise what we see because appraisal is one of our psychological functions, served by particular structures and connections. It is the *individual* who sees, not the eye or the visual cortex. The eye and its connections do not produce a visual image, the *person* sees what is there. Other senses make it possible to experience the world in different ways — to touch, hear or smell things. The person uses his "organed" capacities (or powers) to produce his sensory psychological experience.

In short, an individual functions in various ways, all designed to bring him in contact with the world around him and make it possible for him to act upon it. Experiencing the world or his own body, he is not only acted upon, he *acts* in seeing, hearing, touching. Experience of, and acting in response to outside impressions, eventually leads to overt action; and both experience and action are psychological activities. Only secondarily, and often *post mortem*, can we ever find out what goes on in the brain and what are the structures that seem to be active during experience and behavior. When we interpret and appraise a given situation, we estimate how it will affect *us*, the person, not our brain; and what *we should do* about it, not what muscles should be activated. Relays in the brain are activated and muscles contract in an ordered sequence, but that is done automatically, without our awareness, strictly on the basis of our appraisal and decision. We are aware of our *intentions*, never of the precise neural and muscular patterns needed to carry them out.

Emotion also is not produced by the brain. We experience it when we appraise something as highly desirable or very dangerous. To identify the structures that are active during emotion, we have to be guided by an analysis of our psychological functions as they go into action one after another. Realizing that there must be relays from sensory areas to motor areas if muscles are to be contracted and limbs to be moved, we must look for structures and circuits that can form such relays in the same order in which psychological activities follow one another. When we see or hear something or experience it in another modality, we intuitively appraise it as good or bad (guided by affective memory), and this appraisal is experienced as liking or dislike. Next, we intuitively appraise the conditions and possibilities of action – which determines the type of emotional tendency (fear vs. courage, despair vs. hope). This tendency will lead to action if deliberate appraisal and decision support it. If overt action is not possible or not necessary, the emotional tendency will be revealed in emotional expression and, on occasion, in expressive action (lamentations of grief, exclamations of joy or admiration). Whether action is taken and what kind of action is decided on depends on the person's conscious judgment and deliberate decision which establishes a motive (defined as "a want that leads to action"), while intuitive appraisal produces a felt action tendency that does not necessarily lead to action.*

The appraisal of an object or a situation as good or bad here and now seems to be mediated by the limbic system. The three-layered cortex of this system is arranged in such a way that it borders on every area of the six-layered sensory and motor neocortex. Connections from the neocortical areas to the limbic cortex seem to mediate the appraisal of things seen, heard, touched, smelled, tasted, and the appraisal of body, head and limb movements.

Memory and Imagination Circuits

Since most situations require memory and imagination before they can be appraised for action, there should be connecting circuits that make recall and

---

*For a different view, see Peters (Ch. 13).

imagination possible. On the basis of many research findings we can assume that the visual association cortex serves the registration of visual impressions, the auditory association cortex that of auditory impressions, etc. To re-experience these impressions as *memory* would require a circuit that reactivates the registered "engrams" in the same sequence and the same pattern in which they were originally laid down. In contrast, imagination or fantasy reorganizes experience in ever new and ever changing patterns. Accordingly, the circuit serving imagination would have to be different from that mediating recall.

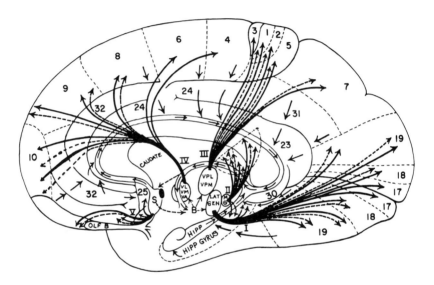

FIGURE 1.   Circuits mediating sense experience and recall. ＿＿ Reception and registration. ＿ ＿ ＿ Recall. Arrows indicate the direction of conduction. Short
arrows indicate the connections for appraisal and recall.
I — visual system. II — auditory system. III — somesthetic system (including
taste). IV — motor system. V — olfactory system. Arabic numerals represent
Brodmann areas.
A — cortical auditory area. B — brain stem. HIPP — hippocampus. LAT GEN
— lateral geniculate nucleus. MGM — medial geniculate nucleus. OLF B —
olfactory bulb. S — septal area. VA — anterior ventral nucleus. VM —
ventromedial nucleus. VL — ventrolateral nucleus. VPL — ventro-
posterolateral nucleus. VPM — ventropostero-medial nucleus. From: Arnold,
1960, vol. 2.

Keeping in mind that it is sensory experience that initiates spontaneous recall and imagination, we realize immediately that the circuits serving these functions must constitute some of the connections between sensory and motor cortex. Since the experiencing subject must appraise the situation in relation to himself, it is really the appraisal of sense experience that should start off further psychological activities. Thus recall would be initiated by the appraisal of anything seen, heard, or otherwise experienced as "good to know" (via limbic system). The recall circuit seems to run from limbic cortex via hippocampal rudiment (indusium griseum) and hippocampus to precommissural fornix, midbrain, sensory thalamic nuclei and the sensory and motor cortical association areas (*modality-specific memory*, see Fig. 1). In addition, an *affective memory* circuit seems to run from limbic cortex via cingulum, postcommissural fornix, mamillary bodies, anterior thalamic nuclei back to the limbic system. An *imagination circuit* carrying visual, auditory, and other sensory and motor patterns, can be found to run from limbic cortex via amygdala and thalamic association nuclei to the cortical association areas (Fig. 2). Thus appraisal (via limbic system) initiates modality-specific and affective recall as well as the expectation of what is to come, via separate circuits.

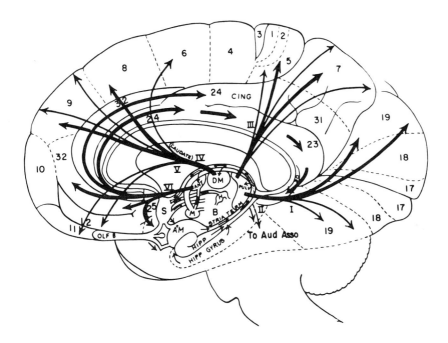

FIGURE 2.   Circuits mediating imagination and affective memory.
I-IV circuits serving imagination: I — visual, II — auditory, III — somesthetic, IV — motor, V — olfactory imagination. VI — circuit mediating affective memory.
AM — amygdala. AT — anterior thalamic nucleus. B — brain stem. CING — cingulate gyrus. DM — dorsomedial thalamic nucleus. H — habenula. HIPP — hippocampus. M — mamillary body. OLF — olfactory bulb. PULV — pulvinar. S — septal area. STRIA-TERM — stria terminalis.

The Action Circuit

The tendency to action, whether called "emotion" or not, also seems to be initiated by appraisal, via the limbic system. An *action circuit* carries the neural impulses via hippocampal system to fornix, midbrain, cerebellum, ventral

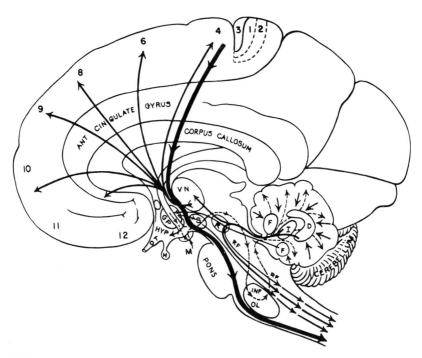

FIGURE 3.   The circuit mediating emotion and action.
————— relay from hippocampus to cerebellum
- - - - - relay from cerebellum to hypothalamic and extrapyramidal effectors.
————— relay from cerebellum to frontal lobe
━━━━━ relay from motor cortex to spinal cord: corticospinal tract.
D — dentate nucleus. F — fastigial nucleus. GP — globus pallidus. H — hypophysis. HYP — hypothalamus. I — interposited nucleus. INF OL — inferior olive. M — mamillary body. OT — optic tract. R — red nucleus. RF — brain stem reticular formation. S — substantia nigra. VN — ventral thalamic nucleus.

thalamus, to the frontal lobe; *motor memory* seems to be registered in the prefrontal area and activated during movement via the action circuit (Fig. 3). *Motor imagination*, finally, seems to employ relays via amygdala, dorsomedial thalamic nuclei, to prefrontal areas. All felt appetitive tendencies, including emotions, seem to be mediated via the action circuit and *registered* in the prefrontal areas, to be *experienced* when relays arrive in the premotor cortex. Since the action circuit activates not only voluntary muscles but also involuntary muscles and glands, the influence of emotion on muscular tension, glandular secretion, blood pressure and heart rate can easily be accounted for; this also accounts for the fact that these emotional effects are cumulative, for they are preserved as dispositional changes in the prefrontal cortex. With every new emotion, the motor effect of similar past emotions is revived – which accounts, for instance, for the steadily increasing muscular changes when fear becomes chronic.

Neurophysiological Patterns in Instinctive Actions

Since appraisal initiates the physiological changes as well as the emotion, we would expect that there is an integrated pattern of emotional expression, hormonal and physiological changes and overt movements characteristic for every emotion. But appraisal and emotion are a part of instinctive as well as emotional behavior: anything that is wanted, attracts – whether it be food, a mate, a warm place to sleep, a vacation, or a beautiful dress. Of course, there is a difference between instinctive and emotional behavior. Instinctive behavior requires a particular physiological state that induces desire and brings man or animal to seek for the desired object. In their natural habitat, animals seek food or mate – not randomly but as if they knew what they wanted; and the observer is never in doubt whether they want either food or a mate. The physiological state, different in hunger and sexual desire, seems to be initiated by hormones that are produced cyclically. When present, the changed hormonal state seems to induce an image of what is needed, which gives direction to the animal's search. As soon as found, the animal appraises the female as good for mating, food as good for eating; this initiates an action tendency accompanied by appropriate physiological changes (e.g., erection, or salivation and secretion of digestive hormones appropriate to the food available).

Physiological Changes in Emotion

Because emotion is always involved in instinctive behavior, it is bound to manifest some of the same physiological changes as the instinctive pattern within which it is embedded. Lust is a parasympathetic phenomenon, and love also seems to have parasympathetic effects. This does not mean that lust is the "basis" or "origin" of love. It merely means that the parasympathetic system is active whenever we appraise something as good, want it and enjoy it. In lust, this wanting is intensified and produces changes not only in heart rate and blood pressure but also in the sexual apparatus which — between puberty and senescence — is predisposed to react because of the secretion of sex hormones.

From this close connection of appraisal with both emotion and physiological changes it follows that different emotions will have different physiological states. Experimental research during the last 25 years has confirmed this view, in contrast to Cannon's emergency theory of emotion which assumed that the physiological state is the same in all emotions and consists of sympathetic excitation which facilitates emotional action. (In fairness to Cannon, it should be said that he only spoke of fear and rage, flight and fight; but at least by implication, the theory was soon extended to all emotions.) Recent research has also shown that even fear and rage can be differentiated physiologically. Though the sympathetic nervous system is active in both, fear is accompanied by adrenaline secretion while rage is accompanied by noradrenaline secretion, with different physiological effects.*

In summary, it is possible to account for the physiological changes in various emotions, and even to work out the neural circuits that trigger them. But only on the basis of a phenomenological analysis of the psychological activities from perception to emotion and action will it be possible to work out a theory of brain function that provides a neural correlate for psychological experience. Without such a theory, the scores of detailed findings resulting from the massive research effort of the last few decades are bound to remain isolated and disconnected nuggets instead of clues to the rich veins of future knowledge.

---

*At the same time, the artificial production of physiological changes ordinarily occurring in fear will not necessarily produce this emotion. Since emotion depends on appraisal, the actual emotional reaction will depend on the way in which the situation is evaluated; and the artificially produced physiological changes (e.g., by an adrenaline injection) will form part of the total situation. Hence, the findings reported by Schachter (see Chapter 7) can be explained easily: a subject will act the fool if he appraises the situation as ridiculous *and* is in an aroused physiological state; he will be aggressive if he finds the situation aggravating *and* is aroused physiologically. In contrast, if he is informed that the physiological state is the effect of the drug injection, he will discount his organic sensations and remain unmoved.

REFERENCES

Arnold, M.B. (1960). *Emotion and personality*. Columbia Univ. Press, New York.

Arnold, M.B. (Ed.) (1968). *The nature of emotion. Selected readings*. Penguin, Baltimore.

Arnold, M.B. (1969). Human emotion and action. In T. Mischel (Ed.), *Human action*. Academic Press, New York.

Brierley, M. (1937). Affects in theory and practice. *Intern. J. Psychoanal.*, 18, 256-68.

Dumas, G. (1948). Emotional shocks and emotions. Transl. Y. Bégin and M. B. Arnold. In M. B. Arnold (Ed.), *The nature of emotion. Selected readings*. Penguin, Baltimore, 1968.

Federn, P. (1933). Die Ichbesetzung bei Feehleistungen. *Imago*, 19, 312-338; 433-453.

James, W. (1884). What is an emotion? *Mind*, 9, 188-205.

Jelgersma, G. (1921). Psychoanalytischer Beitrag zu einer Theorie des Gefühls. *Intern. J. Psychoanal.*, 7, 1-8.

Jung, C.G. (1955). Synchronicity: An acausal connecting principle. In *The interpretation of nature and the psyche*. Pantheon, New York.

Klages, L. (1950). *Grundlegung der Wissenschaft vom Ausdruck* (7th rev. ed.). Bouvier, Bonn.

Krueger, F. (1928). The essence of feeling. Transl. M. B. Arnold. In M. B. Arnold (Ed.), *The nature of emotion. Selected readings*. Penguin, Baltimore, 1968.

Lange, C. (1885). *The emotions* (1885 German transl. Dr. Kurella; 1887, Engl. transl.). Williams and Wilkins, Baltimore, 1922.

Lazarus, R.S. (1966). *Psychological stress and the coping process*. McGraw-Hill, New York.

Leeper, R.W. (1948). A motivational theory of emotion to replace "emotion as disorganized response." *Psychol. Rev.*, 55, 5-21.

Leeper, R.W. (1963). The motivational theory of emotion. In C. L. Stacey and M. F. DeMartino (Eds.), *Understanding human motivation*. Howard Allen, Cleveland.

McDougall, W. (1928). Emotion and feeling distinguished. In M. L. Reymert (Ed.) *Feelings and emotions*. Clark Univ. Press, Worcester, Mass.

Pradines, M. (1958). *Traité de psychologie* (6th ed.). Presses Universitaries de France, Paris.

Shand, A.F. (1914). *The foundation of character*. Macmillan, New York.

Young, P.T. (1961). *Motivation and emotion*. Wiley, New York.

Chapter 13

The Education of the Emotions

Richard S. Peters*

EMOTIONS AS FORMS OF COGNITION

I propose in this paper to confine myself to getting clearer about what is involved in the task of educating the emotions. I do not propose to address myself to further questions about the relevance of empirical work done by psychologists to implementing this task. This would, as a matter of fact, be a very difficult undertaking for two reasons. In the first place, most of the changes in emotion studied experimentally by psychologists could not conceivably be described as "education." Whatever else we understand by "education" (Peters, 1966, Chapter I), at least we think of it as involving a family of experiences through which knowledge and understanding develop. Injecting adrenalin into the body, administering drugs, stimulation by electrodes and various methods of conditioning, do not of themselves bring about knowledge and understanding. They may, of course, provide conditions which facilitate cognitive development. In this respect, like altering the temperature of a room or smiling at children, they may function as aids to education; but they are not themselves processes of education. A psychologist might concede this point about "education" but conclude from it that the task of educating the emotions must therefore be an impossible one; for "emotion" might convey to him only some general state of activation or arousal which had no necessary connection with knowledge, understanding, or belief. In this sphere of behavior, therefore, it would follow for him that people could be stimulated or conditioned but not educated.

This brings me to my second reason for omitting to delve into empirical work

*University of London, Institute of Education.

done by psychologists on emotion, which is that the concept of "emotion" employed by many psychologists fails to do justice to what I would regard as its central feature, namely its connection with a certain type of cognition. If we ask ourselves what we might naturally call "emotions" we would give quite a long list which would include fear, anger, sorrow, grief, envy, jealousy, pity, remorse, guilt, shame, pride, wonder and the like. What sort of criterion underlies this selection? Surely, the connection between emotions and the class of cognitions that are conveniently called "appraisals." These are constituted by seeing situations under aspects which are agreeable or disagreeable, beneficial or harmful in a variety of dimensions. To feel fear *is*, for instance, to see a situation as dangerous; to feel pride *is* to see with pleasure something as mine or as something that I have had a hand in bringing about. Envy is connected with seeing someone else as possessing what we want, jealousy with seeing someone as possessing something or someone to which or whom we think we have a right. And so on. Emotions have in common the fact that they involve appraisals elicited by external conditions which are of concern to us or by things which we have brought about or suffered. (We would not, for reasons such as this, call hunger and thirst emotions.) They differ from each other because of differences in what is appraised. Fear, for instance, differs from anger, largely because seeing something as threatening differs from seeing it as thwarting, and these different appraisals have different consequences both physiologically and in the behavior which may be their outcome. Clues to distinguishing emotions may be provided by overt signs such as facial expressions; but the history of experiments in this field has shown them to be unreliable signs. Also, the fact that we can say that facial expressions are reliable or unreliable as distinguishing marks of the different emotions itself reveals that we have other ways of identifying them. My thesis, however, about the appraisals involved in emotion is not that they provide very valuable evidence as to what the distinct emotions are; it is rather that these different appraisals are largely constitutive of the different emotions. By that I mean that at least a logically necessary condition for the use of the word "emotion" is that some kind of appraisal should be involved, and that the different emotions must involve different appraisals. In other words, emotions are basically forms of cognition. It is because of this central feature which they possess that I think there is any amount of scope for educating the emotions.

Why then have psychologists concentrated on the physiological conditions underlying emotions, on expressions of emotions, and on some assumed link between emotion and action? Partly, I suppose, because Charles Darwin started a tradition of studying facial expressions with his famous, or notorious, experiments with photographs. But more importantly, because of psychology's endeavor to become a proper science based on publicly observable data. Physiological psychology had long been established as a scientifically respectable form of inquiry. It was also thought that concentration on facial expressions or on overt actions—for instance flight in the case of fear—would provide equally reliable data, free from the hazards of introspective reports. It is, I suppose, encouraging to read a long recent article by Leeper, which returns to common-sense in connecting emotions with cognitive cues, but his labored explanation of how psychologists have failed to see this because of the general tendency of scientists to concentrate on what is palpable scarcely holds water (Leeper, 1965, p. 37-40). What Leeper keeps locked in the cupboard is psychology's skeleton, behaviorism, which, as a methodological doctrine, has exercised a baneful and stupefying influence on academic psychology since the early part of this century. It was the concept of "palpability" which went with this particular brand of methodological puritanism, with all its conceptual confusions and antiquated notions of scientific method, that both restricted the questions which psychologists felt they could respectably raise about emotions and which occasioned them to ignore the palpable point that we cannot even identify the emotions we are talking about unless account is taken of how a person is appraising a situation. I am not, of course, denying that there are important questions to ask in these fields—for instance, about the physiology of emotion and about expressions of emotion. I am only commenting on the restrictions placed on investigations into emotional phenomena. (See, for instance, Mandler, 1962.)

There is, too, another important historical point about the restricted study of emotion by psychologists, namely, the tendency to treat fear and anger as paradigms, rather than, say, sorrow and pride. The tendency of psychologists in the behaviorist tradition to confine their work to animals as a matter of fact left them little alternative; for most emotions—for instance, pride, shame, regret, grief—are not experienced by animals because the appraisals involved in them presuppose a conceptual scheme beyond the range of animals other than man. Also, there was a highly respectable ancestry for the study of these two emotions in Darwin's work which gave prominence to them because of their obvious biological utility. But these two emotions are atypical in that they do have definite types of facial expressions connected with them and are accompanied by palpable signs of changes in the autonomic nervous system. Also, if any emotions are closely connected with typical action patterns, these two are. If sorrow were taken as a paradigm, the connection with action patterns would be difficult to discern. And what distinctive facial expressions are connected with envy or pride? Is it plausible to suggest that highly specific physiological changes accompany remorse or regret of the sort that often accompany fear and anger?

EMOTIONS AND PASSIVITY

Suppose, then, that we resist these historic influences, and, sticking to common sense,* insist both on the connection between emotions and distinctive appraisals and on a broad sample of emotions rather than confining ourselves to fear and anger. An interesting point, then, emerges if we study the list, namely, that most of the terms on the list can also be used as names of motives. This is not surprising; for obviously, as the terms "emotion" and "motive" suggest, there is a close family connection between the two terms. This has obviously been another reason which has led countless theorists to postulate an intimate connection between emotion and "motivated behavior," culminating in the historic dispute between Young and Leeper about the facilitating or disrupting effect of emotion on motivated behavior. I have elsewhere summarized most of the important attempts to establish such a connection (Peters, 1961, Section 3), and do not propose to elaborate this theme now. What I propose to do instead is to state briefly what I take to be the proper way of representing the undoubted overlap between these concepts.

My suggestion is that what is common to the two concepts is the connection with distinctive appraisals. In cases where either the term "motive" or "emotion" is appropriate, the situation is appraised in the way which is established by the particular term — for instance, as dangerous in the case of fear, as having done something wrong in the case of guilt. In cases where we apply the term "motive" this appraisal of the situation is regarded as providing the reason why we go on to *do* something. We talk about "motives" only in contexts where an explanation for an *action* is given or demanded; we do not ask for motives for feeling cold, for indigestion or for mystical visions. The explanation takes the form of appealing to a postulated connection between the appraisal and the action pattern in question. If a person's motive for making damaging remarks about a colleague is jealousy, then he must see him as achieving, or likely to achieve something to which he thinks he has a right, and he must act in the light of this view of his behavior.

We talk about jealousy as an emotion, for instance, when a person is subject to unpleasant feelings that come over him when he views his colleague's behavior in a certain light. Perhaps his perception of him is distorted by this view he has of him — perhaps his judgement of his character is warped by it — perhaps he gets into an emotional state at the mere mention of his name. The term "emotion," in other words, is typically used in ordinary language to pick out our passivity. We speak of judgements being disturbed, warped, heightened, sharpened and clouded by emotion, of people being in command or not being properly in control of their emotions, being emotionally perturbed, upset, involved, excited, and exhausted. In a similar vein, we speak of emotional states, upheavals, outbursts and reactions. The suggestion in such cases is that

*For a sustained defense of paying careful attention to the distinctions embodied in the conceptual scheme of common sense see Peters (1958, 1969).

something comes over people or happens to them, when they consider a situation in a certain light, when they appraise it in the dimension suggested by terms such as jealousy, envy and fear. This passivity frequently occurs when we appraise situations as dangerous and frustrating; hence the obviousness of fear and anger as emotions and hence our reluctance to regard benevolence and ambition as emotions, for there are rarely marked symptoms of passivity when we think of people or situations under the aspects connected with these terms.

It is important, to avoid misunderstanding of my analysis of "emotion" which some regard as a trifle eccentric, to be clear about the sort of analysis it is. What I am denying is that the terms "emotion" or "motive" pick out, as it were, distinctive items in the furniture of the mind. I am claiming, on the contrary, that they are terms we employ when we wish to link the *same* mental acts of appraisal with *different* forms of behavior — with actions on the one hand and with a variety of passive phenomena on the other. The appraisals involved, however, need not issue in either motives or emotions. We can say, "I envy him his equanimity" or "I am sorry that you can't come to stay," without acting in the light of the relevant appraisal and without being emotionally affected in any way.

What is common to both "motives" and "emotions," therefore, is the distinctive appraisals which are necessary to characterize these states of mind as being cases of fear, envy, jealousy, etc. The difference lies in the fact that "motive" is a term we employ to connect these appraisals with things we *do*, emotion with things that *come over us*. In strong cases of emotion our passivity is manifest in changes in the autonomic nervous system of which we speak in metaphors which are consonant with our passivity. We boil and fume with anger; we tremble and sweat with fear; we swell and glow with pride; we blush with shame and embarrassment. If the motor system is involved, the manifestations typically exhibit an involuntary character. Our knees knock with fear; we do not knock them. There is, too, the intermediary class of some reactions, which is typical of an uncoordinated, protopathic type, that springs from an intuitive, sometimes subliminal type of appraisal of a situation. An example would be when a person lashes out in anger or starts with fear. These are not reactions to stimuli, like jumping when one receives an electric shock, because of their cognitive core. Neither are they actions in a full-blown sense; for there is no grasp of means to ends, no consideration of possible ends of action. They are what we call "emotional reactions."

This analysis of the similarities and differences between motives and emotions suggests a conceptual connection between "emotion" and "passivity" and between "motive" and "action." It thus denies a conceptual connection between "emotion" and "action" which is so often maintained by both philosophers and psychologists alike. The wide-spread tendency to postulate such a connection is due partly to the overlap between the two concepts already suggested, and partly to the tendency to take some emotions, for instance, fear and anger, as paradigms rather than others. If sorrow, grief and wonder were taken as paradigms, this connection would surely be most implausible, for as Koestler (1966, p. 273-285) puts it: "The purely self-transcending emotions do not tend towards action, but towards quiescence, tranquility and catharsis." There are, of course, plenty of passive phenomena which go with these emotions — for instance, weeping, catching one's breath, a lump in the throat. But one cannot act in an appropriate way out of wonder or grief; one is overwhelmed by them. Perhaps one may *express* one's feelings in a symbolic way, as in mourning, or in some reverential ritual; but the appraisals do not function as motives for appropriate action as in the case of making reparation out of guilt. In the case of motives, the actions are appropriate because they remedy or retain what is unpleasant or pleasant about the situation which is appraised. To run away in the case of fear is to avoid what is unpleasant; to make reparation out of guilt is to attempt to remedy a wrong done. But if a man is overcome by grief because his wife is dead, what can be done of a specific sort, to remedy *that* situation? Expressions of emotion discharge the feeling through some sort of symbolic behavior because there are no appropriate channels through which any relevant action can flow. Furthermore, even appraisals which can function both as motives and emotions do not necessarily lead to action, or even to tendencies to action. Jealousy and envy, for instance, may affect one's perception, judgement and memory; but they may not issue in actions in the sense in which psychologists have thought of actions. They may even be expressed in poetry.

To deny a conceptual connection between emotion and action is not, however, to deny de facto connections. In other words, though it is not part of our understanding of the concept of "emotion" that there must be an action or tendency to action resultant on the appraisal of a situation, actions done out of a variety of motives can be contingently related to emotion; for one of the main manifestations of emotion is their tendency to disrupt, facilitate, heighten and intensify actions and performances. We can act *in* fear as well as *out of* fear; for there is no reason why an appraisal of the situation should not function as both an emotion and as a motive at the same time. The preposition "in" draws attention to the manner of acting rather than to the reason or motive for action which is picked out by "out of." When the same appraisal functions both as an emotion and as a motive then the question is whether the emotional aspect of it is facilitating or disrupting, which depends largely on its strength. (This was one of the points of the controversy between Young and Leeper.) In cases where emotion influences an action or performance done out of another motive, the question is whether the appraisal from which the emotion derives is consonant with, or antagonistic to that connected with the motive for the action. Fear may help a sentry acting out of a sense of duty to spot an approaching enemy long before anyone else; or it may lead him to imagine an enemy. But it is not likely to help him much if he is acting out of sexual desire in an off-duty period. Similarly, fear and envy felt for X are likely to warp and distort the moral judgements which Y may make of his actions. But they might also lead Y to notice aspects of X's behavior which escape the notice of less biased observers. It depends on whether the appraisal involved in the emotion draws the attention away from or towards the relevant features of the situation, "relevance" being defined in terms of whatever criteria make the actions and judgements concerned right or wrong, wise or foolish, valid or invalid, and so on.

EMOTIONS AND WISHES

My account of emotion obviously owes a great deal to Magda Arnold. It differs from her account in not postulating a conceptual connection between emotion and action; for she holds that an emotion is "a felt tendency towards or away from an object" which is preceded by an appraisal of the situation as being of a certain sort that is harmful or beneficial to the agent (Arnold, 1960, Chapters 9-12). There is, however, another feature of her account that would give an additional explanation of the tendency to make a tight connection between emotion and action, namely, the connection which she suggests between emotion and wishing.

"Wish" is a teleological concept which is very closely related to "want." It differs, however, from "want" in that the state of affairs wished for can be very indeterminately conceived. The moon is just the sort of thing that can be wished for, because questions about what one would do with it if one had it do not have to be pressed. Also, mundane questions of taking means to get it, which go along with "wanting" need not be raised. Now "wanting" is conceptually connected with action in the sense that action involves taking the means to a desired end. "Wishing" however, only conjures up the vision of some indeterminately conceived end. But, obviously, the concepts are very intimately connected, and if emotions are conceptually connected with wishes, the tendency to connect emotion with action, or tendencies to action, via the notion of "wanting" would be readily explained.

My contention is that there *is* such a conceptual connection between emotion and wishing. If we consider emotions such as grief and wonder, which are the most intractable ones for those who try to connect emotion conceptually with action, the connection with the weaker teleological concept of "wish" is clear enough. A wife who is mourning for her dead husband *wishes* fervently that he were alive. But what *want* of this sort could issue in appropriate action? A lover, overwhelmed by his love, may wish that he were one with his beloved; but he cannot strictly speaking *want* such a logical impossibility. Yet these are just the sorts of thoughts that come into the heads of those deeply in love. Similarly, in cases where there is a possibility of appropriate action, the appraisal may only issue in a wish; it may not become a motive for action. A person strongly affected by fear or anger certainly has wishes such as "would that I were away from here" or "would that he were dead." But nothing in the way of action or a tendency to action necessarily follows from this appraisal.

Magda Arnold also stresses the immediate, "here and now" intuitive, undiscriminating types of appraisal that are characteristic of emotion. These features of emotion are also emphasized by Sartre, who regards emotion as "an abrupt drop into the magical" (Sartre, 1948, p. 90). This brings out well the connection between emotion and wishes, but it also emphasizes a feature of appraisals which we associate with them when we regard them as emotions, namely, their undiscriminating character. A jealous man's appraisals are not always wild and intuitive, any more than are those of a man who quite sensibly experiences fear when he hears the shriek of a bomb descending towards him. But the more we think of these appraisals as *emotions* and hence stress our passivity with regard to them, the more we tend to think of the appraisals as immediate and "intuitive" and of our reactions as veering towards the involuntary. "Emotional reactions" illustrate both these features. If we jump when we see a face at the window, our appraisal is immediate and intuitive and our jump has an involuntary, protopathic character — quite unlike that of the high-jumper.

I have elsewhere (Peters, 1965, 1969) attempted to generalize this theory of passivity and to connect emotional phenomena via the concept of "wish" with the sorts of phenomena explained by Freud in his theory of the wish, and with theories of the mechanisms underlying perceptual vigilance and defense suggested by more stimulus-response ridden theorists such as Dember. But this is not the place to develop this conceptualizing any further. Enough has been done to enable me to address myself to the question of what must be involved in the task of educating the emotions. If the foregoing analysis is not altogether misconceived, there must be two interconnected aspects of this task. There will first be the development of appropriate appraisals, and secondly, the control and canalization of passivity. I propose to deal briefly with each of these aspects in turn.

THE DEVELOPMENT OF APPROPRIATE APPRAISALS

The Justification of Appraisals

Although it may sound almost indecent to mention it in the company of psychologists, the education of the emotions is inescapably a moral matter. Most emotions and motives are, as a matter of fact, regarded also as virtues and vices—for instance, envy, benevolence, lust, pity. This is presumably because they are consonant with, or conflict with fundamental moral principles such as respect for persons and the consideration of peoples' interests. And there are many emotions which are conceptually connected with general moral notions — for instance, shame, guilt, remorse. There is also the point that "education" suggests the initiation of people into what is worthwhile in a way which involves some depth and breadth of understanding and knowledge. It implies, therefore, not only a view about what is valuable in life, but also the all-pervasive principle of respect for truth. For the endeavor to develop knowledge and understanding would be unintelligible if there were no concern for truth and if educators generally were unmoved by the standards connected with its pursuit, such as those involved in relevance, clarity, and cogency in argument, truthfulness in the production of evidence and impartiality towards people as possible sources of what might be true. Anyone who is concerned with the education of the emotions must necessarily approach his task from the standpoint of a moral position.

It might be thought that psychologists could have little to say about the appropriateness or inappropriateness of the emotions and motives that are taken to be desirable. But this is not altogether true. There are, so it seems to me, at least two respects in which psychologists might have something important to say about this. First, they might produce evidence about what is empirically possible in this sphere, human nature being what it is. There have been philosophers, such as Bertrand Russell (1929) who have held that jealousy is always inappropriate as an emotion, basically because it presupposes unjustifiable claims to a special relationship with another person. If psychologists could show that human beings were unable to avoid appraising situations in this way, that would be an important assertion to make. For there is a sense where "ought" implies "can." It is pointless to tell people that they ought not to feel in a certain way if, in general, human beings cannot avoid being subject to such feelings. This may be untrue about jealousy, but it may well be true about fear and anger, which obviously have a much more solid biological basis. The question then, for the educator, would not be whether, but with and of what, people should be angry or afraid.

Secondly, there is a strong case for saying that psychologists who have concerned themselves with mental health are in a position to offer well-substantiated counsels of prudence about certain emotions. They might say that the influence of some emotions is so all-pervasive that their presence or absence may seriously affect a person's capacity for doing what he thinks desirable, whatever his conception of what is desirable might be. They may say, for instance, that the absence of a capacity for love or the constant presence of a feeling of threat or insecurity might have such an all-pervasive influence on the person's life. Whatever else, therefore, we do about educating children, we should have particular regard for the development of the one and the avoidance of the other; for their presence or absence might be regarded as empirically necessary conditions for the satisfactory development of a whole range of other emotions and motives.

The Conceptual Prerequisites of Appraisals

The point is often made nowadays by educators influenced by Piaget that children cannot form certain concepts unless they have first formed others, though it scarcely needs elaborate experiments to establish this. Nevertheless, even if one regards this as a matter for conceptual analysis as distinct from empirical investigation, it is certainly an important point to make in the sphere of the emotions. For what was made to look, in the writings of classical theorists such as Shand, as a kind of mental chemistry was in fact a crude attempt at making explicit conceptual priorities in the sphere of the emotions. For instance, just as one could not experience pride unless one had a concept of oneself, so one probably has to be able to experience pride before one can be subject to ambition and shame. Guilt presupposes a capacity to feel either fear of another or sympathy for another depending on whether it is the authoritarian or humanistic type of guilt.* Looking at the more complex emotions in this way in terms of the relationship between the concepts involved in the distinctive appraisals, raises in a more modern way the old issue about the possibility of all motives and emotions being generated out of a few simple ones; it also raises difficult empirical questions about the social processes by means of which the rationalization and moralization of appraisals takes place. The development of language is obviously of cardinal importance in this. To enter into the descriptions of a writer such as Henry James or George Eliot is to have one's capacity for making appraisals extended. We tend to think too much of human beings as having the capacity for making discriminations which are put into words by others. It is nearer the truth to say that we learn to make the discriminations by entering into the descriptions. It may, too, take a whole novel such as *Howard's End* to explore the range of an emotion like indignation.

False and Irrelevant Beliefs

Most of our more complex appraisals do not presuppose just other appraisals; they also presuppose empirical beliefs of a more straightforward sort. I may just dislike someone for no apparent reason; but if I am jealous of somebody it is usually because I believe, perhaps falsely, that he has done something, or intends to do something, which threatens my claim to something or somebody. An obvious element, therefore, in the education of the emotions is the attempt to ensure that people's appraisals are not based on false beliefs.

*For the distinction see Money-Kyrle, 1951.

To ensure this is not at all easy. To start with, as I have argued before, insofar as we are subject to something like jealousy as an *emotion*, the appraisal of the situation tends to be immediate and undiscriminating. We are predisposed often to interpret situations in a certain way, especially when we are in a frame of mind which we call a mood, and our beliefs may unreflectingly follow the lines of the appraisal. In a jealous frame of mind all sorts of beliefs are rigged to match our mood. Furthermore, the determination to examine the facts of the matter, to base our appraisals on well-grounded beliefs, is not a disposition that comes naturally to most men. As Bacon argued in the section on the Idols in his *Novum Organum*, the determination to look at the facts, to look for the negative instance which tells against our comfortable beliefs, goes against our inveterate tendency to believe what we wish to be the case. One of the main tasks of the education of the emotions, beginning with the development of what Freud called the ego, which he connected with the sense of reality, must therefore consist in fostering the capacity for objectivity. This is not just a matter of ensuring that children are well-informed; it is more importantly a matter of converting what natural curiosity children have into a concern for truth, and getting them to discipline themselves to submit what they think to public tests.

Psychologists, in my view, have told us too little about the conditions under which reasonableness, in the limited sense of the disposition to base conduct and appraisals on well-grounded beliefs, tends to develop. They have said much more about the antecedent conditions of various forms of irrationality; yet anyone who is seriously concerned with teaching children to be reasonable would like to know how positively to proceed as well as what to avoid. Nevertheless, in the area of irrational conduct, Freud and his followers have invented a technique which is best described as being one of re-education. The point is that the best way of characterizing some forms of neurosis is to say that the patient is a victim of false beliefs.* Of course, according to Freud's definition of "unconscious," the sufferer is not aware of what he believes. Rather, he once believed, for instance, that his father was going to damage him in some drastic way and repressed this belief which occasioned his fear of his father. In later life he has difficulty in dealing with various authority figures. The technique of re-education consists in getting him to recall vividly what he believed about his father and to see that, whether or not this was true of his father, it is not invariably true of authority figures who remind him of his father.

Of course, not all types of irrational conduct have a similar explanation or can be influenced to any great extent by such a process of re-education. An irrational aversion to a type of thing, for instance, a rabbit — to use the classic case — might be set up by an association between that type of thing and an

---

*The writing of both this section and succeeding two sections was helped by a preview which John Wilson of the Farmington Trust, Oxford, was kind enough to let me have of a book he has written on *The Education of the Emotions*.

unpleasant experience, for instance a loud noise. This might establish a nameless dread that was reactivated whenever the individual encountered rabbits or animals with similar characteristics. In such cases, it would be stretching things to say that the person had beliefs about the rabbit which he repressed. And if he was treated by some kind of reconditioning process it would be inappropriate to describe this as a process of *education*. For nothing is done about his beliefs; all that happens is that some different sort of association is established to counteract or inhibit the original one.

I am not, of course, making any claims for the success of psychoanalysis as a technique, or chancing my arm on the extent to which irrational conduct is susceptible of one type of explanation rather than another. All I am claiming is that some irrational conduct and appraisals can be represented as being derived from unconscious beliefs that seem to undergo a kind of irrelevant generalization, and that, insofar as the "cure" consists in getting the patient to understand and to acknowledge this, it can be properly represented as a technique of re-education in the sphere of the emotions.

The Recognition of Emotions

In this process of re-education in psychoanalysis, the patient does not just come to know theoretically that he at one time had some belief about a person or a past event; he is also brought to relive his previous experience which gives him some kind of additional insight into his condition. This kind of distinction is a very important one in the general field of awareness of one's own and other peoples' emotional states. There is a long-standing problem in the theory of knowledge about the status of knowledge of persons which is partly connected with the general problem of criteria of knowledge in this field, and partly with the issue about whether there is any kind of priority to be attached to knowledge of one's own case (see Austen, 1946; Malcolm, 1958; Ayer, 1954 and 1956). But whatever is said about these very difficult matters, there is certainly an important distinction to be made between knowing certain facts about oneself and other people and the more imaginative type of entering into one's own and other peoples' more recondite emotions, for which we use the term "insight."

Many claim that this imaginative ability is encouraged by taking part in games and drama, as well as by literature; but this is an *a priori* type of hunch rather than one substantiated by reliable empirical studies. As, however, one's ability to recognize emotions in oneself is a feature of being educated in this sphere, and as a criterion of being educated emotionally is the tendency for one's appraisals of others to be based on a realistic assessment of their condition, further knowledge about how this imaginative ability is developed is of crucial importance in the education of emotions. In this sphere, we are particularly prone to see what we fear or wish to be the case; our beliefs are likely to follow the lines of our moods and intuitive appraisals. If we lack the capacity for ascertaining what really is the case, we are very likely to remain in what Spinoza called, "The state of human bondage," at the mercy of our own prejudices and passivity.

Emotional Sincerity

Often in such cases, we are not so much victims of ignorance as of insincerity, or mauvaise-foi, about which Sartre has written so much. "Sincere" is applied to people and their speech and other forms of symbolic gestures (for instance, smiles). It can relate either to cases where one does not deliberately mislead people by one's utterances or symbolic gestures, or, more generally, to one's determination to reveal, as well as one can, what one's feelings, beliefs, etc. are. Often one has some strong motive for being insincere — for instance, fear, shame, and the feeling associated with the feigned appraisal helps to develop a tendency towards deceiving oneself as well as others. For any educator, honesty and sincerity must be cardinal virtues, for he is concerned with the development of knowledge and understanding, and if people are concerned with finding out what is true, it must in general be the case that they are disposed to reveal their thoughts and feelings to each other. Without this, no kind of cooperative enquiry can fluorish. How children are best encouraged to develop this disposition is an empirical matter about which it would be rash for a philosopher to make any pronouncement.

THE CONTROL AND CANALIZATION OF PASSIVITY

So much for the appraisal aspect of the education of the emotions. I now propose to make a few observations about the other aspect of it, which is concerned with the management of our passivity. This is, to a large extent, a complementary aspect of the task of developing appropriate appraisals; for the task of freeing people from false and irrelevant beliefs, of enabling them to have insight into themselves and into others, and of encouraging sincerity are made doubly difficult because of the countervailing influence of more primitive, wild types of appraisal that warp and cloud perception and judgment and aid and abet self-deception and insincerity.

The Warping and Clouding of Perception and Judgment

If, as Freud argued, the infant tends to live on in us with the wild and intuitive forms of appraisal characteristic of a more primordial condition of mind, even after the laborious development of the ego and the sense of reality, how can this ever-present influence on our perception and judgement be minimized?

There are, roughly speaking, three ways of tackling this task. The first would be to use some noneducational technique such as conditioning or the administering of drugs. At best these techniques would decrease a countervailing condition, or neutralize an existing condition, which might enable more positive educational techniques, that dealt directly with the development of beliefs and appraisals, to get a firmer grip.

The second approach would be that used by Freud and advocated by Spinoza, namely that of bringing a person to have some kind of insight into the sources of his irrationalities. Even Frued himself, though, never regarded this as a sufficient technique. Indeed he claimed that in some cases it even exacerbates the symptoms, like the distribution of menu cards at a time of famine.

A much more important positive approach is that envisaged by Spinoza in his saying that it takes an emotion to control an emotion. The predicament of most of us, an extreme case of which is presented by the paranoiac, is that we are too much subject to a kind of monadic myopia. Our interpretation of the world is inveterately self-referential. We find difficulty in peering out and seeing the world and others as they are, undistorted by our own fears, hopes, and wishes. Better understanding of ourselves could not, of itself, remedy this condition. There are, however, certain appraisals which lack this self-referential character, notably love, respect, the sense of justice, and concern for truth. The development of what Koestler calls the "self-transcending emotions" is probably the most effective way of loosening the hold on us of the more primitive, self-referential ones. To become effective, they must become stabilized in sentiments, rather than simply issue in sporadic emotions, the term "sentiment" indicating a settled disposition to make appraisals of a certain sort. More precise knowledge about the conditions under which these sentiments are formed would, in my view, be one of the most important contributions which social psychology could make to educational theory.

Motives and the Connection
of Appraisals with Action Patterns

In my preceding analysis of the similarities and differences between the concepts of "emotion" and "motive" I made the point that appraisals can be connected either with our passivity, which may have a distorting and disrupting effect on judgement and action, or with action patterns, in which case they function as motives. So one of the basic ways in which passivity is controlled is to develop appropriate action patterns with which the various appraisals can become connected. Thus a man who is subject to fear will have a settled disposition to act in an appropriate way. His chance of being overcome by passive phenomena is thereby lessened. This transformation of vague wishes into determinate wants and hence into relevant action is of manifest educational importance. To writhe with sympathy, to fume with moral indignation, to squirm with guilt or shame, may be more desirable than to be incapable of such feelings. But, it is surely more desirable still that these appraisals should also function as motives for doing whatever is appropriate. This is particularly important in the context of dealing with tendencies to action which issue from undesirable motives such as envy, hatred and lust. A vague tendency to say "no" to oneself issuing from a feeling of guilt or shame, and unconnected with any disposition to act in an appropriate way, is singularly ineffective. Of more value are tendencies to action issuing from positive sentiments such as respect, benevolence and the sense of justice; for my guess is that the rather negative type of moral education, which issues from the puritan tradition is not particularly effective. In developing these more positive moral patterns of action the transition from second-hand, external sorts of appraisals to first-hand ones, which become linked with settled action patterns, is crucial. Much of what is moral is marked out by generalized appraisals such as "wrong," "good," and "naughty." Terms like these indicate that there are reasons for doing or not doing things but do not intimate at all clearly what the reasons are. Children have to be taught in such a way that they are led to see the reasons for and against courses of action built into them — for instance "that's unfair" and "that is hurting him." The development of such concrete first-hand appraisals, and linking them by on-the-spot training with patterns of action is one of the most important tasks of moral education.

Connected with the puritan tradition is the emphasis on "character," or strength of will, which exhibits itself in higher order traits such as consistency, integrity, determination, and so on. What is called "weakness of will" is explicable in terms of emotions such as fear, anxiety, and lust, which disrupt peoples' well-meaning intentions. Here again, one wonders about the puritan tradition. Strength of character is so often represented in negative terms, as saying "no" to temptation, as standing firm, impervious to social pressure. My guess is that the influence of positive, self-transcending sentiments is just as important in the development of this as either prudence or the more negative superego types of appraisals.

The Expression of Emotions

There is finally the problem of the discharge of passivity through the expression of the emotions. This may take the form of facial expressions and of changes in the autonomic system; or it may be handled in a more controlled way by appropriate speech and gesture of a voluntary sort. It was pointed out that some emotions, such as grief, can only be handled in this way, for there are no appropriate actions in relation to which the appraisals can function as motives.

The control and canalization of emotions through speech and symbolic gesture is an extremely important intermediary in the sphere of emotion, which lies between extreme forms of passivity and appropriate action. In the case of many appraisals, such as those connected with hate, fear, and lust, we would be in a very sorry plight if there were no intermediary between quivering in the passive state specific to the appraisals in question and launching into the relevant actions of murder, flight, and rape. The mechanism of "sublimation" is of obvious relevance here. Much of civilized life, including poetry, manners, wit and humour, consists in devising and learning forms of expression which enable us to deal with emotions in a way which is not personally disturbing or socially disruptive. Control can, of course, go too far. It is interesting to speculate, for instance, about what happens to those who are brought up with a prohibition on the public display of any emotion, either in gesture or in extravagant utterances, such as those of the poet. Do they become stunted in their capacity for experiencing emotion; or does it distort their judgement, facilitate or inhibit their actions in various subterranean ways; or do they tend to form deep and lasting sentiments for people, causes, and places? And what of those who are encouraged always to display their emotions publicly? Is the transience of their emotional states matched by an inability to form stable sentiments? There are a host of empirical speculations in this area, but no well-established knowledge.

UPSHOT

This brings me to my final point which is really the point of writing this paper. Educational problems are not of the sort which can be solved by any one of the established disciplines such as philosophy, psychology, or sociology. They always raise questions to answer which there must be cooperation between people working in different disciplines. I have found that when I have done some work on the philosophical aspects of an educational problem, a host of empirical questions are opened up. If I ask my colleagues in psychology about such issues, they usually reply that no well-designed experiments have been done in this field. In many cases, this lack of research is due not to the fact that it would be impossible to test limited hypotheses, but to the fact that various puritanical traditions in psychology have discouraged work. And so we continue in our abysmal ignorance, dealing with the minds of our children in a haphazard way that would not be tolerated by those who deal with their bodies.

The area of the education of the emotions is a case in point. My contention is that most of the work in this field, with the notable exception of that of Solomon Asch and Magda Arnold, has been hamstrung by the behavioristic and physiological traditions, and by the concentration on fear and anger as paradigms of emotions. My more positive intention has been to construct a conceptual map of the area which reveals, I hope, both what is distinctive of emotional phenomena and what needs to be known if we are to tackle more systematically the cluster of problems connected with this very important area of education.

REFERENCES

Arnold, M.B. (1960). *Emotion and personality*. Cassell, London.

Asch, S. (1952). *Social psychology*. Prentice-Hall, Englewood Cliffs, New Jersey.

Austen, J. (1946). Other minds. In *Proc. Aristotelean Soc., Suppl.*, 20, 148-187.

Ayer, A.J. (1954). Our knowledge of other minds. In *Philosophical essays*. Macmillan, London.

Ayer, A.J. (1956). *The problem of knowledge*. Macmillan, London.

Koestler, A. (1966). *The act of creation*. Pan Books, London.

Leeper, R.W. (1965). Needed developments in motivational theory. In D. Levine (Ed.), *Nebraska symposium on motivation*. Univ. of Nebraska Press, Lincoln.

Malcolm, N. (1958). Knowledge of other minds. *J. Philos.*, 55, 969-978.

Mandler, A. (1962). Emotion. In G. Mandler and E. Galanter (Eds.) *New directions in psychology*. Holt, New York.

Money-Kyrle, R. (1951). *Psycho-analysis and politics*. Duckworth, London.

Peters, R.S. (1958). *The concept of motivation*. Routledge and Kegan Paul, London.

Peters, R.S. (1961). Emotions and the category of passivity. In *Proc. Aristotelean Soc.*, 62, 117-134.

Peters, R.S. (1965). Emotions, passivity, and the place of Freud's theory in psychology. In B. Wolman and E. Nagel (Eds.), *Scientific psychology*. Basic Books, New York.

Peters, R.S. (1966). *Ethics and education*. Allen and Unwin, London.

Peters, R.S. (1969). Motivation, emotion, and the conceptual scheme of common-sense. In T. Mischel (Ed.), *Human action*. Academic Press, New York.

Russell, B. (1929). *Marriage and morals*. Allen and Unwin, London.

Sartre, J.P. (1948). *The emotions*. Trans., B. Frechtman. Philosophical Library, New York.

Part IV

Psychological Approaches
to the Study of Emotion

INTRODUCTION

In this section, Lazarus' paper is a good transition from the cognitive theories of the last section to the experimental study of emotion. As do many contributors to the symposium, Lazarus also reviews past theories of emotion. It is interesting, however, that every reviewer, approaching the field from his own point of view, concentrates on different issues so that each survey adds to those in earlier sections, and all of them give a rounded overview of the field of emotion. Lazarus also discusses some issues raised in previous papers: the problem whether emotions activate, amplify, or motivate (see Tomkins, Leeper, Arnold); and the connection between emotion and the correlated neural or physiological changes (see Pribram, Tomkins, Schachter, Arnold).

According to Lazarus, emotion has several dimensions: physiological, cultural, and cognitive. He suggests ways and means of studying each and describes ingenious methods of studying the cognitive dimension. The immediately following three papers are good examples of the experimental investigation of the cultural dimension: Ewert reports the changing evaluation of their social environment found among pubescent girls; Frijda studies facial expressions in emotion; and Davitz concentrates on the language people use to describe their emotions.

Chapter 14

Towards a Cognitive Theory of Emotion[*]

Richard S. Lazarus, James R. Averill,
and Edward M. Opton, Jr.[†]

This paper will be organized around three interrelated topics. First, we will discuss the concept of emotion and its place in psychology. It will be argued that emotions can best be conceptualized as complex response syndromes. Second, emotions will be viewed from three perspectives, the biological, cultural, and cognitive. The convergence of these approaches will be noted, and a schematic plan outlined which leads towards a cognitive theory of emotion. Third, some methodological issues will be considered, with special attention given to discrepancies among emotional response indices, and to the manner in which investigation of cognitive determinants of emotion can proceed. Empirical research from our laboratory, which lends substance to many of the theoretical issues raised in earlier discussions, will be presented briefly in this methodological section.

THE PLACE OF EMOTION IN PSYCHOLOGY

The question of whether emotion is a useful concept for psychology has been much debated in the last several decades, but without satisfactory resolution. On the one hand, emotions seem of obvious importance in everyday life. On the other hand, attempts to incorporate emotional phenomena into the mainstream

[*]This paper and the research reported within it were made possible partly by a research training grant (RH-4) from the Rehabilitation Services Administration, and by a research grant (MH-2136) from the National Institute of Mental Health.

[†]University of California, Berkeley.

of psychological theory have seemed inadequate to many psychologists, encouraging a distrust of the concept of emotion and to attempts to consider the relevant phenomena under other headings, e.g., motivation and activation.

In considering the place of emotion in psychology, two related questions should be distinguished. First, are emotional concepts important in the description and classification of behavior? Second, are emotional concepts necessary for the theoretical explanation of.behavior — including so-called emotional behavior? Psychologists have usually assumed that the answers to both of these questions must be the same. That is, to the extent that emotions represent a meaningful class of behavior, emotional concepts must play a role in psychological theory; and conversely, if emotional concepts are not theoretically necessary, then emotional behavior need not be considered separately from other forms of behavior. Since both of these inferences are unwarranted, much needless controversy arising from them might have been avoided. We shall argue that emotional concepts represent important substantive areas of psychology and hence they are important for the *description and classification of behavior.* This does not mean, however, that they are necessary in the *explanation* of behavior (except perhaps at a very molar level). Depending on the proclivities of the theorist, other explanatory concepts could be offered to replace them.

This position can be made more clear by drawing an analogy between the role of disease concepts in medicine and physiology and emotional concepts in psychology. No one would maintain that the concept of disease is scientifically meaningless or unimportant. But the concept of disease, or of any particular disease, is not a theoretical construct in physiological theory. Similarly, the concept of emotion can play an important role in psychology without serving as a basic explanatory construct in psychological theory. If we take this analogy seriously, two problems confront the psychologist interested in emotion. The first is the development of an adequate classification scheme for emotional phenomena; the second is the development of psychological principles to explain these phenomena. We do not pretend to have solutions to these problems, but what follows is an attempt to indicate the form these solutions might take. We will begin by reviewing critically but briefly some previous attempts to eliminate the concept of emotion from psychology by subsuming the relevant phenomena under other rubrics, primarily activiation; we will then turn to the problem of classification.

Attempts to Abandon Emotion
as a Substantive Area of Inquiry

As noted elsewhere by the senior author (Lazarus, 1968), the difficult problems involved in defining emotion and in distinguishing it from other phenomena have led many psychologists of diverse persuasions to treat emotions as intervening motivational variables. This made it possible to focus attention, not on the substantive nature of the emotional response, but on the adaptive or maladaptive patterns of behavior which it presumably motivates, e.g., defensive modes of thought or instrumental behavior as studied, for example, in avoidance conditioning. By making emotion an intervening variable, emotional responses went underground, so to speak. An emotion such as anxiety came to be thought of as an evanescent phenomenon, less worthy of study than the adaptive avoidant or defensive response it motivates. With this denigration of emotion as a substantive response, substitute notions emerged, such as drive, activation, and stress which appeared to many to be more scientific and to overcome the awkward definitional problems. In our view, however, these substitutes, while useful for some purposes, have largely begged the basic theoretical and empirical issues concerning emotion.

A particularly timely illustration is the so-called activation theory of emotion. Historically, the notion of emotion as activation can be traced to the assertion by Cannon (1929) that all emotions, if sufficiently intense, are characterized by mass discharge of the sympathetic nervous system. Duffy (1962) too has argued that the physiological differences between emotions are not significant, and that emotional phenomena should be analyzed in terms of a few underlying dimensions, of which activation has received the most attention. The notion of emotion as activation also received strong support when Lindsley (1950), in an earlier edition of this symposium, related emotion to activity of the reticular activating system, a part of the brain stem which had just recently been discovered.

In spite of its mainly physiological origins, the concept of activation received ready acceptance because it could be easily assimilated into the intervening variable approach to emotion, being identified with the concept of drive in learning theory (e.g., Hebb, 1955; Malmo, 1959; Berlyne, 1960). Like the concept of drive, the concept of activation has drawn attention away from emotion as a substantive response, emphasizing instead a single hypothetical dimension of intensity. Differences between emotions have consequently been ignored or assigned little importance.

The ideas of Schachter (1967) represent an interesting recent version of this thesis. (Similar ideas were presented earlier by Duffy, 1941, and Harlow and Stagner, 1933, but without much experimental work to support them.) According to Schachter, the same state of physiological arousal could be interpreted by the subject as joy or anger, or any other emotional state, depending upon the situational context. Thus, although he does not deny the possibility of physiological differences among emotions, Schachter attributes little theoretical significance to such differences, except in those unusual cases where the person becomes confused about the nature of his arousal and hence misinterprets anxiety, say, for hunger. There is no space here to criticize Schachter's formulation (see Averill and Opton, 1968; Lazarus, 1968; Plutchik and Ax, 1967). Our own position to be described below posits a more intimate link between physiological reactions and the cognitive aspects of emotion, each emotion being characterized by its own specific pattern of response, which includes physiological, behavioral, and cognitive components.

It is important to recognize that the two alternatives of emotional specificity and generality in physiological responding are not mutually exclusive. Most regulative processes have both a general and a specific component, and interest in one or the other tends to wax and wane (as it has, for example, in the emphasis on mass action versus localization of function in the brain), depending on technological developments and what appears at the time to be the most fruitful line of attack on the problem. Thus, we see Selye (1950) making his primary contribution in the domain of generality, with the concept of physiological stress and the general adaptation syndrome. Selye certainly does not deny, however, the obvious and important differences in reactions to different stressors, e.g., extreme heat or cold, or in different disease syndromes. Similarly, we have used the concept of psychological stress as a general rubric in our own theoretical and empirical work (Lazarus, 1966), but the use of such a generic term in one context is not to deny the importance of differences between various kinds of stress or emotional responses in other contexts.

Upon reading the literature on emotional differentiation, it is easy to gain the impression that it is primarily an empirical issue whether or not different emotions can be distinguished physiologically. But this is not so. Common sense as well as much empirical research (Averill, 1969; Ax, 1953; Funkenstein *et al.*, 1957; Lacey, 1967) indicates that there are physiological differences between emotions. Not even Cannon (1929) denied this. What he and others after him did deny is that these differences are of theoretical importance. In other words, he claimed that the similarities among emotions are of greater theoretical significance than their differences. No simple empirical demonstration of differences between emotions can disprove this central tenet of activation theory, any more than the existence of different disease syndromes proves Selye wrong with reference to the general adaptation syndrome.

The controversy for and against generality and specificity in emotional responses is much like that between the advocates of a general intelligence factor (Spearman's *g*) and the advocates of independent aptitudes (e.g., Thurstone's Primary Mental Abilities). This is no pseudo-problem, and is still actively debated (cf. Guilford, 1967; McNemar, 1964). Nevertheless, it is a fact that the controversy over the nature of intelligence depends to a large extent on the specific issue being tackled, the types of variables measured, the method of their analysis, and one's general theoretical bias. The same can be said for activation theory. Thus, Berlyne (1967) has recently drawn an analogy between general activation and general intelligence, with the differences between activation patterns corresponding to differences between specific abilities.

To summarize our own position, we maintain that the concept of emotion is empirically and heuristically valid in a descriptive sense. Whether or not emotional concepts will be necessary constructs in psychological theory is another question which cannot — and need not — be decided at the present time. What does seem clear is that emotional phenomena should not be pushed underground, or uncritically subsumed under other rubrics. Rather, the emotions represent a substantive and important, if much neglected, area of psychological inquiry.

The Problem of Classification:
Emotions as Response Syndromes

One of the greatest hindrances to the study of emotions is the lack of an adequate scheme for their definition and classification. The problem is important, because decisions about classification, even implicit, unspoken decisions, have important — one might say "definitive" — consequences for psychological theory and research.

Emotions have been notoriously difficult to define, partially because theorists have assumed that there must be some characteristic unique to emotions which sets them apart from other psychological phenomena. Perhaps we have learned too well the grammar-school injunction that a noun refers to a person, place, or thing. Research, however, has failed to reveal the "thing" to which the noun "emotion" refers. This has led some to suggest the abandonment of the concept, others to blame technological inadequacies. However, such failure stems not from an insensitivity of our physiological recording devices or a lack of acuteness in our introspection; it stems from what Ryle (1949) has called a category mistake, that is, the expectation that words from one logical category will operate like those in another. Emotion-words do not refer to things, in the sense that a table or even an atom is a thing, but rather to syndromes, in the sense that a disease is a syndrome (cf. Averill, 1968b).

An emotion, like a disease, is not defined by any single symptom or set of symptoms, nor has it one center or locus (e.g., in the hypothalamus). For example, subjective experience may serve an important function in emotion, bridging informational gaps for the individual (cf. MacLean, 1960; Simonov, 1969) and providing diagnostic signs for assessment by others (e.g., in self-reports). But subjective experience cannot define emotion any more than it can define disease. Thus, headache is an important diagnostic symptom of brain tumor, yet many brain tumors do not produce headache and many headaches do not indicate brain tumor. Similar considerations apply to physiological changes during emotion and disease, and to behavioral manifestations. Although a disease syndrome is not defined by any single sign or symptom, or any fixed set of symptoms, it remains an extremely important concept. Indeed, a whole branch of medical science, nosology, is devoted to the identification and classification of disease syndromes. A similar nosology for emotional phenomena is needed in psychology.

In addition to referring to syndromes, emotional concepts are also relational; that is, they typically imply an object, just as the concept "answer" implies a question (Tolman, 1923; Kenny, 1963). Moreover, in everyday speech, emotional concepts not only describe behavior, they also help explain it. As such, they may presuppose systems of judgment, e.g., of a moral or ethical nature (Bedford, 1957). Thus, an act of aggression may be committed in anger, jealousy, or even fear; and it may be justified, irrational, or self-righteous, depending upon the circumstances and social relationships involved. Such nuances of ordinary language may seem of little relevance to the scientific study of emotion, but their neglect in a too rapid search for operational precision can lead – and has led – to trivialities and needless controversy (Averill, 1968a). Ordinary language incorporates a great deal of shared experience. The use of a vernacular term in psychological theory must cover at least much of the same territory as the everyday use of the word, and where the ordinary and the scientific meanings diverge, we should be aware of the differences.

The relational nature of emotional concepts is of utmost importance for the development of any classification scheme. Again, we may turn to the analogy between emotion and disease to illustrate how. Disease classifications based primarily on symptomatology, e.g., schizophrenia and cancer, are notoriously unsatisfactory. Without a known etiology, symptomatology provides only an imperfect guide to understanding. We do not wish to imply that the object causes an emotion, as a virus might cause a disease, but only to emphasize that attempts to differentiate between emotions on the basis of response characteristics alone will have only limited success.

The conception of emotions as *response syndromes which are relational* in nature indicates the manner in which their differentiation and classification might proceed. We need not go into details here; suffice it to note that within a given cultural group, at least, there is often considerable consensus with regard to the type of phenomena encompassed by different emotional concepts, e.g., anger, fear, grief, etc. The situation could not be otherwise, or these terms would lose their communicative function and drop from the language. In language as in nature, there is a kind of evolutionary rule, a survival of the fittest. Words that survive must refer to concepts which people find useful in their everyday interactions. Of course, everyday emotional concepts will have to be refined and made more precise for scientific purposes, but this can be done only in conjunction with other technical and theoretical advances in the area (Averill, 1968a).

In the meantime, the psychologist could do worse than to emulate his physiological colleagues in their approach to the differentiation and investigation of disease syndromes. Both diseases and emotions can be classified according to etiology, symptoms, and course of development. No one symptom, or the mere presence of causative agents, guarantees a correct diagnosis; rather, it is the pattern and development of reactions in relationship to eliciting conditions, and to the state of the individual, which allow the inference of disease — and of emotion.

One final point needs to be added. Understanding a syndrome requires analysis of component reactions as well as their synthesis into a conceptual whole. That is, it is only a conceptual convenience to speak of an emotion as though it were a unitary phenomenon. An emotion may be subdivided into many component reactions, which occur concurrently and sequentially, and which are often poorly correlated. A comprehensive approach to emotion should specify the individual and situational factors governing the expression of these component reactions, as well as their integration into coherent behavioral sequences. Such an approach must incorporate a variety of perspectives, three of which will be examined below.

PERSPECTIVES ON EMOTION

Three perspectives on emotion seem fundamental: the biological (including physiological and phylogenetic), the cultural, and the cognitive. They have often been considered mutually exclusive, but we shall attempt to show that they are really complementary, and each leads in its own way to similar conclusions.

The Biological Perspective

The emotions have frequently been classed among the most "primitive," "animal-like," or "instinctual" of psychological phenomena. Yet man appears to be the most emotional of animals, the richness and variety of human experience being as much due to this fact as to man's great intellectual endowment. Indeed, the traditional distinction between the emotional and the rational, deeply rooted in the western philosophic tradition (cf. Beach, 1955), is to a large extent arbitrary and has probably been as much of a hindrance as a help when it comes to theorizing about emotion. The pervasiveness of this distinction, and its mischievousness, is well illustrated in widespread notions concerning the neurophysiology of emotion. It has long been traditional to associate emotions with the viscera, and in previous volumes of this series strong arguments were made to define emotions in terms of visceral activity (Dunlap, 1928; Wenger, 1950). These peripheral definitions have not been widely accepted, partly because of their inherent difficulties, and partly because interest has increasingly turned toward central neural mechanisms. The shift in emphasis from peripheral to central mechanisms, however, has not generally carried with it any change in the tradition of assigning the emotions to more "primitive" structures, e.g., the reticular formation (Lindsley, 1950), the hypothalamus (Bard, 1950), and the limbic system or "visceral brain" (MacLean, 1960). But as Pribram (1960) has pointed out, these supposedly phylogenetically old and so-called primitive structures have undergone evolutionary development just as have cortical structures, and they reach their greatest degree of development in man. Moreover, it now appears that they play as vital a role in cognitive functioning as they do in emotion (Douglas, 1967; Pribram, 1960). Thus, both phylogenetically and physiologically, there seems to be little reason to draw a sharp distinction between the emotional and the cognitive, and to assign to the former an especially primitive function. A similar conclusion has been reached by Leeper (1965) via a slightly different route.

What are the implications of this fact for the psychology of emotion? In the first place, there is no reason to require, as Plutchik (1962) seems to do, that an emotion must be traceable in prototypic form throughout the phylogenetic scale if it is to be considered primary or basic. In the second place, it means that any analysis of emotion, even when approached from a phylogenetic or physiological perspective, will have to incorporate notions which traditionally have been associated with cognitive rather than affective psychology (cf. Pribram, 1967).

The above argument should not be taken to mean that a biological perspective has little to offer in the study of emotion. On the contrary, an examination of the evolutionary significance or adaptive value of the behavior patterns associated with emotions is not only desirable but necessary. For example, when one looks at aggression from an adaptive point of view, there appears to be not one but a variety of response patterns. There is aggression centered around prey capture, aggression in response to pain, aggression in defense of young, territorial aggression, and others still. These different types of aggression can be distinguished not only in terms of eliciting stimuli, but also with respect to response topography and physiological mechanisms (Moyer, 1967). What might be the evolutionary basis of human aggression? Before we can even begin to answer this question, we must cease to consider aggression as though it were a single phenomenon. Any act of aggression may be divided into many component reactions, and each of these may be more or less influenced by a wide variety of biological factors, depending upon the circumstances. That is, all the characteristics of an aggressive act must be detailed before its origins can be investigated in a meaningful way.

To complicate matters further, the characterization of an aggressive act must encompass more than a description of the response and its consequences, no matter how complete from a strictly behavioral or physiological point of view this response description might be. This is evident from the difficulties encountered by such writers as Buss (1961) and Berkowitz (1962) in trying to work out the sticky inferential problem of "intending to harm" as a possible criterion of aggression. In the end, they find no way of eliminating such intent in the definition of aggression. This effectively eliminates the potential elegance that might have been achieved by restricting the subject matter of aggression to overt attack behavior alone.

The situation becomes even more complex when we consider the emotion of anger, for not all aggression can be described as angry. As previously noted, emotional concepts presume systems of judgment. In the case of anger, the role of arbitrariness or justifiability of a frustrating experience has been much debated. It has been argued that frustration is the basic stimulus for aggression, and that arbitrariness does not alter the impulse or instigation to aggression (anger), but merely encourages its expression. Systematic research on such a question must begin by making possible the differentiation, both conceptually and empirically, of aggression as a broad behavioral category from aggression as an aspect of the emotional response, anger. This obviously calls for a theory of anger, and of emotion in general, which exists now in only the most rudimentary form.

The Cultural Perspective

The emotions are deeply rooted in man's cultural as well as his biological heritage. Viable social systems exist under the most diverse political and economic ideologies, e.g., monarchies, democracies, dictatorships, feudalism, capitalism, communism, etc.; but no social system can long survive once it fails to provide for the emotional needs of its citizens (cf. Hebb and Thompson, 1954), or fails to control or channel those emotions in ways tolerable to or advantageous for the social system. The complex interplay between emotion and society has been emphasized especially by the Freudians and neo-Freudians, in fact, by all conflict theories of human personality (cf. Maddi, 1968), as well as by Soviet psychologists under the influence of dialectical materialism (cf. Simonov, 1969). Different societies have molded and shaped emotional experience and expression by a great variety of means, depending upon historical, geographic, economic, and other factors. Four of these means will be described below.

One way in which culture influences emotion is through the perception or *appraisal of emotional stimuli.* Everyone is familiar with anecdotal stories of innocuous stimuli being fear-inducing in one culture or anger-inducing in another, or how foods considered as delicacies by one people are repugnant to another. There is also considerable "hard" data for cultural influences on differential perception. Thus, Segall *et al.* (1966) have presented evidence for cultural differences in susceptibility to optical illusions; Tursky and Sternbach (1967) have demonstrated ethnic differences in psychophysiological response to pain; and Schachter (1967) has made strong arguments for the influence of social context on the interpretation of bodily states during emotion. This is not to say that some stimuli are not biologically more important to some emotions than others, nor that the relationship between emotional stimuli and responses is simply a matter of prior association. We have argued elsewhere against such a view (Averill, 1968b; Lazarus, 1968), but the plasticity of human perception and thought cannot be gainsaid.

Direct influence on emotional expression without the necessary intervention of altered perception is a second way in which culture may influence the emotional response. As La Barre (1947) has pointed out, the outward expression of emotion is subject to great cultural variability, even for those gestures, e.g., crying and laughing, which are generally considered to be biologically determined. Culture molds emotional responses to conform to certain standards, limits the types of responses or emotion-relevant coping possibilities available to the individual, and helps determine the appropriateness or acceptability of the response in relationship to the stimulus situation.

A third way in which culture influences emotion is through the *shaping of social relationships and systems of judgment* which emotional concepts presuppose. In Japanese, for example, there is an emotional concept, *amae*, which appears to have no equivalent in European languages. This is surprising to many Japanese because *amae* seems to be a very basic emotion, observable even in animals; and, according to Doi (1962), it is a key to understanding Japanese personality and political institutions. Roughly translated, *amae* can be described as a wish to be loved or a need for dependency. Unlike the English concept of dependency, however, *amae* generally has a positive connotation. Perhaps both *amae* and dependency can be considered aspects of a more fundamental phenomenon, the need for social attachment. Attachment behavior and its emotional concomitants can be thought of as products of evolutionary pressures toward group living, and is of considerable biological significance in numerous lower species and all higher primates (Hamburg, 1963). How this need for attachment will be expressed in humans depends upon the nature of the culture or social organization. The Japanese culture appears to have given the need for social attachment explicit and generally positive recognition in the concept of *amae*. Western cultures, on the other hand, have tended to place more emphasis on the opposite, and also biologically important, requirement for individual autonomy. Consequently, negative aspects of attachment behavior have come to be emphasized, as in the concept of dependency, and dependency needs are thought of as a childish and often ego-alien property of personality.

The above example also illustrates the complex interplay between the biological and cultural determinants of emotion. Similar analyses could be made of anger, which describes aggressive behavior and feelings occurring under certain culturally prescribed relationships, and of other emotions as well. To use a rather crude analogy, phylogenesis may provide the ingredients for the emotional pie, but culture determines how the pie is cut.

There is still a fourth way in which culture can influence emotion. Certain *conventional forms of behavior*, e.g., mourning rites, courting and marriage rituals, and institutionalized aggression as in athletics and warfare, stem from and help reinforce the particular social structure. These aspects of behavior have generally not been considered under the topic of emotion because often they do not relate specifically to the emotional needs and experiences of the individuals involved and they may not even significantly alter the basic emotional response. Yet the dividing line between social custom and individual emotional expression is not distinct. When a widow wears black and refrains from social contact following the death of her husband, how much of this is an expression of her "true" emotion, and how much an expression of social custom?

We do not wish to imply that the above four ways in which culture may influence emotion are mutually exclusive or exhaustive. What we do wish to illustrate is that emotions are a function of both phylogenetic and cultural factors. The former are frequently emphasized (and therefore have been treated only cursorily here and in the previous discussion), but the latter are often ignored. Neither, however, can be considered more "basic" than the other. Rather, their relative importance will vary depending upon the particular emotion, e.g., fear as opposed to guilt. Moreover, when any given emotion is broken down into its component parts, some of these parts may be primarily biologically determined while others may be traced to cultural origins.

For example, the form of attack in anger (i.e., the method of physical and/or verbal assault) is clearly influenced by cultural factors, while the physiological disturbance, and perhaps even certain of the facial expressive characteristics, may reveal mainly biological determinants. In this connection, Ekman and Friesen (in press) have suggested that while facial expressions may be essentially pan-cultural, the affects which are linked to these expressions, the rules of facial display and the consequences in the behavioral reactions of others, can all vary enormously from one culture to another. This again illustrates the need to analyze complex emotional responses into component reactions before considering biological and cultural determinants. Moreover, both biological and cultural influences must be filtered through the individual psyche, with its peculiar past history, coping resources, and present circumstances. It is to these latter, viewed from a cognitive perspective, that we now turn.

The Cognitive Perspective

A central theme of this paper is that the person or infra-human animal must be regarded as an evaluating organism, one who searches his environment for cues about what he needs and wants, and evaluates each stimulus as to its personal relevance and significance. Emotions should be regarded as a function of such cognitive activity, each particular emotion presumably associated with a different evaluation. Biological and cultural determinants of emotion, as well as the individual's own past history and psychological structure, can operate only through his immediate perception of objects and their significance for him.

The cognitive approach to emotion has been epitomized by Arnold's (1960) use of the concept of appraisal, and Lazarus' (1966; 1968) references to *appraisal* and *reappraisal.* This is not to say that the concept originated with these writers. Indeed, we find it employed, albeit less systematically, in the context of emotion many years earlier, for example, in Grinker and Spiegel's (1945) discussion of battle stress. And even noncognitive theorists such as Duffy (1941) have emphasized the importance of the person's interpretation of the stimulus situation in determining emotional experience and expression.

Extending Magda Arnold's position just a bit, we argue that the pattern of arousal observed in emotion derives from impulses to action which are generated by the individual's appraised situation, and by the evaluated possibilities available for action. In the negative emotions, i.e., where threat is appraised, these involve action tendencies (as Arnold refers to them) such as avoidance or attack. The subjective features of emotion derive from the appraised condition of the organism, including alternatives to action and the coping impulses actually generated, feedback from bodily reactions (Hohman, 1966), and the perceived consequences of the act. The point is that each emotion involves its own particular kind of appraisal, its own particular kinds of action tendencies, and hence its own particular constellation of physiological changes which are part of the mobilization to action, whether or not these action tendencies are actually expressed or inhibited.

Two key ideas are contained in the above position. First, each emotional reaction, regardless of its content, is a function of a particular kind of cognition or *appraisal.* In other words, the emotion of anger requires one kind of appraisal, fear another, grief and joy still different ones, etc. Second, the emotional response itself consists of an *organized* syndrome, each component of which reflects a different but important element in the total reaction. Thus, there are given physiological changes in anger, and these are presumably different from those in fear, etc. (Although, as we have said earlier, a common element of activation may also be identified.) Similarly, the cognitive-subjective component of the emotion reflects an essential element of the total reaction, that is, the perceived danger or threat, or in positive emotional states, an appraised sense of security, mastery, or a desirable bond between individuals. And, since the emotion involves some impulse to action which mobilizes the physiological changes, there are motor-behavioral components as well. True, these may be inhibited in the interest of other social demands, but the action impulses (e.g., to avoid or attack) characterizing different emotions are distinctive to those emotions, and the motor-expressive features (e.g., facial expressions or bodily postures) are in many cases universal in the species, though modifiable by social custom. As noted in the previous section, all three dimensions of reactivity, the motor-behavioral, physiological, and the cognitive-subjective, are integral parts of the emotional response, and, excepting some problems which we will discuss in the section on methodology, the particular pattern which they display provides one of the trademarks of a given emotion.

In considering further the cognitive determinants of emotion, it is necessary to ask two questions. First, what is *the nature of the cognitions* (or appraisals) which underlie separate emotional reactions (e.g., fear, guilt, grief, joy, etc.). Second, what are the determining *antecedent conditions of these cognitions.* Since the analysis is relational or transactional, the determining conditions must be of two types: *situational* (referring to environmental factors) and *dispositional* (referring to the psychological structure of the individual, e.g., his beliefs, attitudes, personality traits, etc.). The problem is to specify the manner in which these situational and dispositional factors interact to produce a given emotional response.

Biological and cultural factors undoubtedly contribute to the development of psychological dispositions. Thus, phylogenesis disposes the organism to respond in a biologically adaptive fashion to certain types of stimuli, i.e., in a manner contributing to species (though not necessarily to individual) survival. In humans, the response may no longer be adaptive due to social evolution, and it may also be greatly modified by individual experience and social strictures, but the biological disposition to respond may nevertheless remain strong. Analogously, through socialization, a culture may impose upon its members certain belief systems, standards of conduct, etc., which shape the appraisal of emotional stimuli (say, by determining what is threatening) and which determine the modes of response that are ego-syntonic or ego-alien.

From the cognitive perspective, then, it is assumed that the person has certain dispositions to search out, respond to, or selectively attend to stimuli of certain types, and that these dispositions may be the product of phylogenetic, cultural, or ontogenetic development, and probably in most instances, the interplay of all three. On the basis of such dispositions, the individual, or a given class of individuals or species, cognitively filters stimulus information, and the resulting appraisal determines whether the situation is evaluated as relevant, threatening, frustrating, sustaining, etc. This appraisal also includes an evaluation of the options for coping and their potential consequences. Cognitive processes thus create the emotional response out of the organism-environment transaction and shape it into anger, fear, grief, etc.

There is one final step in the argument pertaining to the arousal and reduction of the emotional response. Emotional responses are constantly in a state of flux; that is, they may rise and fall, and change in quality rapidly when either circumstances force an alteration of the earlier appraisal, or when defensive modes of thought result in a reinterpretation of the plight of the individual. In short, feedback from the continuous interplay between the conditions causing an emotion and the effects of efforts to cope with them changes the cognitions shaping the emotional reaction.

The senior author has argued elsewhere (Lazarus, 1966; 1968) that there are two basic kinds of processes by which individuals may cope with threat or anticipated harm. The first consists of *direct actions,* such as attack and avoidance, which are designed to alter the organism-environment relationship in such a way as to reduce or eliminate the threat (or, in the case of positive emotions, to sustain or actualize the positive condition). These direct actions may, of course, be inhibited due to internal or external constraints, but the impulses to them, and the accompanying physiological arousal, form an essential aspect of emotion. Sometimes direct action is successful in removing the threat, or in sustaining the desirable condition, but at other times it will fail, or bring in its wake additional threats or harms, and hence new appraisals. Therefore, one way in which emotions can rise and fall, or change in quality, consists in the continuing changes in the organism-environment relationship as a consequence of (direct action) coping processes whose effects on the environment, or on the person, feed back to the appraisal mechanism.

The second type of coping process by which emotional reactions can be aroused or reduced is entirely cognitive, in that it involves no direct actions, merely further evaluations. Elsewhere (Lazarus, 1966; 1968) this has been referred to as *reappraisal.* It is particularly likely as the predominant mode of coping where direct actions are not possible. Reappraisal may proceed from a benign appraisal to a threatening reappraisal, or from an intially threatening appraisal to a benign reappraisal. It may be predicated on objective, new stimulus evidence, and hence involve good "reality testing," or it may represent a "defensive" distortion of reality. The midnight telephone ring might initially be regarded as signalling bad news about someone we love, but be rapidly reappraised as merely a wrong number; or the same telephone ring, expected from a friend and initially responded to as benign, may suddenly convey dreaded information. In the case of an ambiguous cue, one can readily imagine how personality-based belief systems about the environment and one's relation to it could be influential in shaping the initial appraisal, a reappraisal on the basis of additional information, or the direct-action coping process. In any event, the appraisal process must be viewed as a continual searching for, sifting through, and evaluation of the cues which a person or infrahuman animal confronts. Some appraisals are rejected and others accepted on the basis of both the steady inflow of information and the psychological dispositions which influence transactions with the environment. The rises and falls of emotion, and the shifts in its quality, reflect this continuing cognitive activity of appraisal and reappraisal. We know from the clinical research literature that defensive reappraisals are often capable of lowering threat-based emotional reactions even in the absence of real changes in the organism-environment relationship. An illustration of this is found in a study by Wolff *et al.* (1964) of parents with a child suffering from terminal cancer. Those parents who seemed successfully to deny the fatal character of the child's illness also exhibited lower levels of serum hydrocortisone (a measure of stress reaction or negatively toned emotion) than did those not so well defended.

The above brief sketch presents the core of our cognitive approach to emotion. Obviously, much theoretical and empirical work remains to be done. A theory is needed which goes beyond the point of merely stating a frame of reference; it is necessary to detail the cognitive factors involved in particular emotional responses. The literature reveals some efforts to take this step, although there is little consensus. One obstacle has been an overriding (but only partially deserved) distrust of phenomenological approaches, which have been the ones to emphasize cognitive activity as an essential aspect of emotion. There is no reason, however, why cognitive processes cannot be defined as objectively as other intervening psychological variables. If a cyberneticist such as MacKay (1962) can give meanings, albeit somewhat elliptically, to terms like "evaluating" and "significance" in connection with automata or machines, then psychologists should be able to give them scientifically valid meanings when applied to human beings. The important theoretical and research task in a cognitive theory of emotion is to identify the nature of the relevant cognitive processes, to establish their determinants in the stimulus configuration and in the psychological structure of the individual, and to link these to emotional arousal and reduction, as well as to the quality of the emotion experienced.

METHODOLOGICAL PROBLEMS IN RESEARCH ON EMOTION

In this section we shall present some research which deals with two methodological issues central to the above arguments. The first issue concerns the problem of response discrepancies. If emotions are conceived of as response syndromes, what inferences can be made when there is lack of agreement among different measures (e.g., self-report and physiological indices) of ostensibly the same emotion? The second issue concerns the methods by which emotional appraisal can be studied.

Response Discrepancies

One of the most vexing problems in research on emotion is the frequently reported lack of agreement among response indices. Whether emotional responses are divided horizontally into physiological, subjective, and behavioral dimensions, or vertically into relatively discrete acts which encompass all three dimensions, there is typically little agreement among measures (Krause, 1961; Martin, 1961; King, 1968). There are two basic approaches to this problem. The first is to view response discrepancies as due to methodological inadequacies, e.g., uncontrolled extraneous variables, unreliability in measurement, improper statistical analyses, etc. Elsewhere, we have demonstrated that the correlation between two physiological indices of stress (heart rate and skin conductance) can be increased through improved scoring techniques and by using within-rather than between-subject analyses (Lazarus *et al.*, 1963; Malmstrom *et al.*, 1965; Opton *et al.*, 1965). Mordkoff (1964), working in our laboratory, has similarly demonstrated that the near-continuous recording of self-reported affect and within-individual analyses can considerably increase the relationship between self-report and physiological indices of stress.

But even if assessment were completely adequate from a technical point of view, the relationship between different measures of emotion still would be modest. This leads to the second approach, which treats response discrepancies as potential sources of information concerning the individual's attempt to cope with his environment. This latter approach assumes that each response dimension has its own particular adaptive functions. For example, in addition to communicating subjective experience, verbal reports can also dissimulate, and can be used to create any kind of social impression the person desires, consciously or unconsciously. The same can be said of motor-behavioral patterns, although not all emotional responses are equally susceptible to modification. Ekman and Friesen (1968) have reported evidence of micromovements in facial expression which pass so rapidly that they may seem to remain unnoticed when the observer reports, but which may inadvertently communicate, for example, contempt or disgust, which weren't otherwise evident. Ekman colorfully refers to this as the "leakage" of information.

Contradictions may take many forms. For example, the person says he is not angry, but gives motor-expressive evidence (perhaps in the form of Ekman's concept of leakage) through, say, a clenched fist or the facial movements associated with anger, or physiological evidence of anger; or perhaps, as in Grinker and Spiegel's (1954) airmen, the emotional state (in this case, fear) is documented by psychosomatic or other neurotic symptoms which break through in spite of the denial. One can see many permutations and combinations of such contradictions, and it is likely that some are normatively more common and psychologically more interesting than others, reflecting certain characteristic patterns of coping.

Implied in the above argument is that the precise pattern of agreement and disagreement between emotional response indices contains within it information about the kind of transaction which the person is having within himself and with various aspects of his environment. This transaction is inextricably tied up with the emotional response itself, sometimes an integral part of the response (as in the mobilization of attack against harm, or the avoidance of that harm), sometimes a way of covering up or disguising that response, or interpreting it in some way which is ego-syntonic rather than ego-alien. These psychologically meaningful contradictions between response indices must be carefully distinguished from the many artifacts of measurement which also reduce agreement among measures.

The key methodological point is that we must not automatically disregard disagreements among the various emotional indices as evidence either of a shaky conceptual basis for the concept of emotion as a response syndrome, or of the failure of our measurement techniques. Quite the contrary, these very "contradictions" should be *expected* on the basis of what we know about coping with internal and external demands. To repeat an argument made earlier, emotional responses must be broken down into component reactions, and the biological, cultural, and psychological determinants of these reactions examined. The pattern of agreements and disagreements among components may then provide information not only about the kind of emotion being experienced, but also about the way it is integrated with intrapersonal and interpersonal relationships and demands. In short, the assessment of emotion cannot be divorced from other coping processes, but must be seen as one portion of the whole.

Some of these points are illustrated in a recent study by Weinstein *et al.* (1968), who investigated the relationship between defensive dispositions (in this case, repression-sensitization, as measured by the *L, K, Hy-Dn,* and *R-S* scales from the MMPI and the *Gi* scale from the CPI) and the discrepancy between self-report and autonomic indices of stress. In a reanalysis of six previously conducted experiments, so-called repressors showed relatively greater autonomic than self-report reactions to a stressful film, *Subincision*, which depicts crude genital operations among Australian aborigines. Sensitizers, on the other hand, tended to show the opposite pattern of reaction. These results indicate how emotional response measures, even when discrepant, may reflect important psychodynamic processes. That they also may reflect cultural dynamics has been documented elsewhere (Lazarus *et al.*, 1966; Averill *et al.*, 1969).

The Investigation of Appraisal and Reappraisal

It is not enough merely to say that cognition is central to emotion. The problem is to identify the cognitive processes, that is, the appraisals and reappraisals, which determine various emotional responses, and to specify their antecedent conditions. Moreover, concrete operations must be specified for the investigation of these processes. Four basic strategies are available for this purpose, and we shall illustrate each of these with some empirical research, mainly from our laboratory. For other reviews of this research, see Lazarus and Opton (1966) and Lazarus (1968).

Direct manipulation. In a group of studies which appeared beginning in 1964, efforts were made to intervene directly to alter the manner in which subjects appraised or interpreted the events portrayed in stressful motion picture films. In the first such effort (Speisman *et al.*, 1964), three sound tracks were created for the previously described *Subincision* film. These tracks were compared with respect to their capacity to raise or lower autonomic and subjective stress reactions of subjects watching the film. A "trauma" track was found to enhance the stress-producing value of the film, while "denial" and "intellectualization" tracks reduced it. Subsequently (Lazarus and Alfert, 1964), the approach was modified by transforming the sound tracks into orientation passages which were played before the subjects watched the film. Essentially the same results were obtained. The lowering of stress reactions in this way was referred to as "the short-circuiting of threat." This principle of short-circuiting was then extended to another film dealing with wood-shop accidents (Lazarus et al.,1965). And in a more recent study (Folkins et al.,1968), it was demonstrated that the techniques used in desensitization therapy (that is, relaxation and cognitive rehearsal) were also capable of lowering stress reactions, especially the technique of cognitive rehearsal which involves working over an expected trauma through imagery and thought.

The above studies consistently confirmed that the same potentially disturbing movie event produces very different degrees of emotional disturbance in subjects, depending upon how it is interpreted, i.e., on the kind of appraisal the person makes of it. The manipulation of ego-defenses and cognitive rehearsal, moreover, do not exhaust the ways in which emotional appraisal may be directly influenced. Other means which have received experimental investigation include changing the demand characteristics of the situation (Orne, 1962), providing alternative interpretations for one's own reactions (Schachter, 1967), altering the adaptation level or baseline against which incoming stimuli are evaluated (Harvey, 1965), providing knowledge of group norms or performance capabilities (Orne, 1965), and making available alternative response options (Berkowitz, 1967). These different ways are not necessarily mutually exclusive or independent, although the operations involved have generally been quite distinct, reflecting the diverse theoretical orientations of the investigators. Nevertheless, it has been amply demonstrated that the direct manipulation of emotional appraisal is not only feasible but also a strategy of great potential. Unfortunately, most studies using this method have not moved beyond the stage of demonstration. The more difficult task of theoretical analysis and synthesis has barely begun.

Indirect manipulation. Here the role of appraisal and reappraisal in producing or reducing stress or emotional reactions is studied, not by manipulating cognitive processes, but by the manipulation of variables on which such cognitions depend. Anticipation time is one such variable which has recently become the focus of considerable attention; indeed, psychological stress may be largely a matter of the anticipation of harm (Lazarus, 1966). Typically, stress reactions mount as the moment of confrontation approaches, but this general tendency may vary considerably depending upon the duration of anticipation (Breznitz, 1967; Nomikos et al.,1968), prior experience in similar situations

(Epstein, 1967), individual differences in defensive style (Goldstein *et al.*, 1965), and the manner of coping during the anticipatory period (Janis, 1958). Thus, it is evident that cognitive processes underlying emotion may be investigated through the manipulation of anticipation. Such an approach is well illustrated by a dissertation performed in our laboratory by Folkins (in press), who studied variations in stress reactions as a function of anticipation time. Here we will consider inferences based primarily upon the physiological measures of stress obtained by Folkins; ego functioning, assessed from self-report data, will be discussed subsequently.

Briefly, Folkins made his experimental groups await an electric shock for varying periods of time: 5 seconds, 30 seconds, 1 minute, 3 minutes, 5 minutes, or 20 minutes. (Control groups awaited the turning on of an electric light.) The passage of time was indicated by a large clock clearly visible to the subject. Continuous recordings of skin conductance, heart rate, respiration rate, and finger pulse volume allowed an assessment of the ebb and flow of stress reactions during anticipation. In addition to differences in the patterning of stress reactions during anticipation, the six intervals each produced differences in the maximal degree of stress. That is, physiological reactions (peak readings recorded during the last ten seconds prior to the anticipated shock, corrected for covariance with prewarning baselines) increased progressively from the 5 to the 30 second interval, and reached a maximum with the 1 minute anticipation period. Reactions then decreased during the 3 and 5 minute intervals, only to rise sharply again under the 20 minutes anticipation condition.

These results indicate a complex relationship between anticipation time and physiological stress reactions. What makes the same objective threat (electric shock) produce different patterns and levels of disturbance with different periods of anticipation? Presumably, the physiological reactions reflected the subjects' attempts to cope cognitively with the situation, since direct action was not possible in this setting. (The differences between stress and nonstress conditions indicate that responses were not simply a function of waiting for any stimulus.) One might guess that during the 5 second anticipation interval there was no opportunity to comprehend fully the threat and hence only a minor response. With longer periods (30 seconds and 1 minute), the nature of the threat may have been more fully realized but there was insufficient time for adequate countermeasures to be taken. Large stress or "panic" reactions were the result (cf. the report of Fritz and Marks, 1954, that death and injury were higher for persons receiving a 1 minute warning of an approaching tornado than for those receiving no warning). With further increase in time, the subject was perhaps able to reappraise the situation, to assure himself that no great harm could come to him, and consequently there was a diminution in physiological stress response. The 20 minute interval seemed to reverse this pattern of reassurance, however, for reasons which are not altogether clear. Three possibilities seem to exist. First, it is possible that subjects became frustrated, restless, and even annoyed at the very long waiting period. Second, reappraisals could have occurred in which coping strategies originally considered adequate were re-evaluated as ineffective. With sufficient time, a subject's defensive armament might become exhausted in such a process. Third, the long waiting period might itself have become a cue of danger. That is, an event which required a 20 minute wait, could not, indeed, be viewed as minor, and apprehension about the shock might well have risen with such an ominous appraisal. These are, of course, speculations, but they are not without foundation in the self-reports of the subjects.

Inferences from self-report data. After a subject has been exposed to a stressful experience, it is possible to assess through his own self-reports not only the impact of the emotional experience, but also the modes of thought in which he has engaged. This is not the place to discuss the many methodological problems involved in the use of self-report data, or to enumerate their advantages. Rather, we will simply illustrate their application with some concrete examples from our laboratory.

In addition to the previously described physiological measures, Folkins (in press) assessed the psychological changes during anticipation through the use of affect rating scales, a word association test, and a detailed interview, which was analyzed according to a revised version of the Haan-Kroeber model of ego-functioning (cf. Haan, 1969). For the regular experimental groups, this material was collected retrospectively, following the anticipated shock (which was not actually delivered). To control for possible distortion, other subjects were interrupted during the anticipation intervals for on-the-spot assessment of ego functioning.

The responses on the rating scales and word association test indicated a pattern of disturbance similar to that previously described in connection with the physiological data. With reference to ego functioning, moreover, cognitive processes were more flexible and reality oriented during the periods of least disturbance (the 5 second, and 3 and 5 minute anticipation intervals), and more disorganized during the periods of greatest disturbance (the 30 second, and 1 and 20 minute anticipation intervals). The interpretation of these results unfortunately is made difficult by the fact that within any given anticipation interval, between-subject correlational analyses revealed no consistent relationship between ego functioning and stress reactions.

Another example of the assessment of cognitive processes from self-report data comes from one of our earliest studies of film-induced stress reactions (Lazarus *et al.*, 1962). In this study, subjects watched two motion picture films, a benign control film and the *Subincision* film, while autonomic measurements were made during the films. At the end of the *Subincision* film session, subjects were interviewed to determine their reactions and styles of coping. Three basic patterns of response were observed. In one there appeared to be emotional flooding, illustrated by the statement, "It was disgusting; it made me sick to my stomach." A second appeared to involve intellectualized detachment, illustrated by, "It was an interesting anthropological study." A third suggested denial, as in the comment, "It didn't bother me a bit." Incidentally, it was precisely this interview material which led us to develop the denial and intellectualizing sound tracks used in the previously described Speisman *et al.* (1964) experiment.

When we attempted to relate these self-report data to physiological indices of stress, we found no differences in autonomic disturbance during the film between subjects reporting emotional flooding, those exhibiting denial, and those displaying intellectualization. This is, of course, seemingly contradictory to the findings of the studies involving direct manipulations of appraisal, where, for example, denial and intellectualization was imposed on subjects by means of sound tracks or prophylactic orientation passages.

The contradiction between these two methods of approach to the study of cognitive processes underlying emotional arousal or reduction must be explained. Our theoretical solution is to note that a subject will develop successful defenses only when he has time to cognitively rehearse or otherwise prepare for the impending stress (cf. Folkins *et al.*, 1968), or is provided with a ready made form of coping (cf. Lazarus, 1968). An excellent clinical example of a chronic stress situation is reported by Wolff *et al.* (1964). These clinical researchers found that some parents of dying children developed denial defenses, and that these parents showed less stress (evidenced by serum hydrocortisone) than those who were not so defended.

In short, one must be careful to check one method of research on the appraisal process against another, since occasionally, and for reasons related to the different adaptive demands involved, they produce seemingly contradictory results.

Selection of dispositional variables. The final method of studying appraisal and reappraisal involves the selection of subjects who differ in their emotional predispositions. Such differences may be due to biological, cultural, or psychological factors. Thus, different species may show differential tendencies toward aggression or flight as characteristic modes of coping. Even within species there may be considerable differences in emotional dispositions (e.g., beagle dogs are less aggressive than fox terriers, and female mice are less aggressive than males). Such biological predispositions undoubtedly also exist in humans, although their influence is typically obscured by the great variability introduced by cultural and psychological factors. Some of the ways in which culture can influence emotional dispositions have already been discussed. The cross-cultural comparison of emotional reactions under controlled laboratory conditions is little used, but is potentially a very important method of varying dispositional variables (Averill *et al.*, 1969).

One dispositional variable that has been frequently investigated both within and between cultures is defensive style; it effectively illustrates the selection method of studying appraisal. In the study by Speisman et al. (1964), in which prophylactic sound tracks r. 'uced film-induced stress reactions, two kinds of subjects had been selected for treatment — those who could be characterized as having the disposition to cope with threat by denial, and those inclined to employ intellectualizing defenses. An interaction was found between the effects of the two defense-oriented sound tracks and these defensive dispositions; deniers showed more stress reduction than intellectualizers when the denial sound track was played and intellectualizers achieved more stress reduction when they heard the intellectualization sound track.

Actually, the evidence of this interaction was not particularly strong in the Speisman et al. (1964) study. Moreover, although the argument is plausible and has had wide acceptance, until recently there has not been any striking confirmation of the principle that stress reduction by direct manipulation depends on the compatibility of the experimental intervention with the cognitive or defensive dispositions of the subjects. A recent dissertation by Andrew (1967), however, has provided important supportive evidence, and indicates that the principle can also be applied in the clinical context.

Andrew worked with patients anticipating surgery for inguinal hernia. She intervened prior to the operation with a factual instructional statement about the nature of inguinal hernia and the strategy of surgery, an approach similar in method to our use of an intellectualizing sound track or orientation in film-induced stress. By means of personality assessment devices and concepts developed in Michael Goldstein's laboratory at UCLA, Andrew divided the patients into three types, based on defensive style or disposition: those likely to employ avoidant forms of coping; those inclined to sensitizing defenses; and nonspecific defenders who seemed to have no decided defensive preference. She found that given the instructional statement about the operation, avoidant patients were retarded in their objective rates of postsurgical recovery, and needed more medication than avoidant patients not so treated; contrariwise, the nonspecific defenders were facilitated in their rates of postsurgical recovery if they had been given the factual statement; the sensitizers showed no effect of the experimental treatment, and in general, showed the fastest and least complicated postsurgical recovery.

CONCLUDING REMARKS

Historically, emotion and cognition have been viewed as contradictory or incompatible psychological phenomena. Nevertheless, we believe that the resurgence of a cognitive emphasis in psychology — which views man and infra-human animals as information processors and as evaluators of their fate —

and also an increased sophistication concerning the role of biological and cultural factors, are helping to restore the concept of emotion to the center of attention in psychology. The preceding discussions of the place of emotion in psychology, the various perspectives about emotion, and the methodological problems in research on emotion provide a sort of schematic plan for a cognitively oriented theory and research program on emotion. This plan is predicated on the idea that the cognitions determining different emotional responses (syndromes) must be identified, and in turn, this leads naturally to a search for the antecedent conditions, both in the stimulus configuration and within the psychological structure of the individual, which govern the expression of the component reactions. The qualifying word "schematic" attests to the open-ended, provisional nature of this plan, which must be filled in by substantive theoretical propositions about the intervening cognitions of anger, fear, grief, joy, etc., and the conditions under which they will emerge. This brief paper, serving as an overview of a conceptual point of view, cannot serve as the place to fill in the theoretical details, or to attempt to bridge the many gaps in our empirical knowledge. Rather, our aim has been to indicate some lines of convergence in the contemporary study of emotion, and to suggest concepts and approaches which may aid further theoretical and empirical research.

REFERENCES

Andrew, June M. (1967). Coping styles, stress-relevant learning, and recovery from surgery. Unpublished doctoral dissertation, Univ. of California, Los Angeles.

Arnold, Magda B. (1960). *Emotion and personality*. Columbia Univ. Press, New York.

Averill, J.R. (1968a). Operationism, metaphysics, and the philosophy of ordinary language. Psychol. Reports, 22, 861-887.

Averill, J.R. (1968b). Grief: Its nature and significance. *Psychol. Bull.*, 70, 721-748.

Averill, J.R. (1969). Autonomic response patterns during sadness and mirth. *Psychophysiology*, 5, 399-414.

Averill, J.R., and Opton, E.M., Jr. (1968). Psychophysiological assessment: Rationale and problems. In P. McReynolds (Ed.), *Advances in psychological assessment*. Vol. 1. Science and Behavior Books, Palo Alto, California.

Averill, J.R., Opton, E.M., Jr., and Lazarus, R.S. (1969). Cross-cultural studies of psychophysiological responses during stress and emotion. *Intern. J. Psychol.*, 4, 83-102.

Ax, A.F. (1953). The physiological differentiation between fear and anger in humans. *Psychosomat. Med.*, 15, 433-442.

Bard, P. (1950). Central nervous mechanisms for the expression of anger in animals. In M. L. Reymert (Ed.), *Feelings and emotions: The Mooseheart symposium*. McGraw-Hill, New York.

Beach, F.A. (1955). The descent of instinct. *Psychol. Rev.*, 62, 401-410.

Bedford, E. (1957). Emotions. *Aristotelian Soc. Proc.*, 57, 281-304.

Berkowitz, L. (1962). *Aggression: A social psychological analysis*. McGraw-Hill, New York.

Berkowitz, L. (1967). Experiments on automation and intent in human aggression. In C. D. Clement and D. B. Lindsley (Eds.), *Aggression and defense*. Univ. of California Press, Berkeley.

Berlyne, D.E. (1960). *Conflict, arousal and curiosity*. McGraw-Hill, New York.
Berlyne, D.E. (1967). Arousal and reinforcement. In D. Levine (Ed.), *Nebraska symposium on motivation*. Univ. of Nebraska Press, Lincoln.
Breznitz, S. (1967). Incubation of threat: Duration of anticipation and false alarm as determinants of the fear reaction to an unavoidable frightening event. *J. Exp. Res. Personality*, 2, 173-179.
Buss, A.H. (1961). *The psychology of aggression*. Wiley, New York.
Cannon, W.B. (1929). *Bodily changes in pain, hunger, fear, and rage* (2nd ed.). Appleton, New York.
Doi, L.T. (1962). *Amae:* A key concept for understanding Japanese personality structure. In R. J. Smith and R. K. Beardsley (Eds.), *Japanese culture: Its development and characteristics*. Viking Fund Publications in Anthropology, (34) WGFAR, New York.
Douglas, R.J. (1967). The hippocampus and behavior. *Psychol. Bull.*, 67, 416-442.
Duffy, E. (1941). An explanation of "emotional" phenomena without the use of the concept "emotion." *J. Gen. Psychol.*, 25, 283-293.
Duffy, E. (1962). *Activation and behavior*. Wiley, New York.
Dunlap, K. (1928). Emotion as dynamic background. In M. L. Reymert (Ed.), *Feelings and emotions: The Wittenberg symposium*. Clark Univ. Press, Worcester, Massachusetts.
Ekman, P., and Friesen, W.V. (1968). Nonverbal behavior in psychotherapy research. In J. Schlien (Ed.), *Research in psychotherapy*. Vol 3. American Psychological Association, Washington, D.C.
Ekman, P., and Friesen, W.V. (1969). The repertoire of nonverbal behavior categories, origins, usage and coding. *Semiotica*, (in press).
Epstein, S. (1967). Toward a unified theory of anxiety. In B. A. Maher (Ed.), *Progress in experimental personality research*, Vol. 4. Academic Press, New York.
Folkins, C.H. (in press). Temporal factors and the cognitive mediators of stress reaction. *J. Personality and Social Psychol.*
Folkins, C.H., Lawson, Karen D., Opton, E.M., Jr., and Lazarus, R.S. (1968). Desensitization and the experimental reduction of threat. *J. Abnormal Psychol.*, 73, 100-113.
Fritz, C.E., and Marks, E.S. (1954). The NORC studies of human behavior in disaster. *J. Social Issues*, 10, 26-41.
Funkenstein, D.H., King, S.H., and Drolette, Margaret E. (1957). *Mastery of stress*. Harvard Univ. Press, Cambridge, Massachusetts.
Goldstein, M.J., Jones, R.B., Clemens, T.L., Flagg, G.W., and Alexander, R.G. (1965). Coping style as a factor in psychophysiological response to a tension-arousing film. *J. Personality and Social Psychol.*, 1, 290-302.
Grinker, R.R., and Spiegel, J.P. (1945). *Men under stress*. McGraw-Hill, New York.
Guilford, J.P. (1967). *The nature of human intelligence*. McGraw-Hill, New York.
Hann, Norma. (1969). A tripartite model of ego functioning: Values and clinical research applications. *J. Nervous and Mental Diseases*, 148, 14-30.
Hamburg, D.A. (1963). Emotions in the perspective of human evolution. In P. H. Knapp (Ed.), *Expression of emotions in man*. International Univ. Press, New York.
Harlow, H.F., and Stagner, R. (1933). Psychology of feelings and emotions. II. Theory of emotions. *Psychol. Rev.*, 40, 184-195.
Harvey, O.J. (1965). Cognitive aspects of affective arousal. In S. S. Tomkins and C. E. Izard (Eds.), *Affect, cognition and personality*. Springer, New York.
Hebb, D.O. (1955). Drives and the C. N. S. (Conceptual nervous system). *Psychol. Rev.*, 62, 243-254.
Hebb, D.O., and Thompson, W.R. (1954). The social significance of animal studies. In G. Lindzey (Ed.), *Handbook of social psychology*. Vol. 1. *Theory and method*. Addison-Wesley, Cambridge, Massachusetts.

Hohman, G.W. (1966). Some effects of spinal cord lesions on experienced emotional feelings. *Psychophysiol.*, 3, 143-156.

Janis, I.L. 1958). *Psychological stress*. Wiley, New York.

Kenny, A. (1963). *Action, emotion and will*. Routledge and Kegan Paul, London.

King, D.L. (1968). The relatedness of the emotionality variables. *Psychonomic Science*, 10, 367-368.

Krause, M.S. (1961). The measurement of transitory anxiety. *Psychol. Rev.*, 68, 178-189.

La Barre, W. (1947). The cultural basis of emotions and gestures. *J. Personality*, 16, 49-68.

Lacey, J.I. (1967). Somatic response patterning and stress: Some revisions of activation theory. In M. H. Appley and R. Trumbull (Eds), *Psychological stress*. Appleton, New York.

Lazarus, R.S. (1966). *Psychological stress and the coping process*. McGraw-Hill, New York.

Lazarus, R.S. (1968). Emotions and adaptation: Conceptual and empirical relations. In W. J. Arnold (Ed.), *Nebraska symposium on motivation*. Univ. of Nebraska Press, Lincoln.

Lazarus, R.S., and Alfert, Elizabeth (1964). The short-circuiting of threat. *J. Abnormal and Social Psychol.*, 69, 195-205.

Lazarus, R.S., and Opton, E.M., Jr. (1966). The study of psychological stress: A summary of theoretical formulations and experimental findings. In C. D. Spielberger (Ed.), *Anxiety and behavior*. Academic Press, New York.

Lazarus, R.S., Speisman, J.C., Mordkoff, A.M., and Davison, L.A. (1962). A laboratory study of psychological stress produced by a motion picture film. *Psychol. Monographs*, 76, No. 34 (Whole No. 553).

Lazarus, R.S., Speisman, J.C., and Mordkoff, A.M. (1963). The relationship between autonomic indicators of psychological stress: heart rate and skin conductance. *Psychosomat. Med.*, 25, 19-30.

Lazarus, R.S., Opton, E.M., Jr., Nomikos, M.S., and Rankin, N.O. (1965). The principle of short-circuiting of threat: further evidence. *J. Personality*, 33, 622-635.

Lazarus, R.S., Tomita, M., Opton, E., Jr., and Kodama, M. (1966). A cross-cultural study of stress-reaction patterns in Japan. *J. Personality and Social Psychol.*, 4, 622-633.

Leeper, R.W. (1965). Some needed developments in the motivational theory of emotions. In D. Levine (Ed.), *Nebraska symposium on motivation*. Univ. of Nebraska Press, Lincoln.

Lindsley, D.B. (1950). Emotions and the electroencephalogram. In M. R. Reymert (Ed.), *Feelings and emotions: The Mooseheart symposium*. McGraw-Hill, New York.

MacKay, D.M. (1962). The use of behavioral language to refer to mechanical processes. *Brit. J. Philos. Sci.*, 13, 89-103.

MacLean, P.D. (1960). Psychosomatics. In H. W. Magoun (Ed.), *Handbook of physiology*. Section 1: *Neurophysiology*. Vol. 3. American Physiological Society, Washington, D.C.

McNemar, Q. (1964). Lost: Our intelligence. Why? *Am. Psychologist*, 19, 871-882.

Maddi, S.R. (1968). *Personality theories: A comparative analysis*. Dorsey Press, Homewood, Illinois.

Malmo, R.B. (1959). Activation: A neuropsychological dimension. *Psychol. Rev.*, 66, 367-386.

Malmstrom, E.J., Opton, E.M., Jr., and Lazarus, R.S. (1965). Heart rate measurement and the correlation of indices of arousal. *Psychosomat. Med.*, 24, 546-556.

Martin, B. (1961). The assessment of anxiety by physiological behavioral measures. *Psychol. Bull.*, 58, 234-255.

Mordkoff, A.M. (1964). The relationship between psychological and physiological response to stress. *Psychosomat. Med.*, 26, 135-150.

Moyer, K.E. (1967). Kinds of aggression and their physiological basis. Carnegie-Mellon Univ. Report No. 67-12.

Nomikos, M.S., Opton, E.M., Jr., Averill, J.R., and Lazarus, R.S. (1968). Surprise and suspense in the production of stress reaction. *J. Personality and Social Psychol.*, 8, 204-208.

Opton, E.M., Jr., Rankin, N.O., and Lazarus, R.S. (1965). A simplified method of heart rate measurement. *Psychophysiol.*, 2, 87-97.

Orne, M.T. (1962). On the social psychology of the psychological experiment. *Am. Psychologist*, 17, 776-783.

Orne, M.T. (1965). Psychological factors maximizing resistance to stress: With special reference to hypnosis. In S. Z. Klausner (Ed.), *The quest for self-control*. Free Press, New York.

Plutchik, R. (1962). *The emotions*. Random House, New York.

Plutchik, R., and Ax, A.F. (1967). A critique of *Determinants of emotional state* by Schachter and Singer (1962). *Psychophysiol.*, 4, 79-82.

Pribram, K.H. (1960). A review of theory in physiological psychology. *Ann. Rev. Psychol.*, 11, 1-40.

Pribram, K.H. (1967). Emotion: Steps toward a neuropsychological theory. In D. C. Glass (Ed.), *Neurophysiology and emotion*. Rockefeller Univ. Press, New York.

Ryle, G. (1949). *The concept of mind*. Hutchinson, London.

Schachter, S. (1967). Cognitive effects on bodily functioning. Studies of obesity and eating. In D. C. Glass (Ed.), *Neurophysiology and emotion*. Rockefeller Univ. Press, New York.

Segall, M.H., Campbell, D.T., and Herskovits, M.J. (1966). *The influence of culture on visual perception*. Bobbs-Merrill, Indianapolis, Indiana.

Selye, H. (1950). *The physiology and pathology of exposure to stress*. Acta, Montreal.

Simonov, P.V. (1969). Studies of emotional behavior of humans and animals by Soviet physiologists. *Ann. N.Y. Acad. Sci.*, 159, 1112-1121.

Speisman, J.C., Lazarus, R.S., Mordkoff, A., and Davison, L. (1964). Experimental reduction of stress based on ego-defense theory. *J. Abnormal and Social Psychol.*, 68, 367-380.

Tolman, E.C. (1923). A behavioristic account of the emotions. *Psychol. Rev.*, 30, 217-227.

Tursky, B., and Sternbach, R.A. (1967). Further physiological correlates of ethnic differences in response to shock. *Psychophysiol.*, 4, 67-74.

Weinstein, J., Averill, J.R., Opton, E.M., Jr., and Lazarus, R.S. (1968). Defensive style and discrepancy between self-report and physiological indexes of stress. *J. Personality and Social Psychol.*, 10, 406-413.

Wenger, M.A. (1950). Emotions as visceral action: An extension of Lange's Theory. In M. L. Reymert (Ed.), *Feelings and Emotions: The Mooseheart-symposium*. McGraw-Hill, New York.

Wolff, C.T., Friedman, S.B., Hofer, M.A., and Mason, J.W. (1964). Relationship between psychological defenses and mean urinary 17-hydroxy-corticosteroid excretion rates: I. A predictive study of parents of fatally ill children. *Psychosomat. Med.*, 26, 576-591.

Chapter 15

The Attitudinal Character of Emotion

Otto Ewert*

SOME REMARKS ON CLASSIFICATION AND NOMENCLATURE

In spite of different starting points and different approaches, European and American psychology have one thing in common, namely, the unconventional usage of the terms feeling and emotion.

Jaspers (1948, p. 90), for instance, says "as for the term and concept 'emotion,' it is often uncertain what is meant by it in a given case." Referring to American psychology, Rapaport (1942, p. 6) remarks, "There was in indiscriminate application of the words 'emotion' and 'affect,' and their adjectival forms, to almost everything that is not apparently rational or lawful."

The numerous theories of emotion are so confusing and contradictory because each deals with a different subject matter and usually does not clearly explain to what kinds of experience it refers. We do not intend to add another classification to the many already available. However, an analysis of the concept "emotional experience" clearly shows that at least three subordinate concepts have to be distinguished: moods, feelings, and emotions.

To save time, only the most important distinctions will be treated, and these in outline form.

Moods

Moods are background experiences of a diffuse nature. There is no differentiation of experienced self and experienced world. Thus moods do not refer to persons, things or events. They possess no object reference.

*Ruhr University, Bochum, Germany.

Although it is likely that the total state of the organism has something to do with elated or depressed moods, it is possible to distinguish moods from organic sensations. Accelerated heartbeat, retarded respiration, menstrual difficulties, are experienced in the form of organic sensations and differ sharply from elated or depressed moods.

Feelings

By *feelings* is meant the emotional coloring of conscious contents. The difference between a perception, a sensation, and *my* perception, *my* sensation, is grounded in the emotional coloring of conscious contents which makes it appear that perceptions or sensations are pleasant or unpleasant. Wundt has shown a long time ago that sensations are usually accompanied by feelings. These accompany all our experience, conscious or unconscious. In contrast to moods, feelings have an object reference. They refer to something; they possess definite reference points in the individual's environment, which are the content of his perceptions and sensations. A change in perception will change the feeling tone.

While sensations are signs of something, and complex olfactory, taste, and color sensations refer to definite objects, feelings do not point to objects or events in the environment but reveal the individual's reaction to sensations and perceptions. Accordingly, a sugar solution, not too saturated, arouses the sensation "sweet" with the feeling "pleasant" while a more saturated solution may produce the sensation "sweet" accompanied by the feeling "unpleasant." With some restrictions (emphasized by Arnold, 1960), the concepts of adaptation level and level of activation may be used for feelings. Incoming stimuli, just noticeably different from normal experience in the expected direction, will be accompanied by the feeling "pleasant," while more intense changes are experienced as unpleasant. Schönpflug, for instance, has shown in a recent study that sounds which deviate maximally from a given adaptation level, were considered the most unpleasant, while sounds close to the adaptation level were judged as the most pleasant. The judgment pleasant/unpleasant as a function of activation varied under different conditions, according to the adaptation level.

Since sensations are always accompanied by a feeling tone, feelings represent the ground of experience, to use the figure-ground distinction of Gestalt psychology. Lacking form, they usually remain unnoticed. They form the background against which other contents of consciousness stand out.

The close relation of feelings to the individual's reactions to the perceived environment suggests that they serve a biological regulatory function. They facilitate the search for positively valued experiences, and the avoidance of those negatively valued, particularly in the realm of the contact senses (smell, taste, and the skin senses) where the connection with feelings is most easily demonstrated. It is obvious that particularly intense feelings may lead to massive defense reactions or precipitate flight, but also to approach.

Emotions

Against the background of feelings, different kinds of affective experiences stand out which are neither identical with feelings nor can they be called intensified feelings. This requires the introduction of a third kind of affective experience, in addition to moods and feelings. For instance, a man in a state of depression is well able to distinguish between his grief over the death of a member of his family, and the depressive mood which pervades all his conscious experience. In the context of pleasant feelings, anger may be experienced as a relieving outburst; in the context of unpleasant feelings, as hopeless impotence.

Since they are figure, not ground, such well defined affective experiences of grief over the death of a family member, anger at something or somebody, should be called *emotions*, as distinguished from feelings. While feelings accompany the stream of experience and change with changes in stimulation, emotions have a definite beginning and run a characteristic course.

It is not only the figure character of emotion that compels its distinction from feelings. Emotion also is different in having an object reference. While feelings represent the individual's reactions to sensations and perceptions, and function in the service of biological regulation, emotions refer to persons, and to situations relevant to persons. Almost every attempt to classify emotions leads to a differentiation of the various attitudes of an individual to his social environment. Anger, surprise, fear, disgust, contempt, joy, etc., are characteristic attitudes of an individual to other people or social situations. Such reactions to the environment cannot be reduced to biological processes of adaptation, as can feelings. Emotions refer to social rather than biological events. For this reason, the kind and form of such emotional attitudes has to satisfy certain social norms. Research in cultural anthropology has shown that there are "styles" of emotional experience and expressions, so that the socialization process leads the child to form definite attitudes to social situations.

Speaking about emotion as an attitude to the social environment implies that such social situations must be recognized as relevant for the person before they can arouse emotion, a fact convincingly demonstrated by Arnold (1960). Even when the connection between emotion and its situational trigger is not recognized by the individual (as psychoanalysis has shown by many examples), at least he experiences the need to construe a plausible connection *post factum*. On the basis of their experiments, Schachter and Singer (1962) describe such evaluative needs which almost sound like a scientific paraphrase of Heine's Lorelei theme: "Ich weiss nicht, was soll es bedeuten, dass ich so traurig bin (I do not know, what does it mean, that I am so sad)."

The most important of the classificatory distinctions mentioned above may be found in Table I.

TABLE I

DIMENSIONS OF AFFECTIVE EXPERIENCE

Affect	Character of experience	Object reference	Regulation
moods	no differentiation of experienced self and experienced world	none	?
feelings	ground	present	biological
emotions	figure	present	social

THE NEGATIVE PHASE

We have insisted that emotions must be distinguished from feelings because they are the individual's attitudes to his experienced social environment. Such attitudes have their origin in an evaluation of the social situation. An opportunity for testing this hypothesis is provided by the investigation of a phenomenon called by Bühler (1927) and Hetzer (1927) the "negative phase" in the life of girls entering puberty. Hurlock and Sender (1930) have translated the characteristics of the "negative phase" as follows: (from Bühler) "An appearance of disinclination; restlessness; a physical and mental uneasiness which finds expression in obstinacy, wildness, waywardness, and indolence; irritability; melancholia; hatred of self and society as well as hostility toward the latter. During this period their lives are joyless and tiresome; everything is unwelcome and appears evil or bad. Since the process of maturing uses up a good deal of the energy of the person, there results anemia, fatigue, or lassitude. Heightened sensitivity, irritability, restlessness, and the ease with which they can be excited are characteristics of the life of a pubescent." (From Hetzer) " . . . this phase is characterized by passivity and restlessness; loss of interests; desire for isolation; neglect of productive activity; instability; loss of skill of performance; withdrawal from friends, parents and teacher."

Unfortunately, there are hardly any recent studies in this area, and the older studies suffer from considerable methodological deficiencies. Bühler, for instance, used mainly girls' diaries; Hetzer's observations were based on unsystematic observations of girls in orphanages; and Hurlock and Sender were not given permission to interview the girls or have them answer questionnaires; instead, they had to be content with questionnaires answered by educational personnel.

In an attempt to study girls entering puberty, we developed a questionnaire (given to the girls themselves) with six orthogonal dimensions, one of which we have labeled, provisionally, as "negative phase." The following are samples of items with their factor loadings:

My father thinks highly of me .... −0.53
Sometimes I feel like running away from home .... +0.47
My mother thinks highly of me .... −0.51
Sometimes I'd like to be dead .... +0.41

This factor seems to tap a dimension that in many important respects is identical with the "negative phase." Girls with above average factor loadings are significantly different from the mean of the group. They earn significantly higher scores on an anxiety questionnaire (comparable to the Manifest Anxiety Scale), and on introversion (p <.01 in both cases), and have less contact with others (p <.05).

Other data were collected by means of a Guess-Who Questionnaire which was given to several classes of girls. The statements of girls with high loadings on the factor "negative phase" permit the conclusion that early adolescence is characterized by a readiness to react with emotions which impress us as new, no longer childlike, and can best be described as lonesomeness, with a marked element of anxiety. These data are based on tests, Guess-Who and other questionnaires, together with interviews of the girls' mothers.

TABLE II

PERCENTAGE OF Ss WHO ARE ABOVE THE GROUP MEAN ON GUESS-WHO ITEMS

	Guess-who items[*]				
N. P. values	1	2	3	4	5
Extremely high (7-9) N 34	41	38	44	44	41
Middle and low (1-6) N 375	37	23	29	18	33
p	n.s.	.05	.10	.01	n.s.

*Items
1 ... inattentive, reduced achievement
2 ... whispering secrets with older girls
3 ... recently many girl friends
4 ... no interest when class wants to do something together
5 ... no longer participates in pranks

Seen from a biological orientation, as favored by Bühler and Hetzer, we might expect that there would be a relationship between the increased emotionality typical of the "negative phase" and the hormonal changes during puberty. Thus Bühler and Hetzer assume that the menarche occurs during the "negative phase" or toward the end of it. However, a sample of 816 girls for whom we have

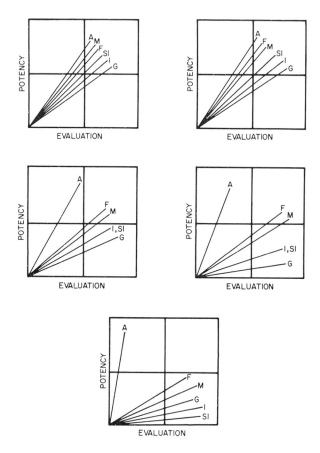

FIGURE 1.   Localization of six concepts in semantic space as found in girls of elementary and secondary school age (10 to 14 years).
I = I myself
M = Mother
F = Father
G = Girls
A = Adults
SI = Self Ideal

anthropological measurements together with the exact dates of onset of the menarche shows no connection between physical maturity and the intensity of the "negative phase."

If, instead, we start from the hypothesis that emotions are attitudes to appropriately appraised social situations, then the readiness for new kinds of emotions, called the "negative phase," should correspond to a changing evaluation of the girls' position in the social environment.

To obtain an operational definition of their position in the social sphere and their possible changes during puberty, we asked the girls to arrange the following terms on the Semantic Differential: "my father," "my mother," "girls of my age," and "adults in general." From a factor analysis done separately for each age group, we derived the factors *evaluation* and *potency*. The dimension *evaluation* is described in pairs of adjectives such as: sociable/unsociable; friendly/unfriendly; shows understanding/does not show understanding. The dimension *potency* is described by pairs of adjectives such as successful/unsuccessful; gifted/not gifted; educated/uneducated. As pictured in the diagram, the distance between the evaluated concepts increases with increasing age. Accordingly, there is an increasing distance between "I myself," on the one hand, and "adults in general," "my father," "my mother," on the other.

The connection between an evaluative attitude and negative phase emotionality is illustrated by the following correlations between various evaluations from the Semantic Differential and the negative phase values derived from questionnaires: "My father" r=-.36; "My mother" r=-.28; "I myself" r=-.24; "adults" r=-.19.

It is interesting that the connection between such evaluation of important persons of one's environment and negative phase emotionality apparently is not the result of stereotyped person perception. Rather, a measure of differentiation of judgment (preference for moderate vs. extreme scale values) shows that the negative phase is positively correlated with more differentiated judgments of persons. Girls with above average values on the factor "negative phase" have higher mean differentiation scores (p <.01). and judge the concepts "father," "mother" and "I myself" in a more differentiated way than the total sample (p <.01).

These results support our initial hypothesis that emotions imply an evaluation of the social situation in its importance for the individual. Such an evaluation is not necessarily an act of discursive reason. Rather, we are dealing here with perceptual judgments, or better, judgments based on social perception. We suggest that the connection between heightened emotionality (defined as "negative phase") and the evaluation of the social environment, as exemplified in our study by evaluations of "my father," "my mother," " girls of my age," "I myself," and "adults in general," can be explained by the experience of a changing social environment and the increasing distance between the individual and his reference persons.

The heightened emotionality characteristic of the negative phase does not seem to be aroused by biological or endogenous psychological processes, but stems from the fact that the individual is embedded in a social context. Societies that do not have conflicts between dependence and independence, or have such conflicts in different form, or at different times, are unacquainted with the heightened emotionality during early adolescence that could be demonstrated in our subjects.

REFERENCES

Arnold, M.B. (1960). *Emotion and personality*. Columbia Univ. Press, New York.

Bühler, C. (1927). Der Pubertatsverlauf bei Knaben und Madchen. *Zeitschrift fur Sexualwissenschaft*, 14, 6-10.

Bühler, C. (1967). Das Seelenleben des Jugendlichen (6th ed.). Fischer, Stuttgart.

Ewert, O. (1965). Gefühle und Stimmungen. In H. Thomae (Ed.), *Handbuch der Psychologie*, vol. 2. Hogrefe, Göttingen.

Hetzer, H. (1927). Systematische Dauerbeobachtungen an Jugendlichen über den Verlauf der negativen Phase. *Zeitschrift für Pädagogische Psychologie und Experimentelle Pädagogik*, 28, 80-96.

Hurlock, E.B. and Sender, S. (1930). The "negative phase" in relation to the behavior of pubescent girls. *Child Development*, 1, 4.

Jaspers, K. (1948). *Allgemeine Psychopathologie* (5th ed.). Springer, Berlin.

Rapaport, D. (1942). *Emotions and Memory*. Williams and Wilkins, Baltimore.

Schachter, S. and Singer, J.E. (1962). Cognitive, social, and physiological determinants of emotional state. *Psychol. Rev.*, 69, 379-399.

Chapter 16

Emotion and Recognition of Emotion

Nico H. Frijda*

Emotions are not only lived and experienced, they are also observed. It may be useful to approach the problem of emotion from the standpoint of the observer — from the point of view of the person "seeing," inferring or supposing somebody else's emotional state.

EMOTION AS SEEN BY THE OBSERVER

What, in fact, does "emotion" refer to when applied to another person? What do we mean when using words like "he is angry " and what can we possibly have in mind when, without using words, we respond appropriately, such as offering comfort on seeing somebody sad.

The statements of experimental subjects give some indications. In an experiment performed a long time ago, subjects were asked for free interpretations of filmed spontaneous expressions (Frijda, 1953). The subjects in that experiment rarely employed simple words like "angry" or "happy," but used, instead, a variety of circumlocutions. Most frequently they described the situation: "You told her a disgusting story," or "She seems to be looking at a tiny kitten."

In other words, recognition of emotion implies a situational reference. Observed emotion indicates the presence of a specific situational valence which is taken seriously by the observed person. To recognize emotion means, at least in part, to make a prediction concerning the situation as the other person sees it.

Other statements of the experimental subjects have a different import. "She has a nasty look — she has a cold expression — she is on the point of bursting

*University of Amsterdam.

out," all seem to refer to forthcoming behavior. To recognize emotion means, in part, to anticipate specific actions, or to anticipate the observed person's response to the observer. Anger is seen as the starting point for beating, or maintaining a stand, or grumbling and scolding. Coldness is lack of sympathetic response when such will be required. Nastiness is a promise of positive disagreeable action, or may already be part of it. To recognize an emotion means, in part, a change in the probability of a whole array of action possibilities.

Finally, some statements are descriptions of feeling, or indicate possibilities of action as seen from the inside: "she has that closed-in feeling, of not knowing what to do." The subjects also report imitative, empathic tendencies. To recognize emotions is, in part, to classify the other person's state in terms of the observer's own experimental or expressive categories or possibilities.

"Emotion" as the meaning of observed behavior is all this — a disposition which can be explicated in one or more of these various ways. Our verbal labels seem to refer to this whole set of possibilities. To "recognize emotion" often is nothing but the implicit notion that such an explication is possible and within reach. Which of the explications becomes actual seems partly determined by the context of observation. In our daily conversational or observational contacts, situational reference is important, while in direct person-to-person interaction, the anticipation of action could be the most appropriate mode. In detached, not directly involved observation, as in the theater or during experiments on the recognition of emotional expression, empathy often comes naturally.

THE RELATION OF BEHAVIOR TO EMOTION

To judge from the preceding considerations, recognizing emotions means observing a state that points beyond its momentarily given behavior pattern, to situational or other cognitive components, as well as to future actions or their likelihood of occurrence. This poses the question: what is the relation between the behavior pattern and the other components? The evidence suggests that there is a one-to-many relation. A given behavior pattern may refer to a whole array of different emotions. This, of course, is the conception of emotion brought forward by Schachter (1964) and others. What is true from the point of view of the subject himself appears to be equally true from the point of view of the observer who recognizes emotion in others. A given expression leads to a variety of interpretations; and situational cues drastically codetermine and canalize the emotional interpretation (Frijda, 1958, 1967).

The fact of such one-to-many relations brings up the question as to the number of related factors. In other words, how differentiated is emotional or expressive behavior, as compared to the differentiation of emotion as implied in the subjects' own, or the observer's, rich descriptive terminology? Is emotional behavior relatively undifferentiated and ambiguous, with the situational and other components responsible for most of the differentiation, or is there rather a relation of one-to-few, one behavior pattern corresponding to only a few different emotional states? Current research favors the first view. As far as facial expression is concerned, variation along a few dimensions seems to account for the variability and coherence in judgement. Schlosberg's (1954) three-dimensional model is the best-known example, though it may underestimate the variety of emotional expression.

Bipolar Scale Studies

Our own research, using judgements on bipolar scales, consistently points to at least five dimensions. This has been true in the reanalysis of older material, and in a study with the photographs used by Schlosberg (Frijda, 1967). It has also been true in a group of four recent studies, where a set of 40 bipolar scales was designed to find more differentiation (Table I).

TABLE I
BIPOLAR SCALES

1.	controlled	— uncontrolled	21.	amazed	— understanding
2.	indifferent	— involved	22.	dull	— clear
3.	aggressive	— friendly	23.	calm	— excited
4.	sleep	— tension	24.	free	— oppressed
5.	abandonment	— reserve	25.	gross	— subtle
6.	authoritarian	— submissive	26.	approach	— withdrawal
7.	startled	— relieved	27.	soft	— hard
8.	artificial	— natural	28.	kind	— unkind
9.	unpleasant	— pleasant	29.	worrying	— lighthearted
10.	closed	— open	30.	moved	— unmoved
11.	energetic	— tired	31.	simple	— complicated
12.	derisive	— mild	32.	disappointed	— hopeful
13.	attention	— disinterest	33.	deep	— shallow
14.	cool	— warm	34.	childish	— adult
15.	admiring	— despising	35.	directed	— undirected
16.	frightened	— carefree	36.	self-assured	— insecure
17.	hesitant	— determined	37.	hurt	— flattered
18.	sad	— happy	38.	introverted	— extraverted
19.	tense	— relaxed	39.	angry	— sympathetic
20.	eagerness	— distaste	40.	content	— discontented

Two of the experiments used photographs of an actress, and two used those of an actor. In all, 62 photographs of the actress were used ("Nelly" series) and 68 of the actor ("Jerome" series). Results are given in Table II. In each of the four analyses the following factors were found after Varimax rotation: (a) pleasantness/unpleasantness; (b) emotional intensity/control or indifference; (c) self-assertiveness/dependence; (d) natural/artificial; (e) attention/disinterest. These five factors accounted for about 85 percent of the variance.

TABLE II

BIPOLAR SCALES: FACTORS

	Percent variance		
	Nelly	Jerome	Congruence coeff.
pleasant-unpleasant	41.1	40.3	.978
emotional intensity-attention	20.8	19.1	.903
self-assured-insecure	13.9	13.2	.950
natural-artificial	4.6	4.8	.795
surprised-not surprised	3.4	1.8	.520
simple-complicated	1.5	4.7	.675
derision-mildness	2.9	—	—
	88.2	82.1	

Factors 1 through 4 lead to coefficients of congruence of about +.80 or more between actors, when data for each actor are pooled, as well as between the two studies of the same actor. The attention factor was noticable only in the "Nelly" studies. Most of it collapsed into the intensity factor in the case of the "Jerome" series (but not in that of Schlosberg's Marjorie Lightfoot photographs, see Frijda, 1967). Rotation to maximum congruence shows the three first factors to be practically identical. The clear presence of a factor of determination and authoritarianism, as an important aspect of perceived emotion, is noticeable in these studies. It was, in fact, suggested by the data from the earlier study and is even more clearly present in the one using the Marjorie Lightfoot photographs (Frijda, 1967). Beyond that, a "surprise" factor seemed to emerge, but no further differentiation of positive or negative emotions as was hoped for in constructing the list of scales.

Still, it may be that these studies reveal less differentiation than emotional expression really contains. An analysis of some of the data in which scales per subject are taken as the variable (not taking the average of the subjects-ratings) suggests a finer structure. In fact, it is possible that the dimensional model itself, inherent in the use of bipolar scales, is not entirely satisfactory. The distribution of expressions in the dimensional space is far from even for some dimensions (Frijda, 1967). Moreover, the increase in the number of factors detracts from the beauty as well as the usefulness of the dimensional model.

Adjective Checklist.

To investigate the possibility of greater and perhaps different differentiation, several studies were undertaken which used a technique similar to that of an old experiment by Osgood(1956), and Osgood and Suci (1955). Subjects were asked to check a list of about 100 adjectives; they were encouraged to check as many

TABLE III
CHECKED TERMS: FACTORS

| | | Percent variance | | |
		Nelly	Jerome	Congruence coeff.
1.	happy	14.1	11.2	.885
2.	sad	9.5	8.2	.892
3.	calm	8.2	5.2	.831
4.	digust	6.8	6.3	.864
5.	surprise	5.8	4.7	.785
6.	bitter	5.7	—	(.690-11)
7.	attention	5.4	5.2	.555
8.	fear	4.7	4.6	.781
9.	pride	4.2	6.1	.683
10.	irony	3.1	3.2	.696
11.	anger	4.5	7.7	.796
12.	insecure	4.2	3.2	.396
13.	moved	2.1	—	
14.	aggrieved	1.9	—	
15.	gay	2.0	—	
16.	pain	1.9	—	
17.	guilty	1.7	—	
18.	scepticism	1.4	1.9	.231
6+.	disinterested	—	4.9	
12+.	distrust	—	2.2	
13+.	childish	—	2.7	
14+.	amusement	—	5.1	
15+.	pondering	—	3.0	
16+.	curiosity	—	2.2	
17+.	reserve	—	2.2	
	total	87.4	84.6	

adjectives per stimulus as they thought appropriate. Deletion of adjectives with low frequency of usage resulted in 76 adjectives for final analysis. The same four sets of photographs as before were used. The result of the two studies of each actor have been analyzed as a whole.

Factor analysis of frequencies of usage of terms per stimulus yielded in both cases at least 18 factors with Eigenvalues larger than 1, all of which were interpretable after Varimax rotation (see Table III). The ten major factors from both actors were quite similar, while the minor ones were different.

All factors were unipolar, as a consequence of the relatively low negative correlations due to the very skewed score distributions. It may seem strange to find 18 unipolar factors as opposed to 4-6 bipolar ones found in the previous experiments.

Cluster Analysis.

Cluster analysis, according to a simple method devised by Elshout and Elshout (1967) gives more insight into the relation between the results of these experiments. Figure 1 presents the cluster analysis of one of the "Nelly" studies as an example of the kind of clusters found.

To begin with, let me point out that the Varimax factors are nearly perfectly reflected in the clusters, since clusters at about the level of average intercorrelations of +.60 contain the variables with factor loadings of about +.60 or higher. These clusters are situated at an intermediate level in a hierarchy of clusterings. Clusters are considered to represent different levels if the average intercorrelations of variables are at least .10 apart. Below the intermediate clusters are finer differentiations, small groups of terms of more restricted common meaning, such as "sweet," "tender," "feminine," and "happiness" (average intercorrelation +.89), or isolated terms. This differentiation is partly due to true differences in usage of the terms or groups of terms, but partly to the unreliability of several of the terms.

Above the clusterings corresponding to the factors are more abstract groupings, numbering 9 or 10 at the highest level. And above these appear in many instances bipolar orderings similar in intent (and sometimes in content) to the dimensions of the previously discussed studies. Many of the larger clusters tend to correlate negatively, with intercluster-correlations of up to (or down to) −.36. (Low negative correlations are included in the diagram because of the above mentioned small magnitude of negative correlations.)

THE HIERARCHICAL MODEL OF EMOTION

These analyses suggest a model of the system of perceived emotions that is somewhat different from the dimensional one. Obviously, it suggests a hierarchical model. In fact, because of the anomalies found in earlier studies (Frijda, 1958), this was suggested before the research reported here was undertaken.

The hierarchical model can be described in two ways. The system of emotions can be seen as a set of discrete states, each of which has among its defining attributes some that represent values of more or less general variables: pleasantness, intensity, degree of attentional activity involved. Other attributes are specific for that group of emotions. Or else, it is possible to conceive of a *n*-dimensional system of emotional space with further differentiations in various regions which are specific for and relevant to each region. There is pleasantness and unpleasantness; and unpleasantness, for instance, may be divided into sorrow and disgust. Perhaps the hierarchical ordering reflects the process of recognizing emotional expression: placing it in a system of gross distinctions and subsequently making finer discriminations.

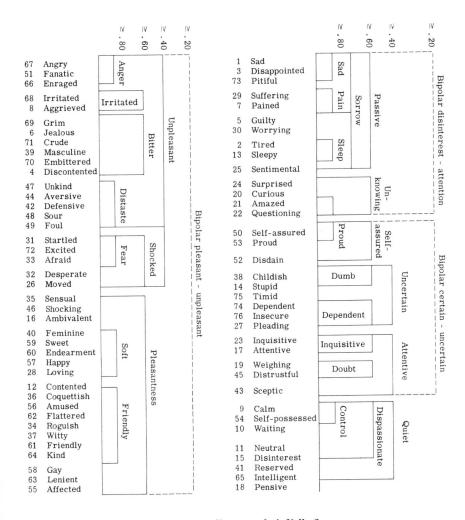

FIGURE 1.   Cluster analysis Nelly 2.

It is rather difficult at this point to say anything definite as to just what are these general dimensions or distinctions. The four analyses, although similar, are not identical, even between studies employing photographs from the same actor. The ordering of the major clusters differs, which may depend on slight differences in the correlation pattern.

It will take some thought to find the most adequate description of these structures. What can be done at this moment is to investigate the way in which the hierarchical ordering and the differentiation at the lower levels are reflected in the facial features. A group of subjects was given the photographs together with a 56-item checklist of facial features, such as "eyes slightly widened" or "head straight, glance straight ahead." Substantial correlations between terms and traits were found which allow the description of the facial patterns leading to the use of each term. These patterns may be highly predictive for the term concerned: weighted addition and multiplication of traits (double weight for those correlating more than +.70, triple weight for those more than +.90) leads to many extremely high correlations. In the two studies for which calculations were made, the average correlations between terms and their best trait combination or single trait are +.78 and +.67 respectively. But significantly correlating traits differ somewhat from experiment to experiment, even when studies with photographs of the same actor are compared. Consequently, it is unclear as yet how stable the predictive value of the various trait-combinations really is.

More relevant to our present concern is the finding that all or nearly all terms in each cluster at factor level have at least one of the correlating facial features in common, which sets them off from all or most other clusters. To what extent finer differentiations are indeed represented by stable patterns remains to be seen.

DIFFERENTIATION OF EMOTIONAL EXPRESSION

There appears to be more differentiation in emotional expression than would appear from dimensional studies. Eighteen different "emotions" (the number of factors and of corresponding clusters) seem at least distinguishable. Moreover, the intensity dimension further differentiates each of them. In fact, it would be surprising if there were fewer distinct patterns. Factor analysis of the facial trait ratings yields ten factors or clusters, most of them bipolar. Obviously, dynamic cues that are absent in photographs will produce further differentiation.

Even so, the general notion of a one-to-many relation (or one-to-several relation) between emotional expression and emotion seems to hold. A large number of correlations between terms is near unity if corrected for attenuation. Several of those are between terms which cannot be considered synonyms or near synonyms, such as, for instance: pleading and pitiful, jealous and embittered, amused and flattered.

Together, the data support the conception that the recognition of emotion consists of categorizing the observed behavioral pattern in terms of a set of general dimensions, of further differentiating within the framework of such general assessment, and of finally specifying, on the basis of situational cues or suppositions, which of the emotions compatible with the given behavioral tendency is actually present.

IMPLICATIONS FOR A THEORY OF EMOTION

The findings have certain implications for a theory of emotion. If distinctions and family resemblances are perceived, they must be there, in the expressive patterns themselves. Efforts to define the various emotions and their relationships may start from there. In fact, the conception of emotion as a behavioral tendency based upon a given situational valence, or tending towards future actions, seems entirely applicable to the analysis of emotion itself. This analysis may be aided by interpretation of the expressive patterns as they appear from the correlations mentioned before. Expressive activity can be interpreted as "positional activity," that is, as manifestation of activity patterns and of modes of relating to the valences or objects involved.

Yet there is a snag in all this. The relation between expressive behavior and emotion is too complicated to permit direct inference to aspects of emotion from experiments such as these. The complexity of this relation becomes evident when attention is directed to the question of how accurately emotion is recognized and also to the study of which expressions in actual fact occur with a given emotion. Every emotion, as defined by the subject himself or by an observer knowing the entire situation, may manifest itself in a very large variety of expressions. Many of these have very little in common, and some will never be recognized correctly when presented without further information (Landis, 1924, 1929; Frijda, 1953). Also, when expressions are presented together with situational cues, nearly every combination makes sense to the subjects; many expressions are compatible with a given emotional complex (Frijda, 1967). There are several reasons for this. Suppression, self-control, and active manipulation of one's own expressive behavior contribute, but so does internalization of the emotion, that is, the transformation of what could have become an acted-out impulse into a representational feeling. Generally, the place of the behavioral tendency in emotion may be quite variable. The protective tendency in overt fear represents a much more defining component in inner apprehension than a merely attentive face. In many of the "higher" emotions (guilt, admiration), the behavioral tendency may be entirely peripheral, irrelevant and unspecific.

These complications may serve as a warning against any attempt to infer the dimensions of emotion directly from the dimensions of recognition of emotional expression. Still, the theory of emotion will have to account for the kind of relations found in recognition studies.

REFERENCES

Elshout, J.J. and Elshout, M. (1967). Marimaxcor: methode voor clusteranalyse van correlatiematrices. Technical Report, Univ. of Amsterdam, Psychology Department.

Frijda, N.H. (1953). The understanding of facial expression of emotion. *Acta Psychol.*, 9, 294-362.

Frijda, N.H. (1958). Facial expression and situational cues. *J. Abnormal and Social Psychol.*, 57, 149-154.

Frijda, N.H. (1967). Recognition of emotion. In L. Berkowitz (Ed.), *Advances in experimental social psychology*, Vol. 4. Academic Press, New York, (in press).

Landis, C. (1924). Studies of emotional reactions. II. General behavior and facial expression. *J. Comp. Psychol.*, 4, 447-509.

Landis, C. (1929). The interpretation of facial expression in emotion. *J. Genetic Psychol.*, 2, 59-72.

Osgood, C.E. (1956). Fidelity and reliability. Pp 374-384 in H. Quastler (Ed.), *Information theory in psychology*. Free Press, Glencoe, Illinois.

Osgood, C.E. and Suci, G.J. (1955). Factor analysis of meaning. *J. Exp. Psychol.*, 50, 325-338.

Schachter, S. (1964). The interaction of cognitive and physiological determinants of emotional state. In L. Berkowitz (Ed.), *Advances in experimental social psychology*, Vol. 1, 49-80. Academic Press, New York.

Schlosberg, H. (1954). Three dimensions of emotion. *Psychol. Rev.*, 61, 81-88.

Chapter 17

A Dictionary and Grammar of Emotion

Joel R. Davitz*

Several years ago, as a result of some work I had been doing on emotional communication, I became interested in the words people use to label emotional states — words like love and hate, joy and sadness. Nowhere could I find an adequate definition of most of these words, yet people use these labels without obvious difficulties in communication, apparently assuming that the meaning of love, hate, joy, or sadness is so clear that they hardly need explicit definitions.

My own thinking about these words, however, was certainly not very clear, and as I frequently do when I am confused about such matters, I began my search for clarity by talking to some of my colleagues. I asked them to tell me what they meant when they said they were happy or sad, or when they used any one of a variety of words to label their emotional states. This approach, I found, was not very profitable. Apparently a psychologist talking to another psychologist about his emotions is not a situation likely to elicit clarity of communication, and I found myself even more confused by my sampling of the current jargon of American psychology.

I was therefore forced to begin talking to nonpsychologists, even to some outside the halls of the university. The conversations changed dramatically. For the most part, people were quite clear about what they meant by various emotional labels, and while they did not always communicate with the verbal grace and precision of my fellow psychologists, they frequently gave rather rich and dramatic definitions of the emotional words they used.

During these conversations it became clear that when most people used a phrase such as "I am happy" or "I am sad," they were referring to *experiences* —

*Teachers College, Columbia University, New York.

not to behaviors, not to situations, and certainly not to measures obtained from an electroencephalogram or a galvonometer. It was in terms of the *experience* of happiness, the *experience* of sadness, hate, or love that my informants defined the meaning of these words. They were obviously unaware of the scientific view that people cannot talk meaningfully about experiences, and they simply didn't realize that their language was supposed to be inadequate to the task of describing emotional experiences. They knew nothing about the rules of American behaviorism, and in their ignorance, with remarkable clarity and consensus, they told me what it meant to experience emotions.

At this point, two alternatives occurred to me. On the one hand, I could discount these conversations as meaningless reports of people who were deceiving themselves, without awareness to be sure, but nevertheless using words without solid, scientific behavioral definitions. Or, on the other hand, I could take these conversations seriously, accept the fact that this is the way in which the language is used, regardless of whether or not it is consistent with current fashion among psychologists. I chose this latter view, and continued this line of exploration, using both interviews and written reports to investigate a wide variety of emotional experiences.

During the course of these early explorations, I began to accumulate a pool of phrases that people used in their descriptive reports, and eventually I developed a checklist of 556 items based on a large number of interviews and well over a thousand written reports. In a sense, this checklist provides a basic vocabulary for the description of emotional experiences.

I then decided to embark on a more formal investigation, with the aim of developing a dictionary which recorded the consensus of reported experiences associated with various emotional labels. Using a critical incident technique and the checklist of descriptive phrases, each of 50 people was asked to describe 50 different emotional states. For each emotional term, an item on the checklist was included in the definition of that term if at least one-third of the respondents checked the item in describing their experiences of the emotion. Thus, the definitions included in the dictionary reflect the independent, intersubjective agreements among my sample of 50 subjects, and the dictionary might therefore be viewed as a product of a consensual or social phenomenology.

DEFINITIONS

Depression

To illustrate the kind of information contained in the dictionary, consider the definition of depression:

"I feel empty, drained, hollow, understimulated, undercharged, heavy, loggy, sluggish; my feelings seem dulled, I am physically less responsive, all excitement, vitality is gone; there is a sense of being dead inside; I feel let down, tired, sleepy; it's an effort to do anything, I have no desire, no motivation, no interest; wants, needs, drives are gone; it's as if everything inside has stopped; I feel mentally dull; my body seems to slow down; there is a sense that somehow I can't experience things wholly, as if there is a lid or some sort of clamp which keeps me from perceiving."

"There is a sense of uncertainty about the future; I feel sorry for myself; a sense of being gripped by the situation; everything seems out of proportion; a sense of being totally unable to cope with the situation, there is simply no place to go, no way of ever getting out, a sense of not knowing where to go, what to do; I lose all confidence in myself and doubt myself; I feel lost; I seem to be caught up and overwhelmed by the feeling; I feel vulnerable and totally helpless, off balance, as if I were in quicksand; the harder I struggle to get out of the feeling, the deeper I'm drawn in; I can't and don't know how to get rid of or pull out of the feeling; I'm completely uncertain of everything; I feel insignificant."

"There is a sense of aloneness, being cut off, completely by myself; I want to withdraw, disappear, draw back, be alone, away from others, crawl into myself; I feel aimless, wandering lost in space with nothing solid to grab on to; I become introspective, turn inwards; everything seems useless, absurd, meaningless, there is a lack of involvement and not caring about anything that goes on around me; there is a sense of being incomplete; as if part of me is missing; a feeling of a certain distance from others; everyone seems far away, as if I'm out of touch, seeing things from far away; there is a sense of unrelatedness to others; I am out of contact, can't reach others; I feel as if I am in a vacuum; I don't want to communicate with anyone; there is a sense of being deserted, betrayed and the world indifferent to me; my body wants to contract, draw closer to myself."

"There is a heavy feeling in my stomach; a sense of loss, of deprivation; there is an inner ache you can't locate; I have no appetite; I can't eat; there is a clutching, sinking feeling in the middle of my chest, there is a heaviness in my chest, I feel as if I'm under a heavy burden; there is a lump in my throat; I'm slightly headachy, as if my brain were tired; I can't smile or laugh; there is a gnawing feeling in the pit of my stomach; a sensation of my heart sinking; it's as if I'm suffocating or something; it hurts to be alive."

"There is a sense of longing, a yearning, a desire for change; I want things to hurry up and begin to change; there is a sense of weakness; it seems that nothing I do is right; I begin to think about what I can do to change the situation."

"I'm easily irritated, ready to snap; I feel choked up, wound up inside."

"I keep searching for an explanation, for some understanding; I keep thinking, 'Why?'; I want to be comforted, helped by someone; I can only think of what caused the feeling; I have a sense of being trapped, closed up, boxed, fenced in, tied down, inhibited; my attention is completely focused on myself, I'm preoccupied with myself."

"The feeling is very deep inside; I seem to feel it at the pit of my being, it's more an 'inner' than an 'outer' feeling; it's a confused, mixed up feeling, involved with other feelings; the feeling seems to linger; to last a long time, with no immediate release; it's a very personal feeling; it's involved with other feelings; the feeling goes slowly, it's a bottomless feeling, there is a sense that the feeling will never end; it all seems bottled up inside of me; it fills me completely."

Happiness

In contrast, happiness is defined as follows:

"There is an inner warm glow, a radiant sensation; I feel like smiling; there is a sense of well being, a sense of harmony and peace within, everything is going right for me; I'm optimistic and cheerful; the world seems basically good and beautiful; men are essentially kind; life is worth living; there is a renewed appreciation of life; I'm optimistic about the future; the future seems bright; I'm loose, relaxed, in tune with the world; there's a feeling of warmth all over; I think about beautiful things; I feel safe and secure, I'm at peace with the world; there is a mellow comfort, a sense of being very integrated and at ease with myself, in harmony with myself; there is a sense of fullness, a sense of smiling at myself; I am free of conflict; there is a sense of 'rightness' with oneself and the world; nothing can go wrong; my movements are graceful and easy, I feel especially well coordinated; there is a general release, a lessening of tension, I am peaceful, tranquil, quiet, completely free from worry; I am really functioning as a unit."

"There is a sense of being more alive, I am excited in a calm way; there is an inner buoyancy, a warm excitement, a sense of vitality, aliveness, vibrancy, an extra spurt of energy or drive, a special lift in everything I do and say; I feel bouncy, springy, effervescent, bubbly, wide awake, with a sense of lightness, buoyancy and upsurge of the body, more alert; there is a particularly acute awareness of pleasurable things, their sounds, their colors, and textures — everything seems more beautiful, natural, and desirable; there is an intense awareness of everything; I seem to experience things with greater clarity; colors seem brighter, sounds clearer, movements more vivid; I seem to be immediately in touch with the world; a sense of being very open, receptive, with no separation between me and the world; a sense that I'm experiencing everything fully, completely, thoroughly; that I'm feeling all the way, all my senses seem to be completely open; there is a strong sense of interest and involvement in things around me."

"I keep thinking how lucky I am; I have a sense of sureness, I feel strong inside, taller, stronger, bigger; there is a sense of being important and worthwhile, a sense of more confidence in myself; a feeling that I can do anything; I feel clean, as if I look especially good; there is a sense of being more substantial, of existing, of being real."

"I feel outgoing, I want to make others happy; there is an intense, positive relationship with another person or with other people; a communion, a unity, a closeness, friendliness and freedom, mutual respect and interdependence; I want others (or the other person) to feel the same as I do; there is a sense of trust and appreciation of another person; a sense of loving everyone, everything."

"I seem to nurture the feeling within myself; I want the feeling to continue, to keep going; I feel like singing, like laughing; there is a sense of accomplishment, fulfillment; there is an excitement, a sense of being keyed up, overstimulated, supercharged."

"It's a very personal feeling; a simple, pure feeling; it's more an 'inner' than an 'outer' feeling; the feeling flows from the inside outwards; the feeling seems to be all over, nowhere special, just not localized."

These examples, of course can do little more than convey the flavor of the dictionary and a sense of the kinds of results obtained as one moves along this line of investigation. However, as suggested by these two definitions, and supported by the others contained in the dictionary, people can indeed describe their emotional experiences with at least a modicum of agreement, and despite the concerns of psychologists about the inadequacies of verbal reports, the English language clearly is flexible and comprehensive enough to permit rich and detailed descriptions of extraordinarily complex phenomena. Of course, not all of the definitions obtained were successful, but on the basis of ratings obtained from independent judges, it seems reasonable to suggest that the great majority of definitions are viewed by nonpsychologists as accurate and comprehensive.

A GRAMMAR

The next, and perhaps most exciting, step in the analysis concerns the structure or grammar underlying the definitions contained in the dictionary. Inspection of the results suggested that certain items occurred together more or less consistently in a number of definitions, and a subsequent cluster analysis of the items clearly substantiated this impression. In fact, the results of the cluster analysis indicated a rational order in the reported experiences which I continue to find astonishing.

Briefly, *phi* coefficients were computed between each item that appeared in the definitions of at least three terms and every other item. Then, a cluster analysis procedure was developed such that in every cluster, the *phi* coefficient between each item and every other item in the cluster was statistically significant at or beyond the .05 level. Thus, when one item in a cluster appears in a definition, other items in that cluster also tend to appear. Similarly, when an item is absent in a given definition, other items in the cluster tend to be absent.

The results of this analysis, summarized in Table I, reveal twelve clusters which, on the basis of content, appear to fall along four major dimensions. The first three are *Hypoactivation*, *Activation*, and *Hyperactivation* — all of which I have included along the dimension of *ACTIVATION*. The next three concern *RELATEDNESS* to the environment, and include *Moving Away*, *Moving Towards*, and *Moving Against*. Next are three clusters which refer to *HEDONIC TONE* — *Discomfort*, *Comfort*, and *Tension*. And finally, three clusters deal with one's sense of *COMPETENCE* in terms of *Inadequacy*, *Enhancement*, and *Incompetence-Dissatisfaction*.

TABLE I
CLUSTERS AND DIMENSIONS OF EMOTIONAL MEANING

Dimension	Clusters		
ACTIVATION	Activation	Hypoactivation	Hyperactivation
RELATEDNESS	Moving Towards	Moving Away	Moving Against
HEDONIC TONE	Comfort	Discomfort	Tension
COMPETENCE	Enhancement	Incompetence — Dissatisfaction	Inadequacy

Naming these clusters and arranging them within the framework of four dimensions obviously involves a certain amount of projection on my part. However, without the opportunity to review in detail the items in each cluster, I can only suggest that the name of each cluster is based directly on the items themselves, and the four dimensions are rather obviously derived from the content of the various clusters.

For me, perhaps the most remarkable aspect of the entire investigation is this structure of emotional meaning. I began by leaving what I thought was the usual line of inquiry into emotional phenomena, and I have finally come full circle to precisely the same kinds of concepts used by previous theorists in their discussions of emotion. *ACTIVATION*, for example, is one of the primary dimensions mentioned by Wundt (1905) in his theory of emotion, and in more recent work it has been emphasized by writers such as Duffy, (1962), Stagner, (1948), Schachter, (1962) and Schlosberg, (1954). *RELATEDNESS* in one form or another plays a major role in the work of Arnold, (1960), Block, (1957), Schlosberg, (1954), Nowlis and Nowlis, (1956). *HEDONIC TONE* has been mentioned in one way or another by Burt, (1950), Harlow and Stagner, (1933),

Young, (1967), and many others. The final dimension, *COMPETENCE*, offers something a bit new in discussions of emotions, though it almost seems as if my subjects had been reading the recent psychological literature and realized that White's (1959) earlier views about the significance of competence are gaining new popularity in current theoretical discussions.

Thus, the professional theoreticians and the nonpsychologists who describe their emotions are not so far apart. It would seem that each of the theorists, probably on the basis of his own life experiences, selected one or perhaps two of the dimensions underlying emotional reports, and built these concepts into a general theory of emotion. For some, perhaps as a consequence of temperament or life style, *ACTIVATION* is all important; for others, *RELATEDNESS, HEDONIC TONE,* or *COMPETENCE* is the central feature of emotion. But if my subjects are to be believed, their reports say that all four dimensions — *ACTIVATION, RELATEDNESS, HEDONIC TONE,* and *COMPETENCE* — are involved in emotional experience and must be considered in any general theory of emotion. Thus, the nonpsychologists tell us that perhaps each of us has been seeing only part of the picture, and we might do well to listen to what these people are saying.

CONCLUSIONS

The implications of this point of view are too numerous to list here, but to illustrate some of these, we might briefly consider the problem of inducing or changing emotional states. Previously, our efforts in this direction have been fairly gross, guided primarily by common sense and pragmatic considerations. If we want to induce fear, we threaten with electric shock; if we want to make someone angry, we insult him; if we want to reduce anxiety, we become "warm and accepting." But the present point of view, while it does not offer an immediate solution, at least indicates the direction we might move to make our efforts more precise and perhaps more effective. Essentially, this view suggests that we define the emotional state we wish to induce or change in terms of clusters or dimensions of emotional meaning, and then design procedures relevant to each of these specific aspects of emotional experience. That is, rather than formulate our goals in broad terms of reducing anxiety or increasing confidence, we might profitably be more precise by thinking of changes along each dimension of emotional meaning. Thus, we might wish to focus our efforts on changing an individual's sense of *ACTIVATION*, or perhaps his experience of *RELATEDNESS, HEDONIC TONE,* or his sense of *COMPETENCE*. This suggests that, instead of dealing with general emotional states such as anxiety, depression, happiness, or love, we might more effectively focus our research on the development of techniques to influence particular dimensions of emotional experience.

It would be presumptuous, I believe, to suggest that anything like a general theory of emotion could legitimately be derived from the kind of data discussed here. But while a careful hearing of what nonpsychologists have to say about their emotional experiences has not led us to a serious contradiction of previous work, it has resulted, at least for me, in clarifying some of the words commonly encountered in discussions of emotion and opened new lines of inquiry for further investigation. Therefore, although I do not recommend speaking to nonpsychologists outside of the university as a steady diet, an occasional conversation now and then can be refreshing.

REFERENCES

Arnold, M.B. (1960). *Emotion and personality.* Columbia Univ. Press, New York.

Block, J. (1957). Studies in the phenomenology of emotions. *J. Abnormal and Social Psychol.*, 54, 358-363.

Burt, C. (1950). The factorial study of emotions. In M.L. Reymert (Ed.), *Feelings and emotions.* McGraw-Hill, New York.

Duffy, E. (1962). *Activation and behavior.* Wiley, New York.

Harlow, H.F. and Stagner, R. (1933). Psychology of feelings and emotions. II. Theory of emotions. *Psychol. Rev.*, 40, 184-195.

Nowlis, V. and Nowlis, H.H. (1956). The description and analysis of moods, *Ann. N.Y. Acad. Sci.*, 65, 345-355.

Schachter, S. and Singer, J.E. (1962). Cognitive, social and physiological determinants of emotional state. *Psychol. Rev.*, 69, 379-399.

Schlosberg, H. (1954). Three dimensions of emotion. *Psychol. Rev.*, 61, 81-88.

Stagner, R. (1948). *Psychology of personality.* McGraw-Hill, New York.

White, R.W. (1959). Motivation reconsidered: The concept of competence. *Psychol. Rev.*, 66, 297-333.

Wundit, W. (1905). *Grundriss der Psychologie* (7th rev. ed.). Englemann, Leipzig.

Young, P.T. (1967). Affective arousal: Some implications. *Am. Psychologist*, 22, 32-40.

Part V

Mood

INTRODUCTION

This section consists of only one paper. Mood is a topic that has aroused sporadic interest but has been investigated haphazardly, without an overall theory to give direction to experimental research. There has been no attempt to provide a systematic framework that would connect mood with feelings and emotions, except for casual references. At the same time, Nowlis' Mood Adjective Check List has obvious connections with Davitz' descriptions of emotions, as reported in Part IV. It is to be hoped that the extensive reference list and the fascinating report of self-regulation of mood will stimulate further research and lead to a theoretical integration of mood within the general field of affect.

Chapter 18

Mood: Behavior and Experience

Vincent Nowlis*

My plan is to discuss four topics related to mood: (a) the renewal of interest in mood during the past two decades as one of the developments in human psychopharamacology; (b) mood theory; (c) mood measurement; and (d) recent developments related to the search for significant relations between private events and both behavioral and physiological events.

DRUGS AND THE RENEWAL OF INTEREST IN MOOD

In 1951 three psychologists, Helen Nowlis, Austin Riesen and I joined G. R. Wendt at the University of Rochester to help initiate a research investigation of the effects of drugs on the social behavior and motivational systems of young men who were college students. We four had been at Yale together in the late 30's, Wendt with a recent Ph.D. from Columbia, the rest of us as graduate students very much involved in learning about learning theory and applying S-R concepts to the analysis of such complex behavior as delayed response and social interaction in chimpanzee and the Zeigarnik effect in Yale undergraduates. At Rochester we carefully worked out a plan to observe the behavior of men in four-man groups in the laboratory and in field situations, to note differences in that social behavior with different drugs and to make inferences about changes in such motivational systems as aggression, anxiety and dependency. The drugs which at that time gave promise of producing both interesting and contrasting effects included the amphetamines, barbiturates and antihistamines. To gain some understanding of these and other drugs in various doses and combinations before administering them to our subjects, we four and a fifth collaborator, Jean

*The University of Rochester, New York.

Cameron, administered them to ourselves every Friday morning and spent the rest of the day, first, in a two to three hour lunch session and then, as far as possible, in our own normal academic, laboratory and domestic routines. As a step beyond the observation of behavior, Wendt suggested, on the basis of experience with a check list of symptoms he had developed in previous work on motion sickness and on drug effects, that we use the list but add to it additional adjectives and phrases which pertain to how people feel when they have had this or that drug. In deciding to ask our subjects, and ourselves, how they and we felt after ingestion of a standard white capsule, we opened a Pandora's box for the contents of which our behavioral training had not fully prepared us.

We assumed that a major goal in the exploratory study of the effects of a psychoactive drug on human behavior is to determine how, in a standard situation, the incidence and intensity of behavioral items change during the period preceding and the period following drug ingestion. With respect to a basic parameter of psychopharmacology, that of dose, we decided on the basis of our own experience that moderate doses would be the most appropriate with which to begin, since certain difficulties attend the use of both small and large doses of such drugs. Small doses are often simply equivalent to what may be called an "impure placebo" — that is, a substance ordinarily active pharmacologically but now present in a quantity so small that both its "main" effects and "side" effects are as placebo rather than as an active substance; such effects appear to be due almost wholly to the subject's expectancies and to the demand-characteristics and other features of the research environment. On the other hand, large doses may produce toxic effects together with unpleasant or strange sensations and feelings; the subject may then begin to concentrate on these and attempt to get relief from them. With the large dose, in other words, any modification in behavior may be largely due to reaction to or concern with these toxic effects.

Our plan was to provide for each subject an optimally moderate dose, which would produce few if any bothersome feelings or organic symptoms and at the same time produce behavioral changes beyond those attributable directly to expectancies and demand-features in the experimental setting. The serendipitous result of this plan was the finding that with moderate doses of certain psychoactive drugs the most dependable and interesting effect was what we had to call a change in mood. Precisely what that mood change was to be (with a certain drug and certain individual) was always somewhat uncertain, since it seemingly depended not only on the drug but also on the immediately preceding mood of the subject, the moods expressed by his partners, and on other external and internal factors (Nowlis and Nowlis, 1956). Basically, however, the subject did typically show a temporary change in the ways in which he was disposed to respond to the world and to himself.

We felt we had to infer that these were changes in mood because of what we saw not only in responses to the adjective check list, but also in spontaneous remarks, expressive behavior, speech, in topics selected for conversation, manner of performing tasks, and, generally, in relatively broad repertoires of behavior and experience. One of our original intents, that of studying a few motivational systems like aggression, anxiety, and dependency, was modified to permit monitoring of the broader spectrum which emerges when we think in terms of mood rather than specific motivations (Harway *et al.*, 1953; Laties, 1961; Nowlis *et al.*, 1953; Wendt and Cameron, 1961).

The unexpected encounter with mood which I have just described happened in our laboratory in the very early 1950's, just at the beginning of the contemporary explosion in the use of the so-called psychoactive drugs. In those days *everyone* knew, as people everywhere have probably always known, that some drugs change mood. It is of historical interest to note, however, that in our culture *at that time* mood change was not as salient in the popular image of drugs as it now is. Mood change was more often recognized casually as a kind of side effect of certain drugs. An interesting theme in the history of pharmacology is the transition of a side effect to a main effect. Drugs are developed, tested and initially marketed on a basis of a capacity for producing certain target or main effects with a minimum of side effects. With extended clinical use, however, an originally underevaluated side effect is sometimes found to be the important or significant or desired main effect. In contrast to our views of a few decades ago, a mood change is now an officially sanctioned and expected main effect of hundreds of important drugs. As example, in section 166.2 of the regulations pursuant to the Drug Abuse Control Amendments of 1965, there are 26 criteria listed to guide the Commissioner of the Food and Drug Administration in determining whether a potentially "dangerous" drug has "stimulant," "depressant," "hallucinogenic," and/or "habit forming" effects. Thirteen of these criteria refer directly or indirectly to specified moods or changes in mood. Are there other areas of psychology in which mood terms will prove to be equally useful?

MOOD THEORY

The term *mood* appears as a nontechnical term in the discourse of all or almost all areas of psychology as well as in everyday discourse. When the psychologist uses the term he rarely defines it, assuming everyone understands it. There are relatively few sustained general discussions of mood. Aristotle, as might be expected, supplies us with the earliest in the *Rhetoric*, which is, in part, a common sense manual of instructions for inducing moods through oratory and drama. The words applied to mood by Aristotle have been variously translated as "mood," "frame of mind," and "disposition." His practical theory is that, having induced a particular mood in the audience or jury, the orator or dramatist will then not only find it easier to elicit certain emotional and other responses in his listeners but can also count on the fact that certain other responses will be less likely than usual to occur. This common sense prototheory is a precursor to the behavioral theories of mood of Ryle (1949) and Skinner (1953), who also see mood as a temporary disposition toward a broad set of behavioral *and* private or subjective events. In relation to our later discussion, it should be noted that in their view, a verbal report such as "I am sad" may occur simply because a sad person may be strongly disposed to say so even though at that moment he may or may not be aware of any subjective feeling or subjective state which he would label "sad." Furthermore, since mood is a disposition, most of the behavioral items toward which one is temporarily disposed may not occur unless strengthened by prompts, probes or other events.

In my own so-called behavioral approach to the concept (Nowlis 1953; 1961; 1963; 1965), mood is a multidimensional set of temporary, reversible dispositions. Within intervals of minutes, hours, or rarely days, mood involves some constancies in behavior and subjective experience. Mood involves the entire person; a person is always in some set of moods. Mood may be estimated on the basis of indices which are otherwise trival. The heterogeneous determinants of mood are often obscure, remote or, though obvious, like the weather or the human situation, may be unaccessible to manipulative control; in such instances mood involves some constraints on behavior and experience. Moods are monitorings. Some of the parameters of mood reflect general patterns of psychobiological function and orientation. Some dimensions are always affective; others are not.

Because of the great importance of affect in psychoanalytic theory, that literature includes many studies of affective moods. The work of Jacobson (1957) is the most thorough psychoanalytic analysis of moods in general. Curiously, because we all start from the same common sense prototheory of mood, all of the features of the behavioral approach are also found in Jacobson's analysis. But she goes far beyond this in relating mood to other psychodynamic processes.

Still other elegant outgrowths from the Aristotelian prototypic stem are found in the existential and phenomenological literature. Since subjective experience is of great importance in these approaches to the study of man, it is that aspect of mood which is elaborately described and analyzed in this literature. For an excellent review of theories of mood, the reader is referred to *Mood and Personality* by Wessman and Ricks (1966). A unique and particularly interesting theory of mood has been developed by Cattell (1963).

In thinking about mood theory, I find that the application of mood terms to behavior and experience has represented a variety of relatively unsuccessful attempts to identify some intriguing yet perversely subtle and obscure ways in which behavior seems to be organized. In formulating future attempts such questions as the following may be helpful:

1. What are the processes which initiate, sustain and terminate an organized pattern of behavior and experience over temporal spans of moderate duration — that is, of durations for which it seems appropriate to use mood terms?

2. If the person is different in every mood, what is the relevance of mood to a theory of the self? Is the manipulation of mood a necessary first step in the experimental analysis of the self?

3. Is it appropriate to assume that mood is always complex and multidimensional and that we should talk about a temporary set of moods rather than about a mood? Or, on the other hand, is a mood simply the one temporarily most obvious or dominant and sustained component in the set of ever fluctuating mood components?

4. Are certain moods and changes in mood properly classed among the major goals of human action? Do they have a reinforcement function? What is their utility?

MOOD MEASUREMENT

Let us now briefly consider mood check lists, since these simple devices are now so widely used. One of the earliest, the Mood Adjective Check List (MACL), was developed at Rochester within a fairly explicit behavioral approach. We can assume that although many of the behavioral items and private events toward which one is disposed in a particular set of moods will not occur (be emitted, be elicited) during any one prolonged observation or testing period, those most likely to occur, since they tend to be least incompatible with other ongoing activities, are feelings and also verbal responses, especially if appropriately strengthened by prompts such as printed adjectives or other verbal responses congruent with the form "I feel. . . ." In selecting verbal responses for mood tests which are to be rapidly and repeatedly administered, we need not be as much concerned with their providing any access to the subjective feeling of the person as with their providing quantitative objective data which vary with mood. Even though superficial, trivial, and often thoughtlessly and rapidly emitted, such responses hopefully are also sincere, dependable and, indeed, susceptible to change in mood.

In putting together a list for factor analytic studies, Russel Green and I (Green, 1964; Nowlis and Green, 1957; Nowlis and Green, 1964) selected four groups of words for the purpose of using each group as tentative definition of a hypothesis about mood. These hypotheses were based on best guesses as to what general patterns of psychobiological function and orientation characterize man. On the basis of watching men for several years as their moods changed in the early drug research, I suggested these four patterns or dimensions: (a) activation and deactivation; (b) positive and negative social orientation; (c) control and lack or loss of control; (d) positive and negative appraisal of how things in general are going — that is, pleasantness and unpleasantness. Each pole of each dimension was then first defined in terms of the kind of behavior and experience toward which a person in that mood would be more strongly or selectively disposed; we then searched for the adjectives which college-educated Americans would apply to their behavior or feelings in that mood. Please note that many of these adjectives are relatively affectless; that is, some have to do more with behaviors and orientations than with affective feelings: e.g., *active, concentrating, self-centered, forgiving*. In other words, we assumed that nonaffective as well as affective events are useful in inferring mood and that some mood dimensions may be relatively free of affect. Our adjectives came from many sources; in particular, just as Harrison Gough got many of his trait adjectives for his ACL from Cattell's list of adjectives, we found many state adjectives for our MACL in the same list (Cattell, 1950).

The list of 130 words was then administered to about 450 college men at the start and finish of six different sessions in which five different mood-inducing films and one aggressive hoax were presented. Five sets of data were independently factor analyzed, yielding 11 factors, most of which could be matched with some confidence across the rotated solutions. The 11 are listed here, together with the original hypothesis each most closely resembles: aggression (negative social orientation), social affection (positive social orientation), surgency (pleasantness), elation (pleasantness), sadness (unpleasantness), vigor (activation), fatigue (deactivation), anxiety (lack or loss of control), concentration (control), egotism (control and negative social orientation), and skepticism (negative social orientation). The results are of interest because they identify a few previously unnoted dimensions of mood which deserve further study, like concentration or like activation (Thayer, 1967; Thayer and Cox, 1969).

The most striking discrepancy between the hypotheses and the empirical factors is the unipolarity of the latter, a finding now replicated many times over. Methodologically, this finding suggests that any initial assumption of unipolarity or bipolarity of scale in this domain of mood, feeling and emotion should first be tested. Theoretically, the finding reminds us that moods often thought to be mutually exclusive may vary quite independently of each other and may thus be simultaneously present with considerable intensity in the same individual, as in the happy yet tearful theater-goer, the hostile lover, the very tired but still overactive child, and the surgent, well-controlled thrill seeker who is also intensely frightened.

Since the typical mood check list, like a short form of the MACL, used in such studies covers about eight dimensions of mood, each defined by as few as three words, we can ask some embarrassing questions. Why would anyone care to obtain estimates of so many aspects of mood? What would lead anyone to rely on three little words for each estimate? Who is knowledgeable enough or clever enough to formulate hypotheses about the changes expected in each of eight dimensions during or after a particular mood-changing experience? The record shows that what has usually happened is that the investigator used the mood scales as a preliminary or supplementary monitor of the effects of a certain kind of treatment in which he was interested and that occasionally he did have hypotheses with respect to changes in scores for one or two dimensions but used the entire list because it is so short or because using the additional words helped to conceal some of his research interests from the subject. Like a pilot's check list, a mood check list is a preprogrammed way of checking and recording pertinent details about the current operational state of the organism. Undoubtedly better check lists, if not better organisms, will soon be available. However useful for monitoring and as an auxiliary index in the testing of hypotheses, they will *not* provide information which in and of itself tells us very much about mood, since their base (very brief and rapid avowals) is too narrow and their reach (number of dimensions) too broad. As Casey Stengel said about baseball players with long arms but very short fingers, they will not make it to the major leagues.

To return to mood check lists in general, what are they good for? There does seem to be a need for them, since we now have them, courtesy of many psychologists, in various formats, with various instructions (momentary mood, mood during the past hour, day, week, year), and with varied numbers of a priori dimensions or empirical factors (aggression alone, anxiety alone, depression alone, these three plus five or six others, etc.). They have been used by people of many ages and occupations and in several languages. Few psychological tests have been used in so many unusual circumstances: under the ocean, underground, in the air while parachuting or orbiting the earth, in modified atmospheres, in countless medical patients in such conditions as asthma, cancer, heart surgery, childbirth, enucleation of the eyeball, and, of course, in healthy individuals in an interesting sample of all the stressful situations known to man. For a review of some of these studies, see Nowlis (1965).*

In summary, to date the MACL and other check lists of mood and of affect have been perhaps most useful in providing a highly convenient mode of communication between investigator and the subject with respect to the way the

*Some of the more recent mood-relevant studies not included in that review will be found in: Agnew, 1964; Appley and Trumbull, 1967; Brown, 1966; Buss and Murray, 1965; Cameron *et al.*, 1967a, b; Constantinople, 1967; Deikman, 1966; Dittman, 1962; Dworkin and Efran, 1967; Fogel *et al.*, 1966; Frank, 1968; Frankenhaeuser *et al.*, 1968; Hall *et al.*, 1964; Heimstra *et al.*, 1967; Hoffer and Osmond, 1962; Kane *et al.*, 1967; Laxer, 1964; Lazarus *et al.*, 1966; Lorr *et al.*, 1967; Lubin, 1965a, 1966; Mahler, 1966; Mayfield and Allen, 1967; Menaker, 1967; Mons, 1967; Mueller, 1965; Myers *et al.*, 1968; Ruff and Korchin, 1967; Schwartz and Dubitzky, 1968; Sem-Jacobsen, 1963; Starkweather and Hargreaves, 1964; Stricker, 1967; Tannenbaum and Gaer, 1965; Tomkins, 1968; Velten, 1967; Weiss, 1966; Weybrew, 1967; Wiltsey, 1967; Zuckerman *et al.*, 1965.

latter feels, but this is also a noisy mode since the subject, to some extent, also tells us how he thinks he feels, things he ought to feel, or wants the investigator to believe he feels.

RECENT DEVELOPMENTS

Where do we go from here? From one point of view the term *mood* is not only nontechnical and pragmatic but also obsolescent. Its usefulness in everyday discourse continues to be more apparent than does its significance in science. A scientific Zeitgeist which fosters analytical thinking leads to experimental investigations of only a few categories of behavior at a time. Such research is now being done, for example, on the phenomena subsumed under such categories as aggression, anxiety and activation but these studies typically make no reference to the mood aspects of these categories. In concentrating on the affective, emotional, and motivational characteristics of such phenomena, can we exhaust the domain of mood without any necessary reference to mood? Even when the inevitable syntheses which follow analysis are done and the whole person and total set of the person are viewed, will mood terms be an essential part of such syntheses? The answer is not clear.

Technological progress often provides completely new modes of observing phenomena. A major difficulty in the study of the private events which, in part, characterize mood (and, indeed, of all private events and subjective states) has been their inaccessibility to observers other than the subject himself. A new area of research based on technical innovations in operant conditioning and self-regulation of various types of brain activity and of other neurophysiological activities now promises to provide more dependable access to those private events. As you know, operant control of such activities has now been demonstrated in animals at the level of the brain, the autonomic nervous system and the single neuron, as well as in man at the first two levels (Fetz, 1969; Katkin and Murray, 1968; Miller, 1969; Shapiro *et al.*, 1969). In particular, the work of Kamiya (1962), originally designed "as a demonstration of the behavioristic equivalent of an introspective act," provides a powerful convergence on private event, trainable verbal report and neurophysiological process, such that facts about all three are obtained at a single level of observation. In developing a mode of research which has been called experiential physiology, B. Brown (undated), Hart (1967), Kamiya (1969), MacDonald and Nowlis (1969), Nowlis and Kamiya (in press), Nowlis and MacDonald (1969) Stoyva and Kamiya (1968), Tart (1969), and others find some temporal correspondences between the report of certain subjective states and the display of EEG alpha activity, particularly prolonged, self-regulated alpha; they also suggest that still other states may be reported during the autoregulation of other EEG patterns. Verbal reports about these states frequently include mood-like terms and are used with some consistency by different subjects. It appears that in contrast to our work, which focussed on some of the "outer" or more public aspects of mood — in particular, on the rapid emission of a series of prompted verbal responses — the Kamiya method provides unique and important access to both inner and outer aspects of mood.

I think that it is neither ironic nor paradoxical that a behavioral method, that of operant conditioning, has suddenly taken on great promise in the exploration of consciousness. In 1956 Gustav Bergmann wrote as follows:

"What follows is the thesis of methodological behaviorism. It must *in principle* be possible to predict future behavior, including verbal behavior, from a sufficiency of information about present (and past) behavioral, physiological, and environmental variables. This is the thesis. Let me state one of its corollaries. Speaking commonsensically or, for that matter, clinically, we often attribute to a person a certain state of mind. We say that he or she perceived something, remembers something, plans something, is sad or gay, and so on. Nor is there any doubt, commonsensically, that we know what we mean when we assert such things, or, for that matter, that sometimes we are even right. It follows that it must *in principle* be possible to coordinate to any such statement another one, however complex, which mentions only behavioral, physiological, and environmental items, such that they are both true or both false. Otherwise one would have to maintain that we can, literally and not metaphorically speaking, directly observe other people's states of mind. Few nowadays are either bold or foolish enough to assert that."

Bergmann's challenge — that what can be done commonsensically can also be done scientifically — has not been directly responded to by many experimentalists. Why? First, because of uncertainty about or distrust of the possible criteria by which to judge whether ". . . we are. . . right" in attributing "to a person a certain state of mind." (After all, some indeterminate proportions of persons are quite unaware of many internal cues and are blind, stupid, mute or wrongheaded in their introspective acts. They should be trained up to certain standards of awareness of and ability to describe private events. But how?) Secondly, because of lack of knowledge about which statement (attribution of state of mind) to coordinate with "another one, however complex, which mentions only behavioral, physiological, and environmental items." Complexity it the key to the problem, since as Ax (in Appley and Trumbull, 1967, p. 361) has pointed out, the physiological psychologist, for example, can effectively monitor only a minute fraction of the complex neurophysiological activities of the person; and the subject, at the same time, can describe only a similarly small fraction of his stream of consciousness. Lack of correspondence may then simply signify unavailability of knowledge about what is indeed to be put into coordinated statements.

Let us note that the Kamiya method certainly does not let us "directly observe other people's states of mind." It does, however, provide partial solutions to both of the above difficulties: (a) training of the subject in improved awareness and discrimination of subjective states as well as in verbal report of such states and (b) a more selective focus on potentially interrelated subjective, physiological and verbal report variables. The method provides what Skinner (1954b, 1961) asked for many years ago: heterogeneous facts obtained at the same level of observation.

Let us apply the general strategy to a very simple case. Isolated on a desert island but with appropriate equipment, how could the color-blind parent of a young child with normal vision teach the child to name colors? One possible solution would be to provide the parent with suitable analogues (such as numbers for wave lengths) on a display yoked to the varying color stimuli in another display. As parent and child view both displays (or each his own) and exchange information and play games with the stimuli, they could develop a common language about the colors which only the child sees and experiences but to which the parent has only indirect access via the colorless but color-related analogue *and* via the increasingly discriminating descriptions by the child of what he sees. It is a variant of this game which is now being played with these analogic displays of internal processes. For the color stimulus, substitute a specific type of brain activity together with its accompanying organismic activities. For the yoked analogue, substitute the EEG display. For the awareness of sensation of color, substitute the awareness of subjective state. For a common language about color stimuli and color sensation, substitute a common language about brain activity and subjective state. There follow both improved awareness and improved control as well as more dependable verbal report.

I started my presentation this morning with a personal account of how a group of behavioral investigators became interested in mood through research on drugs, research in which we examined our own responses to drugs as well as those of our student subjects. I conclude with an account of a recent personal experience. As you would by now expect, when I first heard of Dr. Kamiya's work I decided to take advantage of any opportunity which might present itself to serve as a subject in learning to control subjective states through operant procedures. Other research interests had already led me away from mood research but our son, David Nowlis, is presently working on autoregulation of EEG rhythms in E.R. Hilgard's laboratory at Stanford. Last summer he invited me to be a subject. We arrived at the laboratory on a pleasant Sunday afternoon. Electrodes were placed at several spots on my scalp and I was left in a comfortable chair in a dark room while David and an associate worked with the instruments in the next room, occasionally conversing with each other or with me. It was first determined that I was producing enough but not too much alpha to make the session worthwhile and that this was true whether my eyes were open or closed. Then a circuit was closed which, I was told, sounded a mild tone whenever I did produce alpha. These tones occurred in an irregular manner which at first seemed to have no rhyme or reason. I was permitted to "play" at turning the tone off and on and soon I began to develop some vague hunches about the differences between how I felt as the tone came on and went off and also about how to turn the tone on or off. Then a typical schedule was instituted: keep the tone on as much as possible during a two-mintue period; short rest; keep it off for two minutes. My score, in terms of seconds on or off, was given to me after each trial. Increasing the time the tone was off was easier than increasing the time it was on, but soon I had the tone sounding for most of each two-minute "on" period, and not sounding at all during the other two-minute periods. At one point I heard mildly excited voices in the next room. They seemed to be approving or congratulatory, for, as I later learned, the alpha rhythms had now spread extensively over my head. Interestingly, the tone stayed on despite the pleasant distraction coming from the next room. It seemed to me at the moment that I was in a particularly tranquil, leisurely, relaxed but alert mood and that somehow my introspective acts and attentive acts were compatible with, rather than modifiers of, whatever background CNS activities were regnant at the time. After a final period for free play, the session was ended. It had lasted for about an hour. I feel that in that one session I had learned a little more about controlling or entering alpha and nonalpha than I did about discriminating one subjective state from another, especially when such states were briefly present. With repeated sessions some subjects apparently do learn both excellent control and excellent discriminative ability.

David informs me that former subjects, who were initially paid for their participation, often seek further opportunity to serve as subjects — sometimes offering to do so without pay or even to pay for the opportunity! I suspect that Dr. Kamiya has been urged to design a relatively inexpensive outfit for learn-it-yourself autoregulation of alpha rhythms at home. Having lived through the past twenty years with its increased and in many ways still unsatisfactory use of drugs for the control of mood, let us not be surprised to find that autoregulation of brain and autonomic processes through operant self-conditioning will soon be of wide-spread interest. It has been said that the private sea is the new frontier. We are just beginning to learn how to communicate quickly and effectively while exploring that frontier.

APPENDIX

Pencil-and-paper devices for obtaining self-report of mood or emotional state have taken many forms, many of which can be found among the references. Many colleagues at the University of Rochester helped to design the particular format which has come to be known as the Mood Adjective Check List (MACL).

TABLE I

A SHORT FORM OF THE MOOD ACL

Each of the following words describes feelings or mood. Please use the list to describe your feelings at the moment you read each word. If the word definitely describes how you feel at the moment you read it, circle the double check (vv) to the right of the word. For example, if the word is *relaxed* and you are definitely feeling relaxed at the moment, circle the vv as follows:

relaxed (vv) v ? no (This means you definitely feel relaxed at the moment.)

If the word only slightly applies to your feelings at the moment, circle the single check v as follows:

relaxed vv (v) ? no. (This means you feel slightly relaxed at the moment.)

If the word is not clear to you or you cannot decide whether or not it applies to your feelings at the moment, circle the question mark as follows:

relaxed vv v (?) no. (This means you cannot decide whether you are relaxed or not.)

If you definitely decide the word does not apply to your feelings at the moment, circle the no as follows:

relaxed vv v ? (no.) (This means you are definitely not relaxed at the moment.)

Work rapidly. Your first reaction is best. Work down the first column, then to the next. Please mark all words. This should take only a few minutes. Please begin.

angry vv v ? no	kindly vv v ? no
clutched up vv v ? no	sad vv v ? no
carefree vv v ? no	skeptical vv v ? no
elated vv v ? no	egotistic vv v ? no
concentrating vv v ? no	energetic vv v ? no
drowsy vv v ? no	rebellious vv v ? no
affectionate vv v ? no	jittery vv v ? no
regretful vv v ? no	witty vv v ? no
dubious vv v ? no	pleased vv v ? no
boastful vv v ? no	intent vv v ? no
active vv v ? no	tired vv v ? no
defiant vv v ? no	warmhearted vv v ? no
fearful vv v ? no	sorry vv v ? no
playful vv v ? no	suspicious vv v ? no
overjoyed vv v ? no	self-centered vv v ? no
engaged in thought vv v ? no	vigorous vv v ? no
sluggish vv v ? no	

The particular adjectives which make up the list given in Table 1 consist of some of those which Russel Green and I selected after a number of factor analytic studies (supported through a research contract with the Office of Naval Research) in which large numbers of college students responded to the MACL while in various experimentally induced moods. (When a format similar to that in Table I is used, a score for any factor may be obtained by summing the scores for the individual adjective variables in the factor, letting vv = 3, v = 2, ? = 1, no =.0. Variables presently assigned to each factor are listed below.) An important characteristic of this format is its flexibility of structure (e.g., rating scales can be substituted for check marks) and of content (e.g., instructions can be modified and factor content redefined or extended to include larger numbers of words or phrases). Researchers with an interest in mood often become interested in designing their own list and format and, in this day of easy access to beautifully programmed computers, in developing and testing better hypotheses about mood factors and dimensions. Permission to use the list presented in Table I is, of course, granted.

The following lists , discussed more extensively elsewhere (Nowlis, 1965; Lorr *et al.*, 1967), provide suggestions for further exploration of 12 presently hypothesized mood factors. For each factor the initial group is from the Green-Nowlis studies and is followed by any *additional* words found for similar factors in a sampling of studies done by others. As indicated earlier, Cattell's abundant and prolonged work continues to be an important source of adjectival and other variables for defining mood factors.

Aggression: defiant, rebellious, angry, grouchy, annoyed, fed-up. McNair-Lorr: furious, ready to fight.

Anxiety: clutched up, fearful, jittery. McNair-Lorr: tense, nervous, shaky, on edge. Zuckerman: afraid, desperate, fearful, frightened, panicky, shaky, upset, terrified, worrying.

Surgency: carefree, playful, witty, lively, talkative.

Elation: elated, overjoyed, pleased, refreshed and lighthearted (which also has high loadings on Surgency).

Concentration: cluster 1, careful, contemplative, introspective; cluster 2, clear-thinking, decisive, efficient, attentive, earnest, serious; cluster 3, concentrating, engaged in thought, intent. McNair-Lorr: able to concentrate, able to think clearly, efficient.

Fatigue: drowsy, dull, sleepy, tired. McNair-Lorr: fatigued, worn-out, sluggish, weary.

Vigor or Activation: active, energetic, vigorous, bold, strong, industrious. Thayer: full of pep, peppy, quick, lively (also in Surgency).

Social Affection: affectionate, forgiving, kindly, warmhearted. McNair-Lorr: friendly, cooperative, good-natured, understanding.

Sadness: regretful, sad, sorry. McNair-Lorr: (Depression-dejection) worthless,

helpless, unhappy, discouraged, blue, lonely, gloomy. Also see Zuckerman and Lubin (1965) and Lubin (1966).
Skepticism: skeptical, suspicious, dubious.
Egotism: egotistic, self-centered, boastful.
Nonchalance: nonchalant, leisurely. Thayer: (General Deactivation) at rest, quiet, placid.

REFERENCES

Agnew, N.M. (1964). The relative value of self-report and objective tests in assessing the effects of amphetamine. *J. Psychiat. Research*, 2, 85-100.

Appley, M.H., and Trumbull, R. (Eds.) (1967). *Psychological stress.* Appleton, New York.

Beecher, H.K. (1959). *Measurement of subjective responses.* Oxford Univ. Press, New York.

Bergmann, G. (1956). The contribution of J.B. Watson. *Psychol. Rev.*, 63, 265-276.

Brown, B.B. Identification of subjective feeling states by association with EEG alpha activity represented by a light signal. Undated manuscript. V.A. Hospital, Sepulveda, California.

Brown, C.C. (1966). Psychophysiology at an interface. *Psychophysiol.*, 3, 1-7.

Buss, A.H., and Murray, E.N. (1965). Activity level and words connoting mood. *Perceptual and Motor Skills*, 21, 684-686.

Cameron, J.S., Specht, P.G., and Wendt, G.R. (1967a). Effects of dramamine-analgesic-caffeine combination on moods, emotions, and motivations. *J. Psychol.*, 67, 263-270.

Cameron, J.S., Specht, P.G., and Wendt, G.R. (1967b). Effects of a placebo and an acetominophen-salicylamide combination on moods, emotions and motivations. *J. Psychol.*, 67, 257-262.

Cattell, R.B. (1950). *Personality: A systematic theoretical and factual study.* McGraw-Hill, New York.

Cattell, R.B. (1963). Personality, role, mood, and situation-perception. *Psychol. Rev.*, 70, 1-18.

Clyde, D. (1960). Self-rating. In L. Uhr and J. G. Miller (Eds.), *Drugs and behavior.* Wiley, New York.

Constantinople, A.P. (1967). Perceived instrumentality of the college as a measure of attitudes toward college. *J. Personality and Social Psychol.*, 5, 196-201.

Deikman, A. (1966). De-automatization and the mystic experience. *Psychiatry*, 29, 324-338.

Dittman, A.T. (1962). The relationship between body movements and moods in interviews. *J. Consulting Psychol.*, 26, 480.

Dworkin, E.S., and Efran, J.S. (1967). The angered: their susceptibility to varieties of humor. *J. Personality and Social Psychol.*, 6, 233-236.

Fetz, E.E. (1969). Operant conditioning of cortical unit activity. *Science*, 163, 955-958.

Fogel, M.L., Curtis, G.C., Kordasz, F., and Smith, W.G. (1966). Judges' ratings, self-ratings and checklist reports of affects. *Psychol. Reports*, 19, 299-307.

Frank, K.A. (1968). Mood differentiation and psychological differentiation: some relationships between mood variations and Witkin's research. *Dissertation Abstracts*, 28, 5203-5204.

Frankenhaeuser, M., Mellis, I., Rissler, A., Bjorkvall, C., and Patkal, P. (1968). Catecholamine excretion as related to cognitive and emotional reaction patterns. *Psychosomat. Med.*, 30, 109-120.

Green, R.F. (1964). The measurement of mood. Technical Report, Office of Naval Research: Contract No. Nonr-668(12).

Hall, P., Spear, F.G., and Stirland, D. (1964). Diurnal variation of subjective mood in depressive states. *Psychiatric Q.*, 38, 529-536.

Hart, J.T. (1967). Autocontrol of EEG alpha. Paper presented at the 7th annual meeting of the Society for Psychophysiological Research, San Diego, October.

Harway, V.T., Lanzetta, J.T., Nowlis, H.H., Nowlis, V., and Wendt, G.R. (1953). Chemical influences on behavior: II. Development of methods and preliminary results on the effects of some drugs on emotional and social behavior. Technical Report, Office of Naval Research, Project 144-060.

Heimstra, N.W., Ellingstad, V.S., and DeKock, A.R. (1967). Effects of operator mood on performance in a simulated driving task. *Perceptual and Motor Skills*, 25, 729-735.

Hoffer, A., and Osmond, H. (1962). The relationship between mood and time perception. *Psychiatric Q. Suppl.*, 36, 87-92.

Hollister, L.E. (1968). Some human pharmacological studies of three psychotropic drugs. *J. Clin. Pharmacol. and J. New Drugs*, 8, 95-101.

Jacobson, E. (1957). Normal and pathological moods; their nature and functions. *Psychoanalytic study of the child.* Vol. XIV. International Univ. Press, New York.

Johnson, E., III and Myers, T.I. (1967). The development and use of the primary affect scale (PAS). Research Reports No. 1. Naval Medical Research Institute, Bethesda.

Kane, F.J., Jr., Daly, R.J., Ewing, J.A., and Keeler, M.H. (1967). Mood and behavioral changes with progestational agents. *Brit. J. Psychiatry*, 113, 265-268.

Katkin, E.S., and Murray, E. (1968). Instrumental conditioning of autonomically mediated behavior: theoretical and methodological issues. *Psychol. Bull.*, 70, 52-68.

Kamiya, J. (1962). Conditioned discrimination of the EEG alpha rhythm in humans. Abstract of paper presented at the Western Psychological Association, San Francisco.

Kamiya, J. (1969). Operant control of the EEG alpha rhythm and some of its reported effects on consciousness. In C. Tart (Ed.), *Altered states of consciousness.* Wiley, New York.

Laties, V. (1961). Modification of affect, social behavior and performance by sleep deprivation and drugs. *J. Psychiatric Research*, 1, 12-24.

Laxer, R.M. (1964). Relation of real self-rating to mood and blame, and their interaction in depression. *J. Consulting Psychol.*, 28, 538-546.

Lazarus, R.S., Speisman, J.C., Mordkoff, A.M., and Davison, L.A. (1962). A laboratory study of psychological stress produced by a motion picture film. *Psychol. Monographs*, 76, No. 34 (Whole No. 553).

Larzarus, R.S., Opton, E., Jr., Tomita, M., and Kodoma, M. (1966). A cross-cultural study of stress-reaction patterns in Japan. *J. Personality and Social Psychol.*, 4, 622-633.

Lorr, M., Daston, P., and Smith, I.R. (1967). An analysis of mood states. *Educational and Psychological Measurement*, 27, 89-96.

Lubin, B. (1965a). Adjective check list for measurement of depression. *Arch. Gen. Psychiat.*, 12, 57-62.

Lubin, B. (1965b). A modified version of the self-disclosure inventory. *Psychol. Reports*, 17, 498.

Lubin, B. (1966). Fourteen brief depression adjective check lists. *Arch. Gen. Psychiat.*, 15, 205-208.

MacDonald, H. and Nowlis, D.P. (1969). Terminology, apparatus and procedure in EEG alpha feedback training. Hawthorne House Research Memorandum No. 95, Stanford University.

McNair, D.M., and Lorr, M. (1964). An analysis of mood in neurotics. *J. Abnormal and Social Psychol.*, 69, 620-627.

Mahler, M. (1966). Some preliminary notes on the development of basic moods, including depression. *Can. Psychiat. Assoc.*, 11, (suppl.), 250-258.

Mayfield, D., and Allen, D. (1967). Alcohol and affect: a psychopharmacological study. *Am. J. Psychiat.*, 123, 1346-1351.

Menaker, T. (1967). Anxiety about drinking in alcoholics. *J. Abnormal Psychol.*, 72, 43-49.

Miller, N.E. (1969). Learning of visceral and glandular responses. *Science*, 163, 434-445.

Mons, W.E. (1967). The visual apperception test 1960 of Professor Rafi Kahn, Univ. of Chicago. *Rorschach Newsletter*, 12, 8-9.

Mueller, S.R. (1965). The effects of alcohol upon the alcoholic's conformity behavior and mood states. *Dissertation Abstracts*, 26, 2872.

Myers, T.I., Johnson, E., III. and Smith, S. (1968). Subjective stress and affect states as a function of sensory deprivation. *Proc. 76th Annual Convention Am. Psychol. Assoc.*, 3, 623-624.

Nowlis, D.P. and Kamiya, J. (in press). The control of electroencephlographic alpha rhythms through auditory feedback and the associated mental activity. *Psychophysiology*.

Nowlis, D.P. and MacDonald, H. (1969). Further evidence for rapidly developed control of EEG alpha rhythms through feedback training, and reports of associated mental activities. Hawthorne House Research Memorandum No. 95, Stanford University.

Nowlis, H.H. (1969). *Drugs on the college campus*. Doubleday, New York.

Nowlis, H.H., Nowlis, V., Riesen, A.H., and Wendt, G.R. (1953). Chemical influences on behavior: III. Technical Report, Office of Naval Research. Project 144-060.

Nowlis, V. (1953). The development and modification of motivational systems in personality. In M.R. Jones (Ed.), *Current theory and research in motivation*. Univ. of Nebraska Press, Lincoln.

Nowlis, V. (1959). The experimental analysis of mood (Abstract). XVth International Congress of Psychology, Acta Psychol., 15, 426.

Nowlis, V. (1961). Methods for studying mood changes produced by drugs. *Revue de Psychologie Appliquee*, 11, 373-386.

Nowlis, V. (1963). The concept of mood. In S.M. Farber and R.H.L. Wilson (Eds), *Conflict and creativity*. McGraw-Hill, New York.

Nowlis, V. (1965). Research with the mood adjective check list. In S.S. Tomkins and C.E. Izard (Eds.), *Affect, cognition* and *personality*. Springer, New York.

Nowlis, V. (1967a). Invited commentary. In M.H. Appley and R. Trumbull, (Eds.), *Psychological stress*. Appleton, New York.

Nowlis, V. (1967b). Review of A.E. Wessman and D.F. Ricks, *Mood and personality. Am. J. Psychol.*, 80, 146-150.

Nowlis, V., and Green, R.F. (1957). The experimental analysis of mood. Technical Report, Office of Naval Research: Contract No. Nonr-668 (12).

Nowlis, V., and Green, R.F. (1964). Factor analytic studies of mood. Technical Report, Office of Naval Research: Contract No. Nonr-668 (12).

Nowlis, V., and Nowlis, H.H. (1956). The analysis of mood. *N. Y. Acad. Sci.*, 65, 345-355.

Ruff, G.E., and Korchin, S.J. (1967). Adaptive stress behavior. Pp. 297-323 in M.H. Appley and R. Trumbull (Eds.), *Psychological stress*. Appleton, New York.

Ryle, G. (1949). *The concept of mind*. Hutchinson, London.

Schwartz, J.L., and Dubitzky, M. (1968). Changes in anxiety, mood, and self-esteem resulting from an attempt to stop smoking. *Am. J. Psychiat.*, 124, 1580-1584.

Sem-Jacobsen, C.W. (1967). Brain and consciousness: intracerebral depth electrographic studies in the human brain. Final Report, Grant No. 61-236. New Haven, Connecticut. The Foundations' Fund for Research in Psychiatry, 1963. Cited in Appley and Trumbull (Eds.), *Psychological stress*. Appleton, New York.

Shapiro, D., Tursky, B., Gershon, E., and Stern, M. (1969). Effects of feedback and reinforcement on the control of human systolic blood pressure. *Science*, 163, 588-590.

Skinner, B.F. (1954a). *Science and human behavior.* Macmillan, New York.

Skinner, B.F. (1954b). Experimental psychology. In *Current trends in psychology and the behavioral sciences.* Univ. of Pittsburgh Press.

Skinner, B.F. (1957). *Verbal behavior.* Appleton, New York.

Skinner, B.F. (1961). The flight from the laboratory. In *Current trends in psychological theory.* Univ. of Pittsburgh Press.

Starkweather, J.A., and Hargreaves, W.A. (1964). The influence of sodium pentobarbital on vocal behavior. *J. Abnormal and Social Behavior*, 69, 123-126.

Stoyva, J., and Kamiya, J. (1968). Electrophysiological studies of dreaming as the prototype of a new strategy in the study of consciousness. *Psychol. Rev.*, 75, 192-205.

Stricker, G. (1962). An approach to assessing the meaning of "no change" in a pre-post experimental design. *J. Gen. Psychol.*, 67, 237-240.

Stricker, G. (1967). A pre-experimental inquiry concerning cognitive determinants of emotional state. *J. Gen. Psychol.*, 76, 73-79.

Tannenbaum, P.H., and Gaer, E.P. (1965). Mood change as a function of stress of protagonist and degree of identification in a film-viewing situation. *J. Personality and Social Psychol.*, 2, 612-616.

Tart, C. (1969). *Altered states of consciousness.* Wiley, New York.

Thayer, R.E. (1967). Measurement of activation through self-report. *Psychol. Reports.*, 20, 663-678.

Thayer, R.E., and Cox, S.J. (1969). Activation, manifest anxiety and verbal learning. *J. Exp. Psychol.*, in press.

Tomkins, S.S. (1968). Affects: primary motives of man. *Humanitas*, 3, 321-345.

Velten, E.C. (1967). The induction of elation and depression through the reading of structured sets of mood-statements. *Dissertation Abstracts*, 28, 1700-1701.

Weiss, B., and Laties, V.G. (1962). Enhancement of human performance by caffeine and the amphetamines. *Pharmacolog. Rev.*, 14, 1-36.

Weiss, J.H. (1966). Mood states associated with asthma in children. *J. Psychosomat. Research*, 10, 267-273.

Wendt, G.R., and Cameron, J.S. (1961). Chemical studies of behavior: V. Procedures in drug experimentation with college students. *J. Psychol.*, 51, 173-211.

Wendt, G.R., Cameron, J.S., and Specht, P.G. (1962). Chemical studies of behavior: VI. Placebo and dramamine as methodological controls, and effects on moods, emotions and motivations. *J. Psychol.*, 53, 257-279.

Wessman, A.E., and Ricks, D.F. (1966). *Mood and personality.* Holt, New York.

Weybrew, B.J. (1967). Patterns of psychophysiological response to military stress. In M.H. Appley and R. Trumbull (Eds.) *Psychological stress.* Appleton, New York.

Wiltsey, R.G. (1967). Some relationships between verbal reports of pleasant and unpleasant moods, sleep duration and sleep quality variables in college students. *Dissertation Abstracts*, 28, 346-347.

Zuckerman, M., and Lubin, B. (1965). Normative data for the multiple affect adjective check list. *Psychol. Reports*, 16, 438.

Zuckerman, M., Lubin, B., and Robins, S. (1965). Validation of the multiple affect adjective check list in clinical situations. *J. Consulting Psychol.*, 29, 594.

Part VI

The Role of Feelings
and Emotions in Personality

INTRODUCTION

Perhaps it is significant that of all the participants only two Europeans, one a psychologist, the other a philosopher, have concentrated on the role of feeling and emotion in personality. Wellek, the psychologist, proposes that personality traits vary within a continuum whose poles are opposites. In emotion, this continuum ranges from superficial, though often intense emotional episodes to profound, deeply felt, and personally relevant emotional attitudes. Wellek suggests that individual differences in these dimensions are of great importance for personality assessment.

Strasser, the philosopher, goes one step further and insists that feeling and emotion are the basic modes of experiencing others, and even oneself. This emotional mode of experience, he thinks, is the ground of all knowlege, is direct, immediate, and enables us to develop our objectifying knowledge of the outside world. Emotion, indeed, becomes the ground and foundation upon which our life of reflection is built. Here again, we can see a connection between this view and earlier discussions (Arnold, Lazarus) that emphasized an immediate, direct, unwitting appraisal of things and people, as distinct from the deliberate, reflective judgment of weal or woe that is possible only for the human adult and older child.

279

Chapter 19

Emotional Polarity in Personality Structure

Albert Wellek*

The concepts and terms used in personality study are so vague and ambiguous, particularly when it comes to trait names, that it is difficult if not impossible to prove or disprove the personality theories built upon them.

Consider, for instance, the concept of *will* with its burden of philosophical controversy, consider the term *vitality*, or the terms *feeling* and *emotion* with which we are concerned here. They all indicate concepts fundamental to personality structure, yet are understood differently by each of the theorists using them. Personality descriptions couched in such terms are indispensable for communication yet woefully equivocal, for instance the statements that somebody is "vital," or "willful," or "emotional," or that he has "vitality," "will power," or "vital energy." The same holds for such popular expressions as: "a man of strong determination," "a man of fine feelings," and "a man of heart." Unless such concepts are carefully analyzed, most statements used in personality description and assessment will be ambiguous and vague.

THE PRINCIPLE OF POLARITY

Since 1941, I have tried to clear up these conceptual difficulties by proposing the principle of polarity in personality theory. It means that personality traits vary within a continuum whose poles are opposites. This principle is the key to the system of personality traits worked out in my book, *Polarity in the Structure of Personality*, first published in 1950, with the third revised edition appearing in 1966. (See also Gilbert, 1951.)

*Joh. Gutenberg University, Mainz, Germany.

Along the lines of this symposium, then, I will select from this theory the analysis of emotionality, conceived as an intermediate level within the total structure of personality.

In a controversy with P. Hofstätter of Hamburg, formerly of the Catholic University in Washington, D.C. (Hofstätter, 1956; Wellek, 1956) I discussed the fact that general statements on emotional disposition lack definition and precise meaning. Hofstätter, however, insisted that such statements (e.g., that a person is emotional — *gefühlvoll*) imply a nearly infinite number of test situations in which the subject is expected to behave in the described way. But if that is true, such a statement makes no sense because of the ambiguity of the terms employed. For the purposes of personality assessment, feeling and emotion must be distinguished from "heart" or sentiment (in the sense of the Greek *thymos*, the German *Gemüt*, the French *coeur* or sentiment). Emotions of the heart (*Gemütsgefühle*) have a personal or existential relevance, they are anchored in the "endothymic ground" — in the "core" of personality structure. They differ from superficial, flat, or shallow feelings, and even more from emotions in the narrow sense (as illustrated by the phrase "boiling with rage"). Love, friendship, faithfulness, are emotions of the heart; they concern, involve, and engage a man in his very nature; they may move, touch, stir, or shake him and even change or transform him in his identity. On the other hand, anger aroused by a trifle, or by hurt vanity, is superficial and shallow, no matter how intense. This is true even for the rage and fury that go so far as to want to kill the enemy or destroy innocent objects. Such emotional outbursts touch a man vitally, but never in his very nature, in the core of his being. When his anger, as we say, has "died down," the whole matter will interest him no longer. Often the angry, "choleric" person himself cannot understand how he could have been so enraged a short time ago. Accordingly, we must distinguish the man who is emotionally responsive (*gemütvoll*) from a man who is excitable. Both types are emotional (*gefühlvoll*) but in quite different, even opposite ways.

Forty years ago, at the Wittenberg symposium, Felix Krueger (the successor of Wilhelm Wundt at Leipzig) had emphasized this difference. In the conclusion of his paper he refers to the sometimes tragic "conflict of structural dispositions among themselves, which we experience in depth like other structurally conditioned experiences. . . . (Such) experiences are value experiences as contrasted with momentary excitements; significant emotional insights and profoundly integrative thoughts, in contrast to fleeting hunches or opinions taken over from others; and decisions based on a sense of duty or responsibility. Such structural dispositions are realized whenever the individual is strongly convinced that his whole existence and the level of development he has achieved are at stake in his action. These profoundly emotional experiences are on an entirely different and deeper level than his normal life. They are entirely different from momentary emotions which have warmth and intensity but no depth" (Krueger, 1928, p. 106).

In his phenomenological description of emotion, Krueger envisages a polarity of intensity vs. depth of emotion, of force or vehemence vs. personal relevance. Of course, we must not assume that only profound emotions have personal relevance while explosive emotions are devoid of it. In a way, the reverse is true. Emotional explosions affect a man most intensively, *vitally*. Opposed to this vital engagement, there is another kind of involvement, demonstrated when a man is gripped in his very being by a profound emotional experience. Emotional episodes affect the body; but a profound emotional experience touches a man's psychological existence, his metaphysical core.

This factor of vital organismic relevance, corresponding to the intensity and force of affect, is missing in Krueger's description. Also, he neglects to emphasize that the intensity or force of emotion is identical with its drive aspect. The emotional impulsion, like every other drive, is organismic in nature while emotional depth — as Krueger points out — is a nonorganic, perhaps even a spiritual dimension.

On the other hand, quite a different dimension of emotion is tapped when emotions are classified (Claparède, 1928) according to their degree of organismic adaptation, that is, according to the behavior that accompanies or follows them. Such classification seems to emphasize the drive dimension of explosive affect and its behavioral consequences for the living being. This is not a phenomenological distinction but a classification that uses the drive dimension as a principle.

Even more rigorously than Krueger, I would insist not only on a distinction between intensity and depth of emotional experience, but on an actual antagonism. Explosive emotions tend to be superficial while profound (and thus enduring) emotional experiences tend to be less intense, so compensating for their greater phenomenal and existential breadth. Profound emotional experiences often last a lifetime and may even transcend death, as in the lover's faithfulness to the beloved.

Intensity vs. Depth

In addition, such opposition or polarity involves the manifold variations of emotional attitudes and dispositions. A man's emotional disposition may tend predominantly or almost exclusively toward explosive affectivity or, on the other hand, may tend predominantly or almost exclusively toward profound experiences. When extreme, examples of the first type of disposition are said to demonstrate lack of sensitivity, toughmindedness, or even brutality; examples of the second type, sensitivity, emotional responsiveness, or tendermindedness.

In general, explosiveness of affect seems to be opposed to depth of emotion. Emotional intensity in the widest sense (not merely in the sense of force) is expressed as excitability but also as sentimentality. By sentimentality is usually meant a facile, "gushing" emotional response without solid foundation, sometimes with an affectation, i.e., pretension, of depth. This means lack of genuine feeling, resulting in spurious emotion, in phoniness. The latter involves another polarity, the tension between lower and higher levels of the personality, the Id and the Ego. The disproportion seen in such exaggerated responses creates a typically unconvincing and even ridiculous impression. It is this negative form of exuberance that is meant by sentimentality. (There are positive forms, too, which will be discussed later.)

Accordingly, if we say that a man is emotional, the question is: do we mean that he is sensitive, excitable, or sentimental? Rather thoughtlessly, sensitivity and emotionality are often equated. True, the term emotionality is equivocal; but the second notion, sensitivity, is quite precise, on the supposition that it is understood as *thymos* (Gemüt), i.e., emotional depth.

When a man has emotional depth, he has a readiness to profound experience which penetrates his total personal being. Having both deep and broad foundations in the total structure of personality, profound emotions are both durable and resistant, always ready for new actualizations. Friendship, love, loyalty to friends or country may not be always consciously experienced, simply because such sentiments extend throughout life and may last a lifetime. But they are present as a structural readiness (in the sense of G. Murphy, 1947, or J. Bruner, 1957, who both used this notion, the latter to explain "social perception"). Ready as potencies, they are always at our disposal. This is true also for feelings of value, feelings of significance, a sense of duty, and other sentiments of probity and character (as Krueger pointed out long ago). In all these cases, there is an almost continual transition from the actual or conscious state to a potential or subconscious readiness. Deep feelings of friendship or love, for instance, are not experienced constantly. They lose their state of actuality repeatedly because their intensity may decline to zero at a particular moment or even for longer periods of time. Nevertheless, as sentiments (in the sense of McDougall, 1932) these feelings preserve their structural or attitudinal reality; they represent a readiness to feel such friendship or love, and to act accordingly.

At the same time, not every feeling lacking intensity is profound. There are feelings of indifference, nuances of apathy or unconcern that are neither deep nor intensive. Incidentally, such feelings of indifference are indifferent only with regard to their object, their intentional content. Taken phenomenologically, as states of mind, all feelings and emotions are of concern to the person experiencing them. They have "warmth" at least to a minimal degree, even when they are feelings of indifference; indeed, William James (1890) recognized this relevance and warmth as a basic property of all feelings.

Synthesis of Intensity and Depth

On the other hand, the antagonism of intensity and depth of emotion is by no means total. There is a dialectical synthesis in which emotions are both deep and intensive. Certain types of aesthetic experiences and moral convictions have this character. Genuine *pathos* unites intensity (force) with depth of feeling. False pathos, on the other hand, merely pretends to such synthesis and becomes annoying because it misses out. Aesthetic experiences and strongly held convictions tend to be profound; thus they resolve the opposition between depth and intensity that is the rule in everyday life. Psychologically, it is the essential character of great art, particularly drama and tragedy, that strong emotions lose their trend to superficiality and become both intense and profound. This is of fundamental importance, for it is the essence of dialectical opposition to allow for such synthesis, as it is the essence of polarity to allow for contrast but not to insist on exclusion. This is the *coincidentia oppositorum* of Nicholas of Cusa.

Genuine pathos in the best sense is not appreciated by those whose emotions are sterile or poorly developed. Their thin emotionality cannot stand the two-dimensional expansion toward intensity as well as depth. At best, when stimulated by a concrete situation, their emotions precipitate a momentary explosion which is intense enough but lacks all depth. On the other hand, such people are easily taken in by false pathos, which offers them the illusion of strong emotions without exacting payment in the form of a profound experience of which they are incapable.

In addition to this synthesis of depth and force (in pathos) there is an analogous synthesis of depth and exuberance (in tenderness). Long ago, Kant (1764) insisted that tenderness is a species of the "feeling of the sublime." Tenderness is a tendency toward another, a bridge between lovers, and as such is a structure that offers a kind of synthesis. On the one hand, tenderness is rooted in sentiment (thymos) and in tender feelings for tender things, and so belongs to profound emotional experiences. But on the other hand, being tender and affectionate always means being strongly moved by the realization that the beloved is what he is and that he belongs to us. We are particularly affectionate toward children who move us because they are so small, so sweet, so helpless. A typical form of feminine coquetry tends to expose the softness and weakness of the "weaker" sex so as to arouse protective and tender emotions. (See Konrad Lorenz' "baby stereotype," 1965.) Such tenderness may easily border on sentimentality; but this slightly sentimental coloring of genuine tenderness and affection does not impress us as embarrassing or phony.

At any rate, a touch of emotional intensity (though not of the explosive kind) is contained in the feeling of tenderness, at least as emotional warmth, not to speak of the fact — emphasized by psychoanalysis in its cruder aspects — that an affectionate approach may reach a critical point at which it can easily become aggressive. Because tenderness has the dimension of force of intensity, it may turn into aggressiveness pure and simple. In a much attenuated and playful form, aggression is often expressed in teasing.

We could say that tenderness, in the sense of being moved, is a paradoxically genuine, because profound, form of sentimentality. However, to avoid misinterpreting tenderness as sentimentality and so devaluing it, it must be stressed that this formulation is a paradox. On the contrary, the sublime character of tenderness transcends all sentimentality and slushiness.

Sentiment and Emotional Synthesis

In the realm of sentiment (thymos) there are many forms of experiencing emotional synthesis with their corresponding, subconscious attitudes. Examples are not only pathos in the widest sense, but all awe, reverence, and "holiday" feelings, from worship to ecstatic mystical experiences as Plotinus and the Christian mystics describe them; but also as they are expressed in primitive rites and religions. Moral pathos embraces both genuine enthusiasm and genuine indignation, particularly when it is "holy enthusiasm" and "holy wrath" — opposing *sacra* against *saeva indignatio*. However, the latter also can be genuine pathos, a sublime passion, as demonstrated in the works of great satirists like Jonathan Swift.

In the same category belongs the experience of *being* or *existing* as described by recent German and French existentialists, most clearly perhaps by Jaspers (1946) in his concept of borderline situations (Grenzsituationen) like old age, illness, psychosis and death — the old triad of the Buddha. In such situations a man is shaken to the roots of his being, is stirred by elemental forces, gripped by the strength of his emotions. They confront him with his total helplessness, open up an abyss before him, force him to look into nothingness. He is "hinausgehalten in das Nichts" (held out into nothingness) as Heidegger (1927) puts it. The experience of being thrown into the world, of being doomed to death, is both profound and intense.

In the same way, despair is felt in the depth of the personality while self-hate leading to the desire for self-destruction has great intensity. Depression as directionless mood has *depth*, sadness or sorrow over something loved and lost has *intensity*, although the reasons for such feelings may be rooted deep in the heart. Finally, love and hate must be taken as emotions that offer such synthesis. According to the Swiss philosopher and psychologist Hans Kunz (1946), "Hate may smolder in the depths and consume a man's life yet never reach the surface and be openly expressed." When this happens, hate is rooted in the personality structure and is a subconscious attitude rather than an emotion.

Ambivalence of Feelings

There is still another kind of synthesis of opposites in emotion which combines emotional force and discontinuity, both variants of intensity, not depth. This has been called the ambivalence (Bleuler) or alternance

(Montherlant) of feelings. Ambivalence is experienced particularly in the sexual sphere where lust may turn into pain. Mystical extasis and religious intoxication also reach the point in the "peak experience" where pleasure borders on pain, or the one is interwoven with the other — an insight reached long ago in classical antiquity.

Depth is characterized by breadth and continuity, intensity by its temporal limitation and resultant discontinuity. Intensive emotions are usually shallow and blow over quickly. For the very reason that too much vital energy is consumed in a comparatively short time, the emotion is quickly spent and little or nothing is left. No normal man can rage for hours on end — though a maniac may. Intensive emotions are shock-like, eruptive, explosive, volcanic; they show organic drive. Of course, this affective *disposition* — whether "choleric" or "sanguine" is rooted in personality, is an enduring part of its structure. In crisis situations, for instance, excitability increases; in old age and even maturity, it decreases. Willy Hellpach (1948), the late German psychologist, psychiatrist and minister of state, classified the crises of puberty and climacteric as "thymoses ," i.e., phases of irritability (Zornmütigkeit). On the other hand, the American psychiatrist Hiram K. Johnson (1935) described the process of maturing *after* puberty as a progressive loss of feeling, a flattening of affect.

Antagonism of Intensity and Depth

The antagonism of intensity and depth is also demonstrated in the fact that intensity may be mobilized against depth. Not only may a sudden emotional outburst overrun and even momentarily abolish profound emotional tendencies and commitments — which later is bitterly regretted; but an emotional flare-up may be used consciously or unconsciously to silence deeper levels of feeling. Man defends himself against sorrow by rage.

OTHER POLARITIES

To touch on another polarity: Vanity and pride are the two poles that represent the continuum of self-esteem, as Schopenhauer saw long ago. Vanity has intensity, pride has depth. Vanity is restless, always wanting approval, never satisfied or appeased; while genuine pride is invulnerable and self-reliant. Pride is always "covered" — that is, it is somehow objectively justified, except for its extreme forms which can no longer be called pride but are haughtiness and arrogance.

Still another polarity, related to that of self-esteem, is that of envy and ill-will. Envy, in the proper sense of the word, is intensive, intentional, and even rational: it always applies to a concrete person and is aroused by concrete possessions or gifts we think we lack. Ill-will is undirected, irrational, extensive; it applies to others as such and to possessions as such. Ill-will cannot be mollified as can envy (for instance, when the man we envy no longer possesses what we envied him). Ill-will is a general grudging of everything to everybody. The man who bears others ill-will envies them the good fortune or gifts he has himself, while the envious man envies others only what he does not have. Envy means that a man wants, too, what others have; ill-will means that he wants others not to have anything.

Another similar polarity is that of extraversion and introversion; before C. G. Jung made this polarity famous, Schopenhauer and Kierkegaard had mentioned it. In the area of emotion, one of the poles is empathy, that is, feeling for or with others; the other, self-feeling. Empathy is intentional, directed towards others, and means feeling like others. Self-feeling is nonintentional, turned toward the self, and means feeling as a self.

A third and last polarity may be derived from the concept of personality levels, or the Freudian distinction of the Ego and the Id. Id-feeling (Eshaftigkeit) means warmth and subjectivity, an involvement of the heart. Ego-feeling (Ichhaftigkeit) means coolness, objectivity, personal distance, and emotional control. Klages calls id-feelings "Herzgefühle" (feelings of the heart), ego-feelings "Kopfgefühle" (feelings of the head). Lack of space makes it impossible to discuss these second and third dimensions of polarity more explicitly.

In conclusion, it should be noted that an orthogonal relation, or zero correlation, must be expected between the two poles of each level: intensity vs. depth, extraversion vs. introversion, id-feelings vs. ego-feelings. This seems to hold good also for the more special dispositions or traits, for instance, vanity vs. pride, envy vs. ill-will. Obviously, this does not mean a negative correlation, i.e., an exclusion of one of the poles in our scheme. On the contrary, I have tried to show that a synthesis or combination of polar traits is not only possible but quite usual and has great significance for personality assessment.

CONCLUSION

In general, I have tried to explain polar differences among feelings and emotions as they are experienced phenomenologically. I have also tried to discuss the relation of these polarities as they are seen in personality levels, dispositions, traits and attitudes. Following this basic principle of polarity, it is possible to arrive at a precise system of personality levels and traits, as I have shown in my book (Wellek, 1966). In this way, a logical basis is laid for personality assessment by test and investigation as well as by phenomenological description and intuitive insight. The special task of psychology is to lay bare the framework and core of man's subjectivity. In this paper I have presumed to deal with only a small part of it.

REFERENCES

Arnold, M.B. (Ed.) (1968). *The nature of emotion; Selected readings.* Penguin, Baltimore.

Bleuler, E. (1924). *Lehrbuch der Psychiatrie* (4th ed.). Springer, Berlin.

Bruner, J.S. (1957). On perceptual readiness. *Psychol. Rev.*, 64, 123-152.

Claparède. (1928). Feelings and emotions. In M. L. Reymert (Ed.), *Feelings and emotions.* Clark Univ. Press, Worcester, Mass.

David, H.P. and von Bracken, H. (Eds.) (1957). *Perspectives in personality theory.* Basic Books, New York.

Freud, S. (1955). *Standard edition of the complete psychological works.* Hogarth Press, London.

Gilbert, A.R. (1951). Recent German theories of stratification of personality. *J. Psychol.*, 31, 3-19.

Heidegger, M. (1927). *Sein und Zeit.* Niemeyer, Halle.

Hellpach, W. (1948). Universitas Litterarum. In *Gesammelte Aufsatze.* Enke, Stuttgart.

Hofstätter, P.R. (1956). Zur Frage der Intuition in der Psychodiagnostik. *Studium Generale,* 9, 527-537.

James, W. (1890). *Principles of psychology.* Holt, New York.

Jaspers, K. (1946). *Allgemeine Psychopathologie* (4th ed.). Springer, Berlin.

Johnson, H.K. (1935). The symptom of loss of feelings. *Am. J. Psychiat.*, 91, 1327-1341.

Jung, C.G. (1921). *Psychologische Typen.* Rascher, Zurich.

Kant, I. (1764). *Observations on the feeling of the beautiful and sublime.* (Transl. by J.T. Goldthwaite.) Univ. of California Press, Berkeley, 1965.

Krueger, F. (1928). The essence of feeling. In M.B. Arnold (Ed.), *The nature of emotion.* Penguin, Baltimore, 1968.

Krueger, F. (1953). *Zur Philosophie und Psychologie der Ganzheit.* Springer, Berlin.

Kunz, H. (1946). *Die Aggressivität und die Zärtlichkeit.* Francke, Bern.

Lorenz, K. (1965). *Über tierisches und menschliches Verhalten.* Piper, Munich.

McDougall, W. (1932). *The energies of men.* Methuen, London.

Murphy, G. (1947). *Personality.* Harper, New York.

Scheler, M. (1923). *Wesen und Formen der Sympathie.* Cohen, Bonn.

Wellek, A. (1953). *Das Problem des seelischen Seins.* (2nd ed.). Hain, Meisenheim.

Wellek, A. (1956). Mathematik, Intuition und Raten. *Studium Generale,* 9, 537-555.

Wellek, A. (1957). The phenomenological and the experimental approaches to psychology and characterology. In H.P. David and H. von Bracken (Eds.) *Perspectives in personality theory.* Basic Books, New York.

Wellek, A. (1959). *Der Rückfall in die Methodenkrise der Psychologie und ihre Überwindung.* Hogrefe, Göttingen.

Wellek, A. (1962). The contribution of the perception-typological approaches to the typology of character and the role of sensation, imagination, and thinking in the organizational concept of personality. In *Proc. 16th Intern. Cong. Psychol., Bonn, 1960.* Amsterdam.

Wellek, A. (1963). *Psychologie.* Francke, Bern.

Wellek, A. (1964). Mathematics and Intuition. *Acta Psychol.* (Amsterdam), 22, 413-429.

Wellek, A. (1966). *Die Polarität im Aufbau des Charakters.* (3rd rev. ed.). Francke, Bern.

Wellek, A. (1968). The impact of the German immigration on the development of American psychology. *J. Hist. Behavioral Sci.*, 4, 207-229.

Chapter 20

Feeling as Basis of Knowing
and Recognizing the Other as an Ego

S. Strasser*

Give me leave to raise a problem which, at first sight, has nothing to do with the subject of this Symposium — the problem of how man comes to know and recognize his fellows. I do not think I need to stress the importance of this problem. Without knowledge of fellow men as fellow men, no social, no economic, no political life is possible. Scientific work is likewise not feasible without a team of observers, investigators and specialists. And still we do not know how social life originates, how communities are formed, how communication is possible.

The fact that man is able to know and recognize his fellows has never been doubted. Everyone will also agree that this knowing and recognizing does not cost any effort whatsoever. We do not regard it as achievement of our perceptual capacity comparable to the judgment of distance, or as a feat of our intellect comparable to the solution of chess problems. Knowing and recognizing the other as an ego is a "very natural" process, needing not the slightest exertion. But how it actually takes place we do not know. Many generations of philosophers and psychologists have been at great pains to offer a complicated theoretical explanation for something which in practice is so simple. In this context we should name, amongst others, Stuart Mill (1874, pp. 223-24), Ferdinand Avenarius (1912), the Gestalt psychologists, Theodor Lipps (1912), Edmund Husserl (1950), Norman Malcolm (1967), and Alfed J. Ayer (1967). These authors have come forward with the most astute arguments. Their theories are interesting in many respects. Not one of them, however, provides an explanation of that which needs explaining.

*University of Nijmegen, Holland.

Let me illustrate this by means of some examples. Following Lipps' line of thought, one could say that it is through a "primary instinct" that man knows the mind of other individuals and understands their intimate experiences. However, the question arises why is it that I can empathize with *(einfühlen)* certain individuals, and not with others. Why do I understand the experiences of another person and not those of a cybernetic machine? As long as this is not explained, the concept of "primary instinct" can have no explanatory value. Undoubtedly Scheler (1948) observed something important when he pointed to the phenomenon of sympathy. Yet it remains incomprehensible why I should sympathize with another ego and not with just any organism. It is an uncontended fact that the face of the other person is apprehended as a *gestalt*. However, a tree and a triangle also appear as *gestalts*. The question remains in what respect the *gestalt* of a human face differs from other *gestalts*. In reading the authors I have mentioned and in studying their theories, one cannot escape the impression that the same question is posed over and over again and that only the "languages" and conceptual systems change while the final answer has yet to be given.

MERLEAU-PONTY'S CONCEPT OF
BODY-SUBJECT (CORPS-SUJET)

An exception to this is the philosophical anthropology of Maurice Merleau-Ponty (1962). Why? Because Merleau-Ponty was the first — and up till now the only — philosopher to submit to careful criticism the terms in which the crucial problem was repeatedly stated. What do we actually mean by "the problem of the other ego" is Merleau-Ponty's matter of concern. By this we refer to the question of a being that apprehends itself as a mind just as I am for myself primarily a mind; with respect to this, one still adheres to the old dualistic concept. In other words, by the mentioned authors the ego is seen as a mind that knows itself through reflection; consequently, the intimate knowledge that the ego possesses of its own conscious immanence differs essentially from the knowledge of things, of nature, of the world. One of Merleau-Ponty's great merits is that he ventured to question these seemingly granted suppositions. Is it actually true that I apprehend myself in the first place as a mind, i.e., as a conscious immanence, which through reflection becomes quite transparent? This, the French philosopher strongly denies. In the first place, I apprehend myself as a "grip on the world" or in other words as a being that, through perception, finds his bearings in a world. From the point of view of my existence, my perceptual as well as my practical intentions are meaningful. This meaningfulness is, however, not imparted by a mind but by a body-ego. For indeed the not as yet personal — and in this sense "purely natural" — body is the origin of perceptual, motor, elementary practical, sexual and expressive intentions. This is why Merleau-Ponty speaks of a body-subject that is neither mind nor thing, but that represents a "third mode of existence" (1962, Part One and Two, notably pp. 346-65).

With this we have indeed made some progress as regards our problem. When, in fact, I apprehend myself as a being that can deal with things, that acts in a practical way in concrete situations, that imparts reality with a practical, live meaning, then I apprehend another body-subject in the same manner. In other words, when I perceive a being that flees or defends itself, hides or feeds, then I recognize the being in question as another body-subject. A certain communication between me and the other subject is then possible on a practical live level.

Merleau-Ponty's anthropology takes us so far, and no further. As the French philosopher himself remarked, "Another body-subject is by no means another ego" (1962, p. 354). To another ego belongs also a mind, and how am I to know that another body-subject possesses a mind? In order to explain this, Merleau-Ponty makes use of Husserl's exposition (1950, pp. 138-49); the body of the other ego is present through my perception of the other body; the mind of the other ego is "appresented" through an association with the perceived body (Merleau-Ponty, 1962, p. 356). Basic to this association is the fact that my own mind is on intimate terms with the functioning of my body-subject.

But with this last line of thought we have fallen back into the dualistic rut. Immediately typical doubts will arise: Why do I appresent a mind when I perceive certain body-subjects while this is not so when perceiving other body-subjects? Why do I apprehend snakes or spiders as body-subjects but not as other egos? Merleau-Ponty, incidentally, remarks that a body-subject deals with objects of nature, while another ego deals with objects of culture (1962, p. 354). But this is not satisfactory: in this way the problem is merely shifted. The original question recurs. It now reads: "How do I recognize objects of culture as such?"

DEFINING THE PREMISES

Let us return to our point of departure. When something is so simple in actual practice while so baffling in theory, there is reason to suspect that there is something wrong with the theory. In our case we need not look for logical errors. However, the possibility that the philosophical "language" used to state the problem is unsuitable should be seriously considered. The language which philosophers employ in argument within themselves, amongst themselves and against each other is historically conditioned. The historian will notice that the problem about the knowledge of the other ego simply did not enter into the philosophy of ancient or medieval times. It only arose in modern times. It is common knowledge that René Descartes is regarded as the originator of modern philosophy. The influence he has exerted – even on his opponents – is great.

Undoubtedly, his greatest opponent was John Locke, whose doctrine regarding the two types of experience — "sensation" which provides knowledge of the "outer world" and "reflection" which relates to the "inner world" — nevertheless shows traces of the Cartesian model. For all these reasons we are inclined to state that Descartes, as well as the philosophers and psychologists influenced by him, have made use of such concepts and categories that the problem of the knowledge of the other ego has become insoluble. It is not difficult to demonstrate this. It will be sufficient to formulate two comprehensive statements that characterize Cartesian thought, and the philosophy as influenced by Descartes, in order to understand the consequences of this line of thinking.

The Ego is the Subject
of Cogitationes (Conscious Acts)

The manner in which the ego is a subject has been given greatly differing interpretations. Descartes speaks of a "thinking substance"; Locke of an "inner world"; Kant of an "I think" that accompanies all my conscious acts; Husserl speaks of an ego-pole from which all objectifying intentions emanate. The statement, naturally, may also be reversed. One can also say that the subject of cogitationes is an ego. In a negative formulation it then holds that something which is not the subject of cogitationes is not an ego.

Every Ego Has, through Reflection,
Access to his Own Cogitationes (Conscious Acts)

Here again a reversal is possible. It reads, "That to which, through reflection, I have access are my own *cogitationes.*" Once these premises have been accepted, the conclusion, *"no ego has access to another ego"* is unavoidable. The question is merely whether the above premises hold good. To this we reply with a definite "no." In order to confront our conceptions with Cartesian notions, we shall formulate four theses, which we shall regard as our working hypotheses. (We shall deliberately avoid the terms "mind" and "consciousness" here because they entail the inherent danger of hypostatization. We shall rather speak of "awareness.")

1. *"Awareness" is not an independent subject of functions, acts, intentions, but a mode of existence of an ego.*

2. *The mode of existence that we name "awareness" is not immutable, but, on the contrary, it is highly variable. This variability applies to the degree of "awareness" as well as to its quality.*

3. The following essentially differing forms of "awareness" should be taken into account: *(a) An ego can be aware without possessing an explicit*

self-awareness. In this case it will not reflect upon itself. *(b) An ego can be aware without being directed towards objects.*

4. *The nonintentional, nonobjectifying mode of awareness is genetically the oldest, while the self-aware awareness is the youngest mode of awareness.*

Our theses have not been arbitrarily chosen. They are based, as we shall see, on relatively conclusive psychological results. In the present discussion we must, however, restrict ourselves. We shall, therefore, leave out of consideration the problem regarding the degrees of "awareness." The experiments conducted by Felix Krueger and Friedrich Sander I mention only incidentally: from these it appears that with a low degree of "awareness" there is no question of the apprehension of objects, but rather of a "subjective feeling." I have written about the significance of these experiments in an earlier publication (Strasser, 1956, pp. 40-50).

In the following exposition we wish to give special attention to the content of the last two of our theses. We shall also introduce into our discourse a category whose importance for psychology was indicated by G.W. Allport (1955), the category of "becoming." This implies that we take up the *"genetic standpoint."* We shall ask the question which has been systematically neglected by the philosophers and psychologists influenced by Descartes: which successive shapes does awareness assume in the course of human development? Through which stages does it pass? Which are the essential changes that occur?

THE PREOBJECTIVE STAGE OF DEVELOPMENT

It is significant that the neonate lives through the first weeks of his life predominantly in a state of sleep. Heinz Remplein (1966, pp. 126-55) does not hesitate in using the expression "the age of sleep" *(Schlafalter)* to typify the first two months of the child's life. He who sleeps without dreaming does not react to sensory stimulation, does not notice objects, does not desire anything, does not strive towards anything. The sleeping child preserves and safeguards as it were his frail, early existence by not exposing himself to stimulation. He retreats into unconsciousness.

With reference to those moments when the neonate does not sleep, one can indeed speak of awareness. However, this "awareness" has as yet *no objectifying character.* Psychologists agree that although the neonate reacts to all kinds of sensory stimulation, he is not able to organize his impressions. Paul H. Mussen (1964, p. 32), for example, writes: "Even though a neonate's sense organs function relatively well, it seems unlikely that he *perceives* the world as adults do. Perception involves the organization and interpretation of simple sense impressions. . . ." The psychologist A.M.J. Chorus (1963, p. 27) from Leiden puts it as follows: "Immediately after birth, the suckling can hear, see, smell, taste and feel or touch. Sound, light, hard and soft, wet and dry — all these qualities of surrounding objects get through to him but they do not yet make 'sense' to him; as yet they convey no *meaning* to him; they even disturb him. Initially, he is not able to store and process the outside world with its sounds, colours, and other impressions: he is actually frightened by them." René Spitz (1959, p. 15) puts it yet more strongly when he writes: " ... There is no differentiation between the incoming stimuli; and the behavior which takes place seemingly in response to these stimuli appears to be unspecific."

PRIMACY OF THE SUBJECT-SUBJECT RELATION

The first structurization of the surrounding world (Umwelt) cannot therefore be based on the perception of objects. Is it, then, possible at all? Is it not true that since Aristotle we know that every conception of reality ultimately builds upon sensory data? Although the neonate is not able to process his sensory impressions in such a way that they provide him with objective knowledge, he has still been endowed by nature with a certain equipment. He is full of vital needs and dreads. From an anthropological standpoint the conclusion must be made that the young baby is not by nature an autonomous being. His existence demands a complement in both a positive and a negative sense; on the one hand it requires something that fulfills his essential demands, on the other hand it requires something that averts his vital dreads. This "something" later turns out to be a "someone." In the pattern of our Western Civilization the role of this someone will normally be performed by the mother.

To the young baby the mother is not present as an object with a certain size, shape and colour. She appears to him primarily as a threefold figure. She is, firstly, a bearer of pleasure, delight, comfort. She is, secondly a guarantee of security. She has, thirdly, power over the surrounding world *(Umwelt).*

The first and second of these maternal roles have been recognized by many child psychologists. "Typically, the mother gratifies the infant's primary needs for food, for alleviation of pain, and perhaps even for tactile stimulation. Many of these satisfactions are provided as she feeds the baby," Mussen observes (1964, p. 66). Chorus remarks (1963, p. 44) that the mother "is the being that lets the child share all the good things of life: from her comes warmth, food, ease, dry comfort and that joyful liveliness of laughter and prattle."

With respect to the control of vital dreads, psychologists refer to animal experiments performed by Liddell. From these it appeared that certain experimental procedures which would normally lead to artificial neurosis in lambs and young goats remained without effect if the young animals stayed near their mothers (Liddell, 1954). Remplein observes (1966, p. 183), "The presence of the mother seems to counteract the surge of dread; the child feels secure." The mother, however, would not be the being that "lets the child share all the good things of life" if she did not possess power. What this in effect means is understood by the child only in the next stage, the practical-objectifying stage, of his development. But even as a young baby the child establishes a connection between the appearance of the mother on the one hand, and on the other, to his being satiated, to his being laid dry, to his being immersed in a warm bath. Whoever can transform the pangs of hunger into satiation, unpleasant wetness into comfortable dryness, pain into pleasure, is powerful. The question as to how this is achieved, is not yet asked.

Thus it may be understood that this indispensable, powerful being is the first thing to be known and recognized by the small infant; in other words, *that it is singled out as a special being earlier than all other things,* than all objects of nature and all objects of culture. There is agreement among many psychologists about this matter. W. Metzger (1959, p. 422) expands most on the subject: " 'Mother' is that something which turns all to good. Even from the second week onwards, the voice as well as the visible appearance of this something often begin to differentiate from other — irrelevant — voices and appearances. In the course of the second month the visual acuity and the organization of what is seen generally appears to be well enough developed for this something — although at first only when seen from the front and in upright position — to take on a face with the eyes as focal point. It is the time when the child starts responding to his mother's look with a smile." Remplein (1966, p. 156) describes almost the same facts, to which he adds: "This smile appears only in human interaction . . . . It constitutes a making of contact, at first reactively, later actively . . . . Orientation towards the world of objects does not occur until later." In a similar manner, Wilhelm Hansen (1965, p. 148) notes: "It is consistent with the special situation of the child that it can already make contact with people even before it is able to deal with things." Chorus (1963, p. 46) elaborates on this point: "What is the simplest object to perceive: a point, a ball, a cube or a face? The latter is, no doubt, the most complex of them all. A colored dot will more readily be perceived by the child than a ball; a ball more readily than a cube. This is what — along the lines of adult thought — might be expected, but for the child this definitely does not hold true. The human face is known far sooner by the child; he will respond much earlier to his mother's face than to a colored dot or to a ball." In this context, Spitz (1959, p. 18; see also 1957, pp. 26-30) chooses the term preobjective apprehension: "The establishment of the precursor of the object certainly is preceded by increasingly organized responses to the ministrations of the environment, represented by the mother. This process culminates in . . . the emergence of the smiling response, which represents a conscious reciprocal communication."

PHYSIOGNOMIC PERCEPTION

One might now ask: "How is the mother present to the child in these cases?" But this question is, in fact, misleading, because, in phenomenological literature, "to be present to" is understood to imply the appearance of an object to a subject. Indeed, as adults we can hardly visualize a nonobjective mode of presence. In order to clarify the matter, we shall therefore quote an animal experiment. H. Harlow from the University of Wisconsin "put newly born monkeys with 'mothers' made from wire mesh . . . Some were fed from a bottle attached to the chest of an unadorned wire 'mother,' while the mother of the others was also made of wire mesh, but covered with terry cloth material. The latter structure thus supplied both food and a great deal of tactile stimulation, whereas the former gave food, but not the same quantity and quality of tactile stimulation. Given the choice of going to either 'mother,' baby monkeys characteristically preferred the terry cloth one and spent more time in clinging to her than to the other one, even those babies originally fed by the plain wire mesh 'mother.' When a frightening wooden spider was placed in the cage with a young monkey, he would run to the terry cloth 'mother,' who was apparently the more effective source of security. . . ." Mussen (1964, pp. 68-69), to whom we owe this report of Harlow's experiments, sums up as follows: "The experimenter concluded that tactile stimulation is innately satisfying to an infant animal, so he forms a strong attachment to whatever or whoever offers it."

It should be noted that this conclusion by Harlow is not quite satisfactory. Let us assume for the moment that a real bird-eating spider were used in his experiment instead of a wooden spider. The bird-eating spider would have been able, no doubt, to supply the little monkey with appreciable tactile stimulation, quantitatively as well as qualitatively. Why, then, does the monkey not form an attachment to the spider? Why does it flee from it? Why does the spider induce fear, although the monkey has not had any experience with spiders whatsoever? And what, exactly, is the relation between the feeling of security aroused by the terry cloth "mother" on the one hand, and tactile stimulation on the other?

Here the S-R (stimulus-response) model proves inadequate. With respect to the spider's fear-arousing impression on the monkey we shall have to revert to the concept of "physiognomic perception" which was introduced into psychology by Werner (1948). But another concept of significance in Werner's writings may serve its purpose here: the "syncretic character of primitive organization." Indeed, with reference to the terry cloth "mother" in Harlow's experiment, we may say that in the experience of the baby monkey – just as in that of the human baby – softness, warmth, closeness, mildness and security belong together. One may speak of "signal-properties." Where there is softness and warmth, there one will find comfort, there one will feel safe. The wire mesh "mother" does not possess these properties. As a feeding mother she is therefore liked less, and from her no security whatsoever is expected. Moreover, it is worth observing here, that softness, warmth, closeness, mildness and security form a syncretic whole not only in the primitive apperception of baby monkeys. In the highest spheres of human poetry — including religious poetry — this relationship is present. Perhaps we are not just dealing with signal properties but with attributes which have evolved, not accidentally, into symbols of deep significance for the whole of mankind.

THE ROLE OF FEELING

Without pursuing this matter further, we shall return to the question of how the mother is present to the infant. In order to describe this presence we shall have to use the one appropriate word "feeling." Applicable here are all the meanings of this comprehensive term which was analyzed by Magda B. Arnold (1960, vol. 1, pp. 19-21). "Feeling" indeed refers to tactile impressions; also to other sensory experiences requiring nearness (e.g., the sensation of warmth). Thirdly, the subject feels *himself;* he feels his own state. The baby feels comfortable, satisfied, secure. He feels his own condition, but he only feels this in the contact and through the contact with the mother. His feelings will therefore change completely when this contact vanishes. Because the baby feels his mother, he feels secure. Thus, in the fifth place, we are bound to say: suckling and mother feel *one.* However, this may not be interpreted as being an emotional unity formed by two individuals alone, isolated from their environment. The situation, indeed the whole surrounding world *(Umwelt),* is "felt" to be peaceful, secure, comfortable; in the latter sense we may recognize a sixth meaning of the word "feeling." Remplein (1966, p. 185) correctly observes: "Feeling not only makes man integrated as an individual, it also joins him with his fellow-man into a higher unity. According to our experience even with the adult, intensity of feeling, richness of expression, and coherence with the environment are always geared to each other. How much more so for the child that is an emotional being par excellence!"*

If we attempt to find the common meaning of all these semantic shades of the word "feeling" we shall not easily find a better phrase than that used by Plessner (1950, p. 17) to characterize the essence of feeling: *distanzlose Sachverhaftung.* An illustration of what Plessner means by this "direct intimacy with the object" may perhaps be obtained by means of the analyses given earlier. It refers to the awareness of a contact which excludes all distance. As such, "feeling" in its original form is the opposite of intentional aiming at something, where a "distance" is always presupposed between the aiming subject and the

---

*"Das Gefühl verganzt nicht nur den Menschen, sondern verbindet ihn auch mit dem Mitmenschen zu einer höheren Einheit. Auch beim Erwachsenen sind erfahrungsgemäss Gefühlsbetontheit, Ausdrucksreichtum und Umweltkohärenz gekoppelt. Um wieviel mehr beim Kind, das ein ausgesprochenes Affektwesen ist!"

object at which it aims. Of course, there are also feelings that accompany intentional acts. Such a feeling is, for example, expressed by the sentence: "This color is felt as pleasant." In this case the color is perceived as an object and the perception is accompanied by a certain echo of feeling. However, as long ago as 1956, I pointed out the necessity of distinguishing the latter (secondary) feelings from primary "moods" (Strasser, 1956, pp. 109-117, 127).

When we speak of the "absence of distance," this should not be understood in a spatial sense. Rather, we would say that no medium and no mediator is situated between the feeling subject and the felt object. This explains why the specific subject-object tension does not, as yet, exist. Thus, the situation may best be characterized as follows: *the feeling subject feels himself by the fact that he feels his fellow-subject;* and reversely, the fellow-subject who is felt is present to the feeling subject by the fact that the latter feels himself.

AWARENESS WITHOUT EGO-AWARENESS

Indeed, it need not surprise us that the young child has, in fact, no ego-awareness. We should say, more accurately, that it does not distinguish clearly between "I" and "we," between ego and the surrounding world. "The individual and certainly the child are not autarchic," says Chorus (1963, p. 46). "They live, and can only attain development, *in a human community.* The child does not live as an ego, but it lives as an us, *in a common bond with its whole environment.* And this us of the child is primarily formed by the people around him...." L. J. Stone and J. Church (1957, p. 84) express a similar idea when they write: "Events or objects come into the baby's awareness in terms of immediate threat or gratification to him. Soon after, there may be a connection between things, but the connection is always personal, through the infant. Orange juice may signify that a bath will follow, but these are related as things that happen to *him* in close succession, and not as events in a world.... And there is the difficult part for most adults to grasp: although for the infant everything is related to *my* immediate needs, wants, and experience, there is no *me*. There is simply Hunger and Wetness, and Orange-Juice-Followed-by-Warm-Immersion, all in a context of a familiar person and place; but there is *no* 'I am hungry'...." Remplein (1966) asserts that for the small child the distance between "I" and "You" — which is so typical in the experience of adults — does not exist, especially not in the mother-child relation. Spitz (1957) speaks of reciprocal object relations which always exist between the dyad of the child and the object of his libido. What by Spitz is called a libidinous object, in agreement with psychoanalytic terminology, was specified by us as "fellow-subjects."

On this basis it may be explained why the parents' attitudes, behavior and emotions — which are essentially unintelligible for the child — still exert an influence upon his life. According to Remplein (1966, p. 215) "it is beyond all doubt that the unconscious mind of the child responds to the parents' unconscious sets, attitudes and prejudices like a very sensitive seismograph. It responds to their peace and security, harmony and joy as well as to their irritability and anxiety, their quarrelling and temper." The concept of "contamination of feeling" (Gefühlsansteckung) used by Max Scheler (1948) can be applied here. Scheler points to the fact that the process of contamination occurs beyond the knowledge and intentions of the ego.

According to Hansen (1965), the mother constitutes the first representation of the surrounding world *(Umwelt)* for the child. It depends on her whether his vital needs will be satisfied or frustrated. The mother, therefore, is by no means exclusively the object of love, like the sentimental 18th century authors would have us believe. She can also evoke different emotions. "The giving side (of the mother) arouses his satisfaction − his 'love'," says Chorus (1963, p. 5) with respect to the small child; "and the other, the denying side, evokes his fury − his 'hatred'. In these experiences, no doubt, the basis can be found for the dichotomy in the child's emotional life: love and hate, affection and aversion. We say that the child is ambivalent in his emotions; i.e., love and hate will easily turn into their opposites . . . . "

The mother who gives will arouse libidinous feelings and joy; the mother who denies will evoke aggressive feelings ("hatred") and rage. (Well known is the observation by St. Augustine that one suckling is jealous when the wet nurse feeds another baby.) If a mother maltreats her child, if she does not avert his anxieties, if she withdraws from him, his liveliness may be badly affected. Erikson (1960) and René Spitz (1959) have documented this from their research findings. By her behavior, the mother may thus evoke all the familiar emotions in the small child.

WHAT IS AN EMOTION?

Since the life space of a baby is relatively simple, compared to that of the adult who is entangled in a network of pluriform social relations, it may be useful and instructive in this context to ask the question: what is meant by the term "emotion"? It is definitely not a synonym of "drive" or "need." Hunger, thirst, need of sleep, pain and other afflictions may *cause* emotions but they *are* not emotions. An emotion is not a motive either. A motive is often based on rational considerations and will then lead to coordinated purposeful behavior. This is in contrast to an emotion. Emotional behavior can immediately be recognized as such, just as a typically emotional apperception of the situation will strike us as such. This cannot be explained if one follows Jean Piaget (1954) in assuming that emotionality is no more than a source of energy, whereas the structures are related to cognitive functions.

How does it happen that emotional behavior can easily be recognized as such? We propose to mention the following three characteristics of emotion.

1. Emotions always occur in the context of situations which – to use a modern expression – have an *existential* nature. A baby, for example, is furious not because he is hungry, but because he feels menaced in his existence. Nobody is able to explain to him that he will not succumb to starvation and that his mother is just going to prepare his food. What he feels is a vital need. Similarly, the dread, e.g., the typical dread of the toddler, is a feeling threatened by what is unknown, strange, and oppressive. This is the feature which distinguishes dread from fear. Fear is caused by the perception of a specific danger. We would, therefore, classify fear as an affect and not as an emotion.

2. Emotional behavior is *eruptive* and *expressive* by nature. This is why it stands out, and why it is easily recognized. Negatively, this implies that whoever behaves emotionally, does not act on the basis of reflection, on rational grounds, or after weighing his motives. Neither does he look for the most suitable means to reach a clearly defined goal. These are the reasons why, as R.S. Peters (1965) remarked, the civilized adult gives the impression of passivity when he is overpowered by an emotion.

3. *Emotion is a primitive form of answer given by a subject to a situation.* It is not a "disorganized response" for, as we once remarked (Strasser, 1956, p. 180), a complete disorganization precludes the possibility of giving an answer. Emotional behavior occurs whenever a subject does not apprehend his situation in an objectifying manner, but immediately, in the light of his existential needs and dreads. This is often the case with the young child. But the adult also may revert to such elementary forms of behavior when his existence – actually or seemingly – is at stake. His desire, his hate, his craving and his dread then take on such proportions that he is overwhelmed by them. The "primordial distance" *(Urdistanz)* which, as noted by Martin Buber (1962), charcterizes man as man and enables him to define his attitude towards fellow-subjects, things and situations, completely disappears. And so the objective world built up by the adult loses its meaning for him.

The consequences of this have already been outlined roughly. A man mastered by an emotion acts without due consideration. He will often fail to use the appropriate means in the appropriate order. He does not make decisions "with a cool head." And so he shows that lack of orientation which is so typical of a person stirred by emotion. The so-called panic flight, which was studied by René Déjean (1938), and which differs considerably from purposeful flight is a good illustration. It is also known that a man fighting in a state of fury is in danger of getting the worst of it when his opponent acts with cool calculation and technical ability. On the other hand, emotion may be regarded as an eruption of vital forces capable of impressing, frightening and intimidating a naive opponent.

EMOTIONAL DIMENSIONS

The conception of the nature of emotion as outlined here is related to our conviction that the existence of man has an underlying elementary structure which is not based on objectifying knowledge and discriminatory volition. This structure, therefore, cannot be described by reference to a number of specific objects and purposes; it can, however, be defined by indicating emotional heights and depths. The points of greatest height and depth will then be typical for what we would call an emotional dimension. Let us relate this to our analysis of the early experiences of the child with respect to his mother. As we have concluded, the mother normally provides pleasure and relieves pain; she occasions joy and averts feelings of dread; she is powerful and helps the child that feels powerless; if she fails to do this she provokes his anger and his hate. Correspondingly, we shall distinguish *three basic emotional tendencies:* the innate desire for pleasure and the inclination to turn against whoever frustrates the gratification of this desire; the innate need for security and the aversion from what causes his dread; the desire for power and the tendency to overcome his helplessness (both of which will only become apparent in the practical, objectifying stage of the child's development). These three emotional dimensions we might designate with the Latin names: *libido, securitas* and *potestas.* In behavior they are characterized by the following three contrast pairs respectively: extremes of love and hatred, of elation and dread, of triumph and despair. Of course, all these concepts should be taken in an analogous sense. It is obvious that, for example, the peak of the libidinous gratification of the suckling cannot simply be compared with the paroxysm of love of an adult lover; that the despair of the toddler is of another kind than the despair of a guilt-oppressed adult. Yet we would contend than an analogy exists, seeing that a mature person, when he approaches these emotional high marks and low marks, reverts to the level of behavior which is typically emotional and readily identified as such.

The theory of the emotional dimensions also offers an explanation for the characteristic *ambivalence* of the emotional feelings that has been known in psychiatry since Eugen Bleuler. This ambivalence, as we have seen, also plays a role in the normal child and in the normal adult. Why does love turn so easily into hate, elation into dejection, the feeling of triumphant superiority into the feeling of depressive inferiority? This calls for an underlying structure, indeed a structure that is not based on objectifying knowledge.

Naturally, we would not claim to have presented a brand new theory. The significance of the first two emotional dimensions, that of *libido* and *securitas* was discovered by psychoanalysis, that of *potestas* by individual psychology. We also agree with the position of both these two depth psychological approaches that the early emotional experience of the child can influence the course of his further development. We cannot concede, however, that the construction of an objective world rests solely upon the "sublimation of instincts." In agreement with Merleau-Ponty we see the body and its emotional equipment as "preconditions of reason" *(conditions de la raison)*. In other words, implicitly they are rational. They constitute first sources of meaning; they provide the emotional — or in Werner's words, "physiognomic" — character of reality. Thus they offer foundations for reason when this comes forward as a positive force giving rise to new structures — structures that are based on purposeful action and objectifying knowledge.

OBJECTIFICATION

It is not possible in the scope of the present discussion to give even a brief sketch of the development of awareness. Only by means of a few catch-words can we indicate what, in our opinion, is of importance here. One aspect of this development is the process of objectification, although, in its first stage, this is predominantly a practical exploration of the surrounding world. From the age of three months the child grasps everything, puts things in his mouth, touches and moves everything within his reach. For him, the things are "things of action," as Werner observed (1948, pp. 68-69, 172-73). The Us-ego of the infant is thus changed into an Action-ego. The decisive step in the direction of objectivity is made by the child when he learns to speak. Of all the functions of language, the naming of things is at first the most important. By applying names, the emotional as well as the practical attitude of the child is definitely overcome. If at first the sound "mama" was an exclamation of joy for the baby, later it is the expression of a wish, such as "I want to be picked up"; and ultimately "mama" becomes the name for a person with a specific identity. Of all the new words the child learns, there is one that assumes a special, vital importance: the word "no." "As he becomes aware of his abilities, he wants to exercise them for himself, without help or hindrance or coercion from other people," Stone and Church (1957, p. 112) remark; "perhaps the most striking display of the toddler's autonomy is his intermittent negativism, variously expressed by 'No!'" Remplein (1966) regards the child's obstinacy, occurring in the course of the third year, as a "basic form of personal self-assertion."

Another aspect of this development of awareness is also important from our point of view. Initially, the child imagines his grip on reality, exerted by means of naming, as a magic influence. At the age of seven to eight years, however, this magic notion of language begins to lose ground. As a result of discussions with other persons, the child gradually learns to distinguish between his subjective thought and speech on the one hand and the things that are meant on the other (Piaget, 1947). This process promotes the growth of a more realistic view of the world.

In a sense, the ability and the tendency to reflect constitutes the fulfillment of awareness. This tendency is typical for adolescence. As an adolescent, the young person begins to apprehend himself as an interiority which is unique, different — and therefore separated — from the interiority of other persons. Only then, as Merleau-Ponty (1962) stresses, can there by a *cogitatio* (a conscious act) in a philosophical sense. The child has at first apprehended himself as a practical ego, Remplein (1966) says, but in adolescence man turns his gaze inwards and finds within himself the world of thoughts, feelings, moods, emotions, drives, aspirations and desires; he discovers his inner self *(seelisches Ich)*. "Generally only at the age of 15, the quality truly proper to the individual, that is, the quality of the inner life, begins to expand," remarks P. J. A. Calon (1953, p. 170). Spranger (1953, pp. 34-35) speaks of the discovery of the subject as of a world of his own, a world that is, like an island, forever separated from everything else in the world, from things and people — and on that account the experience of great loneliness. Stone and Church (1957, p. 270) write in less philosophical terminology, but their characterization of adolescence is essentially the same: "The central theme of adolescence is the finding of one's self. This means an intensified self-awareness — largely manifested as self-consciousness — and a new push for independence . . . The older adolescent must now find an identity as himself rather than as a member either of his family or his gang." These adolescents, growing up in the pattern of our Western civilization, do to a certain extent actually live through the content of the contemplations by Descartes, Locke, Husserl and Sartre; many others, however, certainly do not. From this it follows, in a negative sense, that the purely subjective *cogitatio*, the intentional ego-pole, reflection, and the conscious immanence, cannot be designated as *a priori* structures of consciousness as such.

CONCLUSIONS

Our knowledge of the other person as an ego has its roots in the original, nonobjectifying mode of awareness, because that to which a subject is first committed — both in vital and in emotional respects — is his fellow-subject. In order to typify the manner in which the presence of the fellow-subject is primarily experienced, we have used the following formulation: "The feeling subject feels himself by the fact that he feels his fellow-subject." It is not difficult now to understand what direction the further development of awareness takes; what was at first *one* — feeling one's own state and feeling the other — separates out. The subject that feels a fellow-subject begins to realize that he is an autonomous ego that feels a nonego independent of him. In this way, the fellow-subject becomes transformed into a nonego and into an object. In turn, the subject that feels himself becomes a self-aware ego which through thought reflects upon himself. He reflects upon his own ego regardless of the existence of a nonego for him. This leads to the renowned distinction within experience between "sensation" and "reflection" and to the division of the world into an "outer world" and an "inner world."

We have, however, come to the conclusion that the objectifying and reflecting mode of awareness, even in the adult person, is but an "upper layer." Our original feeling and emotional mode of awareness is indeed hidden by it, but it remains there. It rises to the surface whenever the situation appears to the ego in such a manner that he *cannot maintain a distance* (emotion) or whenever, in the nature of things, *no distance exists* (feeling). When I am present to the other, no distance exists. The most elementary of all human experience – we together in surrounding world – is not at first perceived, thought or sought after; it is primarily lived, through feeling.

Thus it is conceivable, on the one hand, that – in a quite natural manner – I can be present to the other as an ego. And thus it is obvious, on the other hand, that a philosophy of immanence and reflection cannot provide an explanation for this presence.

REFERENCES

Allport, G.W. (1955). *Becoming*. Yale Univ. Press, New Haven, Connecticut.

Arnold, M.B. (1960). *Emotion and personality*. Columbia Univ. Press, New York.

Avenarius, F. (1912). Der menschliche Weltbegriff (3rd. ed.). Reisland, Leipzig.

Ayer, A.J. (1967). One's knowledge of other minds. In D.F. Gustafson (Ed.), *Essays in philosophical psychology* (2nd ed.). Macmillan, London.

Bandura, A. and Walters, R.H. (1963). *Social learning and personality development*. Holt, New York.

Buber, M. (1962). Urdistanz und Beziehung. In *Werke*, vol. 1. Koesel-Verlag, Munich.

Calon, P.J.A. (1953). *De jongen*. De Toorts, Heemstede.

Chorus, A.M.J. (1963). *Zuigeling en kleuter* (10th ed.). De Toorts, Haarlem.

Déjean, R. (1933). *L'émotion*. Alcan, Paris.

Erikson, E.H. (1960). The course of healthy personality development. In J.H. Seidman (Ed.), *The adolescent; a book of readings*. Holt, New York.

Erikson, E.H. (1963). *Childhood and society* (2nd ed.). Norton, New York.

Hansen, W. (1965). *Die Entwicklung des kindlichen Weltbildes* (6th ed.). Koesel-Verlag, Munich.

Husserl, E. (1950). *Cartesianische Meditationen*. Nijhoff, The Hague.

Leeper, R.W. (1948). A motivational theory of emotion. *Psychol. Rev.*, 55, 5-21.

Liddell, H.S. (1954). Conditioning and emotions. *Sci. Am.*, 190, 48-57.

Lipps, T. (1912). Das Wissen von fremden Ichen. In *Psychologische Untersuchungen* 1, 4-19. Engelmann, Leipzig.

Malcolm, N. (1967). Knowledge of other minds. In D.F. Gustafson (Ed.), *Essays in philosophical psychology* (2nd ed.). Macmillan, London.

Maslow, A.H. (1954). *Motivation and personality*. Harper, New York.

Merleau-Ponty, M. (1962). *Phenomenology of perception*. Trans., C. Smith, Routledge and Kegan Paul, London.

Metzger, W. (1959). Die Entwicklung der Erkenntnisprozesse. In H. Thomae (Ed.), *Entwicklungspsychologie*. Göttingen, Verlag für Psychologie.

Mill, S. (1874). *An examination of Sir Hamilton's philosophy*. Holt, New York.

Murray, E.J. (1965). *Motivation and emotion* (3rd ed.). Prentice-Hall, Englewood Cliffs, New Jersey.

Mussen, P.H. (1964). *The psychological development of the child* (4th ed.). Prentice-Hall, Englewood Cliffs, New Jersey.

Mussen, P.H., Conger, J.J. and Kagan, J. (Eds.) (1966). *Child development and personality* (5th ed.). Harper, New York.

Peters, R.S. (1965). Emotions, passivity and the place of Freud's theory in psychology. In B. B. Wolman and E. Nagel (Eds.), *Scientific psychology*. Basic Books, New York.

Piaget, J. (1947). *La répresentation du monde chez l'enfant* (3rd ed.). Alcan, Paris.

Piaget, J. (1954). *Les relations entre l'affectivité et l'intelligence dans le développement mental de l'enfant*. Centre de Documentation Universitaire, Paris.

Piaget, J. (1956). *Le jugement et le raisonnement chez l'enfant*. Delachaux Niestle, Neuchâtel.

Plessner, H. (1950). *Lachen und Weinen* (2nd ed.). A. Francke, Bern.

Remplein, H. (1966). *Die seelische Entwicklung des Menschen im Kindes — und Jugendalter* (14th ed.). Reinhardt, Munich.

Scheler, M. (1948). *Wesen und Formen der Sympathie* (5th ed.). Schulte-Bulmke, Frankfurt.

Sears, R.R., Rau, L., and Alpert, R. (1965). *Identification and child rearing*. Stanford Univ. Press.

Spitz, R. (1957). *Nein und Ja; die Ursprünge der menschlichen Kommunikation*. Klett, Stuttgart.

Spitz, R. (1959). *A genetic field theory of ego formation*. International Univ. Press, New York.

Spranger, E. (1953). *Psychologie des Jugendalters* (23rd ed.). Quelle and Meyer, Heidelberg.

Stone, L.J. and Church, J. (1957). Childhood and adolescence. Random House, New York.

Strasser, S. (1956). *Das Gemüt*. Spectrum, Utrecht.

Young, P.T. (1949). Emotion as disorganized response. *Psychol. Rev.*, 56, 184-191.

Young, P.T. (1961). *Motivation and emotion*. Wiley, New York.

Werner, H. (1948). *Comparative psychology of mental development* (rev. ed.). Follett, New York.

Author Index

Subject Index

A

Absence of distance, 300, 306
Abstract concepts, 159
Acceptance of pain, sadness, 142
Acetylcholine, 28
Achievement, need for, 154
ACTH, 75 ff.
Action
  appraisal and, 179
  appropriate, 200-201
  choice of, 175
  circuit, 182-183
  depends on deliberate judgment, 179
  ego, 304
  emotion and, 110, 147, 148, 174-176,
    179, 188, 192, 194, 200-202, 242
  impulse, 175-176
  motive and, 190, 192, 200-201
  tendency and appraisal, 174-176, 179
  tendency as emotion, 124, 174-176
Activation, see also Arousal
  amplification as, 103
  drive and, 209
  EEG, 64
  as emotional dimension, 255-257
  emotions as, 146, 209
  level and feeling, 234
  mood and, 265-266
Activation theory, 5-6, 209
Activators of affect, 108
Adaptation through feelings, 127, 235
Adaptation level and feelings, 234
Adaptive behavior, classes of, 9
Adjective checklist, 245
Adolescence, 236-240, 305
Adrenaline, 28, 34-36, 74-98, 115-118, 184
Adrenaline A, see Adrenaline

Adrenaline B, see Noradrenaline
Affect(s), see also Emotion, Feeling, Mood
  activators of, 108
  amplifier circuits, 102
  appetite and, 45
  archetypal core, 132
  arousal and, 64
  as awareness of stimulation increments,
    39, 108-109
  can become emotion, 133
  characteristics, 108
  classification, 233, 236
  contagion, 107
  containment of, 133
  definition, 105-106, 130-131
  double-bind of, 133
  -ego, 132
  emotion and, 70, 130-131, 133, 233-235
  explosive, 283
  as facial behavior, 106
  as feeling with physiological innervation,
    131
  flattening of, 287
  generality of object, 105
  high-level, 136
  images and, 132
  innate, 107-108
  intensity of, 105
  intensity level, critical of, 64
  Jung's definition, 130-131
  localization of, 133-134
  loss after lemniscal lesions, 103
  major, 107
  measurement (Plutchik), 21-22
  mood and, 264
  as motive, 104, 106, 159
  negative, 107-109
  nomenclature, 233